D0923821

Mysticisms East and West

Studies in Religion and Culture
Series Preface

Perhaps more than ever before, there is a need for Christians to understand the shifting sands of religion and culture. Unfortunately it is with some justification that the church has been criticised, by both insiders and outsiders, for failing to understand the deep social, religious, and cultural changes taking place. This major series invites scholars to provide sensitive, empathetic, reliable, and accessible studies that will advance thinking about important subjects such as fundamentalism, mysticism, globalization, postmodernism, secularization, the religious significance of contemporary film, art, music, literature, information technologies, youth culture, religious pluralism, the changes taking place in contemporary world religions, and the emergence of new, influential, and alternative forms of spirituality. Whilst the majority of the contributors will be Christian thinkers writing with the needs of Christian community in mind, the series will be of interest to all those concerned with contemporary religion and culture.

Christopher Partridge

Mysticisms East and West

Studies in Mystical Experience

edited by

Christopher Partridge & Theodore Gabriel

PATERNOSTER PRESS

Copyright © 2003 The Editors and Contributors

First published in 2003 by Paternoster Press

09 08 07 06 05 04 03   7 6 5 4 3 2 1

Paternoster Press is an imprint of Authentic Media,
P.O. Box 300, Carlisle, Cumbria, CA3 0QS, UK
and
P.O. Box 1047, Waynesboro, GA 30830-2047, USA

Website: www.paternoster-publishing.com

The right of The Editors and Contributors to be identified as the Author of
this Work has been asserted by them in accordance with the Copyright,
Designs and Patents Act 1988.

All rights reserved. No part of this publication may be reproduced, stored
in a retrieval system, or transmitted in any form or by any means,
electronic, mechanical, photocopying, recording or otherwise, without
the prior permission of the publisher or a licence permitting restricted
copying. In the UK such licences are issued by the Copyright
Licensing Agency, 90 Tottenham Court Road, London W1P 9HE.

British Library Cataloguing in Publication Data
A catalogue record for this book is available from the British Library

ISBN 1-84227-092-3

Cover Design by FourNineZero
Printed in Great Britain by Bell and Bain, Glasgow

Contents

Acknowledgements

Our work as editors has been greatly helped by the quality of the material we have received. This has been a fascinating book to edit and we are indebted to those who have so willingly and diligently contributed to it.

In particular, we should like to thank Tom Partridge for producing the Tree of Life glyph for Chapter 8 (Figure 8.1), Tony Graham of the Paternoster Press for his encouragement and seemingly endless patience, and Dr Tony Gray who was involved with the project in its early stages.

Contributors

L. Philip Barnes studied theology and philosophy at The Queen's University of Belfast, University of Hull, and Trinity College, Dublin, where he gained his doctorate in philosophy. He has published widely in such journals as *Scottish Journal of Theology*, *Modern Theology*, *Religion*, and *Religious Studies*. He is currently Lecturer in Religious Studies and Education, School of Education, University of Ulster at Coleraine, Northern Ireland.

Richard Bauckham is Professor of New Testament Studies and Bishop Wardlaw Professor at the University of St Andrews. His most recent books are *Gospel Women: Studies of the Named Women in the Gospels* (2002) and *God and the Crisis of Freedom: Biblical and Contemporary Perspectives* (2002).

Ruth Bradby lived and taught in India for twenty years. She has Masters degrees in both Music and Theology and is currently carrying out doctoral research into alternative spiritualities and popular self-help literature. She has written articles on aspects of Hinduism and also on alternative spirituality.

Arthur Bradley is Lecturer in English at University College Chester, England. His recent academic publications include 'Thinking the Outside: Foucault, Derrida and Negative Theology' (*Textual Practice*, 2002) and 'Without Negative Theology: Derrida and the Politics of Negative Theology' (*Heythrop Journal*, 2001). He is currently writing a book on Derrida, negative theology and modern French thought.

David Burnett is Director of Studies at All Nations Christian College and a Fellow of the Royal Anthropological Institute. He is the author of several books and articles, including *The Spirit of Hinduism* (1992), and *The Spirit of Buddhism* (1996).

Mahinda Deegalle graduated in Buddhist Studies from Peradeniya University, Sri Lanka, in Comparative Religion from Harvard University and has a doctorate in the History of Religions from Chicago University. He is currently Senior Lecturer in Study of Religions at Bath Spa University College, Bath, England. He has published numerous articles on Buddhism in academic journals and edited books, including (ed. with F.J. Hoffman) *Pali Buddhism* (1996).

Colin Duriez is the author of *The C.S. Lewis Encyclopedia* (2002) and *Tolkien and The Lord of the Rings* (2001), and is co-author (with David Porter) of *The Inklings Handbook: The Lives, Thought and Writings of C.S. Lewis, J.R.R. Tolkien, Charles Williams and Their Friends* (2001). As well as a writer, he is a freelance book editor and lectures widely on Tolkien, C.S. Lewis, The Inklings and the Christian imagination.

Mark Elliott, formerly the Assistant Director of the Whitefield Institute, is currently Lecturer in Christian Studies at Liverpool Hope University College. He is interested in studying theology through the history of Christian thought and was contributing editor of a collection of essays on theological anthropology, *The Dynamics of Human Life* (2002). He is the editor of *European Journal of Theology*.

Don Fairbairn is Assistant Professor of Church History and Missions at Erskine Theological Seminary (South Carolina, USA), and visiting Professor of Theology at Donetsk Christian University (Ukraine). He holds an A.B. in English Literature from Princeton University (New Jersey, USA), a M.Div. from Denver Seminary (Colourado, USA), and a Ph.D. in Patristics from the University of Cambridge. He has served as a missionary in two Republics of the former Soviet Union: Georgia and Ukraine.

Theodore Gabriel was born in Kerala State, India, and trained in Anthropology and Religious Studies at the University of Aberdeen, Scotland. He was Senior Lecturer in Religious Studies at the University of Gloucestershire until 2000, and is currently Honorary Research Fellow at the same university. He has carried out research into Islam and Hinduism in Kerala, Lakshadweep and Malaysia, and has published articles on both Islam and Hinduism. Recent publications include: *Hindu-Muslim Relations in North Malabar* (1996); *Christian-Muslim Relations: A Case Study of Sarawak, East Malaysia* (1996); *Hindu and Muslim Inter-Religious Relations in Malaysia* (2000); and (ed.) *Islam in the Contemporary World* (2000).

Ron Geaves is Senior Lecturer and Programme Leader in Religious Studies at the Department of Theology and Religious Studies, University College Chester, England. He has published extensively on the transmigration of religious traditions from the subcontinent to the West. He has a long history of engagement with mysticism across several religious traditions both as a result of academic study and extensive personal 'travel' in the Muslim world and the Indian subcontinent.

Seth Gottesman teaches Judaism and Jewish mysticism in the Department for the Study of Religions, University College Chichester, Chichester, England. He is both a student and a teacher of contemporary practical *Kabbalah* and is currently carrying out research into the contemporary influence of *Kabbalah* in the UK.

Peter Hicks has pastored a number of churches and currently teaches philosophy and pastoral theology at London Bible College, England. His doctoratal research focussed on philosophical concepts in the thought of Charles Hodge. He has written several books and articles in the areas of philosophy and pastoral care, including, *Evangelicals and Truth: A Creative Proposal for a Postmodern Age* (1998).

Dewi Hughes has worked with Tearfund since 1987 in a variety of roles, and is, at present, Theological Advisor to the organisation. Previously, from 1975 he was Senior Lecturer in Religious Studies at the Polytechnic of Wales/University of Glamorgan. He has written several articles and books, including *Has God Many Names?* (1996), *God of the Poor* (1998), and *Castrating Culture: a Christian Perspective on Ethnic Identity from the Margins* (2001).

Helen Marshall is an Anglican priest who has worked in a parish in inner city Bristol, England, and also taught at St Paul's Theological College, Kenya. She is currently working as Chaplain to the Waterloo campus of King's College London, London University.

I. David Miller is Lecturer in Mission Studies at the International Christian College, Glasgow, Scotland. Between 1986 and 1996 he and his wife worked in Japan. For some of that time they were staff members with Kirisutosha Gakusei Kai, the Japanese Christian Students Association (affiliated with IFES). He is now pursuing postgraduate study at Lancaster University looking at conversion among Japanese, comparing those who convert to Christianity with those who convert to Japanese New Religious Movements.

Christopher Partridge is Senior Lecturer in Theology and Contemporary Religion in the Department of Theology and Religious Studies at University College Chester, England. He has published academic articles in the areas of contemporary Christian theology, methodology in the study of religion, and particularly new religions and alternative spiritualities in the West. Recent publications include *H.H. Farmer's Theological Interpretation of Religion: Towards a Personalist Theology of Religions* (1998), (ed.) *Fundamentalisms* (2001), (ed.) *Dictionary of Contemporary Religion in the Western World* (2002).

Introduction

Christopher Partridge & Theodore Gabriel

To have positive religion is not necessary. To be in harmony with oneself and the whole is what counts, and this is possible without positive and specific formulation in words.

Goethe

The Higher part of contemplation, as it may be had here, hangeth all wholly in this darkness and in this cloud of unknowing; with a love stirring and a blind beholding unto the naked being of God Himself only.

The Cloud of Unknowing

For one moment sink into the ocean of God, and do not suppose that one hair of your head shall be moistened by the water of the seven seas. If the vision you behold is the face of God, there is no doubt that from this time forward you will see clearly. When the foundations of your own existence are destroyed, have no fear in your heart that you yourself will perish.

Hafiz

For though she sink all sinking in the oneness of divinity, she never touches bottom. For it is the very essence of the soul that she is powerless to plumb the depths of her creator. And here one cannot speak of the soul any more, for she has lost her nature yonder in the oneness of divine essence. There she is no more called soul, but is called immeasurable being.

Meister Eckhart

Mysticism in the Modern West

'Mysticism' (sometimes identified with 'spirituality') is proving to be the chosen type of religion for future generations of believers in the West.

As traditional institutional religion continues to decline, mystical thought is celebrated as a vital, subversive alternative. There is often a particular rejection of traditional Christian theology because, for example, it is said to stifle spirituality, being fundamentally dualistic, patriarchal and, consequently, ecologically disastrous. This line of thought has been consistently developed by the theologian Matthew Fox, who argues that 'Western spirituality has two basic traditions – that which starts with the experience of sin and develops a fall/redemption spiritual motif; and that which starts with the experience of life as a blessing and develops a creation-centred spirituality.'[1] Creation spirituality, the core of which derives from a particular interpretation of the medieval Christian mystics, Meister Eckhart especially, is understood to be 'a condition sine qua non for ecumenism on a worldwide scale … There will be no worldwide ecumenism without creation-centred spirituality. For ecumenism is not a pious duty or one more commandment, it is an overflow of the relationship we experience with all that is.'[2] (See Richard Bauckham's critique of Fox in Chapter 11.)

Evidence for this religio-cultural shift towards the mystical, the experiential and indeed the creation-centred can be found in bookshops, most of which devote a large amount of shelf space to mystical themes and mystical writers from the world religions. Certainly in the West, there is a remarkable resurgence of interest in teachers such as Kahlil Gibran, Idries Shah, Hazrat Inayat Khan, Alan Watts, Osho and Jiddu Krishnamurti, an emergence of what might be described as a neo-Celtic nature mysticism, massive popular and academic interest in Kabbalah (see Seth Gottesman's discussion in Chapter 8), an increasing number of westerners who turn East because they find the fundamentally mystical thought of Asian religious traditions appealing (see Chapter 7), and, furthermore, numerous westerners who actually become gurus and mystics within Eastern traditions.[3]

This shift (identified by Paul Heelas as the shift from 'religion' to 'spirituality'[4]) is, of course, not new. Whilst, generally speaking, the early modern period did not provide particularly suitable cultural soil for the cultivation of the seeds of Eastern mysticism, there has been a gradual and growing turn to the East over this period. Whether we think of Arthur Schopenhauer's appreciation of Upanishadic philosophy or the promotion of Hindu and Buddhist ideas by the Theosophical Society which, in turn, inspired the emergence of numerous contemporary alternative spiritualities,[5] there has been widening stream of thought throughout the modern period which has criticised Enlightenment rationalism and sought a more mystical form of enlightenment (see Chapter 16). Indeed, the Easternisation of occultism by H.P. Blavatsky (who founded the Theosophical Society in 1875) is a particularly noteworthy point in Western cultural history.[6] After a shaky start, the founders, Blavatsky and Henry Olcott, established the headquarters of the Theosophical Society in Adyar, India. This led to close and formative links with Hindus and Buddhists and eventually to a shift from Western to Eastern esotericism. With its headquarters in India, and as a result of the work of industrious evangelists, such as Annie Besant (who, on Blavatsky's death in 1891, effectively took over the leadership of the organisation), the society became a conduit of Eastern mystical thought to the West. Also of great significance during this particularly fertile period for the emergence of new forms of mystical religion in the West, was the conspicuously positive reception of Ramakrishna's influential disciple, Swami Vivekananda, at the 1893 World's Parliament of Religions in Chicago.[7] Indeed, such was his impact that, 'it is said that to retain a satisfactory audience for a particular session, the chairman's secret was to announce Vivekananda as the final speaker.'[8] After the Parliament, Vivekananda embarked on a nationwide lecture tour in America, which included a brief visit to Britain where he recruited a number of disciples. This culminated in the 1896 with the founding of the Vedanta Society. After returning to India and founding the Ramakrishna Mission Association, he again visited the USA and founded the Vedanta Society of California in 1899. The Easternisation of the West, and with it the 'mysticization' (if another ugly neologism can be excused) of the West had begun in earnest. Several years later in 1907, D.T. Suzuki published his *Outlines of Mahayana Buddhism* and continued, until his death in 1966, to teach Zen Buddhism to increasing numbers of eager westerners. This, in turn, has led to a situation in which there are now many westerners teaching Eastern mystical paths. 'A century ago there were no Western masters – no Westerners who were Hindu *swamis*, Zen *roshis*, or Sufi *sheikhs*. Now there are hundreds. From a standing start the West has produced its own spiritual teachers in traditions that were originally quite foreign ... These people are changing Western culture by making available a view of the human condition which is new to the West.'[9]

Central to much Easternised mystical religion in the West has been an experience-centred vision of religious unity. Indeed, the very idea of the mystical unity of religion has attracted widespread interest in the modern Western world. The popular Christian thinker Bede Griffith's, for example, sets out a 'unifying plan' on the basis of just such a vision of mystical unity in which we all 'direct our minds, our wills and our hearts towards the Infinite and ... allow that Infinite to enter into our lives and transform them.'[10] Again, 'New Age' thinkers Fritjof Capra and David

Steindl-Rast celebrate 'a renaissance of religious experience', 'a new explicit appreciation of religious experience.' They make the point that, 'the deep sense of inner communion with God was thought not so long ago to be the privilege of "mystics". Today, this sense of inner communion is widespread. Today we recognise that every human being can be a mystic of sorts.'[11] (Hughes provides a brief, helpful discussion discussion of Capra at the end of Chapter 16.) Increasingly in the West, religious people are inspired, not by doctrine, not by theological argument, not by philosophic apologetic, but rather by the expectation of mystical *experience*. There is, not only within new religions and alternative spiritualities, but also within traditional religions, a treading of the mystical path. Books such as Canon Peter Spink's significantly titled *Beyond Belief: How to Develop Mystical Consciousness and Discover the God Within*, which claims to help those 'seeking a God they can know and experience directly', and to provide 'guidelines and signposts to help you in your intuitive, spiritual and mystical development',[12] are numerous and popular.

Philosophers and religious studies scholars have also noted that the accounts of mystical experience found within the world religions, whilst distinctive in several respects, do seem to indicate an essentially similar experience. Indeed, Philip Barnes (in Chapter 15) and, from a slightly different perspective which focuses on process and intent rather than simply on the peak experience itself, Ron Geaves (in Chapter 2), cogently argue that there is much to commend the view that the inner mystical experience is fundamentally *the same* throughout the different religions and cultures. There is, it is sometimes claimed, a 'phenomenological unity of mystical experiences'. Whilst, for Barnes, this places a question mark over the value of mystical experience for the Christian, other scholars, such as the American idealist philosopher William Hocking,[13] and, more recently, John Hick, have argued that such phenomenological unity is indicative of something profoundly spiritually positive. For example, Hick makes the following point:

When we study the reports of these outstanding sensitives we find that their experiences exhibit a common pattern, not in their visual and auditory contents but in the 'information' which they express ... [The] hypothesis that I am proposing is that the universal presence of the Real, in which 'we live and move and have our being', generates within certain exceptionally open and sensitive individuals an unconscious awareness of an aspect or aspects of its meaning for our human existence. In cybernetic terms this is 'information' about the significance of the Real for our lives.[14]

(An overview of the modern interest in mysticism and an analysis of the notion that it constitutes the essence of religion, a 'perennial philosophy', is provided by Dewi Hughes in Chapter 16. Indeed, he persuasively argues that such perennialism lies at the core of post-Enlightenment Western thought: 'The interest in mysticism which is becoming more and more pervasive today is not so much a rejection of modernism as the inevitable consequence of it. It is the other face of modernism.'

Of course, along with this Western interest in mysticism, there has been distinctly anti-mystical theologies and philosophies. Many theologians of an earlier generation, particularly those influenced by the anti-speculative thought of Albrecht Ritschl, argued that mystical experiences were not only too bizarre, subjective, and various, but, they were wholly unsuitable sources for either Christian theology or moral guidance. One such theologian was James Denney. Unhappy with certain interpretations of 'mystical union' which 'destroy the personality and individuality of the sinner', he makes a distinction between being 'saved in Christ' and 'lost in God'.[15] Another important British theologian, H.H. Farmer, was uncomfortable with mysticism because such 'religion of introversion' continually faces the danger of shifting away from the sense of responsible personal relationships between the individual and God, and the individual and her neighbour. Instead, the religious life becomes 'an egocentric observation and cultivation of one's own states of mind, and an immoral withdrawal from the problems and challenges of historical existence.'[16] Indeed, for Farmer (and he was not alone – Denney, for one, would have agreed with him), 'mysticism' indicates both the religious impulse towards an impersonalist conception of ultimate reality, and, closely related to this, a particular method of satisfying the human need for unification. 'In essence it is the method of cultivating, usually through highly elaborated techniques of withdrawal and concentration, states of consciousness in which the self, or the world as apprehended by the self, or both of these together, are emptied of that differentiated content which they have in normal, everyday experience.'[17] The problem is that this, more often than not, leads to an impersonalist theology (often with a strong pantheistic/monistic tendency[18]). According to Farmer, any psychological technique which seeks to expunge all differentiations, dualities and tensions from the consciousness

> can only be given a philosophical or metaphysical ground and justification ... by a doctrine in which all such differentiation ... [is] denied significant place in relation to that ultimate reality with which in the end a man must settle accounts. But such a denial necessarily commits you to a fundamentally impersonal view of

ultimate reality and of its relation to men; for it is easy to see that if all distinctions and dualities vanish anything in the nature of an ultimate personal order in which man and God and man and neighbour are in personal relationship with one another vanishes also.[19]

Whilst the above are important Christian theological concerns, we have seen that, generally speaking, the Ritschlian severance of religion from the speculative and the mystical is not popular today. That said, this volume does demonstrate that there is still no consensus amongst Christians over this point. For example, whilst the evangelical philosopher Peter Hicks calls for a renewed appreciation of mystical experience in theology and worship (Chapter 17), and Rev Helen Marshall persuasively argues for the contemporary relevance of the teaching of St. John of the Cross (Chapter 12), Philip Barnes is rather more cautious about the value of Christian mysticism, understanding it to be 'a denial of Christian discipleship' (Chapter 15).

Finally, another area of Western thought in which mysticism is receiving attention, as Arthur Bradley discusses in his particularly thought-provoking chapter (Chapter 14), is modern French philosophy. 'The last few years', he writes, 'have witnessed a sudden explosion of interest in the relationship between the work of Christian mystical theologians like Pseudo-Dionysius and continental philosophers like Jacques Derrida.' Certainly, there are interesting parallels which can be fruitfully explored between the deconstruction of such as Derrida and the negative or apophatic theology of such as Pseudo-Dionysius. (See Don Fairbairn's excellent discussion of apophatic theology in Eastern Orthodox Christianity – Chapter 9.) Bradley examines these parallels and indicates how it might be argued that modern French thought 'saves the name' (Derrida) of Christian mysticism.

Mysticism in the East

In the Eastern traditions the mystical aspect has always been prominent and continues to be so in spite of periods of priestly hegemony and burgeoning of the ritual aspect. Eastern theology has always stressed a pervasive monism as the higher and ultimate reality as against the dualism of the Semitic religious traditions. Ritualism and priestly dominance have always existed side by side with mysticism, though greater respect has always been accorded to the more introspective, meditative and experiential dimensions of religious praxis. Certainly the individual *sadhu* or *sanyasin* who has withdrawn from society and whose focus is in the unity of the *atman* and the *Brahman* than salvation, in the limited sense of experiencing the joys and bliss of heaven, has gained prominence in recent times, and the so-called 'god-men' of whom there are numerous examples have attracted the attention of Westerners considerably in their spiritual quest, again, perhaps a sign of dissatisfaction with the dualistic and doctrinaire tendencies of traditional Christianity. Mysticism is, however, the aspect of religion that draws differing traditions together. A classic example is that of Ramakrishna, the famous Bengali mystic, whose mystical experiences were grounded not only in Hinduism, but also in Islam and Christianity (see David Burnett's interesting discussion in Chapter 6). Ruth Bradby, in her discussion of Hindu mysticism (Chapter 5), shows how the mysticism of Chaitanya (and the International Society for Krishna Consciousness) transcended divisions of caste and religious hierarchy in Hinduism. Since here dogma and doctrine are discounted, and logical rationality is not always the foundation of religious thought, there is a greater potentiality of drawing experience from various religious traditions together. Figuratively speaking, as noted earlier, it has been argued that mysticism is the apex of religious experience to which all religions converge. Speaking of Hinduism, a devout catholic, Roger Murray, writes the following:

> It was in those times of sitting at the feet of the *rishis*, the Vedic seers, and also in times of silence and solitude that must accompany any serious listening to that call, that the need to go beyond *dvandva*, The dualities, became clear. The resonances in our own 'Christian' souls made it impossible any longer to judge this deep Hindu source as being 'outside', another source than ours. Whether it was that extraordinary mystical document, the *Katha* or some other *Upanishad*, or the *Bhagavad Gita* that has sustained countless Hindu men and women on their pilgrimage through life, we were slowly becoming aware that these were our spiritual sustenance as well as theirs.[20]

Moreover, Eastern traditions emphasise the experiential dimension of religion rather than creeds and beliefs. The experience of God is paramount and God is within the individual, indeed the individual is not intrinsically different from God. The ultimate being is impersonal in the sense that it is immanent in creation as well as transcendent. In this state it is beyond worship, beyond limitations of any kind, beyond language and beyond limited conception. Enlightenment, *jnana*, is the ultimate aim of mysticism in all Eastern traditions, be it known as *Brahman* or *Nibbana* (*Nirvana*), not a worldly knowledge which is, in the ultimate analysis, false, created by *avidya* (a knowledge of appearances which are unreal and illusory mediated through the senses), but non-dual, timeless and real, *para vidya* (a transcendental knowledge). It can only be experienced, not described. This is what the Hindu Vedas help devotees to do. Raimundo Panikkar makes the following point:

> The Vedic revelation is not primarily a thematic communication of esoteric facts ... but for the most part the Vedic revelation is the discrete illumination of a veil ... The Vedic revelation unfolds the process of man becoming conscious.[21]

And it can only be experienced and known in a mystical state of being, not in the normal human condition, where the *triputi* (distinctions between the knower, the knowledge and the known) become blurred and transcended, yielding a unity that is the *Brahman*. Burnett's study of Ramakrishna (Chapter 6) talks about the mystical trance (*samadhi*) when he achieves union with the absolute and leaves behind the inert and empty shell of the human body. Amazingly this is an experience he can communicate to others by his touch and even proximity. Such experience of the divine seems to have been lost in the more orthodox forms of all religious traditions, though in the Eastern traditions such events are not rare and are sought after by many. Even ordinary ritual in some traditions exhibits this sort of mystical unity of the human and the divine. The Sufi Dhikr, described by Theodore Gabriel in his essay (Chapter 4) is one such instance when infused by the Divine the Sufi dancers can perform wonderful acts of self-mortification. Another striking example of this is in the Teyyam ritual of the Muttappan in Kerala, where the ritualist who wears costumes representing the deity achieves a mystical union with the divine during which he acts, talks and functions as the divinity in an inimitable way. The Muttapan represents the ultimate, in a limited sense of the supreme beings Vishnu and Shiva, which, in the Vishishtadvaita tradition of Ramanuja, is a clear manifestation of the *Brahman*. A more permanent earthly manifestation of the divine is in the Sai Baba who radiates divine power and aura, and through his many miracles signal this mystical union of the divine and the human in a tangible and durable manner.

So, in the East, theological and doctrinal distinctions give precedence to mystical experience. In the Eastern view truth claims are not important. In the Eastern sense truth is ontic and experiential not epistemic. The opposition is not between truth and untruth, but the real and the unreal as exemplified by the famous passage from the *Brihadaranyaka Upanishad*, beginning *asat ma sat gamaya* (lead me from the unreal to the real). The Sanskrit word for truth, *satya*, has its roots in '*sat*' (essence). Truth is the vision of the real. Truth is *anubhava*, a state of experiencing the real.

As we hve seen, Western Christianity has, to some extent, been suspicious of and even discounted the mystical tradition and focused on a rational approach to unerstanding God. Systematic and scientific theology has been its primary concern whereas in the East it has been expeiencing God. In the East, meditation rather than rational enquiry has been the methodology designed to know or become aware of the truth. Wilfred Felix, an Indian Christian theologian states:

> A second difficulty concerns the exaggerated anthropocentrism of Western Christianity. The Bible does speak about the prominence of humanity as the image of God (Gen. 1:26), and acknowledges his place in creation. However, the concrete development of history in Western Christianity has extrapolated the biblical thought and has paved the way for the emergence of egocentrism and rugged individualism in the modern world ... the anthropocentrism which underlies the present socio-political, economic and military systems is not acceptable to the East whose thoughts and praxis have been animated by a holistic vision of interdependence of the entire reality.[22]

Mahinda Deegalle in his absorbing essay on the mystical experiences of Matala Vanaranta, a twentieth-century Sri Lankan Buddhist monk, recounts the incredible visions and sensations experienced by the monk during various stages of Kasioa meditation.

Again, as we have seen above, increasingly the tide is turning. More and more Christians are now veering away to this perspective of Christ and God. To quote Bede Griffiths again, who was both a Christian mystic and advocate of the marriage of the East and West:

> The Hebrew starts from the transcendence of God and gradually discovers His immanence; the Hindu starts from the immanence and reaches out towards His transcendence. It is a difference of point of view. Each is complementary to the other and opens up a different perspective.[23]

At a first glance, Islam seems to emphasise law and ritual rather than the more introspective and reflective spiritual processes. But Muhammad was himself a mystic, meditating in caves and receiving visions of angels, heavenly books and experiencing a mystical journey to heaven, the *miraj.* Through its initial preoccupation with law and ritual, Islam would probably have become a dry, lifeless and legislative religion, and lost the early fervour which contributed to its phenomenal growth, but for the Sufis who not only revitalised the religion but also effected its spread to hitherto uncharted lands such as South East Asia. Sufism had the advantage that it was ready to absorb into its praxis elements from indigenous religions wherever it went, whether in Bengal or Indonesia or China. Mystical experience thus transcended the creedal, ritualistic and legalistic boundaries that Islam so strictly prescribed, and attracted into its fold people of Hindu, Buddhist and Animistic persuasions. Clifford Geertz in his well-known *Islam Observed*[24] speaks of the famous Javanese Sufi mystic, Sunan Kalidjaga, who had initially been a notorious dacoit. Meeting a Sufi saint in the forest he demanded his money, but was told to look behind. Turning he beheld a tree on which precious stones of all kinds hung like fruits. Amazed and contrite the robber asked the mystic how he could acquire such great powers. The Sufi replied, 'Stand where you are until my return'. Years lapsed and the dacoit was still rooted to the spot when the Sufi saint reappeared suddenly. He asked the robber abstruse questions about the Qur'an and Kalidjaga was able to answer all these questions accurately. This is an illustration of the kind of *gnosis* and unmediated knowledge that, it is claimed, meditation and other mystical practices confer on the seeker after truth.

In the modern world, however, there has been a tendency in Islam to discredit Sufism and attempts to forge a Wahabi model of Islam which would purge itself of the influence of other religious traditions and would seek to be based mainly on the implementation of law. Saudi Arabia and Afghanistan under the Taliban would be classic examples of this trend. But Sufism nevertheless remains strong in many regions and imparts vigour and vitality and also a tolerant view of other faiths to many Islamic communities. Theodore Gabriel in Chapter 4 gives an account of the Sufis of Lakshadweep, a group of Arabian Sea Islands in which Sufism remains a vital part of Islamic praxis and where a puritanical type of Islam has not been able to make much headway unlike most other Islamic nations. Here the traditions of wonder-working Sufi mystics known as Tangals abound and the *dhikr* (literally, 'remembrance of God') remains a central mystical practice.

The Book

The aim of the volume is to provide an overview of a range of mysticisms from both Eastern and Western traditions. Whilst there are numerous books on both 'Western' mysticism, 'Eastern' mysticism, mysticism

within particular religious traditions, individual mystics, or on the philosophical analysis of mystical experience, there are few which bring
together studies in all these areas. Although, of course, a single volume
could not hope to be comprehensive (not even the massive 'World
Spirituality'[25] series achieved this), it is hoped that this volume will provide a relatively accessible introduction both to a range of mysticisms
and also to some of the key religious and philosophical issues related
mystical experience.

The volume is not explicitly separated into discrete parts. Whilst the
reader will notice that an attempt has been made to group the chapters
– in that the volume begins in the East, gradually moves to the West and
to Christian mysticism, and finally concludes with philosophically reflective essays examining the implications and nature of mysticism *per se* –
categorising beliefs into those from 'the East' and those from 'the West' is
not always straightforward and nor is it particularly helpful. For example,
whilst Lakshadweep Sufism, Hindu Mysticism, or the ideas of Tolkien,
Lewis and Barfield might be relatively easy to classify in this way, what
about psychedelic mysticism? What about the Desert Fathers? Are
'Christian' traditions always essentially 'Western'? What about Eastern
Orthodox spirituality? Hence, whilst the volume does have a discernable
structure, we have resisted the temptation to provide neat boxes.

Notes

[1] M. Fox, 'Introduction', in M. Fox (ed.), *Western Spirituality: Historical Roots,
Ecumenical Routes* (Sanata Fe: Bear & Company, 1981), 2.

[2] Ibid., 16.

[3] For an fascinating and encyclopaedic survey the Western reception and transformation of Eastern teachings, see A. Rawlinson, *The Book of Enlightened
Masters: Western Teachers in Eastern Traditions* (Chicago: Open Court, 1997).

[4] Although, bearing in mind the many years of complex discussions of these
terms, particularly 'religion', I have reservations about the too easy usage of
them by Heelas, I recognise the validity and importance of the point being
made. See P. Heelas, 'The Spiritual Revolution: From "Religion" to
"Spirituality"', in L. Woodhead, P. Fletcher, H. Kawanami, & D. Smith (eds.),
Religions in the Modern World: Traditions and Transformations (London: Routledge,
2002), 357–77.

[5] See K. Tingay, 'Madame Blavatsky's Children: Theosophy and Its Heirs', in S.
Sutcliffe & M. Bowman (eds.), *Beyond New Age: Exploring Alternative Spirituality*
(Edinburgh: Edinburgh University Press, 2000), 37–50.

[6] For an interesting and lively, if not particularly sympathetic or objective,
account of the emergence and significance of the Theosophical Society, see

Peter Washington, *Madame Blavatsky's Baboon: Theosophy and the Emergence of the Western Guru* (London: Secker & Warburg, 1993).

[7] For an interesting, though poorly produced and not always legible, collection of documents and newspaper articles relating to the gathering see E. Chattopadhyaya, *World's Parliament of Religions, 1893* (Calcutta: Minerva Associates, 1995). For a discussion of the significance of the gathering for the development of contemporary Western alternative spirituality see L. Woodhead, 'The World's Parliament of Religions and the Rise of Alternative Spirituality', in L. Woodhead (ed.), *Reinventing Christianity: Nineteenth Century Contexts* (Aldershot: Ashgate, 2001), 81–96. For an excellent overview of the Parliament, see M. Braybrooke, *Pilgrimae of Hope: One Hundred Years of Global Interfaith Dialogue* (London: SCM, 1992), chs. 1–3.

[8] Braybrooke, *Pilgrimage*, 32.

[9] Rawlinson, *Book of Enlightened Masters*, xvii.

[10] B. Griffiths, *A New Vision of Reality: Western Science, Eastern Mysticism and Christian Faith*, F. Edwards (ed.) (London: HarperCollins, Fount, 1989), 275. See especially chs. 12 & 13.

[11] F. Capra, D. Steindl-Rast & T. Matus, *Belonging to the Universe: New Thinking About God and Nature* (Harmondsworth: Penguin, 1992), 48.

[12] P. Spink, *Beyond Belief: How to Develop Mystical Consciousness and Discover the God Within* (London: Piatkus, 1996), back cover.

[13] See W.E. Hocking, *The Meaning of God in Human Experience* (New Haven: Yale University Press, 1912), 341–427. See also R. Woods, 'Mysticism, Protestantism, and Ecumenism: The Spiritual Theology of William Ernest Hocking', in Fox (ed.), *Western Spirituality*, 414–36. See also M.L. Furse, *Experience and Certainty: William Ernest Hocking and Philosophical Mysticism* (Atlanta: Scholars Press, 1988).

[14] J. Hick, *An Interpretation of Religion: Human Responses to the Transcendent* (Basingstoke: Macmillan, 1989), 169.

[15] J. Denney, *The Christian Doctrine of Reconciliation* (London: Hodder & Stoughton, 1917), 306–7.

[16] H.H. Farmer, *Revelation and Religion: Studies in the Theological Interpretation of Religious Types* (London: Nisbet, 1954; New York: Edwin Mellen, 1999), 134.

[17] H.H. Farmer, *Reconciliation and Religion: Some Aspects of the Uniqueness of Christianity as a Reconciling Faith*, C. Partridge (ed.), (New York: Edwin Mellen, 1998), 13.

[18] See Denney's thoughts on pantheism in *Letters of Principal James Denney to W. Robertson Nicoll, 1893–1917* (London: Hodder & Stoughton, 1920), 79–82.

[19] Farmer, *Reconciliation and Religion*, 13–14. Cf. Farmer, *Revelation and Religion*, ch. 10.

[20] Murray Rogers, 'Hindu Influence on Christian Spiritual Practice', in H. Coward (ed.), *Hindu-Christian Dialogue* (Maryknoll: Orbis, 1996), 200–1.

[21] R. Panikkar, *The Vedic Experience: Mantra Manjari* (London: Darton, Longman & Todd, 1977), 14.

[22] W. Felix, 'Asia and Western Christianity', *Pacifica* 2 (1989), 270–1.

[23] B. Griffiths, *The Marriage of East and West* (London: Collins, 1982), 26.

[24] C. Geertz, *Islam Observed* (New Haven: Yale University Press, 1968).

[25] Published by SCM Press in Britain and Crossroad Publishing in the USA.

1

It's More than a Zen Thing

The Mystical Dimension in Japanese Religion

David Miller

A shaven-headed monk in black robe sits motionless on the veranda of a Kyoto temple. In front of him stretches out the universe, symbolised in sand and rock. Raked patterns in the sand draw his mind into the Void, into the realisation that all is one, that he himself is not, and that there is only mind. Therein lies enlightenment. All is silent.

For many Westerners this is the archetypal image of Japanese religion and mysticism. Indeed, as far as they are concerned, Japanese religion *is* mysticism. Here in the West, Japanese religion is associated with, and often identified with, the Zen school of Buddhism, which focuses on meditation and the search for enlightenment. Out of Zen come many of the traditional arts of Japan, the tea ceremony, flower arranging, haiku poetry, and the martial arts. All of these speak to Western hearts and minds searching for quietness, tranquillity and a sense of balance, hence the responsiveness to Zen in the West.

Now, in the sense that these things *do* emerge from Zen, and that Zen is arguably the form of Japanese religion which comes closest to the Western understanding of mystical experience, all of the above is true. Indeed, contemporary forms of mysticism in the West have been influenced by Zen teachings and practice through the writings of Japanese such as D.T. Suzuki and Westerners such as Alan Watts and Philip Kapleau. Nevertheless, we are in danger of seriously misunderstanding both Zen and the far wider mystical dimension of Japanese religion if we look at it through Western eyes and try to understand it in Western terms.

In this essay, then, we will first of all attempt to sketch, from a historical perspective, some of the themes in Japanese religion, in particular the mystical elements which are found within its practices. After that there will be a closer look at Zen Buddhism itself. This will be followed by some comment on the mystical elements within Japanese new religious movements, arguably the most dynamic feature of the contemporary religious landscape in Japan.

One more point needs to be made. No doubt in a multi-author volume such as this, contributors will have varying definitions of mysticism. That is inevitable when trying to put into words something which is of course beyond words. In the Japanese context, mysticism should be thought of as something wider than the practice of meditation or the attaining of enlightenment. The definition of mysticism as 'a brief episode or more prolonged state of contact or unity with a transcendent reality, experienced in the source or subject of a profound metaphysical knowledge or insight'[1] is helpful, but in looking at the place of mysticism within Japanese religion it is inadequate. In what follows, practices and experiences other than those traditionally thought of in the West as being 'mystical' will also be considered. These will include experiences of religious ecstasy and possession, as well as the more contemplative experiences normally associated with mysticism. This is because all these various practices and experiences are part of the same phenomenon which ought to be thought of as the mystical dimension in Japanese religion. And as will be seen, running through the various types of mystical experience found in Japanese religion, the more or less common thread is that experience is not sought after for itself, but for what it will bring as a result.

The Mystical Dimension in the Traditional Religions of Japan

Mystical practices in Japanese religion stretch back to the shamanistic origins of Japanese folk religion, the practices which eventually evolved into Shinto. Joseph Kitagawa writes:

> One of the earliest features of Japanese religion was the existence
> of the shamanic diviner, known variously as *miko, ichiko* or *mono-*
> *mochi,* who, in the state of *kami*[2] – possession performed fortune-
> telling, transmission of spirit messages and healing.[3]

From the earliest days, then, the belief that certain people possessed special, spiritual powers was a key concept in the minds of Japanese. In some cases, notably those of the *miko*, the diviners attached either to a particular shrine or to a particular clan, these powers were hereditary. In other cases the powers could be sought after and attained through austere ascetic practices.

These practices continued and were modified after the arrival of Buddhism in Japan, from Korea and China, in the sixth century. Buddhism offered more impressive rituals for reverencing or worshipping ancestors, and in general had a more developed series of doctrines and structures than did Shinto. Indeed, the name *Shinto*, as referring to the original religious practices of the Japanese, only emerged when there came a need to make some differentiation between what was indigenous to the country and what was imported from China and Korea, that is, Buddhism. However, despite its adoption by many of the aristocracy of Japan, for the majority of the population, Buddhist doctrines were too complicated and its formal rituals failed to meet their everyday needs. Thus there emerged a fusion between Buddhism and the traditional folk religious practices of Japan – Shugendo, 'the Way of Cultivating Spiritual Powers'.

Shugendo practitioners were known as *yamabushi*, 'those who live in the mountain'. There were a range of austerities which they undertook in the mountains to gain spiritual power, including fasting, the chanting of spells, solitary meditation, pilgrimages, and standing under waterfalls. Having acquired such powers, they would then come down from the mountains and travel around villages distributing talismans, exorcising spirits and dealing with the harmful influences of these spirits over ordinary people. Meditation was part of their practices, as is revealed in the following excerpt from *The Sutra on the Unlimited Life of the Threefold Body as Taught by the Buddha*. The origin of this piece of writing is unclear, but it does seem to be one of the few Buddhist apocryphal texts[4] actually written in Japan (as opposed to being translated from Chinese). The text is significant in this context in that it gives some indication of the place of meditative practices within the Shugendo tradition. It takes the form of a dialogue between Manjushri (known in Japan as Monju), the *Boddhisatva* of wisdom, and the Buddha, referred to in the text as 'the World-Honoured One', and concerns the origin of the Buddha's teachings and the true nature of enlightenment.

> The World-Honoured One once again said, 'There is nothing that teaches or receives above and beyond the original Buddha of no mind and no thought. Moreover, this is a single Buddha, and there are not two Buddhas. You all should shut your eyes and contemplate the original Buddha that is without beginning and without end' ...
>
> > The supreme path of all Buddhas
> > Has the marks of perfect light and eternal abiding.
> > Those who enter meditative concentration together with
> >   [the Buddha]
> > In the same way realise the mind of enlightenment.[5]

Thus, meditation leading to enlightenment is seen as a key part of Shugendo practice. And the aim of this practice is the acquisition of spiritual power for the benefit of others.

The origins of Shugendo go back to the seventh and eighth centuries CE, and it still continues today. Not only did the *yamabushi* come to be significant figures in Japanese popular religion, but the idea that 'spiritual power' was acquired through asceticism in the mountains also grew in strength. This 'spiritual power' was often thought of as something necessary not just in the area of popular religion, but for developing particular martial and artistic skills as well. The fact that many of the traditional arts of Japan are referred to as 'Ways', the Way of the Sword (*Kendo*), the Way of Tea (*Chado*), the Way of the Bow (*Kyudo*), and so on, in fact indicates a feeling that these are somehow spiritual activities.

In his novel *Musashi,* Yoshikawa Eiji captures some of this expectation. The novel's hero, Musashi, aspires to learn the Way of the Sword. This search involves not only study under other great swordsmen, but the search for enlightenment, acquired through austere practices which will lead him to accomplish his desire. Here Yoshikawa describes Musashi's experience as he struggles to climb the near unconquerable Eagle Mountain.

> The instant he had reached the top, his strained willpower snapped like a bowstring. The wind at the summit showered his back with sand and stones. Here at the border of heaven and earth, Musashi felt an indescribable joy swelling out to fill his whole being. His sweat-drenched body united with the surface of the mountain; the spirit of man and the spirit of the mountain were performing the great work of procreation in the vast expanse of nature at dawn.[6]

The language here describes more than exultation at achieving a great feat. There is clearly a form of mystical union described here, interestingly using sexual imagery, as other mystics have done to describe the intensity of their experiences. The book is a work of fiction, though based on a historical character, but despite this fictional stance, the author is drawing on an understanding amongst Japanese that enlightenment was often achieved through asceticism. And again, this experience was not the end in itself, but the means to a goal. These ideas continue today.

Many schools of Japanese Buddhism appear to emphasise ceremonial and ritual activities. Throughout its history in Japan, and still today, for the majority of Japanese it is a background religion, mainly resorted to at times of death, or in matters related to the care of ancestors. Original Buddhism is atheistic, in that it teaches that all things are one, the

Buddha nature, and that there is no 'other'. However, in practice there appears to be, in Japanese Buddhism, a strong emphasis on spiritual beings and deities who *are* 'other' than the practitioner. This is due in part to the synthesis between Buddhism and Shinto, or rather, to the co-existence of the two religions in Japan, and the resulting identification of Shinto deities with Buddhist spiritual beings which developed over time as Shinto practices remained and learned to co-exist with Buddhism. Emphasis on these spiritual beings is also one of the distinctives of Mahayana Buddhism, which is the dominant form of Buddhism in East Asia, generally.

These spiritual beings are thought of as *boddhisatvas*. They are often referred to as deities, but, strictly speaking, they are different from how deities are often thought of in the West, that is, as those who are distinct from mortal beings. Rather, they are those who have attained enlightenment but who stop short of nirvana, the ultimate state of freedom from all entanglements, so as to be able to help others in their progression. In other words, they are those who have not chosen the easy road of personal satisfaction, but who have taken the hard road of aiding others. Manjushri, referred to above, is one such *boddhisatva*. Kannon, one of the most popular figures in Japanese religious life, is another. Kannon usually appears in feminine form in both Japanese and Chinese[7] pictures and statues, though originally Kannon was a 'he', referred to in Sanskrit as Avalokitesvara, 'the lord who looks in every direction'. His supreme quality is compassion, perhaps the reason why in China and Japan 'he' appears in feminine form. He is also regarded as the manifestation of Amida Buddha, the compassionate Buddha. It is faith in Amida Buddha which underlies the teaching of Jodo Shinshu, the Pure Land School, which is one of the most popular forms of Buddhism in Japan.

Pure Land Buddhism appears to be a contradiction of original Buddhism, which emphasised the unity of all things. It emphasises that salvation, understood as being entry into the Pure Land, is attainable through holding an attitude of thankfulness towards Amida Buddha, and through the recitation at the point of death of the *Nembutsu*. This is the formula *Namu Amida Buddha* ('I take refuge in Amida Buddha'), and recitation of that ensures entry into the Pure Land. This Pure Land is not to be understood as the final goal of Buddhism, which is nirvana, but it is a place where attaining the enlightenment necessary to enter nirvana is easily achieved, as it is a world without struggle and suffering. Parallels are often drawn between Pure Land Buddhism and the Christian concept of salvation by grace. These parallels are rather too simplistic, but it is true to say that in Japan, salvation in Pure Land Buddhism is thought of as being *tariki,* due to a power outside oneself.

Although Zen Buddhism is often thought of as the most mystical form of Buddhism in Japan, in Pure Land Buddhism too a sense of devotion which leans towards the mystical is apparent among experienced practitioners. D.T. Suzuki, the Japanese who more than any other popularised Zen in the West, actually felt that there had been as many cases of enlightenment among Pure Land Buddhists as there had been among Zen practitioners[8] Tucker Callaway was a Presbyterian missionary in Japan for many years who made a sympathetic and insightful study of Zen in particular and Japanese Buddhism in general. He records a poem written by Inagaki Saizo, a teacher in the Pure Land School, which captures this paradoxical feeling of devotion to something other than the devotee yet at the same time a sense of unity. In Buddhist terms, of course, this sense of unity is more than the intimacy of relationship towards which much Christian and Islamic mysticism aspires. It is the actual realisation of how things are, that there is in fact no 'other' and that all things are One. (It should be noted that the poem was written in English, and in style and imagery clearly shows the influence of the Psalms and of the Authorised Version of the Bible in its construction. Nevertheless, the theology that it reveals is Buddhist.)

> O Amitabha,[9] thou art hid from my sinful eye:
> Thou art Spirit: thou art the Law
> Thou art invisible: yet I embrace thee by faith
> Through thy strong Son of immortal love – Sakyamuni![10]
> When I think of thee and thy grace,
> Thou takest to thyself a spiritual form and presentest
> Thyself before mine eyes - a beautiful image,
> Noble and holy, august and supreme.
> I see thy face, not with eyes but in vision;
> The image that I adore and worship is golden and of human form;
> That image is not a mere symbol of thee, much less an idol
> Though it is made of wood or of metal by hand of man.
> I stand in thy presence day and night before thy image:
> I fold my hands before thy face and worship, but not as an idol
>   worshipper.
> Thou art here and there, in the air, and in the earth:
> Thou art anywhere; everywhere is thy mansion in the heights
>   above and in the depths beneath.
> Thou abidest in my heart; thy kingdom is built in my faith:
> When I hear thy commandment and thy Promise,
> Thou appearest before me: showest thyself to the eye of my
>   mind.[11]

Mystical devotion then is a feature of schools of Buddhism other than Zen. Nevertheless, it is Zen which is the form of Japanese Buddhism best known in the West, and to that we now turn.

And so to Zen

> The truth is, Zen is extremely elusive as far as its outward aspects are concerned; when you think you have caught a glimpse of it, it is no more there; from afar it looks so approachable, but as soon as you come near it you see it even further away from you than before.[12]

As mentioned already, Zen Buddhism is the form of Japanese religion which comes closest to Western concepts of mysticism. It is thought of as having meditation and contemplation at its heart, and indeed, Zen practice finds an appeal among many people in the West searching for mystical experience. As the quotation above makes clear, it is not easy to define Zen. Indeed, by its very nature it is almost beyond definition. It is certainly not something which can be grasped solely by intellectual study, but needs to be apprehended intuitively. However, before looking at the mystical aspects of Zen more deeply, it needs to be understood that in Japan, Zen Buddhism bears many similarities, and in society fulfils many similar roles, to other forms of Buddhism.

Zen was first introduced into Japan in the twelfth century at a time of religious and political crisis in Japan. The ruling aristocracy of Japan were seen to be failing, and the Buddhist clergy were morally corrupt. There was also a belief that the Final Dharma age, predicted by Buddhist teaching had begun. The monk Eisai, while studying in China, discovered that Zen Buddhism (in Chinese Ch'an Buddhism) had come to dominate the religious and political scene in China. Eisai saw it could have a similar role in Japan. His *Treatise on Promoting Zen for the Protection of the Country* argues why it should be adopted in Japan to replace the Tendai School which had been the main form of Buddhism up until that time. Eisai saw Zen as being the form of Buddhism which best preserved the essence of the Buddha's teaching. Significantly, he also saw it as providing moral training and discipline which he felt was lacking in contemporary Buddhist practice. In other words, for him, Zen was not simply a vehicle to encourage personal realisation of enlightenment, but something which would have an impact on the nation.

> According to the Benevolent Kings Sutra, 'The Buddha has entrusted the Buddhist teaching on wisdom to all present and future

rulers of petty kingdoms; it is considered a secret treasure for protecting their countries'. The Buddhist teaching on wisdom referred
to here is the teaching of the Zen school. In other words, if people
within a country uphold the Buddhist rules governing moral
behaviour, the various heavenly beings will protect that country.13

It is also highly significant that though the Tendai Buddhist establishment
and the rather decadent court nobility in Kyoto rejected his approach, the
new military government of Japan, the samurai class, adopted Zen and,
together with the Zen monks, established a new pattern for the governing of the country. Other factors, notably Confucianism, also influenced
samurai philosophy, which developed into their code of *Bushido*, the Way
of the Warrior, but Zen remained the underlying religious influence of
this code. Even after the abolition of the feudal system and the formal
end of the samurai class in the middle of the nineteenth century, their
ideals, including Zen, were adopted by Japan's new military classes who
still sought to embody the traditions of *Bushido*.14 For the samurai and
their successors, Zen was as much a way of developing discipline of
thought and subduing the body as a way of attaining enlightenment.

> It is self control, as it is the subduing of such pernicious passions as
> anger, jealousy, hatred, and the like, and the awakening of noble
> emotions such as sympathy, mercy, generosity, and what not.15

Despite its long period of influence over the samurai class, Zen found far
fewer followers among other groups in society, and is actually one of the
smaller Buddhist schools. It is Pure Land Buddhism, referred to above,
with its doctrine of calling on Amida Buddha for salvation, which is the
largest Buddhist school in Japan. It may be that Zen's rather austere teaching and its emphasis on relying on one's own efforts to attain enlightenment lessened its popularity. Nevertheless, in present-day Japan, Zen
Buddhism fulfils a wider role than simply providing a pattern by which
enlightenment can be obtained. In many ways, Zen temples perform similar functions in society as do other temples, notably in providing funeral
services, and dealing with all the rituals surrounding death and the care of
the ancestors. Indeed, only about ten percent of Zen temples in Japan have
a meditation hall. While Zen priests are expected to have completed a
course of meditation training and to have attained enlightenment, the
purpose of this is to qualify them to help others through carrying out their
priestly functions: 'Zen monasticism was and continues to be a highly
ritualised tradition that emphasises public performance and physical
deportment at least as much as "inner experience".'16

It is significant, however, that meditation plays a relatively small part in the overall activity of Zen temples. In tracts which they produce to encourage lay participation in Buddhism, little mention is made of meditation, with far more emphasis being placed on the right observance of rituals and customs, particularly those related to ancestors. Ian Reader provides a translation of the *Shinko jukun,* the 'Ten Articles of Faith', a kind of summary of the life of a Zen adherent, which illustrates this.[17] The first article is this:

> Let us always clean the family Buddhist altar (butsudan) every morning, and, by making a gesture of worship (gassho) and venerating them, let us give thanks to our ancestors.[18]

Of the ten articles, only the last refers to meditation,[19] which is to be carried out on Enlightenment Day, celebrated on 8 December in Japan, but even here it is seen as a ritual way of remembering Buddha, rather than as a means of seeking enlightenment. Another tract, *Jinsei no yasuragi* or *Peace of Mind in Human Life*, stresses the attainment of peace of mind through calm observation of a worshipful gesture, and through thankful remembrance of one's ancestors.[20] The emphasis has shifted away from the idea of enlightenment as a realisation that there is no distinction between oneself and the Buddha-mind to a sense of peace and tranquillity in the midst of a busy life.

In recent years there does appear to have been a small increase in the number of Japanese interested in the meditation practices of Zen, especially among those who have moved to the cities and thus have no established links with a particular Buddhist school. In some areas Zen temples are opening new meditation halls, in an attempt to appeal to those who are seeking a form of spirituality or religious expression which goes beyond the formal or ritualistic approach of much contemporary Buddhism and Shinto. These are the kind of people who might otherwise be drawn to the new religious movements, and Zen temples hope that by attracting them now, they will affiliate to the temple when they come to need their services for funerals and ancestral rites.

Having set Zen Buddhism in its Japanese context, it is time to look more closely at its practice.

Zen in Practice

Zen is both way and goal, both practical technique and mystical experience, both detachment from life and involvement in life, both intellectually demanding and, once grasped, absurdly simple. It sees itself both as a philosophy for all, which need not be linked to any religion, yet at the same time, as we have seen above, it sits within the wider world of Japanese Buddhism. The acceptance of paradox is at its heart.

In essence, Zen aims at the realisation that there is no distinction between one's mind and what appears to be the external world. Everything is a manifestation of one's own mind. More than that, even the sense of one's existence as distinct mind is ultimately illusion. Everything is one, everything is no-thing, everything is 'Emptiness'. This Emptiness is sometimes described by the Japanese word *Mu*. At the simple level it is used as a straightforward negative, but in Zen terms it carries a deeper meaning. Suzuki speaks of this Emptiness as something 'transcending all forms of mutual relationship, of subject and object, birth and death, God and the world, something and nothing, yes and no, affirmation and negation.'[21] In order to grasp this, it is of course necessary to move beyond what Zen sees as the confines of logic, and not just the confines of logic, but the confines of awareness of distinction. It is here that the practice of Zen meditation comes in. Zen understands that in order for this realisation to be attained, in other words, for enlightenment to be grasped, there needs to be a breaking down of the resistance of material logic. Zen training aims to do this and thus may almost be seen as a system to lead the mind to enlightenment.[22]

A key element within Zen is the practice of *zazen*, seated meditation. During *zazen,* participants sit cross-legged in what is known as the lotus position, with both feet resting on the opposite thighs, or the half lotus, with one foot resting on the opposite thigh and the other tucked underneath the opposite thigh. Sometimes the traditional Japanese kneeling position, where both feet are tucked underneath the backs of one's legs, is adopted. Slightly cupped, one hand rests lightly on the other. There are patterns of breathing which are taught to accompany this posture. During these periods of meditation, which often last for about ninety minutes, there is silence in the meditation hall, broken only by the occasional sharp crack of the *kyosaku,* the stick wielded by the instructor. It is sometimes jokingly said that the use of this stick is to waken those who may be nodding off during the meditation, but in fact it is used to try to jolt the mind into enlightenment. (It should be emphasised here that Zen instructors do not use the *kyosaku* willy-nilly, but will only resort to it when they feel that its use is appropriate to the particular student's stage of training.) There are stories of those seeking who have experienced enlightenment after being struck on the head by their teacher, or when their teacher suddenly and unexpectedly shouted at them.

Nor does enlightenment only occur during *zazen*. Students experience it in any number of situations. Zen training is more than meditation. Those who attend residential sessions will also engage in physical labour at the monastery or centre where training is taken place. There will be lectures from the Zen master who is instructing them, and also times of personal instruction, and it may be that during these some word or phrase will suddenly trigger off the experience of enlightenment. There are two main schools within Zen, one known as Rinzai and one known as Soto. Soto emphasises silent meditation, but within Rinzai Zen *koan* are also used to break down the barrier which material logic presents to achieving enlightenment. These *koan* are phrases or short sayings which are presented to the student for him or her to 'solve'. They include, for example, 'What is the sound of one hand clapping?' and 'What is the smell of the colour blue?'

While this may all sound strange, illogical or simply meaningless verbal games, particularly to Western rationalists, there is no doubt that those who have attained enlightenment experience it as a powerful emotional release. Philip Kapleau, in his *The Three Pillars of Zen*, records a number of testimonies of those who have become enlightened.

> All at once I was struck as though by lightning, and the next instant, heaven and earth crumbled and disappeared. Instantaneously, like surging waves, a tremendous delight welled up inside me, a veritable hurricane of delight, as I laughed loudly and wildly. 'Ha, ha, ha, ha, ha, ha! There's no reasoning here, no reasoning at all. Ha, ha, ha.' The empty sky split in two, then opened its enormous mouth and began to laugh uproariously: 'ha, ha, ha.' Later, one of the members of my family told me that my laughter sounded inhuman.[23]

> Abruptly the pains disappear, there's only Mu! Each and everything is Mu. 'Oh, it's this!' I exclaimed, reeling in astonishment, my mind a total emptiness … All is freshness and purity itself. Every single object is dancing vividly, inviting me to look.[24]

Rarely, if ever, is enlightenment achieved without struggle and effort. Not only is there the mental effort involved in 'letting go' of the sense of distinction between things which Zen sees as illusion, but there is also physical effort, and sometimes emotional effort as well, necessary to realise enlightenment. This process is illustrated in a series of pictures known as the Ten Oxherding Pictures,[25] which date from the thirteenth century.

The Ten Oxherding Pictures

The first picture is entitled 'Seeking the Ox', and portrays a man who has turned his back on the ox and, as if he has lost it, goes on his way to look for it, and finds himself confronted by a number of different roads. The significant point about the picture is that the man should have no need to look for the ox in the first place. In the same way, there should be no need to look for what the ox represents, the true nature, the Buddha nature, since all people have it. However, since people are unaware of it and live in a world of confusing choices, they need to seek.

The second picture is entitled 'Finding the Tracks'. This represents the first tentative steps towards enlightenment, the understanding that everything is an expression of the Self. As yet, however, he has not yet begun to experience this.

The next picture is entitled 'First Glimpse of the Ox', the animal seen partially through trees. The seeker comes to some understanding of enlightenment, beginning to grasp his true nature.

The fourth picture, 'Catching the Ox', portrays the man wrestling with the ox to tame it. The seeker has experienced something of enlightenment, though he still struggles with the illusion of distinction between things. As has been noted above, there is often a degree of physical discomfort endured while undergoing Zen training.

The fifth picture is called 'Taming the Ox'. The man leads the ox home, guiding it with a bridle. The seeker has achieved enlightenment, and is becoming increasingly the master of the thoughts which perpetuate the delusion of 'otherness'. After the initial experience of enlightenment, continued practice and instruction are necessary in order to hold on to that realisation.

In the next picture, 'Riding the Ox Home', the man has now tamed the ox so that it will take him home as he sits astride it playing his flute. The seeker has now attained mastery to the extent that he is now undisturbed by any circumstances or thoughts, since he realises that they are all illusion.

The seventh picture is entitled 'Ox forgotten, Self alone', and depicts the man sitting in his hut. Now that the ox is found, tamed and brought home, there is no need for seeking. This represents the stage where the seeker realises that his search for enlightenment as to the true nature of things, and that even the experience of enlightenment itself, is only a stage on the journey.

The eighth picture, 'Both Ox and Self forgotten' is simply a picture of a circle. The seeker is now beyond any sense of pride or accomplishment in achieving enlightenment. All is one, yet at the same time all is Empty. Yet this is not the end of the quest.

Then comes the ninth picture, 'Returning to the Source' which is a picture of a scene in nature. The seeker, who has now found and moved beyond what he sought, can observe the passing of time and the change of seasons with complete calm and detachment. Even enlightenment no longer has any attraction. The person has now realised the purpose of his experiences.

The last picture in the series, 'Entering the Marketplace with Helping Hands', depicts the man going out into the world, free from attachment, simply himself, and therefore able to act to help others in need. This could be said to be the goal of Zen, although to talk of achieving a goal is, in Zen terms, an indication that one has not yet achieved it, since one is still attached to the desire to achieve. Whatever words we use, however, the point is that the practice of Zen and the realisation of ultimate enlightenment does not lead to a withdrawal from everyday life, as in many mystical traditions. Rather, it results in people who are able to live naturally in the world, doing whatever they do as those who are completely free of all attachments.

In some senses Zen is clearly different from some of the other expressions of the mystical within Japanese religion which we have observed. It places emphasis on enlightenment coming from within oneself, because of course there is no 'other'. It is sometimes rather disdainful of other forms of Buddhism which rely on external spiritual sources for help. It is also disdainful of the experiences, visions and sensory experiences which often accompany the progress towards enlightenment. It sees these as inevitable side effects of the meditation process, but of no value in themselves. They may even be negative experiences, in that there is the temptation to become caught up in these *makyo*, as they are known, rather than to continue the search for enlightenment.

Yet in one sense Zen is similar to the patterns we have already observed within other traditions in Japan. The aim of Zen is not the achievement of enlightenment as a goal in itself. As the last of the oxherding pictures makes clear, the ultimate achievement is the ability to live in the mundane world with both complete detachment and total involvement. It is the ability to do this that makes Zen practitioners able to help their fellow beings. Zen is not seen to endow spiritual or magical powers, but in the sense that it is not an end itself but the means to the end of helping others, just as, for example, the *yamabushi* and Shugendo practitioners do, so Zen bears important similarities to other forms of religious practice in Japan.

Reference was made above to the growth of new religious movements in Japan. It is to the mystical dimension of these new religious
movements that we now turn.

Mysticism in the New Religions

The emergence of new religious movements has been the most noteworthy feature of Japanese religious life, since the middle of the nineteenth century and in particular since the end of the Second World War.
Many of these movements claim to be a return to traditional religious
practices, and mysticism, in the sense in which we have already identified this to be a feature of Japanese religion, is a major feature. Tenrikyo
('the religion of heavenly wisdom'), for example, emerged in the middle of the nineteenth century, when Nakayama Miki, in a trancelike state
of spirit possession, announced that she had become the dwelling of
Tenri-O-no-Mikoto 'The Lord of Heavenly Wisdom', and began to
manifest powers of healing. In other words, she stood in the same tradition as the old diviners, shaman and *yamabushi,* those who had gained
their powers through ascetic and mystic practices. Tenrikyo was for many
years regarded as a form of Sect Shinto, and was not recognised as a distinct religious movement until after World War Two.

Soka Gakkai ('value creating society'), the largest of these new movements, emerged as a lay Buddhist movement associated with the
Nichiren School of Buddhism. Its founder, Makiguchi Tsunesaburo, and
his disciple, Toda Josei, were imprisoned by the Japanese authorities during World War II for allegedly being critical of the Emperor system.
Makiguchi died in prison. Toda, in solitary confinement, began to study
the Lotus Sutra in earnest, and to chant the title of that sutra, a key part
of Soka Gakkai teaching. After a long period of chanting, he had a mystical experience when he found himself an observer of what is known
as the Ceremony in Space, an event described in the Lotus Sutra, when
all the boddhisatvas who have gone into the world gather in the presence of Sakyamuni Buddha. Toda's experience was described thus by
Ikeda Daisaku, Toda's successor and current president of Soka Gakkai
International.

> Suddenly [he] found himself in the midst of the air, before he knew
> it, in the huge crowd of people, as many as the sands of sixty thousand
> Ganges, worshipping the brilliant statue of the Dai-Gohonzon.[26] It
> was neither a dream nor an illusion, and seemed as if it lasted only a
> few seconds, or a few minutes, or again as long as several hours. It was
> a reality which he experienced for the first time.[27]

Inspired by this experience, Toda set to the task of expanding Soka Gakkai. From the 1950s it began growing in significant numbers. This was partly due to its aggressive style of proselytisation, known as *shakubuku* or 'breaking down', in other words, vigorous denunciation of other religions and other Buddhist schools. However, it was also because its practices were promoted as leading to health, happiness and the over-coming of obstacles in one's personal life. At the heart of these practices is the chanting of the *daimoku,* the phrase *Namu Myo Ho Renge Kyo* ('Devotion to the Mystic Law of the Lotus Sutra'). This was what Toda was chanting when he had his experience in prison.

At first sight this chanting may not seem to be particularly mystical. Indeed, many of the testimonies of believers talk of chanting *for* something, in much the same way as Christians sometimes speak of intercessory prayer, and sometimes these can seem self-centred and materialistic. Often, however, adherents to Soka Gakkai speak of how chanting has enabled them to overcome negative emotions or difficult experiences in their own lives or in the lives of those round about them. Testimonies of mystical experiences of the sort described above by some Zen practitioners are rarer among Soka Gakkai members. However, the practice of regular chanting, along with devotion to the *gohonzon*, a tablet which is a copy of the original *Gohonzon* which Ikeda records Toda as having seen in his vision and on which are inscribed the words of the *daimoku*, is thought to lead to enlightenment. Chanting is also done not simply for one's own benefit but for the wider good of society. Thus, Soka Gakkai practices too reflect something of the wider mystical dimension of Japanese religion.

Reiyukai ('spiritual friendship society') is another movement which has been inspired by the teaching of Nichiren Buddhism. Healing prac-tices were for many years a key emphasis of this group, as with many new religious movements. It is the way in which the power to heal was gained by members of this movement which is significant here. Reiyukai members who it is felt have reached an appropriate level of spiritual experience are sent to train at Shichimenzan, a mountain sacred to the Minobu sect of Nichiren Buddhism and linked to Shugendo asceticism.

> The idea of a healing power gained through rigorous spiritual training and its link to the cult of the sacred mountain is a major feature of healing in the new religions.[28]

Arguably, the new religious movement which is best known in the West is Aum Shinrikyo (Aum Supreme Truth sect), not for its numbers, but for its use of violence, notably its sarin gas attack which the movement unleashed on the Tokyo underground in March of 1995, killing twelve people and injuring hundreds.[29] This is a long way from the image of the gentle Buddhist mystic, yet in some respects Aum Shinrikyo can be seen as standing in the same mystical tradition which we have already observed in other aspects of Japanese religion. Along with many of the founders of Japanese new religious movements, Asahara Shoko claimed that it was mystical experiences which inspired him to establish a new movement. In his case, he claimed to have received a vision of the Hindu deity Shiva while meditating, and then to have experienced perfect enlightenment while in the Himalayas. He claimed that through adopting the spiritual techniques which he taught, his followers would gain the spiritual power necessary to survive the forthcoming destruction of civilisation which he predicted, and to form the nucleus of a new society. Both in its teachings, which drew on Hinduism, Christianity and Tibetan Buddhism, and in its practices such as yoga, Aum Shinrikyo was noticeably syncretistic, a characteristic shared by many of the more recently established new religious movements, such as Kofuku no Kagaku.

What is important here, however, is that in its meditative techniques and emphasis on the achievement of spiritual power through ascetic practices, it shares the characteristic which we have noted throughout Japanese religion. That is, that the enlightenment achieved through various mystical practices is not an end in itself. Rather, it is what is attained *through* that enlightenment which is important, whether it be the power to heal, to perform exorcisms, or to survive a coming holocaust.

More than a Zen thing …

While the central focus of this essay has been Zen, it is clear that Zen is by no means the only element in the Japanese religious mosaic which involves mystical practice and experience. It is probably fair to say that the elements of Zen which have been imported to the West have been taken out of the Japanese context so that they can become more accessible to Westerners who seek spirituality and mystical experience apart from more formal and ritual observances. Some Christian writers, such as Thomas Merton, have suggested that elements of Zen may be adapted to Christian meditation.[30] So, Zen in the West is not only unrepresentative of Japanese religion in general, but even rather different from Zen in Japan. In the Japanese context, Zen, for all its distinctives, actually is simply one more manifestation of a religious worldview which is aware of the existence of the transcendent, or at least aware that the material is not all that is, and is aware that spiritual powers or insights can be attained through mystical practices. These practices are therefore not ends in themselves, but ways to gain access to that power, as much for the benefit of others as for oneself.

Notes

[1] P. Moore, 'Mysticism and Religious Experience', in Ursula King (ed.), *Turning Points in Religious Studies: Essays in Honour of Geoffrey Parrinder* (Edinburgh: T & T Clark, 1990), 242–53.

[2] *Kami* is the traditional Japanese word for 'deity'.

[3] J. Kitagawa, *On Understanding Japanese Religion* (Princeton: Princeton University Press, 1987), 121.

[4] The 'apocryphal texts' are those which claim to have been inspired while under trance or are in accord with the teachings of the Buddha. For more on this see P. Swanson 'A Japanese Apocryphal Text', in G. Tanabe (ed.), *Religions of Japan in Practice* (Princeton: Princeton University Press, 1999), 247ff.

[5] Ibid., 252, 253.

[6] E. Yoshikawa, *Musashi* (Tokyo: Kodansha International, 1981), 302.

[7] In Chinese 'Kannon' is known as 'Kuanyin'.

[8] Recorded in conversation with Tucker Callaway in Callaway's, *Zen Way–Jesus Way* (Rutland: Tuttle, 1992), 139

[9] An alternative rendering of *Amida*.

[10] Another name for Gautama, the Buddha.

[11] Quoted in Callaway, *Zen Way*, 117, 118.

[12] D.T. Suzuki *An Introduction to Zen Buddhism* (London: Rider, 1969), 43

[13] Excerpt from Eisai's *Treatise for Promoting Zen for the Protection of the Country*, tr. A. Welter, in Tanabe (ed.), *Religions of Japan*, 69.

[14] See for example, Kaiten Nukariya, *The Religion of the Samurai* (London: Luzac, 1973). Originally written in 1913, this is one of the first books on Zen written for an English-speaking audience. See also Brian Victoria, *Zen at War* (New York: Weatherhill Publishers, 1997), which demonstrates a clear link between Zen teachers in the early twentieth century and Japanese militarism.

[15] Nukariya, *Religion of the Samurai*, xv.

[16] R. Sharf, 'Sanbokyodan: Zen and the Way of the New Religions', *Japanese Journal of Religious Studies* 22 (1995), 418.

[17] I. Reader, 'Zen Buddhist Tracts for the Laity', in Tanabe (ed.) *Religions of Japan*, 487ff.

[18] Ibid., 496.

[19] Ibid., 497.

[20] Ibid., 498.

[21] D.T. Suzuki, *Mysticism, Christian and Buddhist* (London: Unwin, 1957), 19.

[22] The Japanese words *satori* and *kensho* are both translated as 'enlightenment', and both are used in Zen writings.

[23] P. Kapleau, *The Three Pillars of Zen* (London: Rider, 1980), 216.

[24] Ibid., 249.

[25] These are found in a number of different Zen texts. I have referred to the pictures and the commentary in Kapleau, *Three Pillars*, 313–23.

[26] This is the object of worship in Soka Gakkai. It is a Buddhist mandala, which, it is claimed was inscribed by Nichiren himself.

[27] Ikeda Daisaku, *The Human Revolution*, Vol. 4, 22 – quoted in D. Montgomery, *Fire in the Lotus* (London: Mandala, 1991), 183.

[28] H. Hardacre, 'The Transformation of Healing in the Japanese New Religions', *History of Religion* 21 (1982), 312.

[29] Following the attack criminal charges were brought against Aum's leaders. Japan's laws on religious freedom made it virtually impossible for the movement to be banned, though many members left. It has now apologised for its actions, and surprisingly continues to function, under the new name of Aleph.

[30] Other Christian writers are less positive about the use of Zen as an aid to Christian meditation. See in particular the discussion in Callaway, *Zen Way*, 150ff.

2

Peripatetic Mystics

The Renunciate Order of the Terapanthi Jains

Ron Geaves

Introduction

This chapter intends to reassess an old premise put forward by Stace (1960), and echoed with qualifications by Parrinder (1976) and Smart (1978), namely that the mystical experience has enough common features, in spite of the obvious differences arising from a multiplicity of religious traditions with diverse soteriological and eschatological doctrines and an awesome range of practices, to be defined as universal.[1] In the process of reasserting a form of universalism, some attention will inevitably be given to Katz's (1978) seminal work in which he argues that mystical experience itself is shaped by the doctrines and practices which the practitioner brings to the experience, as well as differences of interpretation arising from cultural and religious differences.[2] However, the central theme of the following exploration of the Terapanthi Jains is that neither pluralists like Katz, nor universalists like Stace, gave enough consideration to the practitioners' process and intent, and instead focused overwhelmingly on the experience itself, whether union with a theistic deity or annihilation of the self into a non-personal void. Katz does acknowledge that intent is crucial in forming the experience, but then goes on to provide an analysis in which religious difference modifies intent whilst not acknowledging sufficiently the marked commonality within the diversity of process.

Before going on to look at the case study, it is necessary to give some time to the issue of definition. Early definitions of mysticism tended to be concerned with the relationship between the soul and God, and the possibility of direct experience of God.[3] However, T.H. Hughes provides the possibility of a wider definition that focuses on process and intent rather than the end product when he argues that intense concentration of will is one of the foremost characteristics of the mystic. He states that: 'all the faculties are directed to one centre, so that there is a narrowing of the field of consciousness, through the intense concentration of the will to one focal point'.[4] Obviously, there are other fields of endeavour that require from their highest achievers 'an intense concentration of will' and that may go some way to explaining similar unitive experiences in sport, for example. Some reference to the sacred needs to be acknowledged to differentiate mysticism from other experiences of one-pointed consciousness. Perhaps Aldous Huxley, that great champion of the perennial philosophy, provides us with the best working definition to acknowledge all the forms of expression that mysticism can take. Huxley asserts that 'the technique of mysticism, properly practised, may result in the direct intuition of, and union with, an ultimate spiritual reality that is perceived as simultaneously beyond the self and in some ways within it'.[5] Huxley's definition has the advantage of acknowledging both process and eventual apprehension of the sacred without limiting the experience to any one religious tradition.

Parrinder divided mystical experience into two principal areas of monistic and theistic, and acknowledged that Indian yogic systems were the closest to European views of mysticism, even though they were essentially non-theistic, because they incorporated the idea of union.[6] However, Jainism falls outside both categories as it does not acknowledge the existence of an eternal creator God or an all-pervading reality such as Brahman. Moreover, Jainism does not agree with the Buddhist doctrine of *anicca* (impermanence of the self) and asserts that there is an eternal and unique soul in every being. In this respect, it is closer to the ancient Indian tradition of *Samkhya* which divides the cosmos into *prakriti* (nature and transient) and countless individual monads known as *purusha* (eternal and unchanging). Liberation consists of releasing the *purusha* from the bondage of *prakriti* where they then dwell in eternal blissful isolation. This is achieved by the practice of yogic disciplines and asceticism. The Jain assertion of the existence of the eternal soul has led Parrinder to classify the tradition as 'mysticism of the soul'.[7]

However, not all Jains are mystics by any means, and I agree with John Cort that a distinction needs to be made between two arenas of value: one a less delineated tradition of ethics and religious imagination, based around the temple and the veneration of images of the enlightened, whose goal is pragmatic well-being; and the other, a clearly-distinguishable spiritual tradition focused upon a mendicant tradition whose goal is liberation of the soul from matter. [8] However, the original Jain quest as exemplified in the life of its historic founder, Mahavir (d. 527 BCE),[9]

was one of release from bondage through one-pointed practice of meditation and rigorous asceticism. In this respect, I will acknowledge
William James' assertion that religions move from experience to institutional forms and that there is always a dynamic between the two where
individuals and movements attempt to rediscover the experiential
dimension of the founders and early generations of practitioners. This
attempt to rediscover authenticity in a reawakening of the enchanted
universe of the founder can lead to revivals of a mystical or near-mysti-
cal nature that rejuvenate the tradition.

Jainism

Jainism, like many Indian traditions, does not acknowledge a historical
beginning, but rather perceives creation as an endless cycle of existence
formed of two interdependent entities: infinite independent conscious
souls (*jivatman*) and matter (*ajiva*). The souls are held down and trapped
in material existence through *karma*, which is believed to be a form of
subtle matter. Thus all beings, right down to plant life forms, are perceived to be suffering, although the degree of misery is predicated upon
a categorisation of sense beings, in which the five sense beings are the
most conscious, with humanity at the pinnacle. As with other Indian traditions, it is believed that human beings have the capacity to be liberated. In Jainism, this path to liberation was taught by a succession of
enlightened souls known as *tirthankaras* (ford-crossers).[10] It is believed
that throughout all the cycles of existence there have been those who
have discovered the means to release the soul from the bondage of matter through the destruction of all *karma*, and who have turned their
attention to helping others on the path to final liberation. The historic
founder of Jainism was Mahavir, a contemporary of the Buddha, whose
life story bears several resemblances to the founder of Buddhism.
However, Mahavir's journey to enlightenment took a markedly different
route to Siddhartha Gautama in that the primary focus of deliverance
was asceticism.[11]

It is this asceticism that lies at the heart of the Terapanthi revival of
Jain tradition and opens the doors for contemplative life and the possibility of mystical experience. However, it should be pointed out that
Jainism does not deny the existence of God as noted by some commentators. Cort correctly observes that Jains often acknowledge the
enlightened and liberated *tirthankaras* as God, even though they are not
in any sense creators of the universe. Jain understanding of God is anyone who has attained liberation and whose soul exists in independent
but eternal bliss. This state of existence is identical for each liberated soul

and so they continue in timeless identical perfection.[12] Many Jains place these liberated *tirthankaras* at the centre of their worship and venerate them with differing degrees of intensity. Such one-pointed veneration can also lead to loss of individual self and therefore give rise to mystical experience, but the present chapter intends to focus on Jains who do not acknowledge personal worship of images of the *tirthankaras*, but rather focus on their example and teachings.

Mahavir founded four orders (*tirtha*) of Jain life: the male mendicants (*sadhu*); the female mendicants (*sadhvi*); the male laity (*sravaka*) and the female laity (*sravika*). Each of these is expected to pursue the path to liberation by following a number of vows, but the mendicants bear the fullest manifestation of these ethical and spiritual disciplines. There are five great vows that form the foundation of mendicant life. They are: *ahimsa* (non-violence), *satya* (speaking only the truth), *asteya* (not taking that which is not freely given), *brahmacharya* (celibacy), and *apahigraha* (possessing nothing). In addition to the five vows there are three restraints that lead to control of all physical and mental activities:

1. While receiving or placing anything whatsoever, while sitting, getting up, or walking, in all such acts so to restrict bodily operations that discrimination is maintained between what is to be done and what is not to be done – that is called restraint pertaining to the body.
2. Whenever there arises an occasion to speak then to restrict speech – if needs be to keep silent altogether – that is called restraint pertaining to speech.
3. To give up volitions that are evil or are a mixture of good and evil, as also to cultivate volitions that are good – that is called restraint pertaining to mind.[13]

Correct conduct is also maintained through six daily obligatory rituals (*avasyaka*):

1. *Samayika*, a conscious or contemplative attentiveness that must pervade all the mendicant's activities, including sleep.
2. *Caturvimsati-stava*, a recital of hymns that praise the twenty-four *tirthankaras*.
3. *Vanadanaka* or *guru-vandana*, a rite of veneration for one's spiritual preceptor.
4. *Pratikramana*, a prayer rite in which the mendicant confesses all negative actions, speech and thoughts that may have resulted in harm to others.

5. *Kayotsarga*, a form of meditation in which the mendicant mentally abandons the body and focuses on the spiritual heart of one's existence.
6. *Pratyakhyana*, a vow to perform only those actions which destroy *karma*, or at least do not bring any further bad *karma*.[14]

Devout Jain laity will try to observe a lifestyle as close as possible to the mendicants, but their vows are easier and adapted to householder lifestyles. However, many will try to move progressively towards the ideal of total renunciation embodied in the mendicant.

All of the above vows of conduct can be placed under the three great negations that form the foundation of the Jain path to liberation. These are *ahimsa* (non-violence), *anekant* (non-absolutism) and *aparigraha* (non-possession). *Ahimsa* insists upon non-violence to all creatures and the avoidance of causing suffering. Jain *ahimsa* consists of reverence for all life and requires kindness to all living beings achieved through avoidance of mental, verbal and physical injury. Avoidance of violence also includes restricting other's freedom of thought and speech. Jainism believes that *ahimsa* is the highest principle of religion and in many ways the doctrine of *ahimsa* has become synonymous with Jain tradition. My argument is that *ahimsa* for the Jain mendicant becomes more than an ideal of non-violence, and is a strenuous spiritual discipline that develops one-pointed concentration. *Aparigraha* consists of developing the attitude of non-attachment to material possessions and mental attitudes. Ascetics take the vow of *apahigraha* and maintain a strict non-possession of material objects. *Aparigraha* is adapted for lay Jains who ideally maintain a vow of limited possession. This is achieved by setting a limit on wealth and possessions. Once the limit is achieved the rest should be utilised for charitable works. The mendicant's total withdrawal from material possessions once again narrows the field of consciousness by limiting the range of sense experience. These behaviour modifications are under-pinned by the doctrine of *anekant*, the Jain philosophical position of many-sidedness or manifold aspects which asserts that the objects of knowledge are seen from many changing modes of perception. It is only in the state of omniscience that the human being can see things as they truly are. Everyone else possesses only partial knowledge of reality. This doctrine is best expressed in the famous story of the elephant and the seven blind men who can only sense parts of the animal by touch and are not able to describe the totality of the elephant. Ironically, *anakant* places the Jain practitioner in exactly the same universalist position as Stace and the advocates of perennial philosophy. Whereas Stace and others believe that the apparent differences which surround a universal mystical experience can be explained by diverse cultural and religious interpretations, Jains look at monist, pantheistic, panentheistic and monotheistic interpretations of inner experience, and consider it to be the inability of a single point of consciousness to fully comprehend the totality of reality. Thus the Jain mendicant sits lightly with doctrine and prays daily for the well-being and emancipation of all the world's renunciates regardless of religious background. This is especially true of the Terapanthis who regard spiritual emancipation as possible for all human beings regardless of gender or religious persuasion. The Terapanthis, as a reform movement, adhere strictly to the lifestyle listed above and place a major emphasis on the correct performance of *ahimsa, aparigraha* and *anekant*. My argument is that the process of following the strict lifestyle of a Terapanthi mendicant has commonalities with contemplatives of other world religions which will predispose them to similar experiences.

Terapanthi Jains

Jainism is divided into two main groups: the Svetambaras and the Digambaras.[15] The largest grouping, the Svetambaras are also divided between the *murtipujakis* who venerate the images of the *tirthankaras* through temple *puja,* and the Sthanakvasis who refuse to worship images and use the *tirthankaras* as ideal models for Jain practice. The Terapanthi sect is a Sthanakvasi movement formed in the eighteenth century from the life and teachings of Bhiksu (1726–1803).[16] Bhiksu had become the disciple of a Sthanakavasi teacher named Raghunath, but he broke away after accusing the mendicants of the Sthanakvasi tradition of worldliness and lack of commitment to the practices of Jain renunciation. Bhiksu was primarily concerned that the *acharyas* (the mendicant leaders) were settling in monastic communities rather than maintaining a lifestyle of homelessness, walking from place to place each day between the hours of sunrise and sunset. He was also concerned that the monks and nuns were taking food from the laity that was especially prepared for them rather than partaking of food-offerings from meals that the householders had cooked for themselves. Bhiksu taught his revival of strict Jain traditions for forty-four years in the district of Marwar in Rajasthan and upon his death had initiated fifty-six nuns and forty-nine monks.[17]

Since the time of Bhiksu, the Terapanthis have maintained their cohesion and doctrinal integrity through the institution of an unbroken chain or lineage of *acharyas* down to the present day. The present incumbent, Acharya Mahapragya, has led them since 1996 after picking up the challenge on the death of the movement's great reformer, Acharya Tulsi. This unity is reinforced by the institution of a codified *maryada* (rule or code of behaviour) created by the fourth *acharya*. Each year all the mendicants come together just after the period of the traditional *caturmas* (four month monsoon retreat when mendicants do not have to travel) and swear their renewed allegiance to this formal code of conduct. The focus on the teacher/disciple relationship through an unbroken chain of *acharyas* not only helps create cohesion for the Terapanthis, but provides the framework through which disciples can be initiated into a lifestyle of self-discipline under the guidance of a living spiritual leader. The previous *acharya*, Shri Tulsi emphasised this relationship over and above the institutions created by the order when he stated, 'true education does not come from an institute, but instead comes from a teacher's heart'.[18]

Significant developments have taken place under the leadership of Acharya Tulsi (1936–96) and his successor, Acharya Mahapragya (1996–).[19] Both leaders have been strenuous in their attempts to reform Jainism in order to face the demands of a rapidly changing society whilst, at the same time, maintaining and emphasising its eternal principles. The Terapanthi monks and nuns have a reputation for both scholarly achievement and the ascetic lifestyle, but no monastic communities have been established. The mendicants continue to walk barefoot every day from place to place in the prescribed fashion with complete reliance on the charity of the laity for their physical well-being. But unusually, the centre of the organisation of the sect's activities is the educational institution at Ladnun in Rajasthan, the vision of Acharya Tulsi to become the first established Jain university. The other institution of the Terapanthis is the Adhyatma Sadhana Kendra (The Centre of Spiritual Attainment) founded in 1965 by Acharya Tulsi in South Delhi. Although a centre focused upon the spiritual renewal of individuals through retreats and yogic practices and whose mission statements clearly indicate the core teachings of the *acharyas*, the Adhyatma Sadhana Kendra runs a series of workshops and camps in co-operation with the Indian Ministry of Health to introduce those who suffer from diabetes, heart disease, asthma and obesity to the preventative benefits of correct diet, meditation, yoga and other practices, lumped together under 'science of living'. The significant factor here is that the Terapanthis have succeeded in creating a new discourse, borrowing heavily from the existing languages of modern secular education and health to express ancient spiritual practices which do not clash with the emerging discourse of rationalism within modernist Indian thought. This is supported by their rigorous promotion of non-theistic teachings.

Two other new developments have not been introduced without criticism. Acharya Tulsi and his successor have both become aware of the need for the inner spiritual teachings embodied in the lifestyles of Jain renunciates to be promoted around the world to newly emerging Jain communities created by migration. However, Jain monks and nuns are not permitted to travel by any other means than by foot. Thus a new teaching order of renunciates has been created whose vows are less onerous than the full monks and nuns. These *samans* and *samanis* tour extensively, both in India and abroad, promoting the teachings of Jainism with a focus on spiritual practice to both Jains and non-Jains. This universalism was further encouraged by the creation of the Anuvrat programme in India in 1949. The approach to the Anuvrat movement was essen- tially non-sectarian and did not seek to initiate people into the Terapanthis or even Jainism. The movement's ideals were founded upon Acharya Tulsi's emphasis that religion was nothing to do with worship but was the transformation of the individual and society through character building. The movement had a simple dynamic: anyone could volunteer to live a life of mutually agreed minimum restraint through the adoption of a series of vows to follow nine or thirteen point programmes that would lead to the moral and ethical rejuvenation of   society. Both of these ventures attracted criticism that either the teachings of Jainism were being introduced to non-Jains or that the Acharyas were attempting to convert people to Jainism by a back door approach.[20] However, both these reforms which bring the teachings of the Terapanthis to a wider audience, both inside and outside India, are based firmly upon the belief that the spiritual teachings of Mahavir and the *tirthankaras* are a universal method for liberating the soul from the bondage of matter, whose application will work for any human being who practices them, and that they cannot be regarded as the exclusive property of Jainism.

The Teachings

Whilst Acharya Tulsi was attempting to provide ancient Indian techniques of consciousness transformation with a new language derived from the discourse of health, he was also utilising the educational facilities at Ladnun to search the Jain canon of scripture, the Agamas, in order to rediscover the inner practices of early Jain mendicants, used by them to transform consciousness. Alongside this work he began to translate the voluminous and little known Jain canon into vernacular Indian languages and today this activity is extended to English translation. The result of the research into the Jain texts gave birth to the system of practice named *Preksha Dhyana* (meditation on inner vision), a renewed and revitalised system but claimed to be based on very ancient Jain practice. Acharya Tulsi and his successor have devoted their considerable personal and institutional resources to promoting *Preksha Dhyana* throughout the Indian subcontinent. It has been calculated that Acharya Tulsi covered 80,000 miles on foot as he journeyed teaching.

Although *Preksha Dhyana* is promoted in the rational language of science and medicine, its practice is perceived to achieve effects that echo the language of formulated mystical disciplines throughout the world. *Preksha Dhyana* is described as 'a technique of meditation for attitudinal change, behaviour modification and integrated development of the personality. It is based upon the wisdom of ancient philosophy and has been formulated in terms of modern scientific concepts'.[21] It is promoted as a cure for the diseases of modern living:

> On a physical level it helps each bodily cell to revitalize itself. It facilitates digestion, it makes respiration more efficient and improves circulation and quality of blood. On a mental level it proves to be an applied method to train the mind to concentrate. It offers a way to treat serious psychosomatic illnesses without drugs, is an efficient tool for ending addictions and other bad habits, it reveals to one the mysteries of the mind by the realization and real experience of the inner consciousness ... On the emotional level the strengthening of conscious reasoning controls reactions to environmental conditions, situations and behaviour of others, harmonization of the functioning of the nervous and the endocrine system ... And the ultimate eradication of psychological distortion ... On a spiritual level regulation and transformation of blood chemistry ... leads one to attain the power to control the mind and to become free from the effects of external forces compelling one to lose equanimity.[22]

Interestingly, in this promotional language of the Terapanthis there is no sign of the dualism inherent in theistic systems of mysticism or of the intense and passionate longing for union with an ultimate Beloved associated with monotheistic mysticism. Nor is there a dichotomy between religion and science, often found in the West. Chemical transformations of various physical systems are not perceived as a crude reductionist solution to provide an explanation for apparently inexplicable spiritual experience, but, on the contrary, demonstrate that the spiritual and material are holistically bound together within one entity, incorporating both the elements of *purusha* and *prakriti*. Thus we find a system of consciousness transformation that is so profoundly different from the discourses of theistic spirituality as to provide support for Katz's theorising that as intent is radically diverse so must mystical experience be equally heterogenous. However, a closer examination of process reveals startling features of similarity with other contemplative systems.

The word, *preksha* means to 'perceive carefully and profoundly'.[23] In its strictest and narrowest application it is a series of techniques that teach the ability to perceive the subtle experience of consciousness itself as opposed to thought formations. In the language of the Terapanthis it is a technique which is 'basically not concentration of 'thought' but concentration of 'perception'.[24] It is based upon Mahavir's dictum to 'perceive and know' rather than philosophies which claim that either language or thoughts are the basis of knowledge. The emphasis is on the 'here and now' as the only dimension for the experience of reality.

> This is because perception is strictly concerned with the phenomenon of the present. It is neither a memory of the past nor an imagination of the future. Whatever is happening at the moment of perception must necessarily be a reality.[25]

This process of intense one-pointed inner concentration is claimed to be an efficient tool for stilling the wandering mind and leads to equanimity where experience is disassociated from the constantly changing vicissitudes of fortune and the ephemeral world of sense experience with its duality of pleasure and pain. Ultimately, the practice will facilitate the piercing of the 'wall of the container' and reach the soul, but on the way it will assist in purifying the mental state of the practitioner from harmful and disturbing passions such as anger, greed, jealousy, fear and uncontrolled desire.[26]

Similar to the Buddhist practice of mindfulness, *Preksha Dhyana* extends to the daily activities of the practitioner, not only inner contemplation. The practitioners commit themselves to five disciplines which form the heart of the Terapanthi *sadhana*. They are as follows:

1. *Bhavakriya* – this daily discipline to achieve conscious awareness of all one's actions is threefold. First, the practitioner is directed to maintain full awareness of each action they perform rather than mechanical or 'absent-minded' actions. The mind should be kept fully in the action itself rather than wandering in the imagination. Vigilance should be maintained over thoughts, words and deeds.
2. Non-reaction – the will should be trained to direct its efforts into avoiding retaliatory or reactive behaviour, thus cutting down the amount of action which is a result of reaction to stimuli.
3. Amity – the practitioner should engage in developing friendliness, empathy and compassion in all dealings with other sentient beings.
4. Fasting and dieting – not only should the practitioner be strictly vegetarian but the amount of food intake should be controlled, along with periods of complete fasting.

5. Silence – practitioners are encouraged to maintain complete silence or speak only when it is absolutely necessary.[27]

Whilst engaged in these disciplines and sitting regularly to practise the inner meditative focus of *Preksha Dhyana*, the Terapanthi practitioner engages in a process which hopes to achieve a turning of the flow of consciousness from the outside world through the senses to the inner world experienced as subtle vibrations of awareness itself. The end product is described as *Kayotsarga*, which literally means 'an abandonment of the body coupled with a high degree of conscious awareness'.[28]

In addition to inner concentration and the control of one's emotions, actions, thoughts and speech through the five disciplines, the practitioner engages in a series of reflections or meditations as follows:

1. Contemplation of *ekatva* (solitariness) in which consideration is given to the existential state of ultimate aloneness in the universe.
2. Contemplation of *anityata* (impermanence) in which one considers mortality and transience.
3. Contemplation of *asarana* (vulnerability) in which one considers the reality of security endowed by wealth, power and health, as opposed to the security discovered through the transcendental awareness of the soul or self.
4. Contemplation of *samsara* (reality) in which one considers the relationship between the permanent and the impermanent.[29]

When taken together as an integral package combined with the disciplines and restrictions common to all Jain ascetics, the above physical, mental and spiritual practices come together to form a comprehensive, all-inclusive lifestyle and worldview that narrowly restricts the degree of sensory input, and develops a highly concentrated focus upon a restricted or limited range of possibilities concerned with inner purification, inner knowledge and intensity of vigilance. All of this is achieved in a religious environment that gives little support to sectarian or doctrinal differences between religions. The overriding ethos is one of universalism and respect for all the various 'truth stories' or discourses put forward by various religious traditions.

Conclusion

It is not in the scope of this short contribution to embark upon an exercise of comparison with other systems that claim to lead to mystical experience. However, I remain confident that readers will be able to recognise the commonality inherent in this particular manifestation of consciousness-narrowing required of the successful Terapanthi mendicant. Although the Terapanthis maintain a discourse that abounds in imagery drawn from the rational languages of 'science' and 'medicine' rather than the discourse of ecstatic union with a creator-God, the process that leads to the end-product demonstrates marked similarities with the lifestyles of committed followers of Sufi *tariqas* or contemplative Christian orders not to mention other non-theistic systems such as Zen Buddhists or practitioners of Yogic systems.

Although the forms of the disciplines will vary from tradition to tradition, the following features are identified as held in common within contemplative or mystical communities:

1. The narrowing of the field of consciousness so as to direct all the faculties to one centre.
2. The process of mental purification with the ideal of eliminating negative thoughts and emotions.
3. A conscious or contemplative attentiveness during the performance of daily or mundane activities.
4. Restraint on physical and sense activity, often resulting in dietary restrictions, fasting, celibacy, and restrictions upon unnecessary speech.
5. Attempts to achieve inner stillness through meditation, contemplation or prayer.
6. Non-possessiveness which results in either the restriction of material possessions or the renunciation of the idea of ownership.
7. Ethical and moral behaviour embracing the ideal of amity which restricts reactionary or retaliatory behaviour.
8. Daily mental disciplines that attempt to maintain the focus of the practitioner in the 'here and now'.
9. Meditations or reflections upon the 'reality' of existence.
10. A common life – living within like-minded communities of practitioners.
11. Negation of the ego.

My main argument is that the scholarly debate on the universality of the mystical experience has to go beyond the narrow focus upon unitive experience or peak experience and incorporate the day-to-day experience which arises out of process. Katz's focus on intent goes no further than to state the obvious – that there is immense difference between each religion's practice and doctrine. This is to ignore the essential argument of the universalists, that the mystical path within each tradition overrides these differences to arrive at a commonality of inner experience. The diversity of intent may provide manifestations of difference as in Katz's example of Jewish mystics who never proclaim unity with God,[30] but, on the other hand, these differences may be undermined if the process of application of the mystical path demonstrates overwhelmingly similar characteristics.

It is difficult to prove that *samadhi, satori, fana,* and *kyotsarga* are the same experience. The descriptions of experiences contain many differences, even though the similarities are remarkable. However, it seems essential to me that the analysis has to be widened to include the commonality of the process before we can answer the question whether mystics and contemplatives have more in common with each other than they do with the non-contemplative followers of their own respective traditions. The focus on process and intent, rather than solely on peak experiences will provide a fuller account of mystical and contemplative life and the relationship between them and their religious traditions, and will also have the advantage of allowing the debate to acknowledge religious reality rather than the sometimes over-reductionist and deterministic conclusions of psychologists.

Notes

[1] W.T. Stace, *Mysticism and Philosophy* (London: MacMillan, 1960); G. Parrinder, *Mysticism in the World's Religions* (London: Sheldon Press, 1976); N. Smart, 'Understanding Religious Experience', in S.T. Katz (ed.), *Mysticism and Philosophical Analysis* (London: Sheldon Press, 1978). Stace provides a seven point categorisation to assert the universalism of the mystical experience: (1) a unifying vision in which the One is perceived by the senses in and through many objects; (2) the One is apprehended as the inner life, or presence in all things, so that 'nothing is really dead'; (3) the experience brings a sense of reality; (4) there is a feeling of joy and peace resulting in fulfilment; (5) there is feeling of the presence of the sacred; (6) there is a feeling of paradoxicality and (7) the experience is ineffable or beyond description. Stace, *Mysticism and Philosophy*, 131–2.

[2] S.T. Katz, 'Language, Epistemology, and Mysticism', in Katz (ed.), *Mysticism and Philosophical Analysis*, 22–74.

[3] W.R. Inge provided 26 definitions in his Broughton Lectures in 1899 but they all fit the category of union with God. This is not surprising as Inge focused on Christian mysticism. Typical of Inge's collection of definitions are ' Mysticism is religion in its most concentrated and exclusive form. It is that attitude of mind in which all other relations are swallowed up in the relation of the soul to God (E. Caird) or 'Mysticism appears in connection with the endeavour of the

human mind to grasp the divine essence or the ultimate reality of things, and to enjoy the blessedness of actual communion with the highest. The first is the philosophic side of mysticism, the second is its religious side. God ceases to be an object and becomes an experience' (Pringle Patterson). W.R. Inge, *Mysticism in Religion* (London: Hutchinson, 1947), 25.

[4] Quoted in Inge, *Mysticism*, 28.

[5] Quoted in Parrinder, *Mysticism*, 23.

[6] Ibid., 15.

[7] Ibid., 43.

[8] John Cort, *Jains in the World* (Oxford: Oxford University Press, 2001).

[9] There is some dispute over Mahavir's exact dates of birth and death. I have followed Jain tradition (527 BCE) but others have calculated his death as 477 BCE based on Hemachandra's *Parisistaparva* which states that Mahavir attained nirvana 155 years before emperor Chandagupta's coronation. H. Glasenapp, *Jainism: An Indian Religion of Salvation* (Delhi: Motilal Banarsidas, 1999), 31.

[10] Jainism generally acknowledges 24 *tirthankaras* who have existed within this cycle of time. The first or primal *jina* (conquerors) was Rsabhanatha, also known as Adinatha (the First Lord). Other important *jinas* are Shantinatha (the Lord of Peace) and the final three, Neminatha, Parsvanatha and finally Mahavir.

[11] The Buddha shunned asceticism in favour of the middle path after a period of living the ascetic life. Some Jains believe that the Buddha failed as an ascetic after accepting discipleship under Parsvanatha, the *tirthankara* before Mahavir who is also accepted as being an historical rather than a legendary figure.

[12] Cort, *Jains*, 23.

[13] Reproduced from ibid., 24.

[14] Ibid., 25

[15] The main difference in the Svetambara and Digambara concerns the practice of mendicants arising from a dispute over whether they should wear clothes or go naked. The Svetambara wear a simple white robe. There is also a geographical division, with the Svetambara being mainly confined to Gujarat, Rajasthan and the Punjab, whereas Digambaras have traditionally resided in Maharashtra and Karnataka. Digambaras also hold much more restrictive views on the possibility of liberation for the laity and female mendicants.

[16] The term Terapanthi means the 'path of the thirteen'. Thirteen may relate to the thirteen practices of Jain mendicants which the sect wants to restore or, alternatively it may refer to thirteen monks and nuns who originated the community. Others have noted that '*Tera*' also means 'yours' and may refer to Mahavir. The suggestion that the sect belongs to Mahavir reinforces the ideal of revivalism of a primordial or essential Jainism.

[17] A more developed biography of Bhiksu can be found on the website entry for Svetambara Terapanthis <www.philtar.ucsm.ac.uk/encyclopaedia/Jainism/shvter.html>.

[18] <www.terapanth.com/tulsee/tulsee_verdicet.htm>, 5.

[19] These dates are the period of leadership rather than lifespan. There have been ten *acharyas*: Bhiksu (1760–1803), Varimal (1803–21), Raichand (1821–51), Jeetmal (1851–81), Maghraj (1881–92), Manaklal (1892–97), Dalchand (1897–1909), Kalugani (1909–36), Tulsi (1936–96), Mahapragya (1996–). The next acharya has already been chosen by Mahapragya and will be Muditkumar: <www.terapanth.com/terpa_history.htm>, 3.

[20] *The Anuvrat Movement in Retrospect*, <www.terapanth.com/impressions/anumov_4.htm>, 5.

[21] <www.terapanth.com/mahapragya/prekshadhyana.htm>, 1.

[22] Ibid., 12.

[23] <www.terapanth.com/mahapragya/preksha_detail.htm>, 1.

[24] Ibid., 2.

[25] Ibid.

[26] Ibid., 2–3.

[27] Ibid., 4–5.

[28] Ibid., 8.

[29] Ibid., 19–20.

[30] Katz, 'Language, Epistemology, and Mysticism', 34. Katz makes the example that Jewish mystics unlike their Christian counterparts never experience unity with God. He argues that this is proves that experience is modified by intent, as the Jewish doctrine of God's otherness does not allow for the possibility of union. However, Katz may have more usefully drawn upon Muslim Sufis as contrasted with his Kabbalistic mystics. Sufis do describe experiences of union with God even though Islam has a central doctrine of *tawhid* which also posits God's total otherness.

3

The Theravada Monk as a Buddhist Mystic:

Mystical Attainments of a Twentieth-Century Sri Lankan Monk

Mahinda Deegalle

> The most beautiful and profound emotion we can experience is the sensation of the mystical. It is the sower of all true science.
>
> *Albert Einstein*

This essay examines the life of a modern Theravada monk, Venerable Matale Vanaratana (1889–1981), who had written about his mystical attainments. As a representative example of a modern Theravada mystic, Vanaratana's account deserves attention. An analysis of his account of his own mystical experiences (a) enables us to gain some understanding of the lifestyle of a modern Buddhist mystic, (b) provides us with an insight into the meditation exercises believed to be useful for spiritual attainment, (c) identifies certain obstacles along the Buddhist spiritual path, and (d) exposes the particular problems and difficulties encountered by monks who want to follow a mystical path whilst fulfilling the tasks expected of them in Sri Lankan society.

Vanaratana's community life cannot be separated from his mysticism. Hence, whilst some salient features of his mysticism will be analysed, these need to be understood within their historical and literary contexts. In particular, Vanaratana's account will be examined with reference to an authoritative Theravada text, Buddhaghosa's *Visuddhimagga* (*The Path of Purification*). Also important is a recently published Sinhala book – *Kale Suvanda* (*Forest of Fragrance*) – which describes the life of this meditative monk, much of which was lived in the forest and devoted to the practice of *kasina* (whole or universal) meditation.[1]

A Modern Theravada Mystic

The Venerable Matale Vanaratana was born on 3 February 1889 in Matale, Central Province, Sri Lanka. He records that, at a very young age, he was taken away to the Southern Province and ordained as a Buddhist novice (6 June 1906). Venerable Saddhananda, the abbot of Kumara Mahavihara, Dodanduwa and Sunandaramaya Tiranagama, became his preceptor.

Venerable Vanaratana's initial attraction to *kasina* meditation occurred accidentally. On a 'full moon day', when he visited Sunandaramaya, one of his preceptor's sub-temples, its resident monk Venerable Beruvala Vimalasara happened to be explaining the method of developing *kasina* meditation to a layman. Central to that conversation was the use of Buddhaghosa's *Visuddhimagga* as a manual for *kasina* meditation practice. Listening, the young novice became interested and began the initial practice of *kasina* meditation.[2]

The Sinhala book, *Kale Suvanda*, was published in 1999, many years after Vanaratana's death. It was compiled by one of his close lay associates, Mr Haritas Varusavitana, working with materials written by Venerable Vanaratana during his lifetime. In addition to unpublished works, it also included a meditation manual that Vanaratana had written in 1950 for the benefit of those interested in practising meditation. In that publication Vanaratana recorded that he had begun writing about his mystical experiences during meditation twenty-two years after his initial experience, during which he had attained the first *jhana* (state of serene contemplation), which occurred in 1928.[3]

Vanaratana's booklet, *Bhavanavak pilibanda mage atdakim* (*My Experiences in a Meditation*), was printed twice. In 1955, the first printing came with the direction of Venerable Kotmale Amaravansa. Mr D.S. Kottege reprinted it again in 1976. Vanaratana himself recorded that his book was different from those of others because it was based on his own experience in meditation, rather than on accounts written by others.[4] He emphasized the experiential aspects and highlighted the priority given to accounts of *kasina* (whole or universal) meditation that he himself had experienced. Indeed, from a Therevada Buddhist perspective, Vanaratana's book relates some rather unusual material, in that, while it describes Vanaratana's experiences in *kasina* practice, it also contains many episodes of a supernatural nature.

Kasina Meditation Within the Theravada Tradition

The general meaning of the Pali term *kasina* (Sanskrit: *krtsnayatana*) is 'all,' 'whole,' 'entire' or 'universal.'[5] Its mystical and spiritual meanings relate to one form of Theravada meditation practice, the practice of 'calm' (Pali: *samatha*) meditation. As a technical term in Buddhist mysticism, it refers to 'a meditational exercise of total and exclusive awareness of, or concentration on, one of the four elements (earth, water, fire, wind) or one of four colours (dark blue, yellow, red, white) or space or consciousness, leading to *jhana*' (*state of serene ontemplation*).[6] Generally speaking, in the context of Buddhist meditation, the *kasina* (meditation employing visual objects) can be used as a 'device' in 'calm' meditation practice.

Buddhaghosa's *Visuddhimagga*, a fifth century CE, post-canonical work composed in Pali, gives a list of forty subjects of meditation (*kammatthana*) in developing the practice of 'calm' meditation (*samatha bhavana*).[7] The number of subjects of meditation used for 'calm' meditation are as many as forty because it attempts to cater for individual differences in human character and personality. The ten 'devices' (*kasina*) – the first ten items of Buddhaghosa's forty subjects of meditation[8] – are suitable for both the preliminary and the more advanced stages of meditational practice. Before Buddhaghosa, an Abhidhamma text, the *Dhammasangani*,[9] had given a list of only eight *kasinas* omitting 'consciousness' and 'space'. A text which enters into dialogue with Buddhaghosa's work, Upatissa's *Vimuttimagga*, also gave a list of ten techniques of meditation, but in enumerating them it had followed the list given by the following two canonical texts.[10] Among the canonical sources, the *Maha Sakuludayi Sutta* of the *Majjhima Nikaya* and the *Jhana Vagga* of the *Anguttara Nikaya* enumerated the ten *kasinas*, but differed from the *Visuddhimagga* by listing *vinnana* (knowledge) instead of *aloka* (light). The ten *kasinas*, according to Buddhaghosa, are: (i) earth (*pathavi*); (ii) water (*apo*); (iii) fire (*tejo*); (iv) air (*vayo*); (v) blue (*nila*); (vi) yellow (*pita*); (vii) red (*lohita*); (viii) white (*odata*); (ix) light (*aloka*); and (x) limited-space (*paricchinnakasa*).[11] In the Sri Lankan Theravada tradition, as represented by Buddhaghosa, this list of ten *kasinas*, in which *vinnana* is replaced with *aloka*, is accepted. Yogavacara's *Manual of Indian Mysticism* (1896), describes the Sri Lankan tradition as considering the four elements collectively as *bhuta-kasina*.[12] The first four (1–4) of the ten *kasinas*, the four elements, are good for all personality types, the four colours (5–8) are good for 'hate' type personalities, and the last two (9–10) are also good for all personality types. These ten *kasinas* are presented as ways of attaining the four *jhana*s – or states of serene contemplation.[13]

The ten techniques of meditation known as *kasina-mandala* (universal-circles) involve objects such as a blue disc, a circle of earth, or a bowl of water. In the early stages of *kasina* meditation, such physical devices (i.e. coloured discs) can be used as aids. After the initial sight of the coloured disc, practitioners concentrate on a 'circle' until they can visualise a mental image. The image of the circle is acquired with closed eyes and the individual develops the practice until a condition is reached where sense-reaction is suspended. Moreover, this meditation technique also requires the individual to focus on a 'universal' quality such as blueness, earth or water.

Mysticism has played an important role in the history of Buddhism. While authoritative post-canonical texts like Buddhaghosa's *Visuddhimagga* presented the preliminary guidelines for Buddhist mystics in their practice of various meditation techniques, Theravada traditions in South and Southeast Asia have been constantly engaged in the creation of novel meditation techniques. This is evident in the provocative eighteenth century meditation manual, *The Yogavacara's Manual of Indian Mysticism* (1896) – translated as *Manual of a Mystic* (1916) – which is one of the most important Theravada contributions to the study of mysticism.[14] The editor of the Roman script version, Thomas William Rhys Davids (1843–1922), considered it to be 'a unique manuscript' since, he argued, there was 'no other work in Buddhist literature, either Pali or Sanskrit, devoted to the details of *Jhana* (states of serene contemplation) and *Samadhi* (state of even-mindedness when this dualism is ceased)'[15] The manuscript was found in a temple library in Bambaragala Vihara, Teldeniya, Sri Lanka.[16] The author is unknown and the date of its compilation is also uncertain. Whilst Don Martino de Zilva Wickremasinghe (1865–1937) argued for origins in 'the seventeenth, or even of the sixteenth century', it is now generally understood to have been written in the eighteenth century. The arrival of Siamese monks in Sri Lanka in 1753 to revive Buddhism is understood to be the socio-religious context for the origins of both the practices related to *jhana* and also the authoring of this manual. Whilst, in the final analysis, it is impossible to be certain of the Siamese influence on the birth of this text, a consensus has been reached that it is closely connected with the period 'during or just after the above-named' religious revival.[17]

The most important issue for this paper is that the *Manual of a Mystic* contains 'mystic exercises' and becomes representative of a 'mystic faith.' Some of the practices of mystics, such as 'wax-taper exercises', whilst common in esoteric forms of Mahayana Buddhism, are rather novel and unusual for Theravada traditions.

The *Manual of a Mystic* had devoted a section to the ten *kasinas*.[18] With respect to mystical aspects of the language and seeing its ideas from the perspective of a conventional understanding of Theravada practice, Mrs Rhys Davids asserted that one needed 'a catholic intelligence' to decipher the meanings and symbolical significance of the text and its practices.[19]

Vanaratana's Method in Practising *Kasina* Meditation

Vanaratana taught that, before beginning *kasina* meditation, a person should read the relevant chapter in the *Visuddhimagga*[20] where Buddhaghosa sets out the forty objects of meditation (*kammatthana*), including the ten *kasinas*. According to Vanaratana, when Buddhaghosa explained the *kasina* meditation in the *Visuddhimagga*, he had left some space for a meditation instructor to guide the practitioner.[21] From his own experience, Vanaratana asserts the importance of having a teacher before beginning the *kasina* meditation. In Theravada traditions, such a guide in meditation practice is called a 'good friend' (*kalyanamitta*) who guides the meditator through the practice. Vanaratana himself had found a Burmese meditation teacher, Venerable U. Dhammadhara, to be his *kalyanamitta*.[22]

The meditation practice is divided into three stages as (1) *parikamma* (preliminary work), (2) *upacara* (access concentration), and (3) *appana* (absorption). According to Vanaratana, the *Visuddhimagga* did not give an adequate explanation of *appana*. Even when one achieves the first *jhana* of *appana*, he or she may not know it. According to him, the *Visuddhimagga* had not given any signs by which one might recognise the attainment. Thus, he believed that it left space for a meditation teacher to guide the practitioner. For Vanaratana's own practice, he had received instruction from the meditation master and he also had read the relevant descriptions in the *Visuddhimagga*.

Vanaratana's book gives information about the preparation for medi-tation, the way of receiving *kasina* signs (*nimitta*), the way of engaging in meditation, the way of protecting meditation, the way of developing meditation, the way meditation generates results, the pleasure of seeing the birth of wholesome states such as *Saddha* (trust), the way of achiev-ing the first *jhana*, the way of justifying through an act of truth (*sac-cakiriya*) that what one has attained is the first *jhana*.[23] According to the instruction Vanaratana received, when one has achieved the first *jhana* following the *Visuddhimagga*, one can attain the second, third and fourth *jhanas* even without a teacher. According to Vanaratana, the only *jhana* that one cannot attain without teacher's instruction is the first *jhana*.[24]

Vanaratana explains his preparation for *kasina* meditation. As Buddhaghosa had given a detailed description of 'the eighteen faults of a monastery' and 'the five factors related to the resting place',[25] Vanaratana also discusses the importance of finding an appropriate place for meditation. The purity of one's clothes, appropriate observation of the five or ten precepts by the practitioner, and the long practice of 'loving kindness meditation' is equally emphasised. Loving kindness meditation (*metta*) is designed to cultivate universal friendship to all living beings, whether human or non-human, visible or invisible. It is the first of the four Brahma abidings – namely, loving kindness to all beings, compassion in their sorrow, joy in their happiness, and balanced observation of their faults and virtues. If one does not have training in meditation practice, prior to embarking on the practice of *kasina* meditation, one is required to practice the meditation of loving kindness for a week at least. It is essential to observe silence and cultivate mindfulness from the start of meditation and during the practice. Reading books, giving sermons and reciting *paritta* (prayer for protection) should be avoided; meeting with people, conversations, other forms of work, should be avoided; engaging in singing and dancing is also inappropriate.[26] However, daily routine such as the worship service, engaging in *puja*, chanting *paritta* and reflecting on the five recollections (*paccavekkhana*) should be continued. The meditating individual should pay particular attention to the avoidance of conversations that distract him or her from meditation practice. Even in alms-rounds, the practitioner should be careful to avoid distractions. The key factor is keeping one's mindfulness on the object of meditation.

Vanaratana selected fire (*tejo*) *kasina* for his meditation practice. Giving directions to the practice of fire *kasina*, Buddhaghosa stated that the practitioner 'should apprehend the sign in fire.'[27] However, Vanaratana's teacher instructed Vanaratana to adopt the *nimitta* (sign) from the sun. This demonstrates that it is not essential that one adopt the sign from the fire alone. It seems that the sign can be adopted from any bright object – even, for example, a light bulb. However, if one needs to adopt the sign several times because the *nimitta* does not remain firmly in one's consciousness, it is important that the sign is adopted from the same object.

The meditation instructor gave the following advice to Vanaratana: 'You are going to practice *tejokasina*. The sun is the most powerful object of heat in the world. You have to take a sign (*nimitta*) for meditation from the sun. You have to make a determination that with the blessings of the three refuges, your meditation will be successful and five hindrances (*nivarana*) will be removed.' Rather than looking at the sun directly, Vanaratana was asked to look at the sun's rays which appeared through the branches and leaves of jack fruit trees. He was asked to look at the sun for about three minutes without blinking his eyes. His instructor asked him to repeat the word *tejo* (fire) continuously. After three minutes, he was instructed to close his eyes and enter the meditation room repeating '*tejo, tejo*'. Vanaratana sat on a wooden bench covered with a white cloth. He was facing east and repeated '*tejo*' whilst keeping his eyes closed and mentally focusing on a red circle. The colour of the circle gradually changed to blue. Without getting distracted, Vanaratana meditated on the element of fire for two hours.

When one meditates with closed eyes one should look for the sign of the *kasina*. If the sign is found in the mind's eye, then one should meditate with the wish, 'may it develop well.' If the sign does not appear, it should, as noted above, be acquired by opening one's eyes. When the sign becomes fixed (i.e. it appears constantly) the practitioner should, with closed eyes, meditate, visualising it like a picture hanging about three feet in front of him or her. The intention is that, as one meditates, the sign gradually becomes clearer. (Indeed, the sign is believed to become clearer at night.) By the fourth day, the sign became larger like a tea cup. (That is to say, whereas the sign is, in this case, acquired from the sun's orb and is circular, it eventually changes in size and becomes as large as the rim of a tea cup directly in front of the practitioner, and may even acquire a three dimensional image instead of being simply two-dimensional.) When one meditates, the *kasina nimitta* may circulate (i.e. move round and round in circles). One should not allow it to circulate. When '*tejo*' is repeated fast, the sign also circulates fast. While other changes should be allowed, the circulation should be stopped. The repetition of '*tejo*' should not be loud, though it should be audible to someone in the same room. The focus of the mind on the sign gives a sense of pleasure. At the beginning though it was difficult for Vanaratna to focus the mind on the meditation object, later his mind got focused on the object of meditation more easily. By the eighth day, the *kasina nimitta* became larger about eighteen inches in diameter. Its rim also became bright. In the vision, *kasina nimitta*, appearing in front of the face, became brighter. From the rim, a ball of fire moved to the centre, and as it did, the shaking of the *kasina nimitta* stopped. Pleasure was born. When Vanaratana reported these developments to his meditation teacher, he was greeted with praise.

Until the eleventh day, Vanaratana continued his meditation concentrating on *parikamma nimitta* (preliminary sign). On the eleventh day, in the middle of *kasina nimitta*, a fire was born. It was, he reported, about four inches in height. While the *kasina nimitta* did not fluctuate, its size had become about three feet in diameter.

Vanaratana's Mystical Visions

In *Kale Suvanda*, Vanaratana explains the nature of the mystical experience that he had experienced during his practice of the *kasina* meditation.

Vanaratana recorded that his courage and pleasure increased with the appearance of fire within *kasina mandala*. Devotion to *dhamma* increased during the practice and his faith was intensified. When Vanaratana meditated for another two days focusing on that fire, his mental powers became stronger and his concentration was significantly developed. When Vanaratana continued his meditation, pleasure spread within his body like a wave of electricity. His body experienced a comfortable and pleasurable state and he began to have strange visions. He saw a large group of elephants arriving before him with flowers in their trunks and making flower offerings to him. Following the vision of elephants, there appeared various types of animals who came as groups before him. Their numbers were innumerable and he could identify only a few species. Indeed, most of the animals that appeared in his vision he could neither hear nor recognize. Moreover, though he saw many animals in his visions, only a few were pleasant looking, most were extremely frightening and threatening, many being hideously deformed and, in some cases, not even identifiable as animals. The visions that he had were like continuous episodes in a film. When the visions of animals faded away, visions of demons, the dead (Pali: *peta*), and goblins (Pali: *pisaca*) gradually emerged. The visions of demons were followed by scenes of land, roads, houses, streets, rivers, oceans, ships, lakes, ponds, people, and so on. Vanaratana felt that everything on Earth had appeared before him in his visions.[28]

For six days Vanaratana continued meditation, all the time focussing on the fire that appeared in the *kasina mandala* (universal circle of the medita- tional object). Around 9:30 p.m. on the sixth day *saddha* (trust) was intensified.[29] Around 10:30 p.m., a band of elephants appeared in his vision as previously and they paid homage to him. After a while, the fire that was burning in the *kasina mandala* gradually died out. This was followed by a threatening scene in which an attractive blue bowl with a diameter of six feet appeared in front of Vanaratana and pressed hard against his body. This was, in turn, followed by a period of tension, after which he experienced great pleasure as the blue bowl reappeared about three feet from him.

Vanaratana decided to inform his meditation teacher about these visions and experiences. His teacher was delighted, admitting that they were *patibhaga nimitta* (signs of attainment) and explained that it was rare to find such signs.[30]

Conclusion

This essay has focussed on an account of a modern Buddhist mystic in the Sri Lankan Theravada tradition. It has demonstrated that modern

Theravada mystics like Venerable Vanaratana interpret their mystical attainments in the light of textual descriptions found in authoritative texts such as the *Visuddhimagga* and emphasize the continuity of mystical experience through the guidance of a teacher. What the essay demonstrates is that within Theravada Buddhism, though meditation is not the dominant practice but still there is an eagerness for mystical experiences. However, Vanaratana's biography shows that the busy modern village life of the Buddhist monk makes mysticism difficult. This account of Vanarantna's mystical experiences also demonstrates, the criterion of judging the level of mystical attainments from the standpoint of lay observers is the very simple lifestyle of the mystic. However there is much more to this than an austere life.

Notes

[1] The *kasina* (Skt. Kritsna) refers to physical devices, such as coloured circles, used as aids in early stages of meditation. These objects of meditation provide support for acquiring the inwardly visualised sign.

[2] Haritas Varusavitana (ed.), *Kale Suvanda* (Halavata: Merl Varusavitana, 1999), 45–6. In understanding Vanaratana's *kasina* meditation and his mystical experiences, this source will be used throughout this essay.

[3] Ibid., 119. The first *jhana* or state of serene contemplation is characterised by applied thought, sustained thought, rapture, happiness and one-pointedness of mind. Buddhism recognises eight states of *jhana*. These mystic states are not an end in themselves but only a means for emancipation. (See also note 13 below.)

[4] Ibid., 52.

[5] *Kasina* has also been rendered as 'artifices' in *A Buddhist Manual of Psychological Ethics* (*Dhammasangani*), tr. C.A.F. Rhys Davids (London: The Pali Text Society, 1974), 40.

[6] Margaret Cone, *A Dictionary of Pali*, Vol. 1 (Oxford: The Pali Text Society, 2001), 661.

[7] Bhadantacariya Buddhaghosa, *The Path of Purification (Visuddhimagga)*, tr. Bhikkhu Ñanamoli (Colombo: R. Semage, 1956); C.A.F. Rhys Davids (ed.), *The Visuddhimagga of Buddhaghosa*, Vol. 1 (London: The Pali Text Society, 1920), 110.

[8] Upatissa, *The Path of Freedom (Vimuttimagga)*, tr. N.R.M. Ehara, Soma Thera & Kheminda Thera (Colombo: D. Roland, D. Weerasuria, 1961) gives only thirty eight subjects of meditation.

[9] *A Buddhist Manual of Psychological Ethics* (*Dhammasangani*), 40–53.

[10] Upatissa, *Path of Freedom*, 63.

[11] Bhadantacariya Buddhaghosa, *The Path of Purification (Visuddhimagga)*; Rhys Davids (ed.), *Visuddhimagga*, Vol. 1., 118–75.

[12] *Yogavacara's Manual of Indian Mysticism* (London: Pali Text Society, 1896), 48–52.

[13] The second *jhana*, is that state in which the meditator gains 'internal confidence and unification of mind', is without applied thought and sustained thought, and is filled 'with rapture and happiness born of concentration'. In the third *jhana* the rapture fades away and the meditator has in addition equanimity, mindfulness and discernment. In the fourth *jhana* there is 'neither pain nor pleasure' and the mind has 'purity of mindfulness due to equanimity'.

[14] The original Roman script version of the text was produced by the Pali Text Society in 1896 and was the first time that a translation of a Sinhala script text had appeared in the Pali Text Society series.

[15] T.W. Rhys Davids (ed.), *The Yogavacara's Manual of Indian Mysticism as Preached by Buddhists* (London: The Pali Text Society, 1981), vii.

[16] D.B. Jayatilaka,. 'A Dhyana Book', in *Manual of a Mystic: Being a Translation from the Pali and Sinhalese Work Entitled the Yogavachara's Manual*, tr. F.L. Woodward (London: The Pali Text Society, 1982), 143. Sir Don Baron Jayatilaka (1868–1944) recounted his search for this manuscript in his article in *The Buddhist* (*Manual of a Mystic*, vii.).

[17] *Manual of a Mystic*, vii.

[18] Rhys Davids, *The Yogavacara's Manual*, 46–53.

[19] *Manual of a Mystic*, viii.

[20] In chapters 3–9 of *The Path of Purification* (122–84), Buddhaghosa explained various aspects of meditation. In particular, in chapters 4 and 5 he discussed the ten *kasinas*.

[21] Varusavitana (ed.), *Kale Suvanda*, 69.

[22] Ibid., 48.

[23] Ibid., 71.

[24] Ibid.

[25] *The Path of Purification*, 122–6.

[26] Varusavitana (ed.), *Kale Suvanda*, 73.

[27] *The Path of Purification*, 178.

[28] Varusavitana (ed.), *Kale Suvanda*, 88.

[29] Ibid., 93.

[30] Ibid., 94.

4

Islamic Mystics of the Lakshadweep Islands, India

Theodore Gabriel

The Lakshadweep is a group of coral islands belonging to the Republic of India and lying between 120 and 200 miles off the coast of Kerala in the Arabian Sea. There are ten inhabited and seventeen uninhabited islands. The population of about 52,000 are entirely Muslim. They are devout and committed to the prescriptions of the *Shar'ia*, but there is a substratum of Sufism in the practice of Islam in Lakshadweep which is not immediately apparent due to the rigorousness with which the inhabitants follow Islamic laws and regulations.

The Muslims of Lakshadweep are noted for the strictness and intensity of their practice of Islam. But it is the charisma and wonder working powers of the *Tangals* (Sufi *sheikhs*), which have secured them their reputation in the Islamic *umma* (community) of the Indian mainland and even abroad. A number of these individuals proceed on religious journeys (termed *safar* by the islanders) and have followers in places such as Singapore, Sri Lanka and Malaysia. One of them is a teacher in the prestigious Al Azhar University of Cairo, one of the greatest centres of Islamic learning in the world.

What is Sufism?

'Sufism' is the term that indicates mysticism in Islam and originates from early eighth century CE when it crystallised into a specific movement in Islam. The term originates from the Arabic word *suf*, meaning wool, and the name Sufi was given to the itinerant mystics who wore wool to protect themselves from the harsh cold of the Arab nights (in contrast to other Muslims who preferred cotton garments in emulation of the Prophet).

The initial preoccupation of Islam was with law, not with theology or mysticism. The *ulama* seemed to become more and more pedantic as time passed and there was a danger that Islam would become a dry, legislative and ritualistic religion, losing the fervour which contributed to its phenomenal early growth. But even from early days there was a reaction against this legalism and ritualism – a current that stressed the need for mystical inspiration, elevation and personal encounter with God, and which sought to oppose the lapsing of Islam into rigidity and dullness. In fact, Sufism may have prevented Islam from dying out.

Remembrance (*dhikr*) is the keynote of Sufism and all their actions are done in the name of Allah, whether they be spiritual actions such as praying or meditation, or also even mundane acts such as eating. The words *Bismillah* (in the name of God), *Mashallah* (with the help of God), *Al Andulilah* (praise be to God) and *Inshallah* (If God wills) are constantly on the lips of the Sufis.

In the beginning, Sufism was highly antinomian and radical in its understanding of God and his relationship to humanity. Sufism was vigorously opposed and persecuted by the orthodox *ulama* and the Caliphs of Islam. The first martyr to Sufism was Mansur al Hallaj (c.858–922) to whom is attributed the famous saying '*ana al Haqq*' ('I am the Truth', i.e. God). Although the monistic and pantheistic ideas held by some Sufis were considered highly controversial and heretical, al Hallaj was tried and publicly executed by the Caliph, not for his radical theology, but for failing to observe the essential rituals of Islam (the *Ibadah*).

It was the great Islamic theologian al Ghazzali (1058–1111) who was principally responsible for making Sufism respectable and acceptable to the orthodoxy. Al Ghazzali, initially a vehement critic of Sufism, became a champion of the movement. He stressed that mysticism and spirituality should be built on the foundations of strict observance of the external rituals of the *Ibadah*, but should go much beyond merely outward performance.

The Origins of Islam in Lakshadweep

Most scholars agree that the inhabitants of Lakshadweep are descendants of Hindus from Kerala, most probably belonging to the Nair and Tiyya castes, who settled down in these beautiful coral atolls in the second century.[1] The islanders believe that they were then converted wholesale to Islam by Ubaidulla – grandson of Abu Bakr (c.580–634), a companion of Muhammad and one of his earliest converts – who was shipwrecked on the islands in 663 CE. Ubaidulla apparently had a dream in which Muhammad appeared to him and exhorted him to propagate Islam in distant places.[2] Ubaidulla performed great miracles in Amini Island where he was shipwrecked and where the island's inhabitants attacked and tried to kill him. Standing on the beach he stamped on the land and the whole island tilted westwards. He materialised a tiger and caused the aggressors to become temporarily blind. Later he moved to Androth where also he performed astonishing miracles, such as causing an earthquake. Awed by the Hijazi Sayyid's powers and charisma, the inhabitants of the islands accepted Islam wholesale. Ubaidulla married and settled down in Androth. His tomb in Androth is a pilgrimage centre for the islanders and the venue of a colourful and lavish *mowlid* every year.

It is evident that attributing the origins of Islam to a charismatic *Tabiun* from Arabia is one of the reasons for the ascendancy of Sufism in the islands. The Ubaidulla legend lends legitimacy and status to Islam in Lakshadweep. Androth Island, where Ubaidulla lived, abounds with charismatic *Tangals* (itinerant Sufi *sheikhs*) who are much in demand all over South and Southeast Asia. They are mostly descendants of Ubaidulla, and well-known for their wonder-working powers, such as healing, exorcising evil spirits, and conferring many blessings, such as wealth, employment and children.

Ubaidulla is just one of the many Sufi saints who lived in the islands and who is believed to have conferred many blessings on the inhabitants. (I will return to these charismatic personalities below.)

The Sufis of Lakshadweep belong to two *tariqas* (Sufi religious orders), the Quadiriyya and the Riffai, two orders that differ in their orthodoxy and the nature of the *dhikr* performed by them.

The Quadiriyya

The founder of the Quadiriyya, an international Sufi order, was Abdal Quadr al Gilani, who was born in 1077 in Baghdad. It is paradoxical that this Sufi saint originally belonged to the Hambali *madhab*, a school of law, (now known as Wahabi) who are vehemently opposed to Sufism. His praxis and interpretation of Islam does not depart considerably from the orthodox, though he was inclined to mystical interpretation of the Qur'an (*tawil*). His eleven sons were mainly responsible for the propagation of the order and, by the nineteenth century, the Quadiriyya had become popular with several congregations extending from Morocco to South East Asia.[3] The keeper of Gilani's tomb at Baghdad is head of the order and a direct descendant of the founder. However, there is very little administrative control of the congregations, which are mostly self-governing.

The Riffai Order

This order was founded by Ahmad al Riffai, a nephew of Abd al Quadr al Gilani. This is a much more unorthodox and charismatic order noted for their practices of self-mortification, such as walking on fire, eating glass, playing with serpents and piercing the body with sharp instruments. In contrast, the Quadiriyya *dhikr* is staid compared to the Riffai *dhikr* and involves only music and beating of a tambourine. They are less fanatical and stress piety, humility, philanthropy and tolerance.

The thaumaturgical exercises for which the Riffai *tariqua* is noted are attributed by some scholars to the impact of Shamanism during the Mongolian regime of Iraq during the thirteenth century.[4]

Amazingly both orders were introduced to the Lakshadweep islands by Sheikh Muhammad Kasim, an Arab Sufi Sayyid who married and settled down in Agatti Island. He had no progeny from his marriage but later married a lady from a prominent family of Androth, who were descendants of the legendary Ubaid Allah. It is said that the marriage was a consequence of Muhammad Kasim curing this lady of the dreaded disease of leprosy. Muhammad Kasim built the famous Ujjra mosque at Kavaratti Island, noted for its wood carvings.

Sheikh Muhammad died in Kavaratti in 1140 AH. He was buried in Kavaratti near the Ujjra mosque which is the scene of an annual celebration of his *mowlid*. His cap, walking stick and flag are still preserved in the mosque as sacred artefacts. It is believed that prayers to the saint are still efficacious for healing and redressing problems.

The Sufi Leadership

The present heads of the Quadiriyya and Riffai orders are believed to be the descendants of the founders of the orders, and belong to two celebrated families of Kavaratti Island, which is now the capital of Lakshadweep. These families, the Aranikkat and Ekkarpally of Kavaratti, are in reality both descendants of Sheikh Muhammad Kasim who introduced Sufism to the islands, through two of his wives. The Islanders are matrilineal, anomalous in Islam, but most probably a vestige of their Hindu ancestry, since the *Nair* and *Tiyya* castes of North Malabar from where the islanders migrated are matrilinear. So the children take the name of the mother's family, and not of the father. These *sheikhs* visit the other islands once or twice every year. Their representatives in the islands are called the *Khalifa* of the respective order. Upon the *Sheikh's* arrival the *Khalifa* receives him ceremoniously on the beach and he is escorted to the respective mosque to the accompaniment of a *dhikr*. The *dhikr* ceremony is preformed only when these *sheikhs* are present. On Friday, the *sheikh* is ceremoniously escorted to the Juma Masjid where he is presented with oil from giant manta rays caught during the year; this is a valuable commodity in the islands, especially for preserving fishing boats and sailing ships. He distributes part of this to the *Kathib* of the mosque, to his *khalifa* and to the *Amin* (revenue official of the island).

The *murids* (disciples or novitiates) of the two *sheikhs* are expected to obey every instruction given by the *sheikh* and to have implicit faith in him. There are no elaborate initiation ceremonies, but every *murid* is given a *tirassila* (pedigree chart) written in Arabic as a mark of his entry into the order. This is kept as a sacred and secret document throughout his life and is buried along with his mortal remains. The *tirassila* is believed to safeguard the Sufi during his life and to obtain condonation of sins on judgement day.

Sufism and Caste

An interesting fact is that the Quadiriyya and Riffai tariqas of the islands are associated with two different caste groups. Caste is an anomaly in an Islamic community, but the inhabitants of Lakshadweep belong to three castes namely the *Koya*, the *Malumi* and the *Raweri*. Unlike other Muslim groups in the Indian subcontinent, which display caste-like social stratification, caste in the Lakshadweep displays a rigour in the hierarchy, social prohibitions, caste endogamy, concepts of purity and pollution which are identical to the Hindu phenomenon. The Sufi orders of Quadiriyya and Riffai in the islands identify themselves with the high caste of *Koyas* and the inferior caste of *Melacceri* respectively. It is befitting in a way that the Riffai identify themselves with the caste that has for long suffered discrimination and oppression at the hands of the *Koyas*, since the self-mortification acts of their rituals and the intensity of their devotion to God reflect the suffering that they have undergone.

The Dhikr

The word *dhikr* literally means remembrance and in the Sufi context consists of remembering God (Allah) in the words of the *dhikr* song (called *ratib* in the islands). An example of a *ratib* used in Lakshadweep is given below:

> Glory to God, there is no God except Allah
> Mohammed is my guardian, the messenger of Allah.

> O our leader, O, the pivot of power
> O the reviver of religions, our guardian, the messenger of Allah.

> O our former leader, Abdul Quadir Gilani
> The Prophet of Allah is his brother

O leader of the wise, O my leader,
O the greatest one, the Prophet of Allah is his brother
O leader of the wise, O my leader,
O the greatest one, the Prophet of Allah is his brother.

O the sultan of the righteous,
O the leader, O the greatest one, the Prophet of Allah is his brother.[5]

It is evident from this Quadiriyya *dhikr* chant that the remembrance applies not only to God but also to the prophet and to Gilani the founder of the order.

The Quadiriyya *Dhikr*

The Quadiriyya *dhikr* (called *tikkar* by the islanders) seems to be, on the surface, a quiet and rather tame affair compared to the Riffai one. But there is no denying the intense and deep devotion and spirituality expressed through these rituals. It is to be remembered that in the Khilawatiyah and Nashqbandi orders the *dhikr* is almost a silent one and emphasises meditation and concentration on God. An ecstatic state such as the one obviously attained in the Riffai *dhikr* is said also to be achieved in these quietist forms of *dhikr*.

In the Quadiriyya *dhikr* of the islands, the participants, who are dressed in white long shirts, white sarongs and white prayer caps, line up in two rows carrying a tambourine (*daff* in the island language). A Qur'an is placed on a pillow at the end of the rows and the *sheikh* or *tangal* stands in front of the group. The participants bow up and down chanting the *ratib* songs and beating the tambourines. This is a modification of the Middle Eastern Quadiriyya ritual in which the Sufis form a large ring with joined hands, bowing the head and body chanting the *dhikr* songs and stepping to the right.[6] The bowing up and down starts slowly and then gather speed and the music increases in tempo until it reaches a climax of very rapid movements and singing when suddenly the music and the movements stop.

The *dhikr* is based on the Qur'anic injunction that remembrance of God is the believer's cardinal duty (Qur'an: Sura 29:4). Remembrance in practice consists of magnifying, celebrating and lauding God. The most significant act in the *dhikr* is enunciating the unity of God (*tawhid*). The Islamic creed *La ilaha illallah* (there is no god but God/Allah) is intoned many times in the *dhikr*. To the Sufi *tawhid* does not mean the unity of God alone but also his own union with God, an idea not strictly orthodox, but which finds support in verses such as 'God is closer to you than the vein in your neck and knows the innermost whisperings of the human soul'.[7]

The Riffai *Dhikr*

The Riffai *dhikr* is more or less similar to the Quadiriyya. The point of departure is when the music, drumming and genuflecting actions reach a crescendo when some half-naked devotees approach the *sheikh*, who gives them weapons of various kinds. These are swords, daggers, short spears, awls and hammers. The *Khalifa* chanting Qur'anic verses passes his hands over the weapons and the *murids* receive the weapons from him in a reverential attitude. They move backwards from the *Tangal* without turning their backs to him.

The dancers begin to sway from side to side as though they are intoxicated. They seem to be in a state of great ecstasy as they hold their weapons out. They are evidently in an altered state of consciousness. As the music rises to a feverish pitch they plunge the weapons into their stomach, chest, neck, head and all parts of their body. Some pierce their cheeks with awls while others draw the swords over their stomach. Some hold the awl to their forehead and strike it with hammers. In the twilight and dim glow of the kerosene lamps I could not see clearly but they do not seem to feel any pain or adverse effect. It is said that not a single drop of blood is shed. After this act of self-mortification all of them approach the *Tangal* who softly stroke the site of their wounds, which are said to be instantaneously healed so that not even a scar remained as a result of their traumatic acts.

The Tangals

The *Tangals* (an honorific term usually applied to Nampootiri *Brahmins* of Kerala) are the charismatic Sufi leaders of the Lakshadweep islands. The largest number of them live in Androth island and are believed to be the descendants of Ubaidulla who Islamicised the islands. Most of them travel widely on the Indian mainland as well as abroad where they have a big following due to their spirituality and wonder working powers. Legends abound of great Sufi masters who inhabited various islands and performed great miracles. I have already mentioned Sheikh Mohammed Kasim who established the Sufi *tariqas* of Lakshadweep. He was buried in Kavaratti and before his death blessed the women of the island perpetually with freedom from pain in childbirth. This blessing does not extend to expatriate women living in the islands. Kavaratti is the only island in the archipelago where no crows are present. It seems

as Sheikh Mohammed Kasim was on his way to prayer he was defiled
by crow droppings and he cursed the crows of the island which soon
disappeared and never appeared in the island again. Another famous Sufi
saint who lived in Agatti Island was able to walk on the sea. Agatti
Kainjor, as he was called, used to start his nautical jaunt from Agatti
Island immediately after the Subah Namas and was able to reach
Kavaratti Island, a distance of about fifty miles, in time for the *Asr
Namas*.[8] Stranger still is the instance of a child Sufi saint, the Suheli
Kainjor, who could understand many languages. The remarkable ability
of the people of Chetlat Island to climb coconut trees without any
equipment (a skill that I witnessed many times when I lived on the
island), unique in Lakshadweep, is said to be a gift from a Sufi saint who
had lived in the island. Birekkal Muhammad Moula was a saint who
lived in Androth who was believed to possess the ability to see things
happening far away. In contemporary times, as I have already mentioned,
there is still a belief in the power of the Kavaratti *tangals* (who are the
present heads of the Quadiriyya and Riffai orders in Lakshadweep) to
heal instantaneously the wounds suffered by the self-mortifying participants of the Riffai *dhikr*.

The Sufi *dhikr* of the islands and the abilities of the Sufi *sheikhs* give
testimony to the people of the ascendancy of spirit over matter, and how
God is glorified in these rituals and the miraculous deeds of the Sufi
leaders and their followers.

Concluding Comments

There is considerable opposition to Sufism in these islands from the
smattering of Wahabis who live there, who are mainly influenced by
Saudi Arabian ideology, having learnt Arabic under Wahabi teachers in
Kerala who were trained in Saudi Arabia. However, Sufism continues to
be highly regarded in the islands, even in modern times when closer
interaction with secular-minded individuals from the Indian mainland
could have dented their belief in God and the Sufi *sheikhs*. The secular-
ising forces that have accompanied the rapid educational and technological advances made in Lakshadweep seem not to have undermined
the faith of the people and their reliance on Sufi rituals and masters.

The Sufi aspiration is to realise the transcendence of the human soul.
In the *dhikr* and other rituals of Sufism, what the Sufi hopes to achieve
is to raise the souls beyond its bondage to the body and the physical
world and realise its identity with the ultimate. They seek for the extinc-
tion (*fana*) of the created in the uncreated, the temporal in the eternal,
of the finite in the infinite. They demonstrate such transcendence in the

self-mortification acts in which the spirit, through the power of God, triumphs over bodily pain and trauma. The continual chanting of the name of God and Muhammad, the drumming and the dancing helps them in this aspiration of seeking to rise above the limitations of the physical world. Martin Lings[9] points out that the Sufis consider themselves to be returnees – those who have returned to God – an attitude that seeks support from the following verse from the Qur'an:

> Verily we are for God and verily unto him we are returning.[10]

The *dhikr* is a visible testimony to the Sufis' perception of themselves as movers and they consider others, even those who adhere strictly to the *Shar'ia* and the *Ibadah*, the five rituals of Islam, as being stationery.

It is paradoxical that such mystical longings are more pronounced among, not the intellectuals or the more educated elite, but among the rural and comparatively less educated folk of Islamic communities. While Sufism is popular and widely accepted among the ordinary members of the Lakshadweep society, the opposition to it comes from the more intellectual sections of the people, particularly the *ulama* who teach Arabic in the island schools. For them, Sufism is not only heretical, barbaric and contrary to the will of God and the doctrines of Islam, it is totally anathema. They call the Sufis *khurafis* (unbelievers). The Sufi *dhikr* is totally discredited in their eyes. My Wahabi friends decried these practices as *bida* (innovation), not sanctioned by the Qur'an or the Hadith, and Sufi concepts of returning to God and self-extinction and unity with him, as extravagant and heretical. The cutting and wounding of the Riffai *dhikr* they say is an entire hoax, the weapons are blunt and often the mystics' wounds turn septic and they have to be medically treated. To the majority of the Lakshadweep Muslims however the acts are authentic, spiritual and miraculous acts.

The modern movement against Sufism, and elimination of magical acts and syncretism with other religions comes from the more urban and educated sections of the populace, be it in India, Malaysia or any Islamic country, rather than from the rural and less intellectually inclined sections of the public. It may be that Sufi belief and practice is more grounded in religious experience, such as that of the *dhikr*, than in rational theological inquiry. The experience of God in the thaumaturgical acts of the *dhikr*, unmediated by reasoning, is a powerful incentive for the continuance and strengthening of Islamic belief in the islands when it is beset by forces of modernism, such as the secular policies of the Indian government, the scepticism of science and technology, and the materialistic values of twentieth- and twenty-first century 'progress' in the islands. However, it is a fact that the spread if Islam in India and South East Asia was mainly an achievement of Sufi missionaries rather than the more orthodox and conventional Muslims. Its survival and perpetuation in these lands might now also be on the shoulders of the Sufis rather than the intellectually and Wahabi-oriented *ulama* of neo-fundamentalist Muslim sections.

Notes

[1] A.R. Kutty, *Marriage and Kinship in an Island Society* (New Delhi: National Publishing House, 1972), 8. This dating is dependent on the discovery of a cache of old coins in Kadmat Island.

[2] M. Ramunny, *The Laccadive, Minicoy and Amindivi Islands* (New Delhi: Publications Division, Government of India, 1972), 13.

[3] H.A.R. Gibb, *Mohammedanism* (London: Oxford University Press, 1949), 155.

[4] Ibid., 156.

[5] Personal communication from Sri Shamsuddeen Moulavi, Agatti Island (13/5/2001).

[6] A vivid description of the Quadiriyya ritual is given in E.W. Lane, *Manners and Customs of the Modern Egyptians* (London: Alexander Gardner, 1895), 438–9.

[7] Qur'an 50:16.

[8] Satikumaran Nair, *Arabikkatalile Pavira Dveepukal* (Kottayam: National Book Stall, 1972), 298.

[9] Martin Lings, *What is Sufism?* (London: George Allen & Unwin, 1973), 28.

[10] Qur'an 2:156.

5

Hindu Mysticism
Monistic and Dualistic

Ruth A. Bradby

Introduction: Western Perceptions

Hindu mysticism forms part of the public imagination in the West today. Its vocabulary has become common currency in public discourse; its practice is fashionable among the famous, prosperous and intelligent; its metaphors appear in television commercials; and its flowering in popular humour shows that it is now firmly rooted in Western social culture.

A recent cartoon, for example, shows a bored model in an upmarket restaurant asking her eager bespectacled partner to 'Just explain again the bit about the void'. Another cartoon has a cocktail party hostess, surrounded by canapés and socialites, remarking to her otherworldly mystic guest, 'I imagine serenity's pretty much the same, one season to the next?' In a third cartoon, an earnest middle-aged couple tell their son dressed as a Hindu *sadhu*, 'Your father and I just want you to know that we're behind you one hundred per cent should you decide to go back to being a dope addict'. As the cartoons suggest, Hindu mysticism, though commonplace and the subject of affectionate, banal humour, is still viewed in popular culture as slightly ridiculous, incomprehensible and possibly dangerous.

Earlier generations were inclined to feel a mixture of fascination and fear, rather than amusement, when confronted with Hindu mysticism. In his 1924 novel, *A Passage to India*, E.M. Forster describes an expedition made by the Europeans and their Indian friend Dr Aziz to the Marabar Caves. They plan to have a picnic on the hill near the caves, but things start to go wrong. The English girl Adela gets lost in the caves and calls for help. But the English words she speaks get transformed by the cave echo and come back to her as an indeterminate *OM* sound. Perhaps the symbolism that Forster wishes to convey is of Westerners approaching the East with their assumptions of the power of rationality and the potential of language to be used for meaningful communication. Lost in the caves of the orient, they find words transformed into indeterminate sounds, with the mantra-like *OM* sound the only element that can be made out. It is an unnerving experience. Forster's metaphor conveys the popular belief that the East has the power to reduce language – and indeed the whole of human experience and material existence – to one syllable of mystical content.

In the early decades of the twentieth century, when Sigmund Freud was conducting research into personality formation, he identified an early stage which he described as narcissistic omnipotence. He called this state 'The Nirvana Principle'. In Freud's day, the identification of the ego with the universe was regarded by Western thinkers as the defining characteristic of Hindu philosophy and mystical experience. Freud defined the Nirvana Principle as the infant's 'oceanic' feeling of union of the self with the All.[1] This 'limitless extension and oneness with the universe', he argued, described an early developmental state of unified libido before consciousness divided into an awareness of ego and external objects.[2]

The popular cartoons, E.M. Forster's literary symbolism and Freud's 'Nirvana Principle' – disparate as they appear to be – all draw inspiration from a form of Hindu mysticism known as *Advaita* Vedanta, founded by the classical Hindu philosopher Shankara Bhagavatpada (c.700 CE). Shankara has been called both the Aristotle and the St Thomas Aquinas of Hinduism. With relentless logic he constructed a system of strict, idealistic monism (or non-duality) in which salvation or liberation (*moksha*)[3] is achieved through knowledge formed in a mystical experience of the oneness of the soul or self (*atman*) and the Transcendent One (Brahman). Shankara's system continues to be important in India. In the West it has become synonymous with philosophical Hinduism. However, Shankara's monistic mysticism, while significant, represents only one example of the rich diversity of mystical experience within the Hindu tradition.

Outside the intellectual elite, Shankara's *Advaita* has arguably been less influential than the qualified theism of the eleventh to twelfth century mystic philosopher, Ramanuja. Ramanuja reacted against the impersonal logic of Shankara and taught that the world and souls are God's body, agents of his will. His *visistadvaita* ('non-duality in difference') provided the intellectual framework which legitimated *bhakti*, the devotional worship of a personal God. *Bhakti* had been present in Indian literature from the time of the Vedas (c.1500–800 BCE), and had been practised in South India from at least the early centuries of the Christian era. But this movement from below had been viewed by the orthodox as a degraded form of worship fit only for those of low birth. *Bhakti* not only introduced the ideas of spiritual grace and love, but provided a way of liberation open to all castes and to women.[4] After Ramanuja, the orthodox elite of Brahmanism conceded that *bhakti* had a place in Hinduism, as one of the avenues of liberation (*moksha*).

The sixteenth-century mystic Chaitanya represents a third distinct variety of Hindu mysticism. Chaitanya's movement was part of the *bhakti* wave which swept across India after Ramanuja. Like Shankara and Ramanuja, Chaitanya was a *Brahmin* with a classical Sanskrit education. He felt orthodox contempt for *bhakti* until he experienced a dramatic conversion to a *bhakti* form of devotion to Krishna. Chaitanya taught his followers the ideal of a casteless society and a theistic mysticism involving ecstatic self-surrender to Krishna. Chaitanya's mysticism continues to be important today through the Bengal Vaishnavism branch of Hinduism. Chaitanya's Bengal Vaishnavism rather than Madva's *dvaita* (the Hindu tradition often cited in textbooks as an example of dualism) is featured here because an authentic version of it is well known in the West through The International Society for Krishna Consciousness (ISKCON), popularly known as the Hare Krishna movement.[5] It is perhaps significant that the Beatle George Harrison, who began his spiritual journey using Transcendental Meditation, a popular, westernised form of Vedanta, became, through the Hare Krishna movement, a devotee of Lord Krishna by the time of his death in 2001.

This chapter will look at the diversity of Hindu mystical experience described by Shankara, Ramanuja and Chaitanya. Against the background of present day debates about language as a shaper of mystical experience, it will probe the relationship in Hinduism between mystical experience on the one hand and language and scripture on the other. Finally, it will consider the thesis that all mystical experiences are the same,[6] and suggest ways in which the advent of postmodern discourses may bring a fresh approach to old debates about mysticism.

Vedanta: Unity and Diversity

Shankara's monism, Ramanuja's qualified theism and Chaitanya's ecstatic devotionalism are all schools of Vedanta. Vedanta in turn is the sixth of the six systems (*darshanas*) of Hindu philosophy (the others being Nyaya, Vaiseshika, Sankhya, Yoga and Mimamsa) which were defined around the beginning of the Christian era, possibly as a defence against the Buddhist and Jain movements which were considered unorthodox because they did not accept the authority of the Vedas. Vedanta refers to a reflective spirituality which contrasts sharply with the sacrifice and ritual of the fifth system of Hindu philosophy, Mimamsa.

The ritual of Mimamsa, ironically, had provided the continuity between the sacrifices of Vedic times and the more abstract Vedantic system in which the devotee searched within the self for answers to metaphysical questions. In the Vedas, ritual sacrifice came to be understood as a microcosm of the universe and of the person. The Supreme Being, both immanent and transcendent, was believed to be reflected in the inner life of the devotee.[7]

The core belief of the Vedanta system is that there is only one thing that truly exists and that is the Transcendent One, Brahman. Vedanta spirituality broadly refers to the mystical experience of the self's union with the Transcendent One, Brahman, also described as Being, Consciousness and Bliss (*sat, chit, ananda*).[8] Secondly, knowledge of this Transcendent One in Vedanta is said to be dependent upon scriptural revelation. Thirdly, the aim of Vedanta is not disinterested intellectual enquiry, but salvation (*moksha*), that is, liberation from the cycle of rebirth (*samsara*).

The schools of Vedanta had these and other features in common. However, Vedanta should not be seen as a unified system with no important differences. Firstly, the schools of Shankara, Ramanuja and Chaitanya made radically different assertions about the nature of the Transcendent One and about the self's mystical union with the One. Secondly, they differed in their ideas about the nature of material reality. And thirdly, they disagreed about the meaning of liberation (*moksha*) and the method to achieve it.

Shankara and Advaita

Shankara in Context

Vedanta's first interpreter was Gaudapada, who in Hindu tradition was thought to be the teacher of Shankara's teacher. Gaudapada wrote a commentary on the *Mandukya Upanishad*. This text, said to contain the most radical monism of the *Upanishads*, begins with the famous statement: 'OM. This eternal Word is all: what was, what is and what shall be, and what beyond is in eternity. All is *OM*.' Gaudapada argued that if the Transcendent One only is real, then it follows that everything else is unreal. Gaudapada's contribution to Vedantic thought was *maya*, the idea that the external world of sense and experience is illusion, a dream.

In the Vedas, *maya* refers negatively to the evil power of demons and enemies of men (*Rig Veda* I.32.4, *Rig Veda* II.11.5, *Rig Veda* VI.61.3) and positively to creative and magical powers (*Rig Veda* I.167.2, *Rig Veda* III.61.7). The term seems not to have been used as a universal abstraction.[9] Gaudapada used it to mean the unreality of the material world. The logical corollary of this conception of *maya* was the idea that rational thought and sensory experience are untrustworthy agents for experiencing union with the Transcendent. However, Gaudapada did not develop a framework for his concept of *maya*.[10] It was Shankara who constructed a coherent system whereby the Transcendent One, Brahman, could be directly experienced at a level beyond reason and sensual experience.

Shankara's Mysticism

Shankara was a *Brahmin* scholar from South India who is thought to have lived in the eighth to ninth century CE. This was a time of demoralisation for orthodox Hindus because Buddhism had swept across North India and made inroads in the South. To strengthen Hinduism in the face of the Buddhist threat, Shankara is thought to have borrowed from Buddhism ontological concepts (for example, the Buddhist theory of appearance which argues that consciousness alone is real) as well as methods (the establishment of a monastic order and monasteries similar to those of the Buddhists).[11]

Shankara's *Advaita* differed from other systems of Vedanta in his special understanding of ignorance (*avidya*) as the cause of our awareness of the world as separate from Brahman. Shankara used the text from the *Chandogya Upanishad* (6.2.1) again and again. 'Being only was this in the beginning, one, without a second', to show that the only reality is the one Brahman 'without distinctions'.[12] He explained that Brahman, having no beginning, is free from the cycle of rebirth (*samsara*). The appearance of distinctions and the material world around us as separate from Brahman is caused by ignorance (*avidya*). Only the removal of ignorance brings a mystical experience of oneness with Brahman and liberation from the rebirth cycle. How can ignorance be removed?

Shankara argued that ritual and right action (*karma*) cannot lead to liberation. He showed that the path of action, the path (*marg*) used by many Hindus of his time, was futile because the ability to act depends on seeing differences between agents, actions and their results, on believing in cause and effect. Cause and effect was especially problematic for Shankara, because it involves distinctions and therefore is marred by ignorance of Brahman as one. Since all distinctions are the product of ignorance, any positive action will involve distinctions and therefore must be false.[13] Liberation can only come by pure consciousness, unmediated by sensory and mental powers, of the knowledge (*vidya*) of Brahman as one, and of the Self's identity with Brahman.

To remove ignorance (*avidya*) and arrive at right knowledge (*vidya*), Shankara used what some have called the doctrine of 'falsification'. By contradicting worse views, one arrives at better views. For example, regarding the difference between cause and effect, the view that cause transforms itself into effect is worse than the view that it manifests its appearance as effect without itself changing. All views which take causation seriously are inferior to those which espouse non-origination; causal relations involve difference and are thereby tinged with ignorance.

In this dialectical way, the devotee moves step by step closer to *vidya*, true liberating knowledge of the oneness of Brahman. In the end, all positive views are seen to be inadequate because they rely on attributes of Brahman. Brahman is without attributes, incomprehensible, beyond description, ultimately described only by the double negative, 'not this, not this' ('*neti, neti*') repeated in the *Brhadaranyaka Upanishad*.[14] In this way Shankara used a carefully constructed system of logic and inferential argument, developed in the context of commenting on and reconciling the seemingly contradictory scriptural texts, to prove the simple assertion that there is complete oneness between the One Brahman and the Self (*atman*).

However, logic and inferential argument, speculative thought and meditation can only be pointers on the path to pure consciousness of mystical union with Brahman. When the devotee reaches the final stage where he is ready to be liberated, it is a word of scripture, perhaps the famous 'That (Brahman) are Thou' (*Chandogya Upanishad* VI.8.7) which brings mystical consciousness of the oneness of the Self with Brahman and the illusoriness of everything else. Shankara described mystical identity with Brahman as (1) mystical knowledge coming from unmediated contact with the Transcendent One, (2) pure consciousness from which earthly images and concerns have vanished, and (3) an ultimate sense of bliss.[15] Such a person has achieved liberation from the rebirth cycle (*samsara*). He can never truly act again, though he may appear to act, for the individual self does not survive absorption into the Transcendent Self/Brahman.

Shankara dealt with the tension between theistic and monistic texts in the *Upanishads* by suggesting that there are two levels of reality. First, there is Brahman who is identical with the universal Self (*atman*). Brahman alone is real, without beginning and beyond description. Second, there is the deity who may be called many names – Brahma, Shiva, Vishnu, Krishna or Ishwara. This deity is Brahman seen through the veil of ignorance. Deities are present in the texts of the *Upanishads* to help those at lower levels of understanding. The lower level deity has creative powers which produce a plurality of selves and the material world. The individual self (and our consciousness of it as separate from Brahman) belong to this lower level.[16] Commentators after Shankara wondered if the existence of these two levels causes Brahman to be tainted with ignorance. Shankara, however, saw Brahman not as an abstract problem, but as the goal of the mystical journey.

Shankara and Scripture

For Shankara, it is a word from scripture which finally brings liberation (*moksha*), and all Vedantins assert that scriptural revelation is the only fully reliable authority for knowledge of the Supreme Being. Scripture for Vedantins, as for all Hindus, meant first the Vedas (c. 1500–800 BCE). They are *sruti*: that is, they are understood to be eternal, uncreated and authoritative for all Hindus. Secondly, scripture meant the *Upanishads* (c. 800–300 BCE), a collection of speculative texts which present monistic as well as theistic teachings. They are thought of as 'the end of the Vedas', that is, the last of the authoritative revealed scriptures. Vedantins also look to the secondary scriptures (*smriti*), the popular *Bhagavad Gita* and the *Vedantasutras* (or *Brahmasutras*). The Epics and the *Puranas* are said to corroborate the teachings of the Vedas and *Upanishads*. Shankara wrote commentaries on the *Upanishads*, the *Vedantasutras* and the *Bhagavad Gita*. But he looked chiefly to the *Upanishads*.

Shankara constructed his system of idealistic monism by making a synthesis of the seemingly contradictory texts of the *Upanishads*. He was careful to claim the sanction of scripture in all his writing. He argued that scripture is self-validating: 'It is independent, just as the light of the sun is the direct means of our knowledge of form and colour.'[17] Shankara based his arguments on two contentions: that his interpretation of scripture is the correct one, and that this solution is not contradicted by experience. Present day Vedantins follow Shankara in a reliance on scriptural revelation. For example, Vedanta scholar Professor Krishna Sivaraman argues, 'In the final analysis Vedanta, true to its name, relies on the testimony of scripture as the criterion of transcendent experiences.'[18]

Shankara: Concluding Comments

Shankara, popularly thought of as a speculative thinker, might not have viewed himself primarily as a philosopher or a master logician. With Buddhist teaching attracting large numbers of adherents, he was concerned to show the way to a mystical experience of unity with Brahman in the most persuasive way that he could. He might have explained to future generations, who marvelled at the beauty of his arguments, that a consistently logical approach is also the most effective one.

Nor was he the sort of mystic who is unable to act in the practical arena, for he showed a shrewd knowledge of the ways of this world. He established an order of *sannyasin* (those who give up all in search of liberation) and four teaching monasteries, patterned after the Buddhist model, in the four corners of India. He realised, perhaps, that only by institutionalising his speculative mysticism could he ensure that it would be perpetuated to future generations. Shankara was also a creature of his time. Today his order is divided into ten groups, three reserved for *Brahmins* and the rest open to other castes, though not to *dalits* – those still outside the caste structure – nor to women. Shankara himself, however, taught that only male *Brahmins* could become *sannyasins*.

Ramanuja and Visistadvaita

Ramanuja in Context

Ramanuja probably lived in the eleventh to twelfth century CE in Tamilnadu, South India.[19] Ramanuja too was a *Brahmin* of the Vedanta school, and like Shankara, he lived at a time when the orthodoxies of Hinduism were threatened, this time from the missionary religion of Islam. However, from the seventh century, a reaction parallel to Shankara's reaction to Buddhism had spread across South India. This was the *bhakti* movement. *Bhakti* emphasised a personal relationship between the devotee and God, and fervent emotional worship as a response to God's grace. Although viewed with scorn by Sanskrit-educated *Brahmins*, the movement had inspired an outpouring of vernacular poetry, songs and prayers. As the most important temple administrator of his day, Ramanuja was at the pinnacle of the orthodox establishment. Yet he was deeply influenced by the devotional songs and poetry of the Tamil Alvars ('souls submerged in the love of God')[20] as well as by Yamuna, an earlier *Brahmin* Vaishnavite scholar who had tried to incorporate aspects of *bhakti* into Vedanta.[21]

Ramanuja's Mysticism

Ramanuja's mysticism is Vedantic in that it accepted as ultimate reality the single Supreme Self, Brahman. The attainment of Brahman was believed to be the highest goal. However, Ramanuja taught that the individual self is not a fiction to be banished by pure consciousness of the oneness of Brahman. The individual is a final metaphysical fact. His mysticism has been called 'qualified theism' because the individual self is not dissolved but finds perfection through union with God.[22]

Ramanuja's mysticism was a reaction to the cold logic of Shankara's Advaita. Ramanuja was angered by Shankara's teaching that the beloved gods of the Hindu pantheon – Shiva, Vishnu, Ram, Krishna – were consigned to a lower level of reality as part of the veil of ignorance (*avidya*). Nor could he accept a higher reality which meant the abolition of the material world, of the individual, of personality and of the capacity to act and to love.

Ramanuja used his commentary on the *Vedantasutras* to attack Shankara's teachings. In his polemic Ramanuja sarcastically caricatured the main *Advaita* doctrines, appearing to advocate them. There is, he wrote, only one genuine reality called Brahman. Nothing external to him is real. The world which we think we see exists only as an illusion caused by ignorance. All of us are caught in this lost condition of ignorance and therefore are condemned to endless rebirths. Only one thing can bring redemption: knowledge that the world is nothing but illusion, that only Brahman is real and the Self (*atman*) at the base of the soul is identical with Brahman. When this knowledge is realised the veil of ignorance is torn. I realise I am Brahman and all distinctions disappear, especially the distinction between subject, object (cause and effect) and the act of knowing. Likewise all relationships disappear; there is only complete identity.[23] Ramanuja also parodied Shankara's logical system by reducing it to three simple points. (1) Even our senses cannot conceive of real difference or define 'distinction'. (2) Both scripture and logic confirm that Being and knowledge of Being are identical. (3) In the same way, the distinction between a subject and its object which we naively assume does not exist.[24]

Having satirised the arguments of his opponent, Ramanuja denounced them as a web of false teaching and ignorance, and suggested that Shankara had a darkened intellect incapable of logic and unable to understand scripture.[25] Ramanuja argued for a system of 'realism' against Shankara's 'idealism' and 'illusionism'. He taught that distinctions exist: the world in all its variety is real and should be valued. All consciousness presupposes a subject and an object which is different from consciousness as an act. The individual is real and the realisation of Brahman does not mean the self's loss of individuality, but a perfection of it through a mystical experience of communion with God.[26]

Ramanuja agreed with Shankara that Brahman is the ultimate reality, but those texts which indicate that there is nothing *but* Brahman he interpreted as meaning there is nothing *equal to* Brahman. He showed that the *Upanishads* and the *Vedantasutras* teach that Brahman is the same as the personal Lord, Ishawara, and the other deities, and that he has attributes.[27] Ramanuja taught that God is spirit, eternal, loving merciful and righteous. He interpreted the Upanishadic text, 'That Thou art', to convey 'the idea of Brahman having for a body the individual souls'.[28] The world and God are one as the soul and body are one. The world and the individual selves are the body of god, the agent of his will.

Ramanuja scholar S. Raghavachar has shown how Ramanuja saw mystical experience as a journey toward the realisation of God. Ramanuja used the traditional words of Hinduism – karma, jnana and bhakti – but gave them his own meaning and an ascending order of progression as planned stages for the devotee in the journey towards mystical union with God. Perhaps most importantly, he added a new way, prapatti.

Ramanuja defined the first stage, karma (right action) not as ritual duty, or even ethical action, but as all of life's activities which should be sublimated as a path to God. The devotee sees himself as a tool of the divine. All actions should show God's activity in the world. As all of life becomes god-centred, the devotee realises that he has the capacity and desire to know God and is led on to the second state, jnana (knowledge).

For Ramanuja, knowledge of God is a gracious gift from God and causes the seeker to become contemplative, arriving at a new understanding of self and the self's need for God. Knowledge of the self leads to the understanding that peace cannot be achieved except in God. The need of the self for god increases until, finally, the devotee is led on to the highest stage, bhakti.

Ramanuja defined bhakti as a total self-abandonment in the love of God. Bhakti, which in Shankara's scheme was a low form of religion for the ignorant and humble, becomes here the highest stage of mystical God-realisation. However, Ramanuja stressed that true bhakti is based on the previous stage, true knowledge of God, which creates an unquenchable desire in the devotee for mystical union with God. The divinity in this exalted stage becomes the self-revealing lover to the devotee: devotion is a matter of joy and reciprocity.

Lastly, Ramanuja added a new word, prapatti, and a new form of mystical experience to the Hindu tradition. He recognised that the long journey from karma through jnana and finally to the joy of bhakti is difficult. Few were likely to complete it. His new way, prapatti (self-surrender) made no demands on the seeker. Later it became the principal form of bhakti. If a seeker cannot master the disciplined journey leading to bhakti, he may transfer the burden of his inadequacy onto God and seek refuge in God. In place of the staged journey, he may ask God to take responsibility for bringing him to bhakti, mystical union with God.

Prapatti is a once in a lifetime act, not to be repeated. Once God has taken responsibility for the devotee there is nothing more that can be done.[29]

Ramanuja and Scripture

Ramanuja shared Shankara's high view of scripture. The devotee must give himself to hearing scripture (*sravana*), to reflection on it (*manana*) and meditation (*nididhyasana*) in order to embark on the mystical journey. Much of Ramanuja's polemic against Shankara consisted of offering new interpretations of Shankara's proof texts. Like Shankara, he wrote commentaries on the *Upanishads*, the *Vedantasutras* and the *Bhagavad Gita*. He constructed his own logical edifice to explain the difficult monistic texts in the *Upanishads*. But unlike Shankara, he drew most heavily on the *Bhagavad Gita* with its teaching about Krishna as the loving, personal lord to his devotees. He was also influenced by the vernacular Alvar hymns and the *Bhagavata Purana*. Ramanuja wrote nine theological works in Sanskrit. Besides the three main commentaries, he wrote two other short commentaries, three devotional works setting forth *prapatti* as surrender to the deity, and a daily worship manual. As was the case with Shankara, followers of Ramanuja wrote commentaries on all his commentaries and later commentaries on these commentaries were written. These go into extraordinary detail over issues of God's grace and human free will.

Ramanuja: Concluding Comments

Hindus today honour Ramanuja as an important teacher (*acharya*) and the greatest temple organiser within the Vaishnava stream. He is credited with providing the philosophical legitimation for *bhakti* in Hinduism. Ramanuja's God, described as the 'first unambiguously ethical deity in Hinduism',[30] is not abstract, but personal, endowed with goodness, mercy, love, grace, beauty and righteousness.

Ramanuja's *bhakti* had an ethical, emancipatory dimension. Commenting on the *Bhagavad Gita* 9.29, he taught that the great power of *bhakti* meant that God's grace and favour are available to all seekers whatever their caste, education and social class. God's grace draws people to himself regardless of their deficiencies: the only ground for acceptability with God is the individual's need and desire for the love of God. Many of Ramanuja's followers were non-*Brahmins*; they included those from the lower castes. In his temple administration he created ritual duties for *shudras* (the servant caste) though not for women. This tendency in *bhakti* to democratise can be said to have had an influence on political events in twentieth century India. Ramanuja gave a theoretical foundation to Vaishnavism, the branch of Hinduism with arguably the greatest number of devotees in the world today. He stands midway in time, as well as in mystical experience, between the brilliant but frigid philosophy of Shankara and the populist revivalism of Chaitanya.

Chaitanya and Bhakti

Chaitanya in Context

Chaitanya (1485–1533 CE) lived around four centuries after Ramanuja. Unlike Ramanuja and Shankara who had lived in South India, Chaitanya spent most of his life in and around Bengal. Ramanuja had agreed with Shankara that only Brahman truly exists, but he also held that individual selves and the material world are real, though dependent on Brahman for their existence. Hence his view is known as qualified theism. Chaitanya took this view one stage further and propagated a dualistic religion of ecstatic love for a personal god, Krishna.

Like Shankara and Ramanuja, Chaitanya lived during challenging and changing times: the religious and political life of North India underwent great change during his lifetime. Babur established Mugal rule in Delhi in 1526. Guru Nanak, the founder of the Sikh religion, was a contemporary. In 1498, the Portuguese had first landed in India and Catholic missionaries soon followed. Cross-fertilisation of ideas between India and Europe had begun by the start of the sixteenth century, and possibly earlier.

Chaitanya grew up in a *Brahmin* family in Bengal and received a classical Sanskrit education. Like others of his social class he felt disdain for the emotional fervour of *bhakti* worship. However, in 1508 at the age of twenty-two, he went to Gaya to perform memorial rituals for his father. There he experienced a dramatic conversion to *bhakti* when an ascetic South Indian, Ishwara Puri, introduced him to a deep mystical experience of love for Krishna and initiated him into the worship of Krishna.

After this experience, Chaitanya returned home where he joined a group which met each night to sing the praises of Krishna. Their worship of Krishna was accompanied by periods of ecstasy when they were seemingly possessed by the deity. Chaitanya became the charismatic leader of this group. Two years later, Chaitanya completed ascetic vows, renounced home and family[31] and remained a passionate leader of Krishna worship for the rest of his life. He is said to have dived into the sea during an ecstatic episode and to have drowned.[32]

Chaitanya's Mysticism

Chaitanya's mystical spirituality seems galaxies away from that of Shankara. Chaitanya's teaching is thoroughly theistic. Whereas for

Shankara liberation is mystical realisation of the Self's identity with Brahman, Chaitanya taught that all souls are renegades, in need of remembering their real nature as the servants or lovers of Krishna. Traditionally, Krishna was known as one of the incarnations of the god Vishnu. For Chaitanya, Krishna is Lord of the universe, the Supreme Being, the equivalent to Brahman. Indeed, Shankara's transcendent, awe-inspiring Brahman is referred to as the halo of Krishna.[33]

In Chaitanya's mysticism, as with Ramanuja's there are steps on the way to the goal of *bhakti*. Chaitanya defined five kinds of love of Krishna: there is peaceful love (*sadhana bhakti*), love of servant for master (*dasya bhakti*), love of friend for friend (*sakha bhakti*), love of mother for child (*vatsalya bhakti*) and love of woman for lover (*madhurya bhakti*). Of these, *madhurya bhakti* is the highest stage: it is typified by the love of the milkmaids (*gopis*) for Krishna, and the love of Radha, chief among the *gopis*, is the most exalted. In this highest stage Radha forgets that she and Krishna are the subject and object of love as they are caught up together in a mystical experience of love. In this ecstatic state, the lover and beloved seem almost to lose their individuality. God, as Krishna, needs and enjoys communion with humans just as Krishna enjoyed his love-play with the *gopis*. The reciprocity of this mystical experience of knowing, loving and even playing with God made humans in some sense equal with God and, more importantly, equal with one another regardless of caste and gender.[34]

Chaitanya was a passionate devotee of this idealisation of the sexual love between Krishna and Radha. Radha was Krishna's favourite of the *gopis* who left their husbands and came out at night to play with Krishna in the pasturelands near Vrindavan. Chaitanya taught that the Krishna devotee, like Radha and the milkmaids, must have a personal relationship of ecstatic love for Krishna. Chaitanya's mysticism is dualistic: the material world is real, and serves as a snare to distract from the enjoyment of love for Krishna. Humans are of an order of existence different from Krishna and can never become fully divine, just as Radha and the milk-maids could never merge with Krishna as one entity. God and the soul are separate entities: only as separate beings can Krishna and his devotees enjoy one another. However, God and the soul are also seen as made of the same spiritual substance: they are qualitatively one but quantitatively different.[35] Humans are imperfect renegades and they must throw themselves in dependence and self-abasement on the mercy of Lord Krishna. In Chaitanya's Vaishnavism, God as Krishna is then gracious, entering into an ecstatic relationship of love and reciprocity with the devotee.

The fact that the *gopis* left the conventions of married life out of passionate love for Krishna was thought to show the extent of love and devotion which the devotee should feel for Krishna: he is worthy of total abandonment, even if this brings social censure. Chaitanya taught that Krishna should be worshipped as the universal male, and devotees were encouraged to think of themselves as females, following in the footsteps of Radha and the *gopis*. It was not unknown for Chaitanya and his followers to dress as women to heighten the excitement of their devotion as they sang and danced in worship of Krishna.

In addition to the singing and dancing that are characteristic of Chaitanya's Krishna worship, repetition of the name of Krishna and of a personal mantra is important. Belief in the power of the word (*vak*) goes back to Vedic times. The long periods of repetition of the names of God are not to induce trance-like states. The mantra initiation, in which an empowered guru whispers a personal mantra into the ear of the devotee, is thought to open the way to ritual participation in the divine play of Radha and Krishna. Each syllable of the name of Krishna or of a mantra is said to have the power to create the force of God himself within the devotee, and to drive from the mind all that is not consistent with the mystical consciousness of Krishna.[36]

However, the greatest departure in Chaitanya's mysticism is perhaps his view of liberation (*moksha*). In Shankara's *advaita*, liberation came through mystical experience – an intuitive realisation, unmediated by sensual experience, that the Self is identical with Brahman. This brought release from the bondage of endless cycles of rebirth, but, as Ramanuja pointed out, this also meant the end of the individual as such. In Ramanuja's mystical understanding, liberation was gained either through the difficult discipline of the path of action (*karma*), knowledge (*jnana*), and finally *bhakti*, or, through *prapatti*, the total abandonment of the devotee to the grace of God. In both cases, the individual survived to find and enjoy perfection through union with God.

Chaitanya taught that the ecstatic joy of loving communion with Lord Krishna is more than the traditional idea of liberation, that is release from the rebirth cycle. Overwhelming love for Krishna was believed to destroy the cycle of rebirth. But this was seen as an incidental by-product to the more important enjoyment of the reciprocal love relationship with Krishna. Chaitanya is believed to have said, 'At the utterance of the word *moksha*, hatred and fear arise in the mind; at the utterance of the word *bhakti* the mind is filled with joy.'[37] The implications of this view of liberation had the implied corollary that the material world was viewed more positively. It was something not to be escaped from, but to be enjoyed through communion in love and play with Lord Krishna. By transforming *bhakti*, devotion to God into *prema*, love for God, with a greater emphasis on reciprocity, Chaitanya gave a new understanding to the relationship between God and humanity in Hindu traditions.

Chaitanya and Scripture

For Chaitanya, the most important of the sacred texts was the *Bhagavata Purana*. This work probably originated in the Tamil-speaking area of South India in the beginning of the tenth century CE. It encourages believers to aim for ecstasy and in this respect is different from the earlier *bhakti* works such as the *Bhagavad Gita*. A much loved part of the *Bhagavata Purana* is Book 10, which describes the early life of Krishna and gives lengthy details of his love affairs with the *gopis*. The youthful Krishna is a very human character, a likeable rogue. Here Chaitanya saw a representation of the deity with which ordinary people could identify, a person who could share their problems and was worthy of their love.

Chaitanya did not write commentaries on the *Vedas*, *Upanishads*, *Vedantasutras* or *Bhagavad Gita*. The teaching of Chaitanya was given orally to Sanatana Gosvami, his companion and follower. It was written down by Gosvani's brother, Rupa, a scholar who became one of the leading poet-theologians of the Chaitanya tradition. His most famous work giving Chaitanya's teaching is *The Ocean of the Ambrosia of the Rapture of Devotion* (*Bhakti-rasamrta-sindhu*).[38]

Chaitanya: Concluding Comments

Chaitanya was a mystic who had a gift for making mystical experience of God exciting and attractive to ordinary people. Unlike Shankara, Chaitanya did not call for a renunciation of the world. Chaitanya has exerted an enormous influence over the subsequent development of the Hindu religion far beyond Bengal. Scholars have traced Mahatma Gandhi's dislike of caste distinctions, untouchability and the hierarchy in organised Brahmanic religion to his Vaishnava background and to Chaitanya.[39] Chaitanya's disapproval of caste distinctions and disregard for pollution rules were subversive and his mysticism continues to have an emancipatory function today. As noted, Chaitanya's Vaishnavism has become popular outside of India through the International Society for Krishna Consciousness (the Hare Krishna Movement).

Conclusion: Western Perspectives

Western popular perceptions of Hindu mysticism have their roots in the cultural stereotyping of the 'mystic East' by eighteenth and nineteenth century Western scholars. The enlightenment faith in the power of reason and empirical knowledge to understand all reality and to codify it within a universal (albeit Euro-centric) framework, led to the study of the Orient as an academic discipline. As Edward Said has argued, the Western academic discipline of orientalism allowed the cultural stereotyping of the East as 'mystic' in contrast to the implied superiority of the rational, materialistic West.[40]

In the Enlightenment spirit, mysticism also became the object of academic study. In spite of the acknowledged inadequacies of language to describe mystical experience, the mystics had written of their experience to reflect upon it and to commend it to others. The reductionism which grew out of Enlightenment thought encouraged scholars to analyse the writings of the mystics in order to find a universal norm for all forms of mysticism. Mystical experience, isolated from its cultural and religious context, was distilled and defined as a direct apprehension of a dimension of reality which is (1) normally inaccessible to the senses and (2) inadequately described by language. At the end of the nineteenth century, William James identified four characteristics common to all mystical experience: (1) it is 'ineffable', cannot be described by language; (2) it is 'noetic', giving the mystic authoritative knowledge; (3) it is 'transient'; and (4) it renders the mystic 'passive'.[41]

Many followed James in the twentieth century. F.C. Happold's study suggested that all mystics search for unity: monistic mystics seek for absorption into the Absolute, while theistic mystics seek for personal communion with God.[42] Bringing these divisions together, Rudolf Otto's famous study, *Mysticism East and West*, compared the mysticism of Shankara with that of the Christian mystic Meister Eckhart (1260–1327). While avoiding a simplistic perennialism, Otto argued that Eckhart's two levels of God (God and the Godhead) can be compared to Shankara's two levels of reality.[43] In another study, Otto compared *bhakti* with Christian ideas of grace.[44] Later in the twentieth century, Joseph Campbell argued that all understanding of ultimate reality 'displays an order of fixed forms that appear and reappear through all time'.[45] However, most of these thinkers found it difficult not to simplify diverse mystical experiences in order to make them fit into preconceived categories.

Popular Perceptions of Hindu Mysticism

As noted in the Introduction to this chapter, the Western stereotypes of Hindu mysticism found today in popular humour, advertising, films and novels, often assume that a form of Shankara's *Advaita* is the central philosophy of Hinduism. This essentialist view of Hindu mystical experience can be traced back to the orientalist scholars and their influence through education on upper class Indians like Vivekananda, the famous nineteenth-century Hindu philosopher and mystic. Born Narendranath Datta (1863–1902), he took the name Vivekananda after becoming a disciple of the mystical reformer, Ramakrishna. Ramakrishna, an *Advaita sannyasin*, had experienced mystical visions of the goddess Kali and the 'holy mother' Mary but taught that there was no need for a synthesis of faiths. Vivekananda, however, founded the Ramakrishna Mission in India and the Vedanta Society in New York, and reflected his Western education by attempting a synthesis of all religions within Hinduism, the 'mother of religions'. Vivekananda developed this teaching in his missionary journey to America at the end of the nineteenth century and, like the Theosophical Society which had been founded in New York in 1875, taught that Hinduism was the oldest religion and the source of all other faiths.

As Richard King has pointed out, Vivekananda's essentialism operated at three levels. First, Vivekananda taught that Shankara's *Advaita* mysticism is the central philosophy of Hinduism. Speaking in Chicago in the 1890's, Vivekananda argued that the six systems (*darshanas*) of Hindu philosophy are six complementary points of view leading to the same fundamental truth which is the monism of Shankara's *Advaita*.[46] However, it has been argued that this view misrepresents the diversity within Hinduism. The classical Hindu systems defined themselves in opposition to one another.[47] Shankara, for example, wrote against the ritual of the fifth system of Hindu philosophy, Mimamsa. The stereotype also distorts the diversity within the Vedanta system. Ramanuja reacted to Shankara, while Chaitanya's form of *bhakti* was a revolutionary, subversive movement from the bottom which outraged (and meant to outrage) the orthodox elite. Chaitanya even repudiated the traditional Hindu goal of liberation, preferring instead a loving relationship with a personal God in the present.[48]

Secondly, in the Indian context, the Neo-Vedanta movement seemed to absorb Buddhist mysticism. Lecturing in San Francisco in 1900 and in New York in 1902, Vivekananda declared Mahayana Buddhism to be a form of Shankara's *Advaita*. The Buddha was shown to be a reformer within the Vedanta tradition.[49] This position was not taken by Shankara, whose writing is a polemic not just against the ritualism of Hindu Mimamsa, but even more strongly against rampant Buddhism which was seen as the greater threat.

Thirdly, The Neo-Vedanta movement colonised the religious traditions of the world by arguing that Advaita is the mystical truth underlying all religious differences. Again, speaking in New York in 1894, Vivekananda incorporated John 1:1 in his teaching. '"In the beginning was the Word and the Word was with God, and the Word was God." The Hindu calls this *maya*, the manifestation of God … The Word has two manifestations: the general one through nature, and the special one of the great Incarnations of God – Krishna, Buddha, Jesus and Ramakrishna. Christ, like Buddha and Ramakrishna, is knowable. The Absolute cannot be known.'[50] In Vivekananda's scheme, all religions, like the popular deities of Hinduism, are part of Shankara's 'lower level' of reality, helpful to those tinged by ignorance, but inferior to the 'higher level' of reality gained through mystical experience of the self's identity with Brahman. This approach found a perennial universal mysticism in Shankara's *Advaita* Vedanta and located other understandings as inferior.

Perennial Universalism and Popular Hindu-Christian Comparisons

Since Vivekananda's time, Hindu vocabulary and various stereotypes of a form of *Advaita* Vedanta have become integrated into Western cultural discourses. Contemporary alternative spiritualities and the increasingly popular New Age self-help techniques have brought varieties of this form of Hindu mysticism into the market place as a practical resource for all. Christians and others in the West have found helpful and sometimes surprising connections between aspects of Hindu and Christian mystical experience. Some, for example, are moved to awe and wonder by Shankara's vision of the Transcendent as the mysterious One who is beyond all finite understanding and human description. Others warm to Ramanuja's idea of devotion and self-surrender to a personal God who reciprocates with love and grace. They may find in the once-for-all nature of *prapatti* something that seems close to a Christian conversion experience. There also appear to be points of connections between the exuberant joy of Chaitanya's ecstatic mysticism and some manifestations of charismatic Christianity.

However, bearing in mind the nature of this volume, it is worth noting some of the fundamental differences that exist between the Hindu and Christian mystical visions. The following three are perhaps significant in the context of this study. First, Christians traditionally have not seen Christ as unveiling new insights into humanity's already existing relationship with God. They see Christ as establishing the possibility of an altogether new relationship between God and humankind.[51]

Secondly, Christian theologies of creation and the material world are different from the various Hindu understandings of the world as being in some way an illusion or appearance (*maya*).[52] God's creation of the world was pronounced 'good' in the first Genesis creation account. Human redemption is referred to along with redemption or renewal of the creation in New Testament texts. Since Christ's incarnation, the material world is seen to have sacramental value. Christians are able to view the temporal as the potential medium of the eternal, and to believe that the spiritual can be given and received through the material.[53]

Thirdly, in the Christian vision, the individual's relationship to God cannot be separated from horizontal relationships in community. Asceticism and mystical experiences, even love for God, are seen to be hollow hypocrisies if they do not inspire practical love for others.[54] Salvation is not a goal to be attained by deliberate withdrawal from others. It is shown to be received and worked out within a community of faith where the human barriers of race, gender and class do not apply.[55] The values of the new community must then be worked out in the wider world, in a concern for those whom Jesus taught his followers to think of as their neighbours.[56] The Christian love ethic derives from the importance of community in Christian faith. The ethical dimension often associated with many streams of Hindu spirituality – the ethic of non-violence (*ahimsa*) – derives from the importance placed on the final goal of the individual's spiritual journey, liberation from the cycle of rebirth (*samsara*).

Forster, OM and Language

Forster's metaphor of the East's power to reduce all human experience and material existence to the mystical syllable *OM* (sometimes spelled *AUM*) also represents a stereotype of Hindu mysticism. The metaphor perhaps refers to Shankara's *Advaita* teaching that only Brahman truly exists and also to the importance of mantra chanting in many forms of Hindu mystical experience. Whilst it is true that yogic techniques are believed to lead to the silence of the mind in order to achieve the union of the human and the divine within a person, these techniques, such as the chanting of mantras, should not be thought of as mindless distractions. When Chaitanya taught that Krishna's name is more than an arbitrary collection of syllables, that it is itself a portion of his reality and an instrument of his power, he was following in a long line of respected Hindu theologian grammarians. These grammarians, especially the great philosopher of language, Bhartrhari (c. 480 CE), taught that communication is possible because language and meaning are grounded in divine consciousness.[57] The appeal again and again to scriptural authority, the concern to reconcile contradictory texts and the stream of commentaries on Hindu texts as well as the commentaries on commentaries, suggest a respect for the power of language to convey meaningful communication.

Freud, Nirvana and Postmodernism

Freud used Hindu *Advaita* understanding to identify a stage in his theory of personality formation as 'the Nirvana principle'. As a scientist working in the early part of the twentieth century, he subscribed to the Enlightenment faith in a single system of truth based on universal reason which could explain all reality and experience. Mystical experience of union with God, whether Eastern or Western, placed under the searchlight of his scientific method, was seen to be the domain of personalities who had failed to mature. Freud taught that all mystical experience is an illusion. However, since Freud's days, the loss of confidence in many of the certainties of modernity and the advent of postmodern discourses have brought a fresh approach to debates about mystical experience in at least three ways.

First, there is a sensitivity to cultural context and with it a greater respect for the importance of difference. This emphasis on heterogeneity has been associated with the deconstructive approaches of postmodern French thinkers like Jacques Derrida who, in his famous essay, '*Différance*', argued that history writing represents 'the final repression of difference'.[58] For the purposes of this study, the concept of 'difference' involves the demand that the distinctive aspects of a mystical experience as well as the particularies of its tradition and culture must be acknowledged.

This postmodern emphasis on the importance of context has been accompanied by the understanding that the scientist and scholar may not be working from positions of greater objective neutrality than the religious apologist. The context of the scholar may be as important as the context of the object of study: methodological self-consciousness suggests that what the scholar sees depends on where he stands. For example, many of the orientalist scholars (Max Müller, Paul Deussen and Romain Rolland) had been influenced by the German idealism of Kant and Schopenhauer. Thus they were naturally drawn to the *Upanishads* and to Shankara's idealistic *Advaita*, and went on to identify Shankara's monism as the essence of mystical Hinduism.[59] However, to prise an aspect of a mystical tradition away from its cultural and linguistic home may be to eradicate historical realities, to deny the particularities intrinsic to it and therefore to distort it.

Secondly, postmodern discourses have brought a growing understanding of the link between truth/knowledge claims and positions of power. There is a new appreciation for the significance of this relationship, along with a scepticism about the incestuous nature of it.[60] Freud learned about Nirvana and the 'self's oceanic oneness with the universe' from his friend, the orientalist Romain Rolland.[61] Rolland and

Freud, as members of the Western intellectual elite, were able to determine the nature of truth about the 'mystic' East by virtue of their positions of cultural authority. By defining what was the essence (or the highest form) of Hindu mysticism, the orientalist scholars, it is argued, both constructed and maintained control over the object of their study. One cannot but feel sympathy, therefore, for the way in which Vivekananda and the Neo-Vedanta movement turned Western colonial discourses back on the West as a response to the perceived sense of Western superiority.[62] Nevertheless, Vivekananda's essentialism distorted Hinduism's diverse mystical traditions just as the colonial discourses had done earlier.

Thirdly, since French philosopher Jean-Francois Lyotard published his influential *The Postmodern Condition: A Report on Knowledge* in 1979, postmodern thinkers have questioned whether there is any location in the cultural structure which gives those who occupy it an exhaustive vision of the whole.[63] As is well-known, Lyotard observed the decline of universal explanatory theories (or 'metanarratives'), which he considered to be oppressive, and encouraged his readers to see the world as a complex and linguistically dynamic reality which must be interpreted from many perspectives.[64] This approach has fostered a sense of the difficulties of theological claims which attempt to unite all mystical traditions. Is the perennial search for a universal truth common to all mystical traditions informed, at least in part, by the desire for the universal oneness of all mystical experience? The decontextualised, privatised form of *Advaita* mysticism found in many of today's alternative spiritualities may owe more to the Enlightenment desire to create universal frameworks than to the vision of Shankara.

Debates about Hindu mysticism – and debates about the nature of mystical experience itself – are as old as the writings of the mystics and are unlikely to be resolved in our day.[65] However, the representation of *Advaita* Vedanta as the spiritual essence of Hindu mysticism continues to be problematic given the diversity of mystical experience within the Hindu traditions. Shankara's monism, Ramanuja's qualified theism and Chaitanya's dualism, while sharing many points of connection within the Vedanta system, still represent radically different ideas of God, the material world and the nature of liberation. The ethics which flow from these visions are distinctive. To adopt a reductionist approach to the monistic and dualistic streams of Hindu mysticism is to devalue diversity and to celebrate an essence so abstract that it may be unrecognisable to its devotees. To obscure the distinctiveness of those with profoundly different worldviews is to deny the possibility of real communication between those who may have much to say to one another.

Notes

[1] Freud's definition of the 'Nirvana Principle' reveals a Hindu rather than Buddhist understanding of Nirvana. Buddhism defines Nirvana as the realisation that there is no self.

[2] Sigmund Freud, *Civilization and its Discontents* (London: Hogarth Press, 1949), 13.

[3] Hindus sometimes use the language of salvation when speaking of *moksha*, but as the word carries a rather different meaning for Christians, I shall refer to *moksha* as liberation.

[4] R.C. Zaehner, *Hinduism* (Oxford: OUP, 1962), 125–9.

[5] Sean Carey, 'The Indianization of the Hare Krishna Movement in Britain' in Richard Burghart (ed.), *Hinduism in Great Britain: The Perpetuation of Religion in an Alien Cultural Milieu* (London: Tavistock Publications, 1987), 81–99. See also S.J. Gelberg (ed.), *Hare Krishna, Hare Krishna* (New York: Grove Press, 1983).

[6] For an overview and defence of this thesis, see Philip Barnes' essay, 'Dispensing with Christian Mysticism' (ch. 15).

[7] Eric Lott, *Vedantic Approaches to God* (London: Macmillan, 1980), 6–7. Also J.L. Brockington, *The Sacred Thread: Hinduism in its Continuity and Diversity* (Edinburgh: Edinburgh University Press, 1981), 36–7.

[8] Lott, *Vedantic Approaches*, 126–8.

[9] See Paul David Devanandan, *The Concept of Maya* (London: Lutterworth Press, 1950), 20–4.

[10] Ibid., 87–90.

[11] See Ninian Smart's discussion of the connections between Shankara's thought and Mahayana Buddhism. Ninian Smart, *Doctrine and Argument in Indian Philosophy* (London: George Allen and Unwin Ltd., 1964), 101–5. For Shankara's concept of the self compared to Buddhist understandings, see Brian Carr, 'Sankara on Memory and the continuity of the Self', *Religious Studies* 36 (2000), 419–34.

[12] Shankara wrote, 'There can exist nothing different from Brahman, since we are unable to observe a proof for such existence ... Nor can there exist, apart from Brahman, something which has no beginning since scripture affirms that "Being only this was in the beginning, one, without a second." The promise moreover that through the cognition of one thing everything will be known, renders it impossible that there should exist anything different from Brahman.' *Vedantasutras with Sankara's Commentary*, Vol. 2, tr. G. Thibaut (Oxford: Clarendon Press, 1890), 176–7.

[13] Ibid., 320–30.

[14] In his comments on the Upanishadic 'Not this, not this,' Shankara argued that this double negation does not suggest the non-existence of Brahman, or a Buddhist void. Ibid., 166–71; cf. also 332–7.

[15] David Burnett, *The Spirit of Hinduism* (Tunbridge Wells: Monarch, 1992), 180–4. Shankara was reluctant to assign any attributes to Brahman. The formula, 'being, consciousness and bliss' is not found in his best attested works although he used the words separately in his commentary on the *Upanishads*. See Brockington, *Sacred Thread*, 111–12.

[16] Burnett, *Spirit of Hinduism*, 182–183; Brockington, *Sacred Thread*, 109–10.

[17] Lott, *Vedantic Approaches*, 173.

[18] Krishna Sivaraman (ed.), *Hindu Spirituality: Vedas through Vedanta* (London: SCM, 1989), 232.

[19] As with Shankara, scholars are not certain of Ramanuja's dates.

[20] The poems of the Alvars were said to have been used 'to sing the atheist Buddhists and Jains out of southern India'. Zaehner, *Hinduism*, 129. Also S.S. Raghavachar, 'The Spiritual Vision of Ramanuja', in K. Sivaraman, *Hindu Spirituality*, 264.

[21] Brockington, *Sacred Thread*, 132–4.

[22] Raghavachar, *Spiritual Vision*, 262.

[23] Ramanuja's polemic against Shankara is found in the context of his commentary on the first verse of the *Vedantasutra* (*Brahmasutra*) which is, 'then, therefore, the enquiry into Brahman'. *Vedanasutras with Ramanuja's Commentary*, Vol. 3, tr. G. Thibaut (Oxford: Clarendon Press, 1904), 20–30.

[24] Ibid., 30–9.

[25] 'This entire theory rests on a fictitious foundation of altogether hollow and vicious arguments, incapable of being stated in definite logical alternatives, and devised by men who are destitute of those particular qualities which cause individuals to be chosen by the Supreme Person revealed in the *Upanishads*, whose intellects are darkened by the impression of beginningless evil, and who thus have no insight into the nature of words and sentences, into the real purport conveyed by them and into the procedure of sound argumentation ...' Ibid., 39

[26] Ibid., 56–72.

[27] 'Even those texts which describe Brahman by means of negations really aim at setting forth a Brahman possessing attributes.' Ibid., 130.

[28] Ibid., 130.

[29] For Ramanuja's stages of *bhakti*, see Raghavachar, *Spiritual Vision*, 264–70.

[30] Richard Lannoy, *The Speaking Tree: A Study of Indian Culture and Society* (Oxford: Oxford University Press, 1971), 207–8.

[31] Since Chaitanya's *bhakti* was viewed as an alternative to an ascetic withdrawal from life, scholars have puzzled over his embracing the life of a *sannyasin*. Chaitanya is supposed to have said, 'As I must save these men, I have to adopt the life of asceticism. When they see me as an ascetic, they will bow down to me, and in bowing their guilt will be destroyed, and I shall rouse *bhakti* in their purified hearts. Then will these godless men be saved'. S.K. De, *Early History of the Vaisnava Faith and Movement in Bengal* (Calcutta: K.L. Mukhopadyay, 1961), 81.

[32] Ibid., 67–102.

[33] S.C. Chakravarti, 'Bengal Vaishnavism' in K.R. Sundararajan and B. Mukerji (eds.), *Hindu Spirituality: Postclassical and Modern* (London: SCM, 1997), 47–8.

[34] Ibid., 60–1.

[35] Ibid., 47–49. Chakravarti refers to the individual's 'real status as a fragment of the Lord Krishna'.

[36] Neal Delmonica, 'How to Partake in the Love of Krishna', in D.S. Lopez (ed.), *Religions of India in Practice* (Princeton: Princeton University Press, 1995), 244–5. See also H.G. Coward, 'The Reflective Word: Spirituality in the Grammarian Tradition of India', in Sivaraman, *Hindu Spirituality*, 218–20.

[37] Quoted in Zaehner, *Hinduism*, 145.

[38] Chakravarti, op.cit., 49. ISKCON has published new translations of Chaitanya's teaching. See, for example, A.C. Bhaktivedanta Swami Prabhupada, *Sri Caitanya-Caritamrta of Krishnadasa Kaviraja Gosvami* (New York: Bhaktivedanta Book Trust, 1975).

[39] Lannoy, *Speaking Tree*, 389–90. For a different assessment of the ethical dimension in Chaitanya's Bengal Vaishnavism, see De, *Early History*, 552–5

[40] Said defines 'orientalism' as 'the discipline by which the Orient was (and is) approached systematically, as a topic of learning, discovery and practice'. Edward Said, *Orientalism: Western Conceptions of the Orient* (Harmondsworth: Penguin Books, 1995), 73. For a critique of Said's argument, see Fred Halliday, *Islam and the Myth of Confrontation: Religion and Politics in the Middle East* (London: Tauris, 1996), 213–14. See also Robert Young, *White Mythologies: Writing History and the West* (London: Routledge, 1990). Young questions the Eurocentrism of traditional Marxist accounts of a 'single World History' in which the third world appears to be a supplement to the narrative of the West.

[41] James explained the four characteristics as follows: (1) it is 'ineffable', cannot be described by language; (2) it is 'noetic', authoritative for the mystic giving him insights into truth 'unplumbed by the discursive intellect'; (3) it is 'transient', seldom lasting more than an hour; and (4) it renders the mystic 'passive' as he is 'grasped and held by a superior power'. William James, *Varieties of Religious Experience* (New York: Longman, Green and Company, 1902), 380–2. For arguments against a reductionist analysis of James' philosophy, see David Baggett, 'On a Reductionist Analysis of William James' Philosophy of Religion', *Journal of Religious Ethics*, 28 (2000), 423–48.

[42] F.C. Happold, *Mysticism: A Study and an Anthology* (Harmondsworth: Penguin Books, 1963). See also W.R. Inge, *Mysticism in Religion* (London: Hutchinson, 1947); Geoffrey Parrinder, *Mysticism in the World Religions* (London: Sheldon Press, 1976); W.T. Stace, *Mysticism and Philosophy* (London: Macmillan, 1961); Evelyn Undershill, *Mysticism* (New York: New American Library, 1974).

[43] R. Otto, *Mysticism East and West: a Comparative Analysis of the Nature of Mysticism* (New York: Macmillan, 1932).

[44] R. Otto, *India's Religion of Grace and Christianity Compared and Contrasted* (London: SCM, 1930).

[45] J. Campbell, *Oriental Mythology: The Masks of God* (Harmondsworth: Penguin Books, 1962), 3–4. In contrast to most studies of mysticism at this time, Steven Katz challenged the assumption that all mystical experience is the same. Katz, a constructivist, called for greater sensitivity to the cultural particularity of the mystics and argued that pure, unmediated mystical experience is impossible (and meaningless) without its interpretation which must be culturally bound. Katz insisted that his analysis was not founded upon any *a priori* assumptions about the nature of ultimate reality. Steven T. Katz (ed.), *Mysticism and Philosophical Analysis* (London: Sheldon Press, 1978); also Steven T. Katz (ed.), *Mysticism and Religious Traditions* (New York: OUP, 1983).

[46] Swami Nikhilananda (ed.), *Vivekananda: the Yogas and Other Works* (New York: Ramakrishna-Vivekananda Center, 1953), 185–9.

[47] Richard King, *Orientalism and Religion: Postcolonial Theory, India and 'The Mystic East'* (London: Routledge, 1999), 138.

[48] A polemical stance towards other strands of Hinduism continues to be characteristic of the Hare Krishna Movement (a contemporary but faithful version of Chaitanya's mysticism): 'It is true that ISKCON has injected a note of exclusivism into the contemporary Hindu scene but, far from being unorthodox, this exclusiveness was very much a part of traditional Hinduism. Historically Hinduism has been more tolerant of religious differences than Islam or Christianity, but it was never as tolerant as those following the nineteenth and twentieth century reformist sections like the Ramakrishna Mission would lead people to believe ... ISKCON, representing the Chaitanyite tradition of Vaishnavism, rejects this neo–universalistic ethic.' Carey, 'The Indianization of the Hare Krishna Movement in Britain', 99.

[49] King, *Orientalism and Religion*, 138–9. Nikhilanda, *Vivekananda*, 785–92.

[50] Nikhilanda, ibid., 511.

[51] 2 Cor. 5:17.

[52] Rom. 8:20–21, Rev. 21:1. For a theology of nature based on a trinitarian understanding of wisdom, see C. Deane-Drummond, *Creation and Wisdom: Theology and the New Biology* (Edinburgh: T. & T. Clark, 2000). See also Jürgen Moltmann on God's creation as an ongoing event: *The Future of Creation* (London: SCM, 1979).

[53] S.S. Smalley, *John: Evangelist and Interpreter* (Carlisle: Paternoster, 1998), 235–238. Raymond Brown makes the point that John's Gospel, sometimes thought to have less sacramental emphasis than the synoptics, shows a 'sacramental understanding of reality'. The life-giving flesh and blood of Jesus are described as food in Jn. 6:51–58. R. Brown, *The Community of the Beloved Disciple* (New York: Paulist Press, 1979), 52.

[54] Rom. 12:10; 1 Cor. 13; 1 Pet. 1:12; 1 Jn. 4:7–21.

[55] Gal. 3:28; Eph. 2:14–18; 3:14–19.

[56] Lk. 10:30–37.

[57] Coward, *Reflective Word*, 209–26. 'The central contention of the Sphota Theory of the Hindu grammarians is that the overt word sounds simply reflect or reveal, but do not create, the idea … no matter how hard one tries, the whole of the original idea can never be fully reflected in words … but communication is possible because language is divine in nature'. Coward, op.cit., 221. Against this, see Don Cupitt's postmodern critique of modernist theories of mysticism in which he argues that mysticism is a kind of writing: 'The notion that there are or can be, either in mystical rapture or after death, extra-linguistic psychological states or experiences that verify beliefs about God will not bear scrutiny.' D. Cupitt, *Mysticism after Modernity* (Oxford: Blackwell Publishers, 1998), 61.

[58] J. Derrida, *Speech and Phenomena, and Other Essays on Husserl's Theory of Signs*, tr. David B. Allison (Evanston: Northwestern University Press, 1973), 141. Also J. Derrida, *Writing and Difference*, tr. Alan Bass (London: Routledge and Kegan Paul, 1978), 280–91. Derrida coined the term *différance* and suggested that meaning is always 'deferred'. His emphasis on difference is rooted in an anti-metaphysical stance: he argued against the possibility of finding a stable reality behind verbal interpretations. However, Derrida disowned the idea that his writings contain authoritative wisdom, repudiated much that has gone on under the guise of 'deconstruction' by those following him, and did not intend that *différance* should become an important concept. Christopher Norris, *Derrida* (London: Fantana Press, 1987), 11–17.

[59] Paul Deussen, for example, wrote at the beginning of the twentieth century, 'The thoughts of the Vedanta became for India a permanent and characteristic spiritual atmosphere … the original idealsm holds its ground, not annulled by pantheistic and theistic developments'. Paul Deussen, *The Philosophy of the Upanishads* (Edinburgh: T. & T. Clark, 1906), vii–viii. See also King, *Orientalism and Religion*, 128–31.

[60] Michel Foucault, 'Truth and Power', in Paul Rabinow (ed.), *The Foucault Reader: An Introduction to Foucault's Thought* (Harmondsworth: Penguin Books, 1984), 51–75. Also Grace Jantzen, *Power, Gender and Christian Mysticism* (Cambridge: Cambridge University Press, 1995), 12–14.

[61] Sigmund Freud, *Civilization and its Discontents* (London: Hogarth Press, 1975), 2, n.1.

[62] King, *Orientalism and Religion*, 96–117, 156ff.

[63] Jean-Francois Lyotard, *The Postmodern Condition: A Report on Knowledge* (Manchester: Manchester University Press, 1984). Following on from Ludwig Wittgenstein's idea of society as made up of thousands of language games, Lyotard broke with classical Marxist theory of ideology by defining ideology as language games which demand their general adoption and the exclusion (or

'terrorizing') of other language games. John Keane, 'The Modern Democratic Revolution: Reflections on Lyotard's *The Postmodern Condition*' in Andrew Benjamin (ed.), *Judging Lyotard* (London: Routledge, 1992), 88–89. However, by the time of his death in 1998, Lyotard had come to believe that the real enemy of humanity was not grand narratives but the all encompassing embrace of 'techno-science', particularly computers. Jean-Francois Lyotard, *The Inhuman: Reflections on Time*, tr. Geoffrey Bennington & Rachel Bowlby (Oxford: Blackwell, 1991).

[64] Keane, 'The Modern Democratic Revolution: Reflections on Lyotard's *The Postmodern Condition*', 85–88.

[65] For example, Bernard McGinn's multi-volume *The Presence of God: A History of Western Christian Mysticism* is an ambitious history of Christian Mysticism written from an outlook of modernity. The first volume, *Foundations of Mysticism: Origins to the Fifth Century* (London: SCM, 1991) concludes with a long appendix which surveys modern theories of mysticism. In contrast, Michael Stoeber's *Theo-Monistic Mysticism: A Hindu-Christian Comparison* (New York: St Martin's Press, 1994) suggests an interpretive framework which makes sense of the competing claims of monistic and dualistic mystical experiences but avoids the difficulties of constructivism and essentialism. Stoeber develops his argument in the context of a Hindu Christian comparison.

6

The Erotic Mysticism of Sri Ramakrishna

David Burnett

Ramakrishna is the most well-known Indian mystic because his disciples have carefully preserved the story of his life and an account of his teaching. It was his disciple Swami Nikhilananda who wrote the Foreword to the English translation of *The Gospel of Sri Ramakrishna*, which has since become one of the most important texts to frame the Western image of Indian spirituality.[1] Ramakrishna is portrayed as an extraordinary saint who is not a person to understand, but a figure of mystery and awe. He is presented as one of the greatest mystics of modern times who frequently went into *samadhi*, the Hindu equivalent of mystical rapture. Surprisingly, during these states he would sometimes place his right foot in the lap of a young man and caress his penis. Observers were often shocked by this 'sinful' foot, and would angrily confront Ramakrishna when he came out of *samadhi*. Ramakrishna never denied the action nor provided an explanation.

Ramakrishna has been studied from both philosophical and psychological perspectives in an effort to understand the relationship between religious experience and insanity.[2] This essay seeks to address the question of how mystical experiences can be affected by both the culture and the psychological make-up of the person. In order to do this it is necessary first provide a brief background to the life of this very significant modern mystic. This is especially important as the visions of Ramakrishna have often been linked with his childhood experiences.

The Life and Times of Ramakrishna

Like all great stories, that of Ramakrishna commences with a remarkable birth. Kshudiram Chatterjee was a pious *Brahmin* from a village some sixty-five miles northwest of Calcutta. In 1835, when he was about sixty years old, he went on pilgrimage to Gaya, visiting the sacred

footprint of the god Vishnu. It is said that here Vishnu appeared to him
in a dream and said, 'I will be born as your son'.³ Whilst Kshudiram was
at Gaya, his wife, Chandra, who was now forty-five was at home where
she too had a mysterious encounter. It was as if a luminous god entered
her bed and caused her to conceive. On another day, as she was standing in front of the local temple she saw a divine light come out of the
great Shiva *linga* and this rushed towards her. She fell to the ground as if
in a faint. However, the point is that, by the time her husband had
returned home, she had conceived. On 18 February 1836, she gave birth
to a son whom they called Gadadhur (literally, 'Bearer of the Mace')
who some years later took the name Ramakrishna.

Gadadhur was her second son. Her first son Ramakumar had been
born almost thirty years earlier in 1805, and then five years later she gave
birth to their first daughter. Gadadhur grew up as a healthy, fun-loving
boy who seemed to have been spoilt by his father, as might be expected after the earlier dream. Although he was encouraged to attend the
local village school he had little interest in mathematics and science, and
preferred to memorise the tales of the Hindu deities. He was able to
recount from memory many of the great narratives of the Epics, and
even act them out with great accuracy. This illustrated his life long repul-
sion with intellectual abstraction and preference for the ecstatic trance.
Indeed, when he was only six or seven years of age, he fell into his first
trance. This is described in *The Gospel* as follows:

> One day in June or July, when he was walking home along a nar-
> row path between paddy-fields, eating the puffed rice that he car-
> ried in a basket, he looked up at the sky and saw a beautiful, dark
> thunder-cloud. As it spread, rapidly enveloping the whole sky, a
> flight of snow-white cranes passed in front of it. The beauty of the
> contrast overwhelmed the boy. He fell to the ground, unconscious,
> and the puffed rice went in all directions.⁴

Around this time his father Kshudiram died, and this seemed to have
been a major shock to the young boy. He felt even more closely drawn
to his mother, and would help her with her chores around the house and
with worshipping the family deity. With the loss of his father, Gadadhur's
older brother, Ramakumar became his second father. He was a *Sakta*
known for his powers of divination. As the family was struggling finan-
cially he went to Calcutta in 1849 to earn money. During this time
Gadadhur started to become interested in the wandering holy men who
passed near the village on the way to the pilgrimage site at Puri. He
would listen to their telling of the Hindu stories, and would watch them

in their meditation. Gadadhur continued to fall into trances and many of the village people considered him to be an embodiment of Krishna. Older women tended to mother him as the child Krishna whilst younger ones looked upon him almost as Krishna the divine lover. Kripal writes: 'Gadadhur, it seems, entered his trances at least partially to escape these women and their worship. The women, in other words, not only rewarded the trances; they *caused* them.'[5] Gadadhur also began to copy the manners of women and disguise himself as a woman.

In 1855, when Gadadhar had reached sixteen years of age, his bro-ther summoned him to Calcutta because he wanted assistance in his priestly duties. A wealthy widow by the name of Rani had a vision from Kali encour-aging her to build a temple dedicated to her, and promising that if she did this Kali would manifest herself in the temple. The pious woman started to build the temple on the banks of the river. Then she realised that as she was a *shudra*, higher caste *brahmin* priests would not take offerings from her. She eventually gave the temple to a *brahmin* to act as intermediary and invited Gadadhur as priest. He was initiated into the cult of Kali that was strong in Calcutta, and it was at this time he became known as Ramakrishna.

Sometime in the summer of 1856, Ramakumar suddenly died, and Ramakrishna was bereaved of his 'second father.' It was at during this time of grief that Ramakrishna turned to Kali, and sought for *darshan* from her. It is said that he almost gave up eating food, and slept little.

> I felt as if my heart were being squeezed like a wet towel. I was overpowered with a great restlessness and a fear that it might not be my lot to realize Her in this life. I could not bear the separation from her any longer. Life seemed to be not worth living. Suddenly my glance fell on the sword that was kept in the Mother's temple, and I determined to put an end to my life. I jumped up like a mad-man and seized it, when suddenly blessed Mother revealed Herself. The buildings with their different parts, the temple, and everything else vanished from my sight, leaving no trace whatsoever, and in their stead I saw limitless, infinite, effulgent Ocean of Bliss. As far as the eye could see, the shining billows were madly rushing at me from all sides with a terrific noise, to swallow me up. I was panting for breath. I was caught in the rush and collapsed, unconscious. What was happening in the outside world I did not know, but within me there was a steady flow of undiluted bliss, altogether new, and I felt the presence of the Divine Mother.[6]

He came out of the experience uttering the word 'Mother', and his relationship with the goddess became like that between a mother and child. This is the first of his visions of Kali, and as such represents the beginning of his mystical life. Nikhilananda describes this as a 'God-intoxicated State' (*Vyakulata*). Ramakrishna is continually portrayed as seeing this state as one to be intensely desired. Just as a drowning person franticly grasps for air, so a person should seek for a vision of the divine.

Shortly after having these visions of Kali, he began serving Rama. Ramakrishna took up the attitude of the monkey-god Hanuman, the great devotee of Rama, and enacted the role in detail. He tied a cloth around his waist so that it looked like a tail, and ate nothing but fruit and roots. He would call out all the time '*Raghurvir*', and pass much of his time sitting in trees. All his actions corresponded to those of Hanuman. Many people around him, including the temple Director Mathur Babu, thought Ramakrishna was insane.

These recurring states and lack of concern for his physical well-being resulted in failing health. Eventually his mother took him home, but was still concerned about his behaviour. The story is told that in an attempt to cure her son, she undertook a complete fast unto death before the Shiva *linga* of Mukundapur. Hardly had two or three days passed than she had a dream of Shiva who consoled her saying, 'Don't be afraid; your son is not mad; he is in that state on account of a tremendous infusion of the divine spirit in him'.[7] After a few months he showed some improvement.

As he had now reached the age of twenty-three, his mother suggest-ed that he get married. She was pleased that he agreed, and he even indi-cated a little girl of five who lived in a neighbouring village. The mar-riage was duly performed in 1859, but the girl stayed with her parents until she was old enough to take her role as a wife. In fact, the marriage was never consummated. Ramakrishna remained in the village for about eighteen months before returning to take up his ministry at the temple in Dakshineswar.

The Sadhanas of Ramakrishna

On his return to Dakshineswar in 1860, the 'divine madness' reappeared. His aversion to worldly things and his unconventional behaviour reached new extremes. It was during this time that he started to explore new modes of *sadhana*, and was eager to learn from teachers of various sects.

Tantra

First to arrive was Bhairavi Brahmani. The story is told that Ramakrishna was one day picking flowers in the temple garden, when a boat approached. On board was a middle-aged woman in the orange robe of a Hindu nun. Ramakrishna warmly welcomed her, and she soon was listening to his story. After a time studying his behaviour she concluded that he was not merely a special person, but actually an incarnation of God. Under the guidance of the Bhairavi, Ramakrishna began to study the most difficult school of Tantra.

Tantra sees matter as energy (*shakti*) and the absolute (*Shiva*) as consciousness. These figures are usually portrayed in an erotic embrace illustrative of the coming together of *Shakti* and *Shiva*. Practitioners would plunge themselves into the impure in an attempt to be free from it. This often involved eating meat, drinking wine, and having sex with an impure person.

Ramakrisha is said to have had a vision of the Ultimate cause of the universe as a huge luminous triangle giving birth every moment to an infinite number of worlds. He acquired the eight supernatural powers of yoga. Most important, however, was the awakening of the Kundalini power. He first saw this as lying asleep at the bottom of the spinal column, then wakening up and ascending along the *Sushumna* canal, and through its six centres to the *Sahasraara* in the top of the head.[8] One of the results of Tantra for him was an increased respect for women.

Vaishnava

In 1864 a monk named Jatadhari visited Dakshineswar. He carried with him a small metal image of the boy Ram ('Ramlala') in a metal cage. By constant worship of the image the monk had visions of Ramlala like those of a child with an invisible imaginary friend. Jatadhari and Ramakrishna were quickly attracted to each other, but it was to the metal image of Ram that Ramakrishna formed a deeper attachment. The image of the child became so real to Ramakrishna that he considered it to be continually moving and playing in his company. He used to feed him, bathe him, and even admonish him when naughty. So much did this relationship develop that when it came time for Jatadhari to travel on, the child was supposed to have said that he would not leave Ramakrishna. Jatadhari therefore left Ramlala with Ramakrishna.

The highest form of Vaishnava *sadhana* is that of God as beloved and the human soul as lover. In the masculine form Krishna is the personification of the male principle of the universe. The seeker takes up the attitude of Radha, the cowherd girl whose burning love from Krishna makes her forget everything but him. The devotee therefore makes his relationship with Krishna like that of Radha. When Ramakrishna practised this he turned himself into a woman to such an extent that other women of the household felt no constraint in his company. These practices soon brought him visions of Radha, but then he continued in his longing for a vision of Krishna. He finally received a vision in which the form of Krishna actually merged with his own person.

Advaita

Sometime around 1865 when Ramakrishna was about thirty years of age, a naked monk arrived at Dakshineshwar. He was a member of the Naga sect from the Punjab generally known as Totapuri, although Ramakrishna simply called him *Nyanta*, or 'naked one'. He was a firm believer in a formless absolute devoid of duality. He initially made fun of Ramakrishna's beliefs in the gods and goddesses of the *Puranas*. He was however impressed by his spirituality, and asked Ramakrishna if he would like to practice Vedanta. Ramakrishna said he first must ask 'Mother' (Kali). He soon returned smiling saying that she had agreed to him practising this foreign path. It seemed that Bhairavi objected to her new competitor and tried to dissuade him, but Ramakrishna continued.

Totapuri tried to get Ramakrishna to give up the world of *maya*, but the image of Kali kept appearing to him. Finally, Totapuri took a piece of sharp glass and embedded it in his forehead, 'Concentrate on this point!'[9] Once again the goddess appeared, but this time Ramakrishna considered that the new knowledge was a sword and cut the goddess in two. At once his mind ascended past form and merged with the formless Brahman and remained in *samadhi* for three days. Within three days Ramakrishna attained what it had taken Totapuri forty years to accomplish. At the end of the third day Totapuri chanted '*Hari OM*' and he came back to normal consciousness.

Totapuri normally stayed at a place for no more that three days because of the danger of becoming attached. Determined to establish his new disciple he actually stayed eleven months, and in that time he also learned a lesson about *maya*. Totapuri was suffering from dysentery, and struggling to hold to the unreality of the pain whilst in *samadhi*. He finally decided to commit suicide. At night he walked out into the river, but he found that instead of the water getting deeper it continued to remain at waist level. Almost at the other shore his mind was suddenly dazzled by a great light and he saw 'the Ma', the Mother of the Universe. She was the divine energy – she is everything. One cannot even die without her consent! He had previously mocked Ramakrishna's worship of Kali, but now he realised that she was indeed the great *Shakti*.

On Totapuri's eventual departure Ramakrishna fell into a deep *samadhi* that was to last six months. Flies entered his nostrils and ears, his hair grew matted, and his bowel functions were uncontrolled. He had to be forcibly fed. Jensen sees this as a reaction to another male figure who 'died' leaving him bereft.[10]

Islam

Towards the end of 1866, Ramakrishna is said to have begun to practice the mystic practices of Islam. Under the direction of his 'Mussalman' guru he dressed as a Mussalman and chanted the name of Allah. He started praying in the form of Islamic *salat*, and neglected the Hindu deities including even Kali. He took up residence outside the temple, and stopped visiting the Hindu temple. After three days he had a vision of a radiant figure, 'perhaps Mohammed'.[11] The figure gently approached him and became lost in Ramakrishna, and passed into communion with the absolute. For most Muslims this would have been a heretical experience. However, his interpreters believed he had achieved the very centre of Islam: 'The mighty river of Islam also led him back to the Ocean of the Absolute.'[12]

His Wife as the Embodiment of the Divine Mother

In 1872, his wife who was by then eighteen was anxious to meet her husband because she had heard stories from people who had questioned his mental state. She therefore went to Dakshineswar where her husband welcomed her. He began teaching her, and was pleased that she was of a spiritual inclination. It is said that he soon began to worship her as the embodiment of the divine. On the new moon of May 1872, an auspicious night for the worship of Kali, he made Sarada Devi occupy a special seat in his room and began to worship her from 9.00 p.m. They were both said to have been in an exalted state of consciousness, and when he recovered he surrendered himself and the results of his various *sadhanas* to her as Divine Mother. The young woman was from that time known by the title of Holy Mother.

Christianity

In November 1874, Ramakrishna was seized by an irresistible desire to learn about Christianity. He began listening to the readings from the Bible by Sambhu Charan Mallick, a literate follower of Ramakrishna. Ramakrishna was said to have been fascinated by the life and teaching of Jesus. While sat in the house, his eyes became fixed on a picture of the Madonna and Child. The figures in the picture took on life, and rays of light emanated from them and entered him.

> In dismay he cried out, 'O Mother! What are you doing to me?'
> And, breaking through the barriers of creed and religion, he entered a new realm of ecstasy. Christ possessed his soul. For three days he did not set foot in the Kali temple. On the fourth day, in the afternoon, as he was walking in the Panchavati, he saw coming

towards him a person with beautiful large eyes, serene countenance, and fair skin. As the two faced each other, a voice rang out in the depths of Sri Ramakrishna's soul: 'Behold the Christ, who shed His heart's blood for the redemption of the world, who suffered a sea of anguish for love of men. It is He, the Master Yogi, who is in eternal union with God. It is Jesus, Love Incarnate.' The Son of Man embraced the Son of the Divine Mother and merged in him.[13]

Nikhilananda continues:

Sri Ramakrishna realized his identity with Christ, as he had already realized his identity with Kali, Rama, Hanuman, Radha, Krishna, Brahman and Mohammed. The Master went into *samadhi* and communed with the Brahman with attributes.[14]

The identities of Kali, Rama, Hanuman, Radha, Krishna, Mohammed, and Christ are considered to be the attributes, or visual expressions of the ultimate reality, Brahman.

The Coming of the Disciples

Ramakrishna became increasingly well known in the region of Calcutta and people began to visit him sometimes out of sheer curiosity. He had a vision in which Kali promised that many disciples would come to him. Initially he was disappointed by those who came. We are told that he longed for them saying, 'Come, my boys! Oh, where are you? I cannot bear to live without you!'

The first to come were Ram Chandra Datta, a young doctor, and his cousin Manomohan Mita who came to Ramakrishna in 1879. A few months later Surendranath Mitra came, then Balaram Ghose (later called Premananda) and Mahendra Nath Gupta (simply known as M), the author of *The Gospel of Sri Ramakrishna*.[15] The number of disciples continued to increase over the following months until there were sixteen. They included Narendranath who, in 1893, took the name Vivekanada and became famous for his presentation of the Vedanta tradition at the World Parliament of Religions in Chicago (1893). Ramakrishna seems to have made a distinction between those disciples who dedicated themselves completely to him and those who merely admired him from distance.

The first encounter of Narendranath (Vivekananda) is one of the best known, possibly because he is portrayed as an educated sceptic. Narendranath was born on 12 January 1863 into a wealthy family. As he

studied Western philosophy at college he became more and more confused in his beliefs. Finally, in his third year at college, when he was
eighteen years of age he came to Ramakrishna. The context reveals the
clash of philosophies that many Hindus were facing in their contact with
Western society.

Ramakrishna first saw the boy at a gathering of the Brahmo Samaj[16]
where he sang. He was immediately taken with Narendranath. He asked
the leaders to bring the boy to Dakshineshwar. however, he seemed
reluctant to go with them. After about six months he did travel to
Dakshineshwar, and Narendranath records that Ramakrishna took him
to the north porch and closed the door to seclude them from others. He
then grabbed his hand and began to shout, asking why he had been so
long in coming to him. He then suddenly changed and folded his hands
in homage and began to venerate the boy as the ancient sage Narayana.
Narendranath was clearly frightened and puzzled. Ramakrishna then
changed again, bringing sweets to him and behaving normally with
everyone else. Understandably, Narendranath did not return to
Ramakrishna for some time believing him to be insane. However, he
finally did return and had an equally unusual encounter. Ramakrishna
quickly approached him and placed his right foot on his body, and
immediately the boy entered *samadhi* (deep concentration) with a total
loss of control. Narendranath called out for help, Ramakrishna laughed
and touched his chest with his hand and the experience ended.
Narendranath left confused and perplexed wondering how this madman
could induce such an effect with his foot and hand. Soon Narendranath
returned for a third visit. As they sat talking Ramakrishna stood up and
walked towards him, and once again he extended his right foot and
touched him. Narendranath lost consciousness. When he came to,
Ramakrishna was passing his hand over his chest and smiling.

The homosexual connotation that runs through much of
Ramakrishna's relations, especially with the teenage disciples has long been
a problem for scholars. Ramakrishna used various techniques to arouse the
disciples. Nudity was one of them. Ramakrishna would often dance naked
surrounded by his male disciples, and sometimes the boys would dance
naked. For Ramakrishna nudity was an expression of the mystical state. He
would ask to examine the bare chests of men and boys, and sometimes ask
them to walk naked in his presence. Ramakrishna also paired his disciples
up into 'masculine' and 'feminine' in order to awaken their devotion and
love. (He believed that such as sexual lust was overcome when women
were regarded as embodiments of Kali.) He would also dress and behave
like a woman in their presence, a practice that again needs to be understood in the context of his mystical devotion to Kali, the Divine Mother.[17]

In April 1885, Ramakrishna noticed an inflammation of the throat that was aggravated by a long *samadhi*. It turned out to be cancer of the throat, and he was taken to Calcutta for better treatment. Eating became painful and he gradually became weaker. Finally on Sunday, 15 August 1886 his pulse became irregular, and he moved into 'the *samadhi* from which one never returns.' The following day his disciples took his body to the cremation ground on the banks of the Ganges.

These young disciples were to be the one's who would take the message of Ramakrishna to the world. The power of Ramakrishna was said to have passed into Vivekananda who set up the Ramakrishna Mission in 1897 with the aim of undertaking social service and spiritual visions.[18] It now has 131 branches in India and in different parts of the world. It has an extensive web page that continues to present the message of Ramakrishna to the world.[19]

Issues of Mysticism

The story of Ramakrishna is truly remarkable, and raises many significant issues with regard to the understanding of the nature of mysticism.

The Cultural Context

Philosophers and theologians generally acknowledge that religious experiences are shaped by particular social contexts. In the nineteenth century, the British dominated Bengal from their main headquarters in Calcutta. This city was the meeting point of East and West. The British built grand buildings on the style of London from which to run their profitable trade from India to Europe. Christian missionaries had entered the region and were preaching a theistic message. Although they made only few converts they did undermine the confidence of many Hindus in their own traditions. This is clearly illustrated in the account of Narenda who struggled with Western teaching and his Hindu traditions.

The Hindu response was the teaching of *advaita* (non-duality), which teaches that all the gods are essentially unreal. The polytheism that the missionaries mocked was merely a symbolic expression of the greater reality of monism. The only way to liberation was to break out of the bonds of ignorance by realising one's own self in Brahman. All the texts beyond the *Upanishads* were therefore claimed to be unnecessary additions, and not the real essence of the Hindu tradition. The experience of oneness with the absolute is therefore the ultimate experience. *Samadhi* was therefore perceived as a means that surpassed the philosophical exposition of religion presented by Western scholars and missionaries.

Nature of Samadhi

Ramakrishna was certainly a remarkable person, in that he could very easily move into the mystic state (*samadhi*). However, even though he could easily enter such states, it is notable that to enter another mystic path, he needed to be taught by an exponent of that particular way and sometimes even be initiated into the tradition. He could quickly move along the path to the higher states, but he had to begin at the entrance of the particular school.

Essentialism, also known as 'perennial philosophy', assumes that behind the variety of descriptions of visions and revelations of mystics there is an invariant common core of experience.[20] This is essentially unaffected by the individual mystics particular historical situation, social status or religious commitment. The content and context, experience and interpretation are seen as being independent of each other. Religious doctrines therefore relate to mystical experiences only as post-experiential role. Contextualists, on the other hand, argued for a relationship between context and content, and religious doctrine and religious experience was one of reciprocity. In other words, religious doctrine does shape the landscape of the mystic's vision.

Ramakrishna's experiences would therefore suggest a contextualist view of mysticism rather than one that is essentialist. In other words, there would not seem to be one common mystical experience as proposed by Underhill and others in the *philosophia perennis*.[21] Visions experienced cross-culturally show some similarities such as light and spatial dimension. However, many elements emerge from the person's own religious and cultural tradition as with the role of Kali and Hanuman in Ramakrishna's case.

The *Kalika Purana* describes a ritual, which is part of the *Bhakti* tradition that allows an adept to become identified with the goddess. Men or women of any caste may perform the ritual at any time. The ritual requires flowers, some food and water, and an image of the deity. The adept begins to worship the goddess first externally and then as if she is within the individual. The worshipper essentially dies to be recreated as the goddess. The goddess becomes identified with the worshipper.[22] Ramakrishna gradually internalised Kali to such an extent that she became a part of his ego, and he merged with her. Ramakrishna was therefore operating with the religious milieu of a common religious tradition of that area of India.

Sexual Imagery

Raab points out that, 'Psychological explanations of Ramakrishna's religious experiences tend to associate them with the losses of his father and brother, and subsequent yearning for his mother.' The loss of the two important male figures in his life was compounded by the fact that in Hindu society boys are often separated from their mothers when about five years old, and are subject to the demands and constraints of male companionship. His visions are therefore considered to be an attempt to cover or displace early memories. The resulting childhood trauma resulted in a confused sexual role, and a secondary transsexual identity that resulted in his cross-dressing.[23]

The chapter began with the account of how Ramakrishna would place his right foot provocatively in the lap of a young male disciple. Kripal in his study of the life of Ramakrishna advances the thesis, 'that Ramakrishna's foot points to a secret of which he himself was not aware, namely, that his mystical experiences and visions were constituted by erotic energies that he neither fully accepted not understood.'[24] The foot seemed to invoke both feelings of devotion and shock among the disciples who struggled to understand its significance. Kripal argues that the foot was a symbol of Ramakrishna's descent back to the social world. With the young disciples of the 1880s he could finally remain in a human community.

> Like the goddess herself, arousing Shiva from his deathlike slumber with her beautiful feet, Ramakrishna awakens his disciples into radically new forms of consciousness with his foot … He was the goddess standing on top of the ithyphallic god.[25]

How were Ramakrishna's homosexual desires related to his mysticism? As we have seen, Tantra and Bengali Vaishnava dominated Ramakrishna's view of the world. In his devotion to the goddess Kali, he rejects the role of lover and takes the role of a child. Later in his devotion to Krishna, in which there is the role of a female lover of the god, he finds it easy to adopt that role of lover. As Kripal concludes:

> Ramakrishna's homosexual tendencies, in other words, deeply influenced, indeed determined, the manner in which he created his own self-defined 'states' out of the symbols of his inherited religious tradition. His homosexual desires, if you will, created the symbolic contours and shape of his mysticism.[26]

This would suggest that mystical experiences are arguably not just culturally conditioned, but are influenced by the individual's personality. In the case of Ramakrishna, his homosexual tendencies were a source of empowerment.

The Question of Empowerment

Sexual imagery is known in other traditions including Christianity as with Teresa and St John of the Cross. Ramakrishna approached it from the Tantric path that was part of the Hindu social context in Bengal. His sexual tendencies did not merely form the symbolic shape of his mysticism, for his homoerotic energies themselves empowered others. How was it that a touch from his right foot would cause his disciples to explode into altered states of consciousness?

The erotic was an integral part of his life. It is said that the very pores of his body shook with pleasure and power. Here were personal symbols of the erotic that carried meaning to society. Deep sexual energies were realised as the *sakti* that was to awaken the divine. The nature of this process was unknown to Ramakrishna himself who spoke of a 'secret' far beyond analysis. Mystical experiences seem to provide a way of uncovering the vein of creativity that lies deep in all of us.

The Teaching According to his Disciples

After his death the disciples of Ramkrishna formulated his teaching in a way that is attractive to both East and West. The main elements of that teaching are summarised as follows:

1. The ultimate Reality is one, but is known through different names.
2. God can only be realised through sincere struggle.
3. God-realisation is the supreme goal of life.
4. All religions are true in so far as they serve as different paths to the same reality.
5. All souls in their true nature are divine.

The school of thought provoked by Ramakrishna was that all religions are essentially different paths to the same goal. Today booklets produced by the Ramakrishna movement continue to stress this teaching in the selected saying of the master.

> All religions are true. God can be reached by different religions. Many rivers flow by many ways but they fall into the sea. There all are one.
>
> A truly religious man should think that other religions also are paths leading to truth. We should always maintain an attitude of respect towards other religions.
>
> Every man should follow his own religion. A Christian should follow Christianity, and a Mohammedan Mohammedanism. For

the Hindu, the ancient path, the path of the Aryan Rishis, is the best.[27]

Religion is expressed not merely in the forms of creed or dogma, but as spiritual experience. Religion makes no sense unless its truths are experienced. His teachings therefore provided a significant answer to the dominant views of Western Christianity that were challenging Indian society in the nineteenth century. *The Gospel of Sri Ramakrishna* provided a polemic carefully crafted to appeal to certain sections of European society. It is not surprising that Ramakrishan's sexual orientation was carefully omitted from the English text.

Conclusion

There is little doubt that Ramakrishna's behaviour was at times pathological, and even people within his own society believed him to be mad. However, the relationship of his madness to his mystical experience is not clear, and we are not in a position to come to definitive conclusions about the nature of his madness. One thing that can be said is that his madness was special, in that for some members of his society in the midst of the social confusions of nineteenth century Bengal it effected healing. Ramakrishna worked out his own mental illness through religious symbols that also brought healing to others. He was a 'wounded healer' that led many who faced similar social and religious crises to a new sense of meaning and hope. His mystical experiences open new responses from ancient Hinduism as the people of India came in contact with Western culture and Christianity.

Notes

[1] Nikhilananda, *The Gospel of Sri Ramakrishna* (New York: Ramakrishna-Vivekananda Centre, 1942).
[2] Kelley Ann Raab, 'Is There Anything Transcendent About Transcendence? A Philosophical and Psychological Study of Sri Ramakrishna', *Journal of the American Academy of Religion* 63 (1995), 321–41.
[3] Nikhilandanda, *Gospel*, 2.
[4] Ibid., 3.
[5] J.J. Kripal, *Kali's Child* (Chicago: University of Chicago Press, 1995), 58.
[6] Nikhilandanda, *Gospel*, 19–20.
[7] Advaita Ashrama, *Sri Ramakrishna: A Biography in Pictures* (Calcutta: Advaita Ashrama, 1976), 34.
[8] Nikhilananda, *Gospel*, 35.

[9] Ibid., 49.

[10] Kripal, *Kali's Child*, 153.

[11] Nikhilananda, *Gospel*, 58

[12] Ibid.

[13] Ibid., 59.

[14] Ibid.

[15] Ibid., 112.

[16] The Brahmo Samaj was a Hindu society (*samaj*) formed in 1828 by the Hindu reformer Rammohan Roy (who had been influenced by both Islamic and Christian teaching) to promote theism and restore religious purity. The Brahmo Samaj sought to express their worship in Western forms with hymns and readings. Unlike Hindu worship, the Brahmo Samaj was also keen to avoid the use of images in worship. Roy 'accomplishes his aim through the worship of the one God of all religions with readings from the Vedas and the *Upanishads*, hymn singing and expository sermons. Though lacking popular appeal because of its intellectual bent, the Brahmo Samaj did succeed in creating an atmosphere of liberalism and rationality and in providing a meeting place for people of similar religious views and a forum for the reinterpretation of the Hindu tradition.' Glyn Richards (ed.), *A Source-book of Modern Hinduism* (London: Curzon Press, 1985), 3.

[17] See Ramakrishna, 'The Divine Mother', in Richards (ed.), *Source-book*, 67–8.

[18] C.V. Matthew, 'Ramakrishna Movement: Its Legacy to Hindu Spirituality and India', *Dharma Deepika* 1 (1995), 33–48.

[19] See <www.ramakrishna.org/> See also K. Klostermaier, *A Survey of Hinduism* (Albany: State University of New York Press, 1994^2), 437ff.

[20] See Chapter 16 below.

[21] E. Underhill, *Mysticism* (London: Methuen, 1960).

[22] D. Kingsley, 'Blood and Death Out of Place: Reflections on the Goddess Kali', in S. Hawley & D.M. Wulff (eds.), *The Divine Consort: Radha and the Goddesses of India* (Boston: Beacon Press, 1982), 116–20.

[23] Carl Olson, *The Mysterious Play of Kali: An Interpretative Study of Ramakrishna* (GA: Scholars Press, 1990).

[24] Kripal, *Kali's Child*, 238.

[25] Ibid., 241.

[26] Ibid., 319.

[27] Swami Lokeswarandanda, *The Ramakrishna Movement* (Calcutta: Ramakrishna Mission, 1996), 5–6.

7

Sacred Chemicals

Psychedelic Drugs and Mystical Experience

Christopher Partridge

Psychedelic religionists believe that mystical experiences can be induced by the careful use of hallucinogens. Hallucinogens are substances which, when taken in small doses, cause a chemical reaction in the brain, the effect of which is an alteration in the user's perception, mood and thought processes.[1] However, unlike some drugs, hallucinogens are not often associated with memory loss or confusion. That is to say, although it is not always the case, generally speaking, most people under the influence of hallucinogens will be aware of what is going on around them and will be able to reflect, often in detail, on the experience after it has passed. Indeed, there is usually a heightened sense of awareness, a belief that one's perception is sharper, deeper and more responsive to one's environment. Moreover, along with exaggerated sense perception, there is often a feeling of transcending the mundane and a consequent belief that the scales have fallen from one's eyes.[2] Because of this, some users of hallucinogens interpret their experiences as explicitly religious. Reflecting this understanding of *induced* or *provoked* mysticism, such substances are sometimes termed 'entheogens',[3] which literally means 'that which engenders god within'.[4]

Bearing in mind that similar experiences have been sought and attained, often at great personal cost, by disciplined mystics and ascetics throughout religious history, it is unsurprising to learn that some religious devotees have turned to this less demanding but apparently equally effective psychedelic route. Indeed, Richard Rudgley claims, with some justification, that, not only have 'most communities ... used psychoactive substances in both secular and sacred contexts', but also 'our own usage [in the contemporary West], which is almost exclusively secular, makes our culture in certain important respects the exception rather than the rule. Few societies pursue intoxication in the arbitrary and hedonistic fashion prevalent in the modern West.'[5] Paul Devereux makes a similar point: 'Our modern culture stands out in the long record of human history because of its difficulty in accepting, in an orderly and integrated way, the role natural substances ... have played in aiding mind expansion.'[6]

What follows is principally a phenomenological study of entheogen spirituality. However, the essay also seeks to provide some cultural and, particularly in the final section, theological reflection on mystical experience provoked by hallucinogens.

Premodern Psychedelia

Perhaps the most obvious early mention of hallucinogens in the world's sacred writings appears in the Rig Veda (c.1200–900 BCE). Of its 1,028 hymns, 120 are devoted to Soma, a psychoactive plant which was visualised as a deity.[7] From the imagery used in the hymns, it seems clear that, after it was pressed in wooden bowls, filtered through woollen gauze, mixed with milk, and consumed, the resulting effects were dramatic.[8] As the Indologist Wendy Doniger O'Flaherty comments, 'Soma can be dangerous ... but the effects of drinking [it] are usually admired, or at least sought after: a sense of immense personal power ... the assurance of immortality ... and the hallucinations of trance ...'[9] It is perhaps worth quoting a couple of short passages from the Rig Veda to illustrate this:

> I have tasted the sweet drink of life, knowing that it inspires good thoughts and joyous expansiveness to the extreme, that all the gods and mortals seek it together calling it honey. When you penetrate inside it you will know no limits ... We have drunk the Soma; we have become immortal; we have gone to the light; we have found the gods ... The glorious drops I have drunk set me free in wide space.[10]

Again, in another hymn, one of the Vedic gods (probably Indra), incarnate in the intoxicated worshiper, rejoices in his own abilities which have been strengthened by the drug/god soma:

> In my vastness, I surpassed the sky and this vast Earth. Have I not drunk Soma?
> Yes! I will place the Earth here, or perhaps there. Have I not drunk Soma?
> One of my wings is in the sky; I have trailed the other below. Have I not drunk Soma?

I am huge, huge! flying to the cloud. Have I not drunk Soma?
I am going – a well-stocked house, carrying the oblation to the
gods. Have I not drunk Soma?[11]

The point is that the plant Soma, which was central to much Vedic spirituality, seems to have been given its privileged position because of its
powerful hallucinogenic properties. Although there is no scholarly consensus as to which plant soma is,[12] the point is simply that at this early
period of Indian religious history, we have evidence of the religious use
of psychoactive substances.

Of course, this religious attitude to drugs can be found in many other
cultures throughout history and across the globe.[13] For example, Siberian
shamans utilise the fly agaric mushroom (*Amanita muscaria*) and the
female shamans of Korea induce states of trance by drinking large
amounts of alcohol. Again, the Aztecs worshipped, along with the mushroom *teonanacatl* and the vine *ololiuqui*, the highly hallucinogenic *peyote*
cactus which they revered as 'the flesh of the gods'. Although, for obvious reasons, attempts were made by Spanish missionaries to stamp out a
religion which operated with this understanding of divine flesh, peyote-
based spirituality (which had been driven underground) emerged again
during the nineteenth century. In more recent years, Michael Harner in
particular has shown the importance of hallucinogenic plants within the
belief systems of some indigenous peoples. They invest individuals with
powers otherwise unattainable and allow access to the spirit world.[14] It
has also been practised by the North American Indians of the Plains (the
Native American Church).[15] Indeed, it seems to be increasing in popularity. According to Cheryl Pellerin, the Native American Church 'had
13,000 members in 1922. Today, membership is 250,000. U.S. Indians
who live far from the peyote's natural habitat use mescal buttons, which
they legally buy and distribute through the U.S. postal service.'[16] As to
the religious significance of peyote for the Native American Church,
Robert de Ropp comments,

> from the moment when the gatherers of the cactus set off in search
> of the plant, the whole enterprise is suffused with a sense of the
> sacred … The anthropologist J.S. Slotkin [whose work clearly
> impressed Aldous Huxley[17]] … defined the peyote religion as
> Christianity adapted to traditional Indian beliefs and practices.
> According to these beliefs, the Great Spirit created the universe and
> controls the destiny of everything therein. The Great Spirit put
> some of his supernatural power in the peyote, which he gave to the
> Indians to help them in their present lowly circumstances. By eat-

ing peyote under the proper ritual conditions a person can incorporate some of the Great Spirit's power, just as a white Christian
absorbs that power from the sacramental bread and wine.[18]

This sacramental understanding of hallucinogens (sometimes understood as divine power within the substance which, when imbibed, leads
to a religious experience) is a common theme in psychedelic mysticism.[19] Nevertheless, whether understood precisely in this way or not,
the point is that, as Ninian Smart notes, 'there has over a long period
been experimentation with psychedelic drugs ... Naturally early attitudes to [hallucinogenic] plants differ rather from modern ones. The
visions could be attributed to the divine nature of the plants themselves.
It is more "modern" to think that their effects come from being windows, so to speak, of vision – as though the mind is already at some level
in touch with transcendental powers to which drugs can clear a pathway.'[20] It is to the development of this latter, more 'modern' understanding that we now turn.

Aldous Huxley and the Dawn of the Psychedelic Revolution

Although drug-provoked spirituality has a long history, and although the
modern Western psychedelic story can be said to have begun in 1938
when Albert Hofmann, a research chemist working for Sandoz Pharmaceutical Laboratories in Switzerland, produced LSD-25 (lysergic acid
diethylamide), contemporary psychedelic mysticism began to seriously
coalesce in the 1950s.[21] Humphrey Osmond, a British psychiatrist working in Canada who had used LSD to treat alcoholics, introduced Aldous
Huxley to the use of mescaline. During this decade, several other key
figures, such as Huxley's friend Gerald Heard,[22] began exploring not
merely the psychological and psychiatric potential of hallucinogens, particularly LSD (the study of which had been going on for some time[23]),
but also their mystical potential. They became convinced that the altered
states of consciousness produced were in fact mystical states and that hallucinogens provided a gateway to a larger, truer grasp of reality.

However, one of the first tasks to be faced was the very practical one
of describing the drugs which could be used in this way. Both Huxley
and Osmond sought a term which did not carry the medical and pathological baggage that the available pharmaceutical terms did, but would
rather indicate their mystical and visionary potential. Huxley sifted
through his Liddel and Scott's Greek lexicon and eventually came up
with the term 'phanerothyme' which simply means 'to make the soul

visible.' In a letter to Osmond he introduced the new term in the
following rhyme:

> To make this trivial world sublime,
> Take half a gram of phanerothyme.

Osmond, however, had his own ideas and responded with the following:

> To fathom Hell or soar angelic,
> Just take a pinch of psychedelic.'[24]

As Peter Haining comments, 'Neither the scientist nor the writer could
have known that not only had they invented the label for the generation that would experiment with the psychedelics ... in what became
known as "tripping", but that in those few lines they had effectively
launched the literature of psychedelia.'[25]

Of this literature, it is arguably Huxley's own volume *The Doors of
Perception* that is, as Jay Stephens says, 'the most famous book on the psychedelic bookshelf'. Taking him only a month to write, it is essentially
an exploration of the implications of his own psychedelic experience.
The revealing title of the book is lifted from William Blake's *Marriage of
Heaven and Hell*: 'If the doors of perception were cleansed, everything
would appear to man as it really is – infinite.' When the doors of perception were cleansed for Huxley in Los Angeles, on the morning of
6 May 1953 after ingesting 300 milligrams of mescaline, he was literally
lost for words and awed by what he felt and saw. It wasn't simply that he
was struck by the rainbow brilliance of the world he had entered, but,
more profoundly, he was moved by his sense of oneness with reality, a
reality which he perceived to be essentially divine. As he stared at a glass
vase containing three flowers, the cleansing power of mescaline allowed
him to perceive, as he put it,

> what the iris, rose, and carnation so intensely signified was nothing
> more, and nothing less, than what they were – a transience that was
> yet eternal life, a perpetual perishing that was at the same time pure
> Being, a bundle of minute, unique particulars in which, by some
> unique and yet self-evident paradox, was to be seen the divine
> source of all existence. I continued to look at the flowers, and in
> their living light I seemed to detect the qualitative equivalent of
> breathing – but of a breathing without returns to a starting-point,
> with no recurrent ebbs but only a repeated flow from beauty to
> heightened beauty, from deeper to ever deeper meaning. Words like

Grace and Transfiguration came to my mind, and this of course is what, among other things, they stood for. My eyes travelled from the rose to the carnation, and from the feathery incandescence to the smooth scrolls of scented amethyst which were the iris. The Beatific Vision, *Sat Chit Ananda*, Being-Awareness-Bliss – for the first time I understood, not on the verbal level, not by inchoate hints or at a distance, but precisely and completely what those prodigious syllables referred to.[26]

He then goes on to focus on the legs of a bamboo chair.

How miraculous their tubularity, how supernatural was their polished smoothness! I spent several minutes – or was it several centuries? – not merely gazing at those bamboo legs, but actually *being* them – or rather being myself in them; or still more accurate (for 'I' was not involved in the case, nor in a certain sense were 'they') being Not-self in the Not-self which was the chair.[27]

As I will argue below, mescaline had allowed him to experience the essential elements set out in his anthology of mystical writings *The Perennial Philosophy*.[28] It animated ideas and presuppositions which were, until his psychedelic experience, principally abstract concepts. Just as virtual reality equipment allows the architect to walk around and experience buildings which are as yet only ideas and plans, so mescaline added depth to Huxley's two-dimensional, fundamentally Indian worldview. Reality was experienced as 'a continuum, a fathomless mysterious and infinite Something, whose outward aspect is what we call Matter and whose inwardness is what we call Mind.'

Without rehearsing the valid criticisms of Huxley's naïve equation of theistic and non-theistic mystical experience by R.C. Zaehner and others,[29] my aim at this point is simply to draw attention to the fact that he is clearly claiming his psychedelic experience to be directly analogous to those reported by the mystics. This, we will see, becomes a common theme in subsequent psychedelic mysticism. Psychedelics, it is claimed, provide a profoundly religious, yet instant, mystical experience. For Huxley, mescaline introduced him to the Beatific Vision which is, he perceives, what mystics in the Indian religious tradition apprehend when they speak of Being-Awareness-Bliss. In a few short minutes he had begun to experience 'eternal life', 'pure Being', and 'the divine source of all existence'. He had entered into what mystics down the ages longed to experience.

Hence, it is not surprising that it wasn't long before Huxley was arguing that training in mysticism can, in his words, be 'speeded up and

made more effective by a judicious use of the physically harmless psychedelics now available'. Whilst he was careful not to recommend
alcohol, cocaine and other harmful substances, because he was
convinced (wrongly[30]) that certain hallucinogens were not harmful
(particularly LSD and mescaline), he suggested that people should
experiment with them. Indeed, he criticised the church for 'not "baptizing" mescaline or similar drugs and incorporating them into
Christian worship'[31] and firmly believed that psychedelics would one
day be central to all   religion.

As to how hallucinogens actually induce genuine mystical experiences, following the philosopher Henri Bergson, Huxley believed the
brain and central nervous system to be what he calls a 'reducing valve'.
In other words, the brain functions as a filter allowing access only to that
information which is practically useful for survival on the planet. There
is, however, a great deal of unfiltered information out there. This broader range of unfiltered knowledge and consciousness is what Huxley, following the philosopher C.D. Broad, refers to as 'Mind at Large'.[32]
According to Broad,

> each person is capable of remembering all that has ever happened
> to him and of perceiving everything that is happening everywhere
> in the universe. The function of the brain and nervous system is to
> protect us from being overwhelmed and confused by this mass of
> largely useless and irrelevant knowledge, by shutting out most of
> what we should otherwise perceive or remember at any moment,
> and leaving only that very small and special selection which is
> likely to be practic-ally useful.[33]

Hence, Huxley points out that, although 'each one of us is potentially
Mind at Large', the business of survival means that our brains allow us
only the knowledge we need to sustain physical existence. The world we
perceive is actually a reduced world sustained by a tiny supply of consciousness from Mind at Large.

Hence, when, for example, mystics, psychics, people under hypnosis,
or those who practise spiritual disciplines have an awe-inspiring experience of a larger spiritual environment, what they have done is simply
circumvented the reducing valve and exposed themselves to more of
Mind at Large. According to Huxley, there flows into the minds of such
people, 'not indeed the perception "of everything that is happening
everywhere in the universe" (for the by-pass does not abolish the reducing valve, which still excludes the total content of Mind at Large), but
something more than, and above all something different from, the care-

fully selected utilitarian material which our narrowed, individual minds regard as a complete, or at least sufficient, picture of reality.'[34] This, of course, according to Huxley, is exactly what happens when one takes psychedelics; the reducing valve is circumvented.

(Interestingly, John Hick also follows C.D. Broad's thought fairly closely at this point: 'The filtering function of the brain and nervous system, and of our own conceptual frameworks, protects our individuality by screening out the virtual infinity of information flowing around us all the time. For a finite consciousness is constituted by a grid that excludes all except a minute aspect of reality. From this point of view, the mind/brain functions as a kind of reducing valve, evolved to keep out far more than it lets in.' He then turns to discuss the efficacy of psychedelics, which he explains in a way not dissimilar to Huxley: 'In altered states of consciousness this filtering mechanism is partially suspended, releasing a flood of information not normally available to us. Drugs which act directly on the brain to inhibit its normal screening function have for this reason long been used for religious purposes.'[35])

In a later essay, Huxley argues (in a passage which, again, reminds one of Hick's appropriation of Kantian epistemology[36]) that between every human consciousness and the rest of the world,

> stands an invisible fence, a network of traditional thinking-and-feeling patterns, of second-hand notions that have turned into axioms, of ancient slogans revered as divine revelations. What we see through the meshes of this net is never, of course, the unknowable 'thing-in-itself' ... What we normally take in is a curious mixture of immediate experience with culturally conditioned symbols, of sense impressions with preconceived ideas about the nature of things.[37]

As to how we can break through this epistemic fence, Huxley's answer is, principally, 'by the practice of pure receptivity and mental silence.' By evacuating our minds we 'cleanse the doors of perception and, in the process, make possible the emergence of other than normal forms of consciousness – aesthetic consciousness, visionary consciousness, mystical consciousness.'[38] Whilst humans need conceptual thought for everyday living, such meditative practice will eventually allow us access into that which he terms 'Not-thought', that which is not conditioned by culture, thought and language.

In a similar way to meditation, psychedelics enable people to breach the fence between their conditioned minds and the larger spiritual environment, thereby giving them access to 'a new direct insight into the very Nature of Things'.[39] They help to clear the path to the apprehension of Mind at Large, to 'an "obscure knowledge" that All is in all – that All is actually each.' This, he says, is as near as 'a finite mind can ever come to "perceiving everything that is happening everywhere in the universe".'[40] This, as far as Huxley is aware, is the most developed stage of mystical awareness. Initially and most commonly psychedelics simply introduce a person to the aesthetic consciousness, in which the beauty of the world is perceived. This may, in turn, modulate into visionary consciousness, in which the world will 'reveal itself as not only unimaginably beautiful, but also fathomless mystery … New insights into a new, transfigured world of givenness, new combinations of thought and fantasy – the stream of novelty pours through the world in a torrent, whose every drop is charged with meaning.'[41] Finally, some individuals will experience the facts of the universe directly and without symbolic mediation. It is at this point that the individual experiences that 'obscure knowledge' of 'the divine ground of all being … the Suchness of all.'[42] The experience has now deepened into mystical consciousness.

> The world is now seen as infinite diversity that is yet a unity, and the beholder experiences himself as being at one with the infinite Oneness that manifests itself, totally present, at every point of space, at every instant in the flux of perpetual perishing and perpetual renewal. Our normal word-conditioned consciousness creates a universe of sharp distinctions, black and white, this and that, me and you and it. In the mystical consciousness of being at one with infinite Oneness, there is a reconciliation of opposites, a perception of the Not-Particular in particulars, a transcending of our ingrained subject–object relationships with things and persons...

In brief, the effect of psychedelics is to reduce the efficacy of the neural filter, breach the fences of our culturally conditioned worldviews, and break down what Huxley refers to as 'the confining stockade of verbalised symbols'. In performing this function, they facilitate access to Mind at Large and increase the likelihood of mystical experience.

This understanding, or variants of it, can be found in much subsequent psychedelic mysticism. Indeed, it is difficult to underestimate the significance of Huxley for the development of psychedelic spirituality in the West. Although notable people such as Hofmann, Osmond, Heard, and the influential Czech psychologist Stanislav Grof[43] publicly worked with LSD and other hallucinogens, it seems clear that psychedelic religious experience gained a kudos that would have been denied it had it not been for Huxley. His ideas, expounded in eloquent and informed prose, found their way into the minds of those who would not normally have considered psychedelic mysticism worthy of critical scrutiny. For example, I'm not sure R.C. Zaehner would have ever written *Mysticism, Sacred and Profane* or *Drugs, Mysticism and Make-Believe*,[44] let alone taken mescaline himself, had he not read *The Doors of Perception*. And it is doubtful that he would have read that book, which he admitted was 'an important book',[45] had it not been penned by one of the finest writers of the twentieth century.

Psychedelic Mysticism for the Masses

The psychedelic mysticism of the fifties was essentially an elitist spirituality. As John Cody has observed, Huxley and his friend Gerald Heard 'carried out a cautious strategy toward psychedelics that was intended to prevent damaging publicity by stressing respectable research under expert direction. They also confined distribution to a hand-picked coterie of the gifted and influential'.[46] Indeed, the modern history of psychedelics might have been very different had Huxley been interested in socialising psychedelics. However, as Huxley wrote in a letter to Osmond, 'The last thing I want is to create an image of myself as "Mr LSD". Nor have I the least desire (being without talent for this kind of thing) to get involved in the politics of psychedelics.'[47] This was certainly not the case for the man Allen Ginsberg called 'a hero of American consciousness ... faced with the task of a Messiah',[48] namely, Timothy Leary.

Although, as a psychologist at Harvard University, Leary's interest in psychedelics was initially academic, it rapidly became both more recreational and more spiritual. He was particularly impressed by *The Tibetan Book of the Dead* (significantly, one of Huxley's favourite sacred texts).[49] Traditionally, *The Tibetan Book of the Dead*, or the *Bardo Thödol*, is read to a dying person as a guide to equip them for a forty-nine day journey between lives. It is believed to help the dying overcome attachment to their bodies and families.[50] However, as Leary's colleague at Harvard, Richard Alpert, recalls, *The Tibetan Book of the Dead* provided 'the most vivid descriptions of what we were experiencing with psychedelics but hadn't been able to describe.'[51] (Indeed, on a trip to India, Leary's friend, Ralph Metzner, introduced a Tibetan Buddhist teacher, Lama Govinda, to LSD. The result was highly significant. 'For the first time, after thirty years of meditation, the Lama had experienced the *Bardo Thödol* in its living sweating reality.'[52] Consequently, writes Leary, 'when word came to the philosophic community of India that a group of Harvard psychologists was using the ancient Buddhist text as a manual for drug-induced satoris, there was great interest.'[53] 'You', said Lama Govinda to

Leary, 'have been an unwitting tool of the great transformation of our age.'[54])

Motivated by Leary's drive and charismatic personality, the sixties psychedelic revolution quickly became a large and influential subculture. The term 'psychedelic' rapidly expanded to include all forms of culture which were thought to inspire, or to be inspired by, the use of hallucinogens. A great deal of time and creative energy was invested in the production of particularly music and visual art which would encourage successful psychedelic experiences. Whether one thinks of bands such as the Incredible String Band, the Grateful Dead, the Velvet Underground, early Pink Floyd, and the Doors (who took their name from Huxley's book, *The Doors of Perception*[55]), or records such as the Beatles' *Sergeant Pepper's Lonely Hearts Club Band* (on the cover of which, along with pictures of Mahatma Gandhi, Sri Yukteswar, Sri Lahiri Mahasaya, and Sri Paramahansa Yogananda, was also a photograph of Aldous Huxley), or the work of writers such as William Burroughs, Jack Kerouac, Hunter S. Thompson, and Allen Ginsberg, or the vibrant poster art of the period, it all reflected the impact of hallucinogens and, indeed, the Eastern-influenced religious thought of Huxley and Leary.

Again, regarding Huxley's significance, it is worth pointing out that, although this revolution may have happened without Huxley, there is little doubt that Huxley's essays The *Doors of Perception* (1954) and *Heaven and Hell* (1956) had a shaping influence upon it. Indeed, it is arguable that the turning East in the sixties can be traced back, to a large extent, to the influence of Huxley, whose whole psychedelic experience was coloured by his attraction to Indian mystical thought. One only has to read Leary's 'Homage to Huxley' to gauge his significance for the sixties subculture.[56] It is certainly the case that 'Leary saw a world modelled after Huxley's *Island*, in which the educational potential of psychedelics was obvious. But Huxley's fantasy offered no guidance on the important problem of how the moksha medicine could be introduced to a complex society like the United States.'[57] This was to be Leary's self-appointed role.

This brings us to the formation of the International Foundation for Internal Freedom (IFIF). Leary came up with the idea of 'a new profession of psychedelic guides' who, he said, will have 'the patience of a first-grade teacher, the humility and wisdom of a Hindu guru, the loving dedication of a minister-priest, the sensitivity of a poet, and the imagination of a science fiction writer.'[58] The result was the IFIF, a psychedelic organisation which was to be made up of small communities controlled and supplied with LSD from a centre based in Boston. Leary's vision was that, through a process of growth and division, the world would be covered with small IFIF cells spreading the psychedelic gospel. Hence, with the emergence of the IFIF, psychedelia became effectively a new religious movement seeking to evangelise America. As Leary candidly admits, 'In 1961 we estimated that 25,000 Americans had turned-on to strong psychedelics ... at a rate of cellular growth we expected by 1967 a million Americans would be using LSD. We calculated that the critical figure for blowing the mind of the American society would be four million LSD users and this would happen by 1969.'[59] As is evident in the writings from the period, it was clearly believed that humanity was on the verge of a new age of drug-provoked, Indian-influenced, expanded, mystical consciousness.

Although the IFIF proved to be short-lived, the psychedelic fire had taken hold.[60] Sixties beatnik culture had turned East, enthusiastically converted to psychedelia, and, for the most part, accepted Leary's philosophy of 'turn on, tune in, and drop out' – which was effectively the new psychedelic mantra. Leary explains the thinking behind the mantra: 'Drop Out – detach yourself from the external social drama which is as dehydrated and ersatz as TV. Turn On – find a sacrament [namely LSD] which returns you to the temple of God, your own body. Go out of your mind. Get high. Tune In – be reborn. Drop back in to express it. Start a new sequence of behaviour that reflects your vision.'[61] In other words, for Leary to drop out is quite literary to form a 'cult',[62] an alternative, counter-cultural, drug-based religious community. He writes, 'Quit school. Quit your job. Don't vote. Avoid all politics. Do not waste conscious thinking on TV-studio games. Political choices are meaningless ... Dismiss the Judaic-Christian-Marxist-puritan-literary-existentialist suggestion that the drop-out is escape and that the conformist cop-out is reality. Dropping out is the hardest yoga of all.'[63] Having said that, he goes on to argue that 'tuning in' is the gradual manifestation in society of psychedelic culture. 'Slowly, gently start seed transformations around you. Psychedelic art. Psychedelic style. Psychedelic music. Psychedelic dance.'[64] This is essentially Leary's 'politics of ecstasy' which he preached right up until his death of prostate cancer in Los Angeles, June 1996.[65]

As to how far Leary's psychedelia can be described as 'religious', aside from the perennial problems surrounding the definition of 'religious', this is difficult to determine. It is true to say that he was not as driven by Eastern mysticism as, for example, Huxley or Alpert/Ram Dass were, in the sense that there was a strong tendency in Leary's more science-based thought to interpret the mystical consciousness in physical terms. In his significantly entitled book *Your Brain is God*, this is made explicit. He declares, for example, 'your are a God, act like one',[66] and speaks of

prayer as 'ecstatic communication with your inner navigational comput-
er'.[67] Again, he writes, 'control your own brain, be your own Divinity,
make your own world. Master the God technologies … Live out your
own highest vision.'[68] Furthermore, in his final book, which contemplates his imminent death from cancer and the meaning of life, the discussion of religious themes tends to be pseudo-scientific and anthropocentric, focusing on such as brain chemistry, rather than union with
an external spiritual reality.[69] Hence, although he was happy to speak of
death as 'a singular transcendent experience', even as 'the ultimate trip
to higher realms of consciousness',[70] and although he believed there to
be 'something' beyond death, nevertheless, he writes the following:

> when the body stops functioning, consciousness advances to the
> nervous system, where it belonged all our lifetime. Consciousness
> just goes home to the genetic code where it belongs … When con-
> sciousness leaves the nervous system and fuses with the genetic
> code we receive all life since and before our embodiment. I predict
> that dying is a merging with the entire life process. In other words,
> we become every form of life that has ever lived and will live. We
> become the DNA code that wrote the entire script. Consciousness
> returns to the genetic code.[71]

Hence, whilst happy to work with ideas such as universal consciousness,
Leary's mysticism is certainly not the Indian-inspired acosmic monism
or idealism informing many forms of 1960s psychedelic mysticism.
Indeed, he explicitly states that, when those using LSD report 'retro-
gression and reincarnation visions, this is not mysterious or supernatural. It is simply modern biogenetics.' That is to say, 'Built within every
cell are molecular strands of memory and awareness called the DNA
code … Your body carries the protein record of everything that's happened to you since the moment you were conceived as a one cell
organism. It's a living history of every form of energy transformation
on this planet back to that thunderbolt in the Precambrian mud that
spawned the life process over two billion years ago … [C]ountless
events from early and even intra-uterine life are registered in your brain
and can be flashed into consciousness during an LSD experience.'[72]
Again, it would seem that, for Leary, psychedelics do not induce mystical experiences as these have been understood by the mystics down the
ages, but rather 'take you beyond the senses into a world of cellular
awareness.'[73] Arguably, therefore, if it is to be understood as mysticism at
all, Leary's psychedelia should perhaps be understood as a form of phys-
icalist/pseudo-scientific nature mysticism. One is made aware of one's

unity with a greater whole, but that whole is none other than 'life'. We are thinking more in terms of DNA rather than Brahman-Atman identification (as in the Vedantic thought that informed Huxley's perennialism).

This, however, as noted above, was not the interpretation given to psychedelic experiences by many during the sixties. The psychedelic experience was understood to be explicitly spiritual and mystical. For example, Paul McCartney, who might be considered typical of many at the time, makes the following statement: 'God is in everything. God is in the space between us. God is in that table in front of you. God is everything and everywhere and everyone. It just happens that I realised all this through acid [LSD], but it could have been through anything. It really doesn't matter how I made it … The final result is all that counts.'[74] The point is that psychedelics were clearly believed by many to induce a monistic or pantheistic mystical experience and, in turn, provide a broader, more spiritual worldview.[75]

Psychedelia and Rave Culture

In more recent years we have witnessed what might be described as the third phase of the modern psychedelic revolution (the fifties being the first, and the sixties the second), namely a particular stream of 'rave' or 'club' culture. It is not difficult to trace the continuity between the psychedelic hippy culture of the sixties and certain aspects of eighties and nineties rave culture.[76] Indeed, not only is there a recent CD setting contemporary dance music to the words of Leary,[77] but also there are a range of groups and musicians who betray the influence of Leary and the psychedelic subcultures of the sixties. For example, the following words are taken from the Porcupine Tree's *Voyage 34* album: 'the LSD trip is a pilgrimage far out beyond your normal mind into that risky and revelatory territory which has been explored for thousands of years by mystics, visionaries and philosophers.'[78] Again, one could cite numerous 'trance' music pieces which are explicitly psychedelic (for example, 'Sex, Drugs and Acid Trance' by the S.U.N. Project,[79] 'Acid Munchies' by Optica,[80] 'LSD' by Hallucinogen,[81] or almost anything by Shamanic Tribes on Acid[82]). As Sheila Whitely observes in her discussion of contemporary music and culture:

> … there is a strong sense of shared identity between the sixties hippy philosophy and that of nineties alternative culture. Similarities are present in the music, the influence of the drug experience, an awareness of the destruction and ruination of the

Earth and the poisoning of the seas. New Age Travellers share the
hippy philosophy of alternative family groupings and the freedom
to opt out of mainstream society, whilst free festivals and raves provide the space both to trip out and experience a range of house and
ambient bands. Publications, such as the Freak Emporium provide
guidance to a range of psychedelic music, magazines and books,
whilst Bush Telegraph provides features on cannabis and the dream
mechanism, homeopathy and growing hemp in the UK. Collective
experience, music and drugs appear, once again, to provide the
means whereby young people can explore the politics of consciousness, to set up an alternative lifestyle.[83]

Indeed, there is an interesting geographic connection between the hippie culture of the sixties and psychedelic rave culture, namely Goa. This
Christian state in India to which many hippies travelled in the sixties
and seventies has again emerged as an important destination for the
devotees of a particular type of Western subculture. Hippie culture has
been transformed into trance culture. The music has changed, but the
Indian-inspired psychedelia is still intact. As Ben Osborne comments:

Still catering for cheap drugs, the ultimate Goan pilgrimage is to
a Full Moon party. Here you can trip to the deep throb of electronic music until the first rays of the Asian dawn lift the dew
from the palm leaves … [Goa] became a fixed stop-off point on
the international party trail from Ibiza to Amsterdam, New York,
and Mikanos, but differed from these scenes largely through its
base in psychedelic drugs.[84]

Having said that, whilst Indian-inspired beliefs were central to both earlier psychedelic mystical experience and the much more recent Goan
psychedelia (as the covers to the compilation CDs of 'Goa trance' music
clearly indicate), generally speaking, contemporary psychedelia tends to
be far more eclectic and certainly more Pagan and Earth centred.[85]
Indeed, shortly before his death, Leary himself declared that, 'as
Americans, we are proud to point out that the 1960s drug-culture's
giddy, wild, confused eruption of philosophy and spiritual anarchy
played an important role in stimulating and provoking the new
Scientific Paganism of the 21st Century.'[86] He is, he says, 'delighted to
discover that certain ancient religions, mainly pagan, in millennia past
had anticipated what our scientists are now discovering.'[87]
    A good example of this type of essentially Neo-Pagan, 'shamanic'
spirituality is that developed by the late Terence McKenna, probably the

most important contemporary psychedelic thinker. Without going into
the intricacies of McKenna's rather obscure fungi-centric philosophy, it
is essentially based on the belief that the evolution of human consciousness was kick-started by the ingestion of hallucinogenic mushrooms, the spores of which originally travelled through space.[88] 'Space',
he tells us, 'is a vast ocean to those hardy life-forms that have the ability to reproduce from spores, for spores are covered with the hardest
organic substance known. Across the aeons of time and space drift many
spore-forming life-forms in suspended animation for millions of years
until contact is made with a suitable environment.'[89] Indeed, Mckenna
claims that humans have a very basic and important relationship with
mushrooms. In a sense, humans are beings with a mushroom consciousness. If I have understood him correctly, we are spiritual beings
because our early ancestors ate hallucinogenic mushrooms. There is, in
other words, a chemical origin to the sense of the sacred in human history. Hallucinogens are the principal motivating factors behind the
development of the religious consciousness in the human race; powerful visionary experiences caused humanity to look beyond the physical world and to interpret life religiously. (Similar theories about the
origins of particular religious traditions have been posited by scholars
such as John Allegro[90] Mary Barnard,[91] and especially the Harvard
mycologist Gordon Wasson.[92])

McKenna's basic thesis (which Leary clearly found persuasive[93]) is
simply that psychedelic mysticism takes us back to our roots. The feeling of oneness with nature is by no means coincidental. Hallucinogenic
plants encourage the re-emergence of the archaic consciousness of primal peoples. Hence, he claims that 'the 20th century mind is nostalgic
for the paradise that once existed on the mushroom dotted planes of
Africa where the plant-human symbiosis occurred that pulled us out of
the animal body and into the tool-using, culture-making, imagination-
exploring creature that we are.'[94] Indeed, much of McKenna's work
focuses on what he calls 'the Archaic revival': 'a revival of the Archaic –
or preindustrial and preliterate attitude toward community, substance
use, and nature – an attitude that served our nomadic, prehistoric ancestors long and well, before the rise of the current cultural style we call
"Western". The Archaic refers to the Upper Paleolithic, a period seven
to ten thousand years in the past, immediately preceding the invention
and dissemination of agriculture. The Archaic was a time of nomadic
pastoralism and partnership, a culture based on cattle-raising, shamanism, and Goddess worship.'[95]

In his Preface to the revised edition of what has become the hallucinogenic mushroom grower's bible, *Psilocybin: Magic Mushroom Grower's*

Guide (originally published in 1976), McKenna claims that (partly as a result of this book) 'more people are now actively engaged in a religious quest using psilocybin than ever before in history. This is a complete rebirth of a religious mystery and it has taken place in less than a decade!'[96] However, the point is that he clearly understands hallucinogens, particularly mushrooms, to be central to authentic mystical experience. For example, in a recent dialogue with a Buddhist, when questioned as to whether he sees any contradiction between Buddhism and exploring psychedelics, he simply responds, 'No, I would almost say, "How can you be a serious Buddhist if you're not exploring psychedelics?"'[97]

Whether influenced by McKenna or not (and he seems to have a large and growing following), as in the sixties, psychedelic mysticism has largely been propagated through music. As already indicated, within what might be termed 'rave culture' an eclectic, but essentially Neo-Pagan, psychedelic spirituality is emerging.[98] Indeed, groups such as the Shamen are explicitly indebted to McKenna and even include samples of him expounding his ideas in their music.[99] Psychedelicists like McKenna and Fraser Clark (who is also greatly indebted to McKenna[100]) believe rave culture to be extremely important for the progress of psychedelia. In Clark's words,

> With the advent of rave ... the sheer number of personal experiences ensured that, by the mid-1990s, the drug war was won, bar the official shouting. For the new generation, the subject today has shifted from being an issue to being close to a mere topic, like sex has become, and dancing, and petting, and nudity, and all the rest during our recent long, slow, ambient evolutionary 'return march' through the final nano-second of outdated 'history'.[101]

And he has a point, in that, nowadays, many are using psychedelics along with virtual reality apparatus, trance music, ambient music, dub music, all of which are often brought together at gatherings to be utilised in what are understood to be the new sacred spaces and rituals.[102]

Simon Reynolds comments that, 'instigated by anarcho-mystic outfits like Spiral Tribe and by neo-hippy travellers on the "free festival" circuit ... the techno-pagan spirit' evolved. Spiral Tribe, he points out, "preached a creed they called Terra-Technic, arguing that ravers" non-stop ritual dancing reconnected mankind with the primordial energy of the Earth.'[103] Indeed, more established new religionists, such as the followers of the Indian guru Rajneesh/Osho, have strong links with some forms of contemporary dance culture, particularly the trance music scene[104] (which out of all the genres of music in the contemporary dance scene is most linked to psychedelics). As Jane Bussmann comments in her overview of rave culture:

> Having the doors in their minds opened wasn't enough for some people: they wanted the back wall knocked out and a psychic patio built. Just like John Lennon, Peter Sellers and London's happening scene of the sixties, people are finding themselves cross-legged on the floor all over again. Shamanism, yoga, Sanjasin [sic], paganism, Special Brew … now there are all kinds of ways to get on a spiritual one …[105]

Of course, the controversial drug central to rave culture in the 1980s and 90s was 'E' or 'Ecstasy' (MDMA – methylene-dioxymethamphetamine). However, whilst Mary Anna Wright comments that 'the Ecstasy experience involved intense insights into the depth of the human psyche that touched on a spiritual revelation or metanoia',[106] generally speaking, it would seem that, whilst mood altering, Ecstasy did not have the same sort of 'spiritual' or psychedelic impact that LSD did in the 1960s. It tended to lead simply to egoistic hedonism, rather than a spiritual quest. (Users I have spoken to agree with this assessment.) I am not arguing that psychedelics don't engender hedonistic or egoistic attitudes (for they clearly do), but only that they also, because of their particular hallucinogenic properties, tend to contribute to a more spiritually reflective disposition. This can be observed in, for example, the underlying philosophy of the hippy-punk-influenced anarchic 'sound system', the Spiral Tribe, who developed 'an alternative lifestyle, based around psychedelic drugs, tribal techno music, and New Age belief systems'.[107] Matthew Collin makes the following insightful point:

> What seems to have had a far stronger effect on the development of Spiral Tribe, its belief system and its *modus operandi*, is a much more powerful drug than Ecstasy, one which turns minds inside out and worlds upside down, asking questions and demanding answers – LSD. Whereas Ecstasy invokes intense happiness and empathy, but doesn't necessarily force you to re-evaluate your way of life, the wild hallucinations brought on by a heroic dose of LSD can push the human ego to the brink of dissolution. Spiral Tribe wanted to tap the potential that was being filtered out by the central nervous system, to short circuit years of conditioning. Their insistence was that pleasure in itself just wasn't enough. [In the words of Mark Harrison of Spiral Tribe] 'MDMA has its place, but once you've taken it a couple of times, its lessons are learned very quickly and

it becomes unnecessary … From what I've seen, I don't think it has very much to show you, whereas I don't think you can go wrong with LSD and magic mushrooms. They are much more important … LSD and magic mushrooms have a much more creative influence, not just on raves, but on life, on one's understanding of oneself and the world around.' Looking back on Harrison's account of the Tribe's spiritual awakening at the Longstock festival, it can easily be seen in the context of a revelatory, life-changing LSD experience.[108]

(Is it a coincidence that, in the above passage, the comments about the filtering function of the central nervous system sound very much like those of Huxley? Here again there is evidence of the enduring influence of Huxley on psychedelic counter-cultures.)

It should be noted that there is, amongst the more spiritually-minded 'ravers', certainly in Britain, an unhappiness with what is understood to be the commercialisation of rave culture. Increasingly rave and dance music/culture is becoming too closely associated with, if not the product of, 'big business'. As such it is being shunned within some alternative/counter-cultures. For example, some interesting research recently carried out in Australia found that a distinction was being made between 'raves' and 'doofs', the latter being non-commercial, 'psychedelic gatherings' or 'bush parties' organised at grass roots level for those 'in the know'. Moreover, these psychedelic gatherings are more explicitly Pagan in orientation than raves and engender a stronger sense of community in participants.[109]

Finally, having drawn attention to the use of psychedelics by some Pagans, I should also point out that many Pagans, particularly those that belong to organised groups, consider the use of drugs to be detrimental to spiritual progress. For example, Tanya Luhrmann found that 'participants never took drugs during rituals, or indeed outside them, although for some of them, youthful experience with consciousness changing drugs had lead them to magic because they realised, they said, that they could change their perception of reality. Robert, a member of the coven I joined, told me that taking drugs in rituals was like taking a helicopter to the top of Mount Everest. Part of the experience lay in the climb.'[110] (Huxley, of course, took the opposite view, in that he was happy to forego climbing experience in favour of a helicopter trip.)

Psychedelic Mysticism and Religious Experience

In a recent issue of the influential New Age journal *Gnosis* there is an anonymous essay by a person who describes herself as a Christian psychedelicist. However, the author, unhappy with Judeo-Christian understandings of God, describes a non-personal pantheistic (or perhaps panentheistic) spiritualit:. 'I hesitate to use the word "God" in this article because it comes loaded with so much doctrinal meaning. I will use the word "god", however, as it most accurately expresses my sensation of holiness. I do not mean a personal deity; to me it is best thought of as a force or energy such as gravity or magnetism or light.'[111] Similarly, concerning her actual experience under the influence of psychedelics, she makes the following observation: 'a sense that holiness permeates everything even though we are usually not aware of it: a feeling of love, blessedness, and adoration, a feeling that I am being blessed without being particularly deserving and am returning this love toward god; and what I will call a sense of mystical oneness, in which any sense of separation between myself and god disappears.'[112] The author then goes on to point out that if mysticism is 'the belief in an ultimate unity of the universe that can be directly experienced', then mysticism is central to psychedelicism. This pronounced monistic tendency is common in psychedelic literature. Although defining mysticism is not an easy task, if we broadly understand the mystical experience as a direct experience of, or an experience of unity with Ultimate Reality, then psychedelics clearly do engender mystical perception. That is to say, whether the experience develops in an explicitly monistic direction or not, psychedelics do tend to transform the religious impulse into what might be described as a 'mystical experience'.

As to whether the experience is actually a 'religious' experience, or simply the result of distorted perception, the question is, needless to say, very difficult to answer, in that, like consciousness, a first person phenomenon such as mystical experience is difficult to analyse using third person discourse. However, it certainly would seem to be the case that psychedelics do have, in some cases, a 'religious' impact. There is clear evidence that psychedelics do generate what are understood by users to be religious experiences. Certainly the work done by the psychologists Robert Masters and Jean Houston led them to accept such claims: 'In our experience, the evidence would seem to support the contentions of those who assert that an authentic religious experience may occur within the context of the psychedelic drug-state.'[113] This was, according to Leary, certainly the claim of Lama Govinda. Similarly, I have spoken to a person who claims to have had an encounter with Jesus (which eventually led to conversion) whilst under the influence of *psilocybin* ('magic mushrooms'). Again, in the essay by the anonymous psychedelicist, the author insists that, 'In a very real sense, LSD helped me find god – the god within – and I feel I am a better person for it. I am eternally grateful for the blessings and spiritual richness psychedelics have brought into my life. Without them I would be without god. I know many of my co-religionists feel the same.'[114] Similarly, in a lecture sponsored by the American Lutheran Church's Board of Theological Education entitled 'The Seven Tongues of God', Leary provides the following short account of his first experience.

> ... I ate seven of the so-called sacred mushrooms which had been given to me by a scientist from the University of Mexico. During the next five hours, I was whirled through an experience which could be described in many extravagant metaphors but which was, above all and without question, the deepest religious experience of my life ... I have repeated this biochemical and (to me) sacramental ritual several hundred times, and almost every time I have been awed by religious revelations as shattering as the first experience.[115]

Leary then goes on to relate aspects of his research, commenting that this has involved 'several thousand people from all walks of life, including more than 200 full-time religious professionals, about half of whom profess the Christian or Jewish faiths and about half of whom belong to Eastern religions.'[116] These included divinity college deans, chaplains, religious editors and, he says, 'several distinguished religious philosophers.' The result was that (and in Leary's opinion this is a conservative estimate) 'over 75 per cent of these subjects report intense mystico-religious responses, and considerably more than 50 per cent claim that they have had the deepest spiritual experience of their life.'[117] Elsewhere, he claims that

> Five scientific studies by other investigators yield data which indicate that if the setting is supportive, but not spiritual, between 40 to 75% of psychedelic subjects will report intense life-changing philosophic-religious experiences. If the set and the setting are supportive and 'spiritual', then from 40 to 90% of the experiences will be revelatory and mystico-philosophic-religious ... How can these results be disregarded by those concerned with philosophic growth and religious development? These data are even more interesting because the experiments took place in 1962, when individual religious ecstasy – as opposed to religious piety – was highly suspect and when meditation, jogging, yoga, fasting, body consciousness, social-dropout-withdrawal, and sacramental – organic – foods were surrounded with an aura of eccentricity, fear, clandestine secrecy, even imprisonment.[118]

Again, the research done by Masters and Houston demonstrates that it is very common for the psychedelic experience to be interpreted mystically and for apparently non-religious people to adopt a more spiritual worldview as a result of a psychedelic experience: 'between thirty-two and seventy-five percent of psychedelic subjects will report religious-type experiences if the setting is supportive; and in a setting providing religious stimuli, from seventy-five to ninety percent report experiences of a religious or even mystical nature.'[119] Indeed, there are very few people, as far as I can gather, who use hallucinogens and do not have a mystico-religious worldview and interpret their experiences in that way. As I have indicated, it is probably not going too far to say that psychedelic mysticism had much to do with the West turning East in the sixties; certainly they are mutually supportive. This is supported by a leader of a Zen Buddhist community in Colourado, Richard Baker Roshi. Reflecting on the 1960s, he makes the following comment: 'We were in San Francisco right in the middle of the whole scene from '61 on. What Suzuki-Roshi and I noticed was that people who used LSD – and a large percentage of students did – got into [Zen] practice faster than other people ... My feeling is that psychedelics create a taste for a certain kind of experience.'[120] Surya Das, a Buddhist teacher, makes a similar observation: 'I think it is interesting to note that when I get together with my fellow Western dharma teachers, and we consider how our personal paths began (in this life at least) – very few willingly disclose that they actually entered the dharma through the portal of drugs, and the writings of A. Huxley, C. Castaneda,[121] Ram Dass, T. Leary, R.D. Laing, etc. Yet I feel quite certain that psychedelic experience has been a great gate to the dharma for many of our generation.'[122] Clearly there are devotees from a range of traditions who do understand psychedelics to provide authentic, revelatory, life-changing religious experiences.

In the final analysis, it is hard to ignore the fact that hallucinogens do seem to lead to a more 'religious' worldview or to a quest which might be termed 'spiritual'. Indeed, over a century ago now, William James was impressed by the fact that even nitrous oxide and ether 'stimulate the mystical consciousness to an extraordinary degree.' He claimed that he knew people who were convinced that 'in the nitrous oxide trance we have genuine metaphysical revelation.'[123] Similarly, W.T. Stace's work on mysticism led him to the following conclusion regarding the chemically-induced experience: 'It is not a matter of it being *similar* to mystical experience; it is mystical experience.'[124] Again, Stace insists, 'The fact that the experience was induced by drugs has no bearing on its validity.'[125]

Analysis

Whilst comparative studies such as Stace's are impressive, in the final analysis, it is difficult to see how the matter might be conclusively settled. That said, it does deserve some consideration. To this end, and also in an attempt to draw the various lines of thought together, I want to make six points.

(1) To begin with a rather general introductory point, it is difficult to avoid the evidence that psychedelic experiences tend to be of the more monistic type. Indeed, although Zaehner is often too sweeping in his judgements, he was probably correct to coin the term 'panenhenism'[126] ('all-in-one-ism') to describe much psychedelic mystical experience. He even went so far as to suggest that drug-induced mysticism is never fully theistic, in the sense of being an experience of an encounter with a personal God. Although we will see below that Zaehner was wrong to claim that no psychedelic experience is fully theistic, it is certainly true that many psychedelicists report experiences which are more accurately described as panenhenic. Even the Christian psychedelicist mentioned earlier who claims that the Bible is central to her beliefs, says that psychedelics produce 'a sense of mystical oneness, in which any sense of separation between myself and god disappears.' Significantly, we noted her insistence that, in using the term 'god', she is not referring to 'a   personal deity'. Using typically panenhenic language, she writes, 'to me it [by which she means "God"] is best thought of as a force or energy such as gravity, magnetism or light.'[127] Again, this is supported by the work done by psychologists such as Robert Davidson,[128] and Masters and Houston. According to the latter, 'The subject experiences the world as transfigured and unified. He describes himself as having been caught up in an undifferentiated unity wherein the knower, the knowledge, and the known are experienced as a single reality.'[129]

(2) As Michael Stoeber points out in his comparative study of Hindu and Christian mysticism

> mystical experiences are influenced in part by subjective, psychological processes that are grounded in and dependent upon the individual's socio-religious history … [The] emotional and cognitive frameworks of the mystic do influence the kind of experiences she can have. The socio-religious history of the mystic affects not only the way she will interpret the experience, but also the experience itself.[130]

My point is simply that, if this is true of mysticism *per se* (as I believe it is), then it is particularly the case with psychedelic mysticism. It is no coincidence that the man who produced *The Perennial Philosophy* went on to have an essentially Indian pantheistic or panenhenic psychedelic experience. This is where the evidence runs counter to Zaehner's argument in *Mysticism, Sacred and Profane*. Whilst many psychedelic experiences have been similar to Huxley's, others operating within different contexts and with different worldviews report more theistic visions, such as those experienced during the Peyote rituals of the Native American Church. The anthropologist James Slotkin records that, during these rituals the celebrants 'see visions, which may be of Christ himself … Sometimes they become aware of the presence of God and of those personal shortcomings which must be corrected if they are to do his will.'[131] And as Masters and Houston have pointed out, not only are 'the Peyote rituals of the *Native American Church* … frequently productive of theistic religious experiences', but also 'the phenomenon of specifically theistic versions of psychedelic mysticism is an ancient and widespread tradition.'[132] The point is simply that, whilst I would argue that psychedelic experiences are undoubtedly heavily weighted towards panenhenism, contexts, presuppositions, worldviews etc. all contribute to the final shaping of an individual's psychedelic experience.[133]

(3) This emphasis on the importance of contexts, and emotional and cognitive frameworks, not only causes problems for aspects of Zaehner's thesis, but also it undermines the ideas posited by such as McKenna, who claims that religious consciousness was introduced into the human race when evolving humanity ingested psychedelics. For example, John Bowker has persuasively argued that 'LSD does not induce "religious experience" but … it initiates a state of excitation and arousal which is labelled and interpreted by available cues.'[134] Hallucinogens act 'not as innovatory of concepts in abstraction but as reinforcement or confirmation of concepts already formed, or in the process of formation.'[135] Again, Seymour Kety points out that 'no drug ever introduces a new function into an organism; it merely accentuates or inhibits or otherwise modifies a function which already exists. We cannot expect drugs to introduce anything new into the mind or into behaviour, but merely to accentuate or to suppress functions in behaviour which are already present.'[136] Hence, my point is that, rather than psychedelics introducing religious consciousness into the human race, it is far more likely that psychedelic visions have been stimulated by existing religious ideas. As noted above, psychedelics are virtual reality chemicals which fill out two-dimensional theories and doctrines. Psychedelic mysticism is Feuerbachian projection in multicolour. As the normal constraints of the mind are repressed, as plausibility structures bend, and as the dreamlike psychedelic world dawns, one's longings, desires, theories, and beliefs are

allowed to take shape and assume the appearance of objective reality. The psychedelicist is not seeing a new world revealed, but a familiar world through different eyes.

A further implication of this thesis is that Huxley was mistaken in believing that psychedelics enable one to transcend the constraints of culture and language. Psychedelics, dependent as they are on the contents of memory and context, simply make this world *appear* bigger, rather than introducing us to a bigger world.

(4) It should be noted that, whether by sleep deprivation, starvation, isolation, long periods in the sun, staring at an object for long periods of time, repetitive dancing, and many other often obscure and extreme activities, most mystics down the ages have altered their body chemistry in order to achieve the desired mystical effects. Hence, bearing in mind that there are parallels between chemically-induced experiences and other mystical states, are psychedelicists not simply promoting a less arduous way of changing body chemistry and thereby triggering an experience which aids reflection on already existing religious concepts? It seems to me that it is difficult to argue that this is not the case. As a major study of altered states of consciousness demonstrated in 1985, 'the basic dimensions of an LSD experience are a lot like experiences that come from ... non-drug experiences like sensory deprivation or some kinds of sensory overload.'[137] However, I would suggest that, rather than signifying the validity of psychedelics, this places a question mark against some of the mystical experiences produced by extreme asceticism of all varieties. Now, I should say that I am not seeking to simply dismiss all mystical experiences which occur during periods of ascetically-motivated deprivation. My point is simply that, because one would expect people who deny themselves food, sleep, or light for long periods of time to have, for clear physiological reasons, strange experiences (just as people who swallow hallucinogens have strange experiences), the fact that they then do have these experiences means that it would be naïve to simply accept them as the results of a genuine encounter with God. It is very likely that these experiences are little more than the result of altered brain chemistry.

(5) I want now to briefly introduce two useful categories developed many years ago by the English theologian H.H. Farmer: namely 'substantival' religion and 'adjectival' religion.[138] First, substantival religion is, Farmer says, 'religion as constituted by the awareness of the specifically religious objective reality.'[139] In other words, substantival religion is a person's actual awareness of objective, divine reality/God. Secondly, adjectival religion is, to quote the philosopher A.A. Bowman (to whom Farmer is indebted at this point), 'those manifestations which are best

denoted by the epithet *religious* — a religious emotion, disposition or movement.'[140] More specifically, 'adjectival' elements in religion are the 'subjective' elements. These elements are helpful, and even necessary, in that they satisfy fundamental human needs, such as feelings of security, belonging, release, withdrawal from the stresses of everyday life. And, of course, all religion does have adjectival elements in it. For example, I suspect that few Christians have not felt uplifting emotion and a release of stress when singing a favourite hymn in a large congregation. We all do have certain non-religious needs met when we worship. However, the satisfaction of such needs can be experienced apart from any substantival experience of God, and therefore 'apart from the religious consciousness as such'. In other words, all sorts of secular stimuli can engender feelings which we also experience in a religious setting. And whilst substantival religion (religion in which God is involved) may relate itself to these adjectival elements, in that we can be drawn into a deeper experience of God by listening to a particularly moving piece of music or by contemplating the majestic architecture of a cathedral, adjectival religion does not *necessarily* connect with substantival religion.

This substantival-adjectival distinction is useful because it draws attention to the fact that, in Farmer's words, 'profound needs and satisfactions of the human spirit ... can manifest themselves with great power in other contexts than distinctively religious ones.'[141]

That this is so means that certain complications arise which need to be taken into account when assessing the value of psychedelics for inducing mystical experience. When a person's 'needs and their satisfaction are present, particularly if they are present in an intense form, it is easy to suppose that the reality of living, substantival religion is also present in a correspondingly intense degree: whereas, in fact, it may not be present at all, or, if present, only in a quite fleeting and incidental way.'[142] That is to say, because people are aware that certain adjectival elements are often associated with substantival religion, they far too readily assume that the latter is being experienced when they experience the former. Hence, in using hallucinogens a person will provoke changes in the body's chemistry which may in turn lead to adjectivally religious experiences containing little or no substantival content. (As I have already noted, it would be foolish to claim that this is always the case. The 'outsider'/observer is certainly not in a position to assess the content of the 'insider's' experience. I am simply arguing that it is a possibility, perhaps even a probability, that such experiences are wholly adjectival.) Just because I see a bright light, have a strange vision, feel a deep sense of warmth and love, does not mean that I have encountered God.

Bearing the above in mind, it is interesting to note that, near the end of their study, Masters and Houston make the following observation: 'Although the experiences of introvertive drug-state mysticism are integral level experiences, they rarely yield any such radical transformation of the subject's inner and outer life as ordinarily results from the integral level religious experiences.'[143] They surmise that the reason for this 'may be that those few subjects who are sufficiently prepared for and able to attain to introvertive mystical states are already persons of exceptional mental and emotional maturity and stability. The present potential of the person has already in large measure been realised. It is also possible, however, that the aforementioned tendency of these subjects to avoid or minimise the work with psychodynamic materials may preclude the possibility of a transforming experience.'[144] There is, of course, another explanation: there is rarely a 'radical transformation of the subject's inner and outer life' simply because there is a lack of substantival religious content in psychedelic experience, hallucinogens being substances which distort one's perception of reality, rather than being 'sacred' chemicals which engender a divine-human encounter. That said, the problem of the cognitive labelling of experience precludes the possibility of certainty in these matters. In the final analysis, I am not in a position to judge the substantival religious content of another's experience.

(6) Finally, was Huxley right to criticise the church for 'not "baptizing" mescaline or similar drugs and incorporating them into Christian worship'? Clearly there are problems with the psychedelic approach to spirituality for the Christian. The fact that one is so much at the mercy of emotion, instant ideas, and distorted sensory input which gives the material world an appearance of liquidity and malleability makes it very difficult to understand how one might focus on a personal God in any meaningful way. In other words, the subjective so dominates the psychedelicist's mind that the object of worship is transformed or distorted in ways which, whilst awe-inspiring, uplifting and inspirational, are not determined by the object of worship and are thus, arguably, only tenuously 'Christian.'

To develop this line of thought a little – because adjectival elements can arise as a result of that which is *other than* an encounter with God, when they are incorporated into substantival religion they are, argues Farmer, 'prone to act as a disturbing or corrupting or enfeebling factor in it, bringing with them, as it were, an alien influence from their alien origin.'[145] This, I would argue, seems to be the case with psychedelic religion. For example, whilst Zaehner was wrong to claim that psychedelic mysticism is necessarily panenhenic, in that some psychedelic experiences can be described as theistic, we have seen that there is certainly a panenhenic pull, a tendency toward an understanding of unity with nature and the Divine.

The Christian psychedelicist mentioned earlier stressed exactly this. The Christian God of the Bible, she claimed, 'is best thought of as a force or energy such as gravity or magnetism or light', a force with which she believed herself to be united. However, this, I would argue, is problematic, because central to Christian spirituality is a personal relationship with a personal God. Although context is important and may help to shape the experience in a personalist direction, psyche-delics do seem to erode the sense of a divine-human 'I–Thou' relationship. They thereby introduce a 'corrupting or enfeebling factor' into Christian spirituality. As such hallucinogens strike at the heart of a religion which is concerned with the personal and the reconciliation of persons, rather than panenhenic unification, identification, and absorption. In short, because psyche-delic mysticism tends to erode the 'I–Thou' character of divine-human relations, it is not a path Christians would be wise to tread. Indeed, in response to Richard Baker Roshi's comment that 'psychedelics create a taste for a certain kind of experience', I would simply point out that it is a taste for a kind of experience which runs counter to the central pillars of Christian spirituality.

Notes

[1] See C. Pellerin, *Trips: How Hallucinogens Work in Your Brain* (New York: Seven Stories Press, 1998). Pellerin provides an accessible, entertaining, slightly anarchic introduction to the neuroscience behind psychedelics and an overview of current scientific research in the area.

[2] These perceptions were demonstrated in the TV documentary series *Sacred Weeds* (London: TVF/Channel 4, 1999 – repeated 2002), the purpose of which was to monitor the physiological and psychological effects of a variety of legal hallucinogenic substances on willing human subjects.

[3] See A. Hofmann, 'Foreword', in A. Melechi (ed.), *Psychedelica Britannica: Hallucinogenic Drugs in Britain* (London: Turnaround, 1997), ix; R. Jesse, 'Entheogens: A Brief History of their Spiritual Use', in *Tricycle: the Buddhist Review* 6.1 (1996), 61–4.

[4] Anon., 'Psychedelics: a First-Ammendment Right', in *Gnosis* 26 (1993), 31.

[5] R. Rudgley, *The Alchemy of Culture: Intoxicants in Society* (London: British Museum Press, 1993), 144.

[6] P. Devereux, *The Long Trip: A Prehistory of Psychedelia* (London: Penguin, Arkana, 1997), ix. See also P. Devereux, *Places of Power: Measuring the Secret Energy of Sacred Sites* (London: Blandford, 1999), 199–202.

[7] For a good, concise discussion of the significance of Soma in early Vedic ritual see J.L. Brockington, *The Sacred Thread: Hinduism in Its Continuity and Diversity* (Edinburgh: Edinburgh University Press, 1981), 16ff. See also G. Flood, *An Introduction to Hinduism* (Cambridge: Cambridge University Press, 1996), 43–4.

[8] '…[soma] produced hallucinations of the kind made familiar by modern experiments with a variety of drugs and herbs.' A.T. Embree, *The Hindu Tradition* (New York: Vintage, 1972), 21.

[9] W.D. O'Flaherty, in *The Rig Veda: An Anthology*, tr. W.D. O'Flaherty (Harmondsworth: Penguin, 1981), 119.

[10] Rig Veda 8.48.

[11] Ibid., 10.119.

[12] Because of its extraordinary hallucinogenic properties, Gordon Wasson (whose principal area of research was the traditional use of hallucinogenic mushrooms in Mexico) has argued that soma may have been the fly agaric mushroom (Amanita muscaria). However, this has been disputed for the very good reason that it does not grow in India. Having said that, it does grow in the mountains of Afghanistan and the Veda does indicate that it grew high in the mountains. Hence, J.L. Brockington suggests that 'The Aryan incursion into India [through Afghanistan] resulted in the progressive loss of contact with the areas from which the soma plant was acquired and consequent loss of knowledge of its actual nature, which seem to have coincided with a steady increase in elaboration of the ritual.' Brockington, *The Sacred Thread*, 17–8. See also G. Wasson, *Soma: the Divine Mushroom of Immortality, Ethno-Mycological Studies* 1 (New York: Harcourt, Brace & World, 1968); and T. McKenna, *The Food of the Gods* (London: Rider, 1999), ch. 7.

[13] See, for example, Rudgley, *Alchemy of Culture*.

[14] See e.g. M. Harner, 'The Sound of Rushing Water', in A.C. Lehmann & E.J. Myers (eds.), *Magic, Witchcraft & Religion: An Anthropological Study of the Supernatural* (Mountain View: Mayfield Publishing Co., 1997[4]), 122–127. The article first appeared in *Natural History* 77:6 (1968), 28–33.

[15] Perhaps the most important study of this Native American use of peyote is still David Aberle's *The Peyote Religion Among the Navaho* (Norman: University of Oklahoma Press, 1982[2]).

[16] C. Pellerin, *Trips*, 130.

[17] See A. Huxley, *The Doors of Perception and Heaven and Hell* (London: Flamingo, 1994), 45ff.

[18] R.S. de Ropp, 'Psychedelic Drugs', in M. Eliade (ed.), *Encyclopaedia of Religion*, Vol. 12 (New York: Macmillan, 1987), 47. This article has been reprinted in A.C. Lehmann & J.E. Myers (eds.), *Magic, Witchcraft and Religion: An Anthropological Study of the Supernatural* (Mountain View: Mayfield Publishing Company, 1997[4]), 128–33.

[19] For example, we will see below that Timothy Leary referred to LSD as a sacrament, as did Michael Hollingshead (founder of London's World Psychedelic Centre) and others within psychedelic religious groups such as the Polytantric Church. On Hollingshead, see A. Melechi, 'Acid Virgil: the Michael Hollingshead Story', in A. Melechi (ed.), *Psychedelica Britannica*, 87–104.

[20] N. Smart, *Dimensions of the Sacred: An Anatomy of the World's Beliefs* (Berkeley: University of California Press, 1996), 192.

[21] See A. Hofmann, *LSD: My Problem Child* (New York: McGraw Hill, 1980).

[22] On Heard and psychedelics, see J.V. Cody, 'Gerald Heard: Soul Guide to the Beyond Within', in *Gnosis* 26 (1993), 64–70.

[23] For a discussion of the therapeutic use of LSD, see R. Sandison, 'LSD Therapy: A Retrospective', in A. Melechi (ed.), *Psychedelica Britannica*, 53–86.

[24] P. Devereux, *The Long Trip*, xvii–xviii.

[25] P. Haining, 'The Psychedelic Generation: A Retrospective Introduction', in P. Haining (ed.), *The Walls of Illusion: A Psychedelic Retro* (London: Souvenir Press, 1998), 9.

[26] Huxley, *The Doors of Perception and Heaven and Hell*, 8.

[27] Ibid., 11.

[28] A Huxley, *The Perennial Philosophy* (London: Chatto & Windus, 1946).

[29] See particularly R.C. Zaehner, *Mysticism, Sacred and Profane* (Oxford: Oxford University Press, 1961).

[30] See e.g. R.J. Strassman, 'Adverse Reactions to Psychedelic Drugs: A Review of the Literature', *Journal of Nervous and Mental Disease* 172 (1984), 578–9.

[31] Zaehner, *Mysticism, Sacred and Profane*, 19.

[32] Huxley, *The Doors of Perception and Heaven and Hell*, 11.

[33] C.D. Broad, quoted in ibid., 11.

[34] Ibid., 12–3.

[35] J. Hick, *The Fifth Dimension: An Exploration of the Spiritual Realm* (Oxford: Oneworld, 1999), 100.

[36] J. Hick, *An Interpretation of Religion: Human Responses to the Transcendent* (London: Macmillan, 1989), 240–9.

[37] Huxley, 'A Visionary Prediction', in Haining (ed.), *Walls of Illusion*, 212.

[38] Ibid., 215.

[39] Huxley, *The Doors of Perception and Heaven and Hell*, 15.

[40] Ibid., 14.

[41] Huxley, 'A Visionary Prediction', 219–20.

[42] Ibid., 220.

[43] Stanislav Grof, whose work has significantly influenced the development of 'transpersonal psychology', was convinced that LSD facilitated access to the subconscious. He thus argued that the drug had great therapeutic value. See S. Grof, *Realms of the Human Unconscious: Observations from LSD Research* (New York: Viking, 1975).

[44] R.C. Zaehner, *Drugs, Mysticism and Make-Believe* (London: Collins, 1979).

[45] Zaehner, *Mysticism, Sacred and Profane*, 3.

[46] Cody, 'Gerald Heard: Soul Guide to the Beyond Within', 68.

[47] Huxley, quoted in J. Stevens, *Storming Heaven: LSD and the American Dream* (London: Flamingo, 1993), 288.

[48] A. Ginsberg, 'A Tale of the Tribe (from Preface to "Jail Notes")', *Beyond Life With Timothy Leary* (Mercury Records, 1997).

[49] See T. Leary, R. Metzner & R. Alpert, *The Psychedelic Experience: A Manuel Based on the Tibetan Book of the Dead* (New Hyde Park: University Books, 1964).

[50] The translation used by Leary, that by W.Y. Evans-Wentz, is still in print: *The Tibetan Book of the Dead* (Oxford: Oxford University Press, 2000³). This edition includes C.G. Jung's interesting 'Psychological Commentary', tr. R.F.C. Hull, xxxv–lii.

[51] R. Alpert, quoted in Stevens, *Storming Heaven*, 262.

[52] T. Leary, *Flashbacks: An Autobiography* (New York: Tarcher/Putnam, 1990), 212.

[53] Ibid., 214.

[54] Ibid., 215.

[55] Although the book does not use the term 'psychedelic', it is often cited as one of, if not *the* founding text of psychedelia.

[56] T. Leary, 'Homage to Huxley', in *The Politics of Ecstasy* (London: Paladin, 1970), ch. 18.

[57] Stevens, *Storming Heaven*, 264.

[58] Leary, quoted in ibid., 264.

[59] Leary, quoted in ibid., 269–70.

[60] For a brief socio-historical overview of this period, see H.W. Morgan, *Drugs in America: A Social History 1800–1980* (New York: Syracuse University Press, 1981), ch. 8.

[61] Leary, *The Politics of Ecstasy*, 183.

[62] Although there are problems with the term 'cult', my use of it here follows the sociological definition provided by Roy Wallis: a form of religion which does not consider itself to be the sole repository of truth and salvation, but is considered to be deviant religion, rather than respectable religion, by outsiders. See, R. Wallis, *The Road to Total Freedom: A Sociological Analysis of Scientology* (London: Heinemann, 1976), 13.

[63] Ibid., 185.

[64] Ibid., 185.

[65] Although Leary is now dead, a virtual Leary will still invite you into his home, show you around, and impart to you his psychedelic philosophy: see www.leary.com.

[66] T. Leary, *Your Brain is God* (Berkeley: Ronin Publishing, 2001), 85.

[67] Ibid., 74.

[68] Ibid., 85.

[69] For example, he contemplates the possibility of eternal life in the form of his consciousness downloaded onto the Internet.

[70] T. Leary, *Design for Dying* (London: Thorsons, 1997), 131.

[71] Ibid., 133.

[72] Leary, *Politics of Ecstasy*, 115. See also Leary, *Your Brain is God*.

[73] Leary, *Politics of Ecstasy*, 114.

[74] Paul McCartney, quoted in ibid., 93.

75 There were others, of course, who rejected this use of psychedelics and took them as an alternative to religion. Duncan Fallowell, for example, makes the following comment: 'The worst thing about the sixties was the growth of religion, a mental disease if ever there was one. I was never tempted to seek out a guru. It seemed to me that the whole object of approaching reality, which was part of taking acid, was to leave all this mumbo jumbo behind.' J. Green (ed.), *Days in the Life: Voices from the English Underground 1961–1971* (London: Pimlico, 1998), 297.

[76] See S. Whiteley, 'Altered Sounds', and S. Reynolds, 'Back to Eden: Innocence, Indolence and Pastoralism in Psychedelic Music, 1966–1996', in Melechi (ed.), *Psychedelica Britannica*, 121–142, 143–165.

[77] *Beyond Life with Timothy Leary*. If I am not mistaken, the following hip-hop track also puts the words of Leary to music: 'The Time Has Come' by U.N.K.L.E. vs the Major Force Orchestra. This can be found on *Headz: A Soundtrack of Experimental Hip-Hop Jams* (Mo Wax, 1994).

[78] S. Whiteley, 'Altered Sounds', 138.

[79] S.U.N. Project, 'Sex, Drugs and Acid Trance', *Trancentral Eight* (Kickin Records, 1998).

[80] Optica, 'Acid Munchies', *Goa Trance*, Vol. 2 (Rumour Records, n.d.).

[81] Hallucinogen, 'LSD', *Twisted* (Dragonfly Records, 1995).

[82] E.g. Shamanic Tribes on Acid, *The Mad Hatter's Acid Tea Party* (Kinetix, 1998)

[83] S. Whiteley, 'Altered Sounds', in Melechi (ed.), *Psychedelica Britannica*, 139.

[84] B. Osborne, *The A-Z of Club Culture* (London: Sceptre, 1999), 113–4.

[85] See, for example, Jim DeKorne, *Psychedelic Shamanism: the Cultivation, Preparation and Shamanic Use of Psychotropic Plants* (Port Townsend: Loompanics Unlimited, 1994).

[86] Leary, *Your Brain is God*, 17.

[87] Ibid.

[88] See particularly McKenna, *The Food of the Gods*; and also his *The Archaic Revival: Speculations on Psychedelic Mushrooms, the Amazon, Virtual Reality, UFOs, Evolution, Shamanism, the Rebirth of the Goddess, and the End of History* (San Francisco: Harper, 1992).

[89] T. McKenna, 'Foreword', in O.T. Oss & O.N. Oeric, *Psilocybin: Magic Mushroom Grower's Guide. A Handbook for Psilocybin Enthusiasts* (Quick American Publishing, 1986), 14.

[90] See J. Allegro, *The Sacred Mushroom and the Cross* (London: Hodder and Stoughton, 1970).

[91] In her essay 'The God in the Flowerpot', Barnard makes the following comment: 'When we consider the origin of the mythologies and cults related to drug plants, we should surely ask ourselves which, after all, was the more likely to happen first: the spontaneously generated idea of the afterlife in which the disembodied soul, liberated from the restrictions of time and space, experiences eternal bliss, or the accidental discovery of hallucinogenic plants that give a sense of euphoria, dislocate the centre of consciousness, and distort time a space, making them baloon outwardly in greatly expanded vistas...The experience might have had, I should think, an almost explosive effect on the largely dormant minds of men causing them to think of things they had never thought of before. This, if you like, is divine revelation' – quoted in J. Bowker, *The Sense of God: Sociological, Anthropological and Psychological Approaches to the Sense of God* (Oxford: Oxford University Press, 1973), 142.

[92] According to Wasson, 'our remote ancestors, perhaps 4000 years ago, worshipped the mushroom.' Indeed, according to Leary, 'Wasson suggested that every major world religion had originated in the botanical hallucinations of some early visionary. He recited and then translated the ancient names for mushrooms in various Middle Eastern and oriental languages, proposing that they all implied a religious experience – food of the gods, flesh of the gods. Even the name of Jesus Christ in Aramaic, he claimed, was derived from the word for psychedelic mushroom.' Leary, *Flashbacks*, 92, 93.

[93] 'Terence McKenna, among others, has speculated that the evolution from pre-human to human was the result of the synergy of mind-altering plants and the human mind. It seems like a good guess' (Leary, *Design for Dying*, 87).

[94] Idem., <www.deoxy.org/mckenna.htm> (24/4/1999).

[95] Idem., *The Food of the Gods*, xvi.

[96] Idem., 'Preface to the Revised Edition', in O.T. Oss & O.N. Oeric, *Psilocybin*, 8.

[97] Idem., 'Sacred Antidotes: an Interview with Terrence McKenna', *Tricycle: the Buddhist Review* 6:1 (1996), 97.

[98] The Shamen, for example, are clearly sympathetic to the views of McKenna, who appears on their album *Boss Drum* (One Little Indian Ltd, 1991).

[99] E.g. 'Re-evolution', on *Boss Drum*; and 'Re-evolution (Shamen mix)', on *The Shamen Collection* (One Little Indian Ltd, 1998).

[100] See e.g. Frazer Clark's explicit indebtedness to McKenna in F. Clark, 'The Final Word on Drugs', in Melechi (ed.), *Psychedelica Britannica*, 185–204.

[101] Ibid., 199.

[102] An understanding of the spaces made for raves as being sacred sites and of dance itself as being a spiritual activity is increasingly common. 'Our new sacred site is the dance floor and even though the structure of the temple has changed the sacred earth beneath our feet is still the same' Chris Dekker in the booklet accompanying the compilation dance CD *Sacred Sites* (Return to the Source, 1997).

[103] S. Reynolds, 'Back to Eden: Innocence, Indolence and Pastoralism in Psychedelic Music, 1966–1996', in Melechi (ed.), *Psychedelica Britannica*, 159.

[104] J. Bussmann, *Once in a Lifetime: the Crazy Days of Acid House and Afterwards* (London:Virgin Books, 1998), 135.

[105] Ibid., 147.

[106] M.A.Wright, 'The Great British Ecstasy Revolution', in G. McKay (ed.), *DIY Culture: Party and Protest in Nineties Britain* (London:Verso, 1998), 228.

[107] Osborne, *Club Culture*, 273.

[108] M. Collin, *Altered States: the Story of Ecstasy Culture and Acid House* (London: Serpent's Tail, 1998²), 204–5.

[109] See D. Tramacchi, 'Field Tripping: Psychedelic *communitas* and Ritual in the Australian Bush', *Journal of Contemporary Religion* 15 (2000), 201–213.

[110] T. Luhrmann, *Persuasions of the Witch's Craft: Ritual Magic in Contemporary England* (Cambridge: Harvard University Press, 1991), 222.

[111] Anonymous, 'Psychedelics: a First-Ammendment Right', 31.

[112] Ibid.

[113] R.E.L. Masters & J. Houston, *The Varieties of Psychedelic Experience* (London: Anthony Blond, 1966), 257.

[114] Anonymous, 'Psychedelics: a First-Ammendment Right', 32.

[115] Leary, *The Politics of Ecstasy*, 13–4.

[116] Ibid., 14.

[117] Ibid., 14.

[118] Leary, *Your Brain is God*, 11–12.

[119] Masters & Houston, *Varieties of Psychedelic Experience*, 255. This view is supported by Jane Dunlap's psychological study in which she makes the following interesting comment: 'What has been amazing to those of us experimenting with hallucinogens has been the apparent ability of many people in all walks of life to have a sudden partial lifting of the veil between what we usually call consciousness and a mental state in which such great unity and completeness is felt that a permanent attitude of optimism toward life may sometimes be crystallised in a moment…[M]any subjects have reported religious revelations in which God became a reality. Furthermore, their lives have been significantly and permanently changed by the realisation of a kind of divine love which they found within themselves.' J. Dunlap, *Exploring Inner Space: Personal Experiences Under LSD-25* (Harcourt, Brace & World, 1961), 8–9. Perhaps the most famous experiment of this nature was that carried out by Walter Pahnke in Boston University's Marsh Chapel, namely 'the Good Friday experiment' (sensationalised in the press as 'the miracle of Marsh Chapel). The subjects received either psilocybin or a partial placebo (which was designed to produce only very mild effects). The results of the experiment, which were written up in Pahnke's Harvard University doctoral thesis on drug-induced mysticism, demonstrated that significantly more of those who received psilocybin reported religious

experiences than those who had received the placebo. See W.N. Pahnke, 'Drugs and Mysticism', in B. Aaronson and H. Osmond (eds.), *Psychedelics: The Uses and Implications of Hallucinogenic Drugs* (London: Hogarth Press, 1971), 145–65. For Leary's comment on the experiment see Leary, *Your Brain is God*, ch. 2.

[120] Richard Baker, Ram Dass, Joan Halifax & Robert Aitken, 'The Roundtable', in *Tricycle: the Buddhist Review* 6.1 (1996), 103.

[121] Although there is not space to explore at the controversial writings of the anthropologist Carlos Castaneda, his work should be noted as one of the most significant influences upon modern psychedelia and particularly contemporary neo-shamanism. I remember as a teenager in the 1970s spending many hours reading and subsequently discussing with friends accounts of Castaneda's experiences under the direction of Don Juan, a Yaqui Indian sorcerer/shaman. Using particularly peyote, Castaneda claims to have encountered 'a separate reality' populated by spirits, as well as shamans who were able to change into animals. Although Castaneda's first book led to a doctoral thesis, there has been some debate over the veracity of his accounts. Some scholars have simply claimed that the books are little more than imaginative stories, rather than anthropological accounts. Whatever the truth of the matter, his still significant influence is hard to underestimate. He published six books: *The Teachings of Don Juan* (London: Arkana, 1970); *A Separate Reality* (London: Arkana, 1973); *Journey to Ixtlan* (London: Arkana, 1975); *Tales of Power* (London: Arkana, 1990); *The Second Ring of Power* (London: Arkana, 1990); *The Eagle's Gift* (London: Arkana, 1992); *The Art of Dreaming* (San Francisco: HarperCollins, 1994); *Magical Passes* (San Francisco: HarperCollins, 1998); *Fire From Within* (London: Pocket Books, 1998); and *The Wheel of Time* (London: Arkana, 2000).

[122] Surya Dass, 'What Does Being a Buddhist Mean to You?', *Tricycle: the Buddhist Review* 6.1 (1996), 43.

[123] W. James, *Varieties of Religious Experience: A Study in Human Nature* (London: Longman, Green & Co., 1902), 387.

[124] W.T. Stace, quoted in Bowker, *Sense of God*, 144. See also Masters & Houston, *Varieties of Psychedelic Experience*, 312.

[125] Stace, quoted in Leary, *The Politics of Ecstasy*, 69.

[126] Zaehner, *Mysticism, Sacred and Profane*, 28.

[127] Anonymous, 'Psychedelics: a First-Ammendment Right', 31 (my emphasis).

[128] See R. Davidson, 'Appendix', in Dunlap, *Exploring Inner Space*, 210–6: 'On numerous occasions…volunteers have reported sudden insights into the essential unity of all life and the dissolution of their usual thinking in terms of opposites: good-bad, beautiful-ugly, love-hate' (215–6).

[129] Masters & Houston, *Varieties of Psychedelic Experience*, 308.

[130] Michael Stoeber, *Theo-Monistic Mysticism: A Hindu-Christian Comparison* (New York: St Martin's Press, 1994), 1–2.

[131] J. Slotkin, quoted in Masters & Houston, *Varieties of Psychedelic Experience*, 257.

[132] Masters & Houston, *Varieties of Psychedelic Experience*, 257.

[133] As Hick concludes his comparative study of mystical experience, the 'observable facts suggest that mystics within the different traditions do not float free from their cultural conditioning. They are still embodied minds, rooted in their time and place. They bring their Hindu, Buddhist, Jewish, Christian, Muslim or Sikh sets of ideas and expectations with them on the mystical path and are guided by them towards the kind of experience that their tradition recognises and leads them to expect' (*An Interpretation of Religion*, 295).

[134] J. Bowker, *The Sense of God*, 150.

[135] Ibid., 153.

[136] S. Kety, quoted in ibid., 153.

[137] Pellerin, *Trips*, 110. The research was carried out by Adolf Dittrich and involved 1133 individuals from Britain, Switzerland, Germany, Italy, Portugal, and North America. See A. Dittrich, 'Psychological Aspects of Altered States of Consciousness of the LSD Type: Measuring Basic Dimensions and Predicting Individual Differences', in A. Pletscher & D. Ladewig (eds.), *50 Years of LSD: Current Status and Perspectives of Hallucinogens* (New York: Parthenon, 1994), 101–18.

[138] I have discussed these more fully in *H.H. Farmer's Theological Interpretation of Religion: Towards a Personalist Theology of Religions* (New York: Edwin Mellen, 1998), ch. 5.

[139] H.H. Farmer, *Revelation and Religion: Studies in the Theological Interpretation of Religious Types* (Lewiston: Edwin Mellen Press, 1999), 164.

[140] A.A. Bowman, *Studies in the Philosophy of Religion*, Vol. 1 (London: Macmillan, 1938), 4.

[141] Farmer, *Revelation and Religion*, 165.

[142] Ibid., 165.

[143] Masters & Houston, *Varieties of Psychedelic Experience*, 311.

[144] Ibid., 311–12.

[145] Farmer, *Revelation and Religion*, 165.

8

Making Sense of Jewish Mysticism

Traditions of Kabbalah in the Contemporary World

Seth Gottesman

Introduction

The post-war world has witnessed a growth of interest in what is loosely termed *Kabbalah*, the study and practice of Jewish mysticism. In accordance with the post-religious orientation of contemporary Western culture, this new interest has attracted a wide range of individuals and groupings from far beyond the confines of mainstream Judaism and the traditional place of mysticism within communal religious practice.[1] Contemporary interest in *Kabbalah* now ranges from renowned scholars of religion and literature critics through to Jewish psychotherapists, New Age seekers, a broad variety of Pagans, and even media pop icons such as Madonna and Mick Jagger.[2] All are now making use of this long established tradition in new, diverse and interesting ways that present many questions for both students and scholars of contemporary religion and spirituality. These questions are of particular interest to contemporary practitioners of Jewish mysticism themselves, including the traditionally religious, where this approach to Judaism still thrives and provides personal meaning. Therefore any study needs to explore the characteristics of Jewish mysticism that are to be found within mainstream Judaism as well as within the various 'New Age' locations where emerging forms of *Kabbalah* are open to all spiritual seekers, not just those who are ethnically Jewish.

What is Jewish Mysticism?

So just what is Jewish mysticism? What are its specifically Jewish components? And what makes these components mystical? The term *Kabbalah* simply means 'that which is received' and implies an ongoing tradition of mystical interpretation. However, a summary reading of the numerous texts now available on the subject will quickly reveal a number of key concepts that are to be found in both traditional and 'New Age' forms of Jewish mysticism. It is these varied, but inter-related elements that are particular to Jewish mysticism and help to define, or characterise, its unique approach. These key elements can be listed as follows:

(1) The universe is an emanation that emerges from within the divine source of all being, the *Ayin* or 'no-thing' (the nature of which is beyond human understanding). For the creation to occur, *Ayin* must first become *Ayin Sof*, or absolute and limitless potential. Within this absolute potential a 'space' is then made into which the creation, in the initial form of limitless divine light or *Ayin Sof Aur,* can then emerge.

(2) The divine emanation includes, as well as the earth, the invisible realms of heaven and hell. The process of emanation is described in Genesis. However the initial source of creation, the *Ayin-Ayin Sof-Ayin Sof Aur* relationship, is not dealt with in Genesis as it belongs to the oral tradition of Torah. Consequently, the Jewish mystical understanding of creation is significantly different to an understanding that is only derived from a reading of Genesis, a text located within a wider 'mystical' context of oral explanation and interpretation.

(3) Unlike the divine trinity of *Ayin, Ayin Sof* and *Ayin Sof Aur*, the divine emanation can be conceptually understood and represented. This is most commonly seen in the well known 'Tree of Life' diagram based upon ten 'qualities' of being or *Sephirot*; Crown, Wisdom, Understanding, Mercy, Judgement, Beauty, Reverberation, Endurance, Foundation and Kingdom. The divine emanation is now understood as a set of eternal relationships occurring between these qualities that the 'Tree of Life' diagram seeks to represent in a form that is deliberately speculative and open-ended in character, rather than fixed (see Figure 15.1, p. 134).

(4) There are an additional 22 links or paths that can be superimposed upon the 'Tree of Life' that correspond with the 22 letters or character 'symbols' of the Hebrew alphabet. Each symbolic letter has its own meaning and represents a further divine quality of being. Both systems (letters and sephirot) inter-locate to create a combined symbolic representation of the created cosmos that is again quite deliberately open to variant and speculative interpretations.

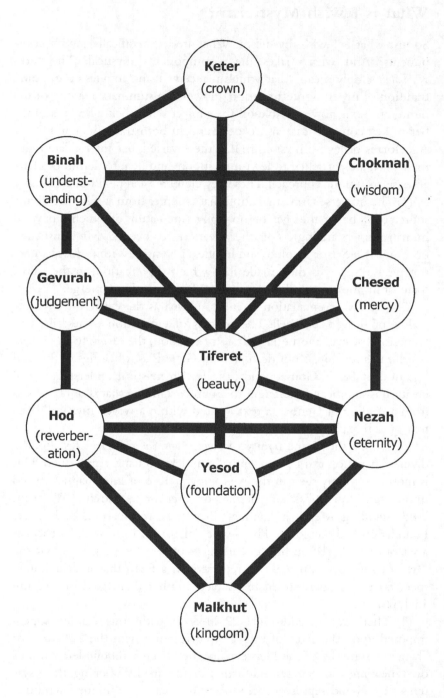

Figure 8.1: The kabbalistric 'Tree of life' glyph

(5) Common to both symbolic systems is the view that the emana-tion/creation has a fourfold structure arranged in a descending hierarchy beneath the eternal realm of *Ayin/Ayin Sof/Ayin Sof Aur*. These overlapping levels consist of the spiritual realm (*Atzilut*), the men-tal realm (*Beriah*), the psychological realm (*Yetzirah*), and the material realm (*Assiyah*). Perceiving this fourfold structure in all areas of life is an important goal for the Jewish mystic, given that it is the basic pattern or template used by deity to create the cosmos or macrocosm. Given that human beings are created in the image of God (also in accordance with this fourfold pattern) we are able to perceive the harmonic functioning of the universe, both within ourselves and also outside of ourselves in the material and non-material worlds of existence. (6) Bearing the above in mind, the Jewish mystic seeks to reflect this divine order within the fourfold microcosm of their own life, a macrocosm-microcosm relation-ship comparable with other forms of mysticism found within the major world religions (e.g. Islamic Sufism). This process of mystical 'orienta-tion' is developed and supported through individual engagement with the symbolic systems noted above, but in a manner most appropriate to each individual and their cultural location. This will inevitably result in a diversity of differing forms of mystical practises which include intel-lectual speculation, a variety of systems of meditation, different forms of devotional prayer and also practical magic.

Differing approaches to the concepts and beliefs outlined above do go some way to explaining the diversity that characterises Jewish mysti-cism, a diversity that is, in many ways, actually resistant to any definitive definition. That is to say, any fixed definition is problematic given the emphasis that Jewish mysticism places upon personal interpretation and resulting individual practises. This mystical individualism ensures that spiritual insights do not remain at a purely conceptual level. That the mystic strives to move beyond the purely conceptual and theoretical is clearly in accordance with a fourfold understanding of the nature of the cosmos that descends from the spiritual realm through the intellectual, emotional and material realms.

Jewish mysticism, therefore, should not be understood simply as a body of historical and contemporary mystical texts. Having said that, these texts do build upon and continually add to an established and evolving body of individual thought and practises. Some texts, such as the medieval *Zohar* (the 'Book of Splendour'), have exercised a greater influence than other texts during certain historical periods, but the indi-vidualistic nature of Jewish mysticism ultimately prevents fixed defini-tions or any claims to the exclusive validity of a particular approach or interpretation. Rather, it is the common body of mythic and symbolic systems of thought outlined above that characterise Jewish mysticism, together with an acceptance of the individualistic nature of mystical practise in establishing a personal relationship within the cosmos as a whole. Indeed, this perspective goes some way to explaining Jewish mysticism's growing popularity in a New Age setting, in that it openly embraces and celebrates personal interpretation and diversity in a highly eclectic manner. In other words, *Kabbalah* lends itself to certain forms of contemporary Western 'Self spirituality'. Here the practice of *Kabbalah*, now often accessed through 'teach-yourself' book form or weekend workshops can be compared with other 'dislocated' spiritual practises such as Yoga or Chakra-based systems for understanding health and spiritual well-being.[3] According to Waren Kenton, a contemporary practitioner, popular author and teacher of *Kabbalah*

> *Kabbalah* is the inner and mystical aspect of Judaism. It is the perennial Teaching about the Attributes of the Divine, the nature of the universe and the destiny of man in Judaic terms. Imparted by revelation, it has been handed down over the centuries by a discreet tradition that has periodically changed the mythological and metaphysical format to meet the spiritual and cultural needs of different places and epoch. This long and broadly-spread history has given *Kabbalah* a remarkably rich and wide variety of images of reality which appear to the unversed eye as strange, obscure, and even at times contradictory or corrupt.[4]

The above definition also acknowledges that much of the mystical approach is also to be found within the symbol and stories of the Hebrew Bible or *Tenach*. However, an essential difference between Jewish mysticism and mainstream Judaism lies in the interpretation of this same material (e.g. the mystic's understanding of the cosmological levels or realms of being that describe a fourfold universe is distinctive). Therefore, Jewish mysticism stands as a particular interpretative stance within mainstream Judaism, with results that may clearly distinguish it from mainstream Judaism, even though common sources or core texts are often shared.[5] As Warren Kenton's definition suggests, this diversity can be understood in terms of differing mythological or symbolic values when compared to conventional religious Judaism, despite many shared 'Judaic terms'. Indeed, as noted above, Jewish mysticism not only exists within mainstream Judaism as a particular interpretative perspective, but it is increasingly the case that it operates effectively within a wider community of 'mystically orientated' individuals who are interested in practising *Kabbalah* as a highly personal form of spirituality, free from the limitations of traditional religion.[6]

The Contemporary Study of Jewish Mysticism

The wide availability of easily obtainable publications has now resulted in a number of popular texts that claim to either teach or explain Jewish mysticism. Many of these popular texts seek to relate *Kabbalah* to traditional Judaism, often as a means to reinvigorate Jewish interest in what many see as a declining faith in the West. However, other texts seek to reinterpret mystical material and practices in a manner appropriate to today's world. One such explanatory text, now over fifty years old, is Gershom Scholem's *Major Trends in Jewish Mysticism*[7] which legitimised the study of Jewish mysticism for a post-war generation engaging with Eastern religious mystical thought as part of the emerging counter culture. Prior to this publication, the historical study of Judaism had, as a nineteenth-century post-enlightenment and rational discipline, ignored or rejected the significance of mysticism and mystical texts. As well as being a widely popular book on the subject, the quality and scholarship apparent in *Major Trends* also redefined the historical study of Judaism. Scholem clearly recognised the power of conceptual ideas, especially when expressed in new, radical and esoteric forms such as devotional mysticism, an understandable position for a Jewish historian born in Germany in the early twentieth century:

> If the great task of Jewish scholarship in our generation, the task of rewriting Jewish history with a deeper understanding of the interplay of religious, political and social forces, is to be successfully carried out there is an urgent need for a new elucidation of the function which Jewish mysticism has had at varying periods, of its ideals, and of its approach to the various problems arising from the actual conditions of such times.[8]

Scholem explored the relationship between Jewish mystical literature and Jewish history. Mystical texts, he pointed out, often interpreted (within mysticism's broader cosmology) biblical monotheism in a way that contextualised it and made it relevant to a particular age. This included the second century *Sefer Yetzira* ('Book of Formation'), a mystical interpretation of Genesis which taught that the universe was created from thirty-two paths consisting of the ten *sephirot* and the twenty-two letters of the Hebrew alphabet, which, as we have seen, are key defining characteristics of Jewish mysticism. This literature emerged as part of the rabbinical codification of both oral and written material that had previously 'free-floated' within Jewish culture at various levels, including that of folk tradition and superstition. Scholem provided clear insights into the rabbinical transformation of Judaism that was occurring in the early centuries of the common era, as well as an understanding of the nature of mystical material that existed prior to the development of rabbinical Judaism.[9]

Scholem's most significant contribution to the study of Jewish mysticism is his work on the medieval *Zohar* text and the later sixteenth century exile-cosmology of the *Kabbalist* Isaac Luria. In his study of the *Zohar* he provides a convincing argument that the emergence of the rational, intellectual approach to interpretation favoured by many Rabbi's, although successful in its own terms, was somewhat limited in its approach to cosmology. Therefore, to balance the rabbinical transformation of the faith, the *Kabbalah* emerged as a form of interpretation that fully embraced the cosmological dimension of existence in which ordinary, everyday life was seen as an essential part of the divine whole. Thus, the contrasting intellectual and mystical approaches to faith were successful in different ways because they addressed different human needs:

> Mystics and philosophers are, as it were, both aristocrats of thought; yet *Kabbalah* succeeded in establishing a connection between its own (mystical) world and certain elemental impulses operative in every human mind. It did not turn its back upon the primitive side of life, that all important region where mortals are afraid of life and in fear of death, and derive scant wisdom from rational philosophy.[10]

In contrast to purely intellectual interpretations of faith, the emerging *Kabbalah* fully embraced the problem of evil in the world and its mystical yet practical answers quickly proved to be successful throughout all levels of Jewish society. Mystical texts, such as the 'theosophical' *Zohar*, would become highly popular throughout the expanding Jewish world. But of equal significance at this time were charismatic individuals such as the *Kabbalist* Abraham Abulafia who sought a more emotional and ecstatic approach through the contemplation of Hebrew letters, and what we might now recognise mental free-association techniques and Hebrew 'mantra' meditations. Here Jewish mysticism is clearly characterised by differing approaches emphasising either the 'contemplative' and the theosophical[11] or the 'ecstatic' and the emotional, a situation inevitably resulting in a variety of different mystical practies. For example, the highly complex exile-cosmology of Isaac Luria, with its close connection to Gnostic thought through the concept of a 'hidden' creator, found favour amongst speculative, theosophical mystics including the seventeenth-century Jewish false messiah, Shabbetai-Zvi. But rather paradoxically Luria's approach to *Kabbalah* found its greatest expression amongst the nineteenth-century eastern European Hasidism with its simple, joyful and emotionally ecstatic approach to mystical experience.[12] Where the traumatic experience of a destructive false messiah within the global Jewish community saw a backlash against dangerous mystical speculation (and a discrediting of speculative mystical interpretation in general prior to the European enlightenment) Hasidism utilised aspects of Luria's 'irrational' yet complex cosmology to empower this emerging form of devotional Judaism. Over two centuries Hasidism has withstood condemnation from within the Jewish world, violent persecution, exile and ultimately the Holocaust. It has also played a significant role in the rebuilding of post-war Judaism and its characteristic fervour and enthusiasm, particularly apparent in the Lubuvitcher community, is a direct result of its mystical cosmology and the personal response that this demands.[13]

A later generation of scholars acknowledge their debt to Scholem and urge the reading of his key works in any 'serious' study of Jewish mysticism. But there is also some criticism of Scholem, not least, it is argued, because he provides an inadequate conceptual framework within which a student might explore and examine the deeper meaning of mystical symbolism. This, it could be argued, is simply the result of the inevitable limits of any historical approach which necessarily seeks to locate ideas in history, rather than explore deeper meanings and significances. More recent scholars, such as David Blumenthal, have sought to broaden the historical perspective with an experiential approach to the texts themselves which asks these 'deeper', more personal questions:

> In approaching this selection, the reader will want to study it carefully. Not all of it will be clear, but with work, most of it will yield to human understanding. Note the fusion of numerological, body and theosophic techniques and themes ... There are also questions the reader will want to pose: Why is this material so involved, so complex? What is the mystic trying to achieve? To what would this praxis lead if it were given free rein to follow its own inner logic? Does it correspond to our conception, or awareness, of the divine? Why? Why not? Can a 'modern' person be this kind of mystic? Why? Why not?[14]

However, the study is again ultimately limited in that it confines itself to the 'canonised' traditional texts and, at times, is rather dismissive of more contemporary works that may lack the 'classical purity' of the *Zohar* (now legitimised for academic study by Scholem). These contemporary texts, with their emphasis on popular psychology and self-development, although clearly Jewish mystical texts, are rejected on the grounds of literary quality. A similar self-limitation in definition is apparent in the work of literary critic Harold Bloom, who also derives his stance from that of Scholem. Whilst it is unsurprising that Bloom, in his definition of Jewish mysticism, should emphasise theosophical texts such as the *Zohar* as being the most important within the tradition, this is done at the expense of other equally important texts derived from the less intellectually oriented ecstatic approach.

> Mysticism is a word that I have avoided in this essay, for *Kabbalah* seems to me more of an interpretative and mythical tradition than a mystical one. There were *Kabbalistic* ecstatic's, and sub-traditions of meditative intensities, of prayer conducted in an esoteric manner. But *Kabbalah* differs finally from Christian or Eastern mysticism in being more a mode of intellectual speculation than a way of union with God.[15]

Here Bloom suggests that biblically-based symbolism and theosophical interpretation is at the heart of Jewish mysticism, which is largely understood as a creative tension between monotheism, Gnosticism and Neoplatonism.[16] This definition, derived from Scholem's historical interpretation of Jewish mysticism as a history of conflicting ideas, again locates a 'pure' *Kabbalah* in the historic past. This focus upon the intellectual aspects of *Kabbalah* results in the reduced status of ecstatic and meditative practices, such as numerology and meditations on the Hebrew letters, although these have often been central aspects of mystical thought and practise at certain periods in history (including today). Again, this stance is dismissive of contemporary *Kabbalistic* texts, even if they are seen to be 'palpably sincere and even authentically enthusiastic in their obfuscations.'[17] Bloom welcomes the work of Scholem as necessary for all 'rational students' of the subject. However, not only did Scholem never claim to be an 'insider', a practising *Kabbalist*, but the Jewish mystical tradition clearly does contain 'irrational', ecstatic and devotional material which an approach such as Bloom's can too easily overlook or, even, dismiss. In the final analysis, the outcome of Scholem's dominance in this area, in terms of academic study, is a tendency to locate Jewish mysticism as a quasi-intellectual tradition from the historical past, rather than understanding it to be an important contemporary manifestation of mystical religion.

Hence, whilst Scholem's work is important, there is a need for students of Jewish mysticism to move beyond it and to recognise the need for the study of contemporary *Kabbalism* which is often characterised by irrationalism, ecstatic spirituality, warm devotion and postmodern eclecticism.

The 'New Kabbalah'

Perhaps a key factor in this neglect of contemporary *Kabbalah* by scholars of Jewish mysticism is that they often seek to establish connections between their historical studies and the wider Jewish world of today. Many contemporary *Kabbalists* have a limited or confrontational relationship with the Jewish world and often choose to locate themselves some way outside of the traditional Jewish religious community. Hence, practical *Kabbalah* can be observed in the ultra-orthodox approach of the Hasidim, and also within the world of New Age spirituality. Certainly Jewish mysticism is much more than Bloom's 'mode of intellectual speculation', the range of contemporary practises extending from contemplative meditation through to the making and wearing of magical amulets and even psychotherapeutic techniques for personal self-healing.

Such diversity goes back to the differing theosophical and ecstatic approaches to Jewish mysticism, for just as the *Zohar* can be legitimately seen as the essential theosophical text, so the ecstatic practises of Abraham Abulafia from the same period are also vital to an understanding of the ecstatic approach. The key here is not what Abulafia taught in terms of Hebrew letter meditations, but rather that each of his students was asked to develop a deeply personal relationship with the practices of mystical speculation, and that these students were often drawn from beyond the confines of traditional Judaism. Abulafia's decision to teach women and non-Jews, much to the outrage of the mainstream Jewish world, can be seen in relation to the development of Christian and magical *Kabbalah*, two important traditions that are also worthy of study in their own right. It, in addition, is Abulafia's approach to Jewish mysticism, an approach which makes use of the language and spiritual concerns of the age in a contextualised and highly individualistic manner, which enables Jewish mysticism to stand on its own terms, firmly outside of the body of mainstream communal Judaism.

It is the continuation of Abulafia's approach that now characterises the practise of *Kabbalah* in its contemporary New Age location as a spiritual tradition open to all. Therefore, within contemporary *Kabbalah* it is also possible to determine some specific themes, the first of which is a growing proliferation of accessible modern texts and study group 'workshops' that are largely open to all. These modern practises still rely upon a cosmological perspective, as seen, for example, in the comparative approach of the spiritual healer Caroline Myss in her comparisons between the Tree of Life, the Hindu *chakra* system and the Christian sacraments in understanding energy centres for esoteric healing.[18] But for many contemporary practitioners the most important task is to explain the symbolism of Jewish mysticism in terms of contemporary psychology:

> One of the unique aspects of *Kabbalah* is that it is a living tradition. It is – and always has been – adaptable to the needs and circumstances of successive generations. While in the past it has proven both a rich source of mystical lore and a firm foundation for a system of practical magic, it is now being reinterpreted by modern masters as a means of self-analysis and self-development. Contemporary *Kabbalists* highlight the tradition's potential for personal development, concentrating on the ever reverberating parallels between the physical, the psyche and the spirit. Such teachings lie at the heart of the true tradition.[19]

It is not unusual for contemporary texts on the *Kabbalah* to make reference to Scholem and his groundbreaking historical research, for he too recognised the psychological nature of Jewish mystical symbolism, even though as a historian he was unwilling to explore its deeper meanings at a psychological level. However, modern *Kabbalists* have no such reservations and teacher-authors such as Paul Roland, Warren Kenton and Perle Besserman all emphasise an accessible psychological dimension. That said, there are a variety of interpretations and definitions of Jewish mysticism that point to different understandings of the relationship between *Kabbalah* and popular psychology. Besserman and her own teacher, the highly influential Areyeh Kaplan, emphasise the practice of meditation as the ultimate purpose and orientation of *Kabbalah* and its mystical symbolism, a psychological understanding being a necessary stepping stone to the final mystical goal.[20] Indeed, Besserman, for example, suggests that there is a hierarchy of *Kabbalistic* activities, the highest being the spiritual act of meditation, which directly corresponds with a fourfold understanding of creation.[21]

A similar position is explored by Charles Poncé who, like Besserman, makes reference to Scholem's work and also acknowledges the limitations of the historical approach.[22] However, following a Jungian interpretation of Jewish mystical material, Poncé is concerned about any limitations imposed upon the spiritual tradition of *Kabbalah* when it is reduced to mere clinical psychology.[23] His position also goes some way to explain modern *Kabbalah's* location within the 'New Age' spiritual communit, in that it offers a speculative yet personal mythology that attracts both Jews and non-Jews alike, while traditional forms of religion, such as Judaism continue to lose relevancy in the western world.

> The findings of modern researchers imply that if a mythology can no longer be experienced by the individual at the collective level, within the context of a societal or communal myth, and if this type of thinking and experiencing is essential to being, then one can usually find the impetus or spirit behind these old systems of trans-formation manifesting itself in new forms. The purpose, therefore, in studying such systems as the *Kabbalah* is to reacquaint modern man with the nature and structure of the mythical dimension.[24]

It is this emphasis upon the symbolic and mythical dimension within Jewish mysticism, clearly related to modern psychology by Warren Kenton, Perle Besserman and others, that is the focus of these new forms of *Kabbalah*. But even in these contemporary, post-religious forms, Jewish mysticism remains the personal study of mystical material and its resulting practises.

Conclusion

To clearly define the *Kabbalah* is, if not quite an impossible task, a very difficult and complex one. This is because there is a need to recognise the limited, personal perspectives of practitioners and scholars when attempting any such definition. The attempt to characterise Jewish mys-ticism encouraged in this study is one that seeks to move away from spe-cific definitions and instead looks at the totality and function of Jewish mysticism as a whole. In many ways this view is in accordance with the functional definition offered by Scholem: 'Jewish mysticism in its vari-ous forms represents an attempt to interpret the religious values of Judaism in terms of mystical values.'[25] Jewish mysticism is a mode of spir-itual expression that embraces individualism and diversity as it seeks constant re-expression in the most appropriate manner. Unlike Bloom, I would argue that it is a tradition that is not designed to function in a purely abstract, intellectual manner. Rather, Jewish mysticism always seeks a place in the practical world of human needs and human experience. In pursuit of this goal these mystical values are now increasingly 'going it alone', divorced from their relationship with the religious values of traditional Judaism. Consequently, the practice of *Kabbalah* is increasingly successful in the contemporary world where the language of psychology (often transpersonal psychology), rather than that of traditional religion, seeks to relate people to their inner selves and to establish for them a place within the cosmos.

Yet some accommodation between both traditional and mystical parties is still possible, as is demonstrated in the work of Howard Cooper, who is both a Rabbi and a psychotherapist. In *A Sense of Belonging*, a penetrating analysis of contemporary British Judaism, Cooper recognises that behind the outward practise of traditional faith there lies an inner, personal world of symbolic meaning and personal interpretation. This inner world is as subject to growth and change as the human body itself, a process he seeks to capture in deeply mythic and therefore *Kabbalistic* language: 'The ancient Hebrew writers conveyed the complex moral and psychological realism of their ideas through storytelling. The importance of this cannot be overstated: to convey mythology through narrative necessitates that the meaning of events is not fixed ... Meaning was a process that required continual revision.'[26]

The tradition of Jewish mysticism in all its forms is about the ongoing construction of personal meaning, but it needs to be recognised that this is a process that goes far beyond the limits of an abstract, intellectual exercise. This results in a tradition that can happily incorporate complex, and at times apparently contradictory, material. And yet the function of this tradition, whether encountered 'inside' mainstream Judaism or 'outside' in the post-religious world of New Age spirituality is, in essence very simple. Jewish mysticism is recognition of the importance of constructing effective personal meaning within one's life whilst simultaneously establishing a relationship with the divine processes of the cosmos. This has always been, and remains, the core purpose and practise of Jewish mysticism because all life including our own participates in the radical monotheism of 'one being' as found in the declaration of Jewish faith, the *Shema*: 'Hear O' Israel, the Lord is our God, the Lord is One.'

Notes

[1] T. Eagleton, *The Idea of Culture* (Oxford: Blackwell, 2000), 40.
[2] C. Graham & M. Martin, 'Can the Kabbalah Save the Jaggers?', *The Mail on Sunday* (16 January, 2000), 3.
[3] C. Myss, *Anatomy of the Spirit* (New York: Bantam Books, 1997), 72–80.

⁴ W. Kenton, *Kabbalah: Tradition of Hidden Knowledge* (London: Thames & Hudson, 1979), 4.

⁵ Ibid., 12–14.

⁶ P. Besserman, *Kabbalah and Jewish Mysticism* (Boston: Shambhala, 1997), 145.

⁷ G. Scholem, *Major Trends in Jewish Mysticism* (New York: Schoken Books, 1995).

⁸ Ibid., xxvi

⁹ Ibid., 47.

¹⁰ Ibid., xxvi.

¹¹ The term 'theosophical' often tends to be associated with the occult and spiritualistic ideas and practises of the Theosophical Society. However, this is not the sense in which it used here, which is much closer to the definition provided by the *Oxford English Dictionary*: 'wisdom concerning God or the divine.' More precisely, it can be understood as structured philosophical speculation combined with mythic, symbolic and poetic elements based upon personal experience. See R.E. Montgomery, *The Visionary D.H. Lawrence: Beyond Philosophy and Art* (Cambridge: Cambridge University Press, 1994), 169–70.

¹² D. Cohn-Sherbok, *Jewish Mysticism: An Anthology* (Oxford: Oneworld, 1995), 173–4.

¹³ K. Hanson, *Kabbalah: Three Thousand Years of Mystic Tradition* (Tulsa, Oklahoma: Council Oak Books, 1998), 213.

¹⁴ D. Blumenthal, *Understanding Jewish Mysticism: A Source Reader* (New York: KTAV Publishing House Inc., 1978), 172.

¹⁵ H. Bloom, *Kabbalah and Criticism* (London: Continuum, 1999), 47.

¹⁶ Ibid., 15.

¹⁷ Ibid., 17.

¹⁸ Myss, *Anatomy of the Spirit*.

¹⁹ P. Roland, *Kabbalah* (London: Piatkus, 1999), 27.

²⁰ P. Besserman, *Kabbalah and Jewish Mysticism* (Boston: Shambhala, 1997), 28–9.

²¹ Ibid., 124–38.

²² C. Poncé, *Kabbalah: An Introduction and Illumination for the World Today* (London: Quest Books, 1979), 260–2.

²³ Ibid., 263.

²⁴ Ibid., 258.

²⁵ Scholem, *Major Trends*, 10.

²⁶ H. Cooper & P. Morrison, *A Sense of Belonging: Dilemmas of British Jewish Identity* (London: Weidenfeld & Nicolson, 1991), 195.

9

Eastern Orthodox Mystical Theology

Don Fairbairn

In a volume such as this, one of the significant difficulties is that of how to categorise various kinds of mysticism as Christian or non-Christian. Of course, the forms of spirituality discussed in part three are clearly non-Christian, but what of those in part two? Is the mysticism of the Desert Fathers or of John of the Cross really Christian? In one sense, we can say that these forms of spirituality are Christian, because they spring from the Christian tradition. But Protestants, and especially evangelical Protestants, often find these forms of spirituality to be so suspicious that we are reluctant to call them Christian at all. In fact, some of us may want to say that no form of mysticism is really Christian.

The difficulty of categorising a form of mysticism as Christian or non-Christian is especially acute when one considers Eastern Orthodox mystical theology. Many Westerners argue that Orthodox spirituality is actually a thinly-disguised form of Neoplatonic philosophy. In that pagan philosophical system (somewhat akin to Eastern monism), the human soul was thought to bear an essential connection with the divine realm, and salvation consisted of the soul's struggle to escape the prison-house of the body and return to union with the divine. A person under-took this struggle by seeking to mortify the desires of his or her body in order to achieve a state of *apatheia* (passionlessness), so as to participate in the divine realm through *theosis* (usually translated 'deification'). In some ways, Orthodox mysticism sounds very similar: it speaks of the struggle to attain *apatheia* and of an upward ascent of the soul to one-ness with God. It insists on a true union of the creature with God and describes salvation with the term *theosis*. It is certainly tempting for Westerners to regard Eastern Orthodox mysticism as nothing more than a baptised form of Eastern pagan philosophical spirituality.

But in other ways, Orthodox mysticism sounds decidedly theistic and Christian: it insists that God is absolutely transcendent and that no creature can participate in his essence at all; it argues that only the incarnation of God the Son avails to bring people into union with God; it resolutely denies that deification involves any form of absorption of the mystic into God; and ironically, it insists that Western Christians are the ones who are too philosophical in our spiritual approach. According to Eastern theologians, the Western church has lost sight of the true God of the Bible in the midst of its philosophical descriptions of what sort of character God should have. In contrast, Eastern theologians insist, Orthodox mysticism provides the means to a vision of the true God himself, the way to genuine union with him.

What then is one to make of Eastern Orthodox mysticism? Is it a sub-Christian spirituality which has drunk too deeply from the wells of pagan philosophy and Asian monism and whose Christian appearance is largely a veneer? Is it a truly Christian approach to spirituality, one from which Western evangelicals can learn? Or is it *the* truly Christian approach to union with God, a deeply biblical mysticism which serves as an indictment of our superficial spirituality? In order even to begin considering such questions, one must attempt to fathom three key Eastern Orthodox mystical ideas, all of which will sound very foreign to Western ears and will be easy to misinterpret. These are the concept of apophaticism (negative theology), the idea of *theosis* or deification as the vision of divine light, and the distinction between the essence and energies of God. In this essay, I will consider these three ideas and will then offer an evangelical appraisal of Orthodox mysticism. As I attempt to explain Eastern Orthodox mystical theology, I will rely on the writings of three major shapers of the mystical tradition: the anonymous sixth century Syrian writer known as Pseudo-Dionysius,[1] the seventh-century Greek theologian Maximus Confessor, and the fourteenth-century Greek monk Gregory Palamas. I will also use the writings of four twentieth-century Eastern Orthodox theologians who have done much to revive the Orthodox mystical tradition and interpret it to a Western audience: Vladimir Lossky, Alexander Schmemann, John Zizioulas, and John Meyendorff.

Apophaticism and Union with God

One of the most striking differences between the Eastern and Western churches is that in the West, mysticism has usually been seen as somewhat of a fringe movement; whereas in the East, it lies at the very heart of Orthodox spirituality. Historically, the Western church has been preoccupied with institutional questions, and the authority figures have usually been the members of the church hierarchy: the bishops and priests. More recently (that is, in the last 800 years or so), it has been the

teachers and scholars, the 'learned theologians' who have been held up
as the shapers of Christian life and doctrine. Consequently, the Western
approach to Christian life tends to be very knowledge-based. We study
the texts of the Bible and listen to what our teachers say about those
texts so as to learn the truth, and we seek to apply that truth to our lives.
We believe that knowledge *about* God will lead us to knowledge *of* God.
The mystics, the people who have sought a more direct experience of
God apart from rational knowledge, have normally had somewhat of an
uneasy relationship with the institutional authority figures. They have
usually been seen as a threat, since they held their own experience of
God to be more normative than the official teaching of the church.

However, in the East, monasticism has long provided the spiritual
ideal which Christians have sought to emulate, and as a result, most of
Orthodox theology has grown out of the mystical striving for union
with God which characterised early Eastern monastic life. Monasticism
effectively began in the Egyptian desert in the third century, and for the
Desert Fathers, Christian life was not primarily a quest to *learn about*
God, but rather a struggle to purify oneself so as to be able to *see* God.
Toward the end of the fourth century, Evagrius Ponticus provided the
classic articulation of the monastic life by dividing it into three steps:
praktike, *psychike*, and *theologike*. *Praktike* was the preliminary step of rid-
ding oneself of vices[2] and acquiring virtues, so as to achieve the calm-
ness of soul and freedom from passion known as *apatheia*. *Psychike* was
the more advanced step of struggling directly with demons, once one
had achieved a measure of success at mastering one's own passions. The
final step of *theologike* consisted of pure contemplation of the Trinity.[3]
Evagrius and the Egyptian Desert Fathers believed that this contemplation was contentless – a union with God which derived not from rational knowledge (and the pride which could accompany it), but from
ignorance.[4] This focus on union with and vision of God rather than on
knowledge, inherited from the early monastic movement, was to form
the heart of Eastern mysticism.

In the early sixth century, Eastern mystical theology began to come
of age through the writings of Pseudo-Dionysius, who adopted an
Evagrian spirituality and sharpened the idea that union with God came
from ignorance, not knowledge. Pseudo-Dionysius begins his short treatise *Mystical Theology* with a poem:

> Trinity! Higher than any being, any divinity, any goodness!
> Guide of Christians in the wisdom of heaven!
> Lead us up beyond unknowing and light,
> up to the farthest, highest peak of mystic scripture,

> where the mysteries of God's Word
> lie simple, absolute, and unchangeable
> in the brilliant darkness of a hidden silence.
> Amid the deepest shadow
> they pour overwhelming light on what is most manifest.
> Amid the wholly unsensed and unseen
> they completely fill our sightless minds
> with treasures beyond all beauty.[5]

In this poem two things are especially noteworthy. First, the writer sees
Christian life as an ascent to the mysteries of God. He refers to the
Trinity as a guide and beseeches God to lead Christians upward. Here
the writer clearly reflects the Evagrian spirituality which he has inherited from monasticism. Second, and much more striking, Pseudo-
Dionysius delights in using paradox to describe God. The Trinity is
higher than any divinity, that is, beyond any idea of divinity we can har-
bour in our minds. But not only is God beyond our comprehension; he
is even 'beyond unknowing.' His mysteries lie in 'brilliant darkness' and
'pour overwhelming light' from 'deepest shadow.' God's mysteries grant
us 'treasures beyond all beauty,' but only when our minds have become
'sightless.'

In these paradoxes we find a window into the world of Orthodox
mystical theology. The mystic does not seek to learn more about God,
so as to move closer to a full comprehension of his character. Rather,
one attempts to strip one's mind of any idea of God (what the writer
calls 'any divinity'), to become blind to any philosophical speculation
about who God is. God is darkness, shadow, and we can enter the shadow and be united to him only when we render ourselves sightless.
There, in the darkness of ignorance, we shall find the overwhelming
light of God's presence. Following this poem, Pseudo-Dionysius restates
his idea more prosaically:

> My friend, my advice to you as you look for a sight of the myste-
> rious things, is to leave behind you everything perceived and
> understood, everything perceptible and understandable, all that is
> not and all that is, and, with your understanding laid aside, to strive
> upward as much as you can toward union with him who is beyond
> all being and knowledge. By an undivided and absolute abandon-
> ment of yourself and everything, shedding all and freed from all,
> you will be uplifted to the ray of the divine shadow which is above
> everything that is.[6]

Maximus Confessor (one of the great heroes of the Eastern church
because of his role in the seventh century monothelite controversy)

writes similarly that it is precarious to speak of God verbally and is much safer to contemplate him without words and only in the soul. He asserts that only one 'who has gone beyond the whole nature of the intelligible and the sensible realities and has purified himself from every particularity stemming from his origin, can encounter God with a soul naked and stripped of representations of him.'[7] Twentieth-century theologian Vladimir Lossky explains this idea more fully when he asserts that a knowledge-based theology would see the theologian as the subject of an inquiry and God as its object. In contrast to such a view, mystical theology is no longer aware of the distinction between the subject (the theologian) and the object (God). He continues, 'God no longer presents Himself as object, for it is no more a question of knowledge but of union. Negative theology is thus a way towards mystical union with God, whose nature remains incomprehensible to us.'[8]

What Lossky calls 'negative theology' goes by the more technical name 'apophatic theology' or 'apophaticism.' This is an approach to theology and spiritual life which proceeds by declaring what is not true of God, rather than by affirming what is true of him (an approach which is called 'kataphatic theology'). Instead of listing and explaining the attributes of God (as a Western theologian would probably do), an Eastern theologian is more likely to consider aspects of our world which show imperfection or incompleteness and to declare that God does not have these qualities. God is not limited; he is not temporal; he is not sinful, etc. Of course, Western theology does this as well, but there are two crucial differences between the way East and West use such negative techniques. First, when Westerners assert that God is beyond our comprehension, we are usually making a statement about the limits of *our* knowledge and ability to grasp God's character; we are not making a statement about *God himself*. We believe that God *could* be perfectly understood, but *we* cannot understand him, since we are too limited. However, when Orthodox mysticism declares God to be incomprehensible, it is making a statement about God himself. In God's essence, in the mystery of the inner life of the three trinitarian persons, there is *nothing to understand*; all is darkness and mystery. The second difference grows directly out of the first: If Westerners seek to describe what God is not, it is for the purpose of being able eventually to say what he is. For example, if we say that God is not limited, we are in effect asserting that he is present everywhere, able to act everywhere, able to know all things about all places and times, etc. But when an Eastern Orthodox mystic describes what God is not, the purpose is quite different. The mystic seeks not simply to rid his or her mind of *false or inadequate* concepts of God (so as to replace them with true, adequate concepts), but rather to rid the mind of *all* concepts of God. Through such concentration on what is not true of God, a person eventually reaches the point at which he or she can no longer make negations: in the face of God's mysteriousness one cannot declare whether some quality is true of him or not. In a very striking summary, Lossky asserts, 'The apophaticism of Orthodox theology is a prostration before the living God, radically ungraspable, unobjectifiable, and unknowable.'[9]

To a Western Christian, this may seem close to agnosticism, as if Orthodox mysticism did not believe we can actually know anything about God's character. This is not the case, as Pseudo-Dionysius makes clear in a treatise on the divine names. He writes that we come to union with God only through the power given to the biblical writers,

> a power by which, in a manner surpassing speech and knowledge, we reach a union superior to anything available to us by way of our own abilities or activities in the realm of discourse or of intellect. This is why we must not dare to resort to words or conceptions concerning that hidden divinity which transcends being, apart from what the sacred scriptures have divinely revealed.[10]

A bit later in the treatise, he continues:

> With a wise silence we do honour to the inexpressible. We are raised up to the enlightening beams of the sacred scriptures, and with these to illuminate us, with our beings shaped to songs of praise, we behold the divine light, in a manner befitting us, and our praise resounds for that generous Source of all holy enlightenment, a Source which has told us about itself in the holy words of scripture.[11]

These important passages indicate that apophatic spirituality does not reject *all* knowledge about God, for the writer directly states that the Source of enlightenment (God) 'has told us about itself.' Rather, apophaticism rejects any knowledge about God which comes from non-biblical sources. When Pseudo-Dionysius refers to 'our own abilities' and 'the realm of discourse or intellect,' he is criticising the arrogance which leads us to think that we can understand God on our own, using our own minds and processes of rational enquiry. We can know something about God, but what we know comes from revelation, from Scripture, not from what the West would later call 'natural theology.'

Modern theologian Alexander Schmemann offers a very helpful explanation of the difference between rational knowledge derived from philosophical enquiry and personal knowledge derived from revelation:

Holy' is the real name of God, of the God 'not of scholars and philosophers,' but of the living God of faith. The knowledge about God results in definitions and distinctions. The knowledge of God leads to this one, incomprehensible, yet obvious and inescapable word: holy. And in this word we express both that God is the Absolutely Other, the One about whom we can know nothing, and that He is the end of all our hunger, all our desires, the inaccessible One who mobilizes our wills, the mysterious treasure that attracts us, and there is really nothing to know but Him.[12]

Here Schmemann contrasts the concept of God which one gains from philosophical reasoning (kataphatic theology) with the true God, the living God of faith. Rationally or philosophically, we can know nothing about God, since rational argument leads us only to an idea of the sort of God who is philosophically plausible, not to the true God. And in fact, there is nothing about God's essence and inner life which is accessible to rational investigation; there is nothing to know. However, through a mystical spirituality founded on Scripture, we can know the true God. The apophaticism of Orthodox mysticism is a way of acknowledging that God is incomprehensible and beyond us, while still seeking to be united to him.

Theosis and the Vision of Divine Light

If Orthodox spirituality revolves around the struggle to purify one's soul and strip one's mind of knowledge so as to be united with God, I need now to consider what such union entails, and I will do so through an examination of the Orthodox understanding of *theosis* or deification. In the early Eastern church (and to some degree in the early Western church as well), two of the biblical concepts which received great attention were the statement in Psalm 82:6, 'You are "gods"; you are all sons of the Most High,' and the declaration in 2 Peter 1:4 that through God's promises we may 'participate in the divine nature and escape the corruption in the world caused by evil desires.' These passages provided the basis for the patristic belief that human beings were called to become gods in some sense, to become partakers of the divine nature, and the idea of deification was one of the primary concepts by which the early church expressed its understanding of salvation. Maximus Confessor was one of the key writers who combined the patristic idea of deification with apophatic theology and Evagrian spirituality. He explains as folows:

> When we fulfil the Father's will he renders us similar to the angels in their adoration, as we imitate them by reflecting the heavenly blessedness in the conduct of our life. From there he leads us finally in the supreme ascent in divine realities to the Father of lights wherein he makes us sharers in the divine nature by participating in the grace of the Spirit, through which we receive the title of God's children and become clothed entirely with the complete person who is the author of this grace ...[13]

Notice that as in Evagrius and Pseudo-Dionysius, so also in this passage salvation is an ascent of the Christian to God, an ascent which becomes possible as the believer fulfils God's will through moral purification and holy conduct. This ascent enables one to share in the divine nature, and Maximus interprets this to mean that the believer is fully clothed with the person of Christ. Elsewhere, he elaborates further, 'In Christ who is God and the Word of the Father there dwells in bodily form the complete fullness of deity by essence; in us the fullness of deity dwells by grace whenever we have formed in ourselves every virtue and wisdom, lacking in no way which is possible to man in the faithful reproduction of the archetype.'[14] Here we see that Maximus maintains a distinction between God/Christ and the believer; it is not true that Christians are absorbed into God or become gods in essence. However, the fullness of deity which dwells essentially in Christ comes to dwell in the mystic by grace.

This deification, this 'fullness of deity' which the mystic acquires by grace, includes several aspects. First, it means that by grace the Christian gains some of the qualities which characterise God. It is important to note that the expression 'partakers of the divine nature' in 2 Peter 1:4 comes at the beginning of a discussion of godly characteristics which people should strive to acquire: goodness, knowledge, self-control, perseverance, godliness, kindness, and love (2 Pet. 1:5–9). Therefore, deification consists partly of partaking by grace and one's own action in those qualities which God shares with humanity. A second aspect of deification is human partaking in God's immortality, sharing in his eternal existence. 2 Peter 1:4 describes partaking of the divine nature as escaping corruption, and one of the major ideas of the early church was that humanity was called to move from a mortal, corruptible state to an immortal, incorruptible one. This aspect of deification corresponds to what evangelicals call 'eternal life,' sharing God's immortality and enjoying his presence eternally. A third component of deification is fellowship or communion with God. Modern Greek theologian John Zizioulas writes that *theosis* 'means participation not in the nature or substance of

God, but in His personal existence. The goal of salvation is that the personal life which is realised in God should also be realized on the level of human existence.'[15] What Zizioulas means by God's personal life is the communion, the fellowship which the persons of the Trinity share with one another. When Orthodox mystics speak of becoming sons of God (one should remember that Ps. 82:6 links being 'gods' with being 'sons of the Most High'), they are referring to believers' sharing in the sonship which God the Son has with his Father, the communion within the Trinity.

In Orthodox mysticism, these three aspects of *theosis* are all subsumed under a broader concept, that of divine light. To the Orthodox, God's characteristics or qualities, his immortal existence, and his personal communion within the Trinity are all associated with the fact that God is light. It is light which shines forth from God, enabling believers to acquire his characteristics. It is light which conquers the darkness of death and brings immortality. It is light which shines forth from Father to Son and Spirit. When the mystic is purified to the point of being able to see the divine light, he is able to share in divine life. The concept of God as light is prominent in the Johannine writings of the New Testament, and has long been a major part of Eastern Orthodox mysticism. (One should remember that Pseudo-Dionysius' poem quoted above is full of light/darkness imagery: the mysteries of God lie beyond light and reside in brilliant darkness.) The centrality of divine light in Orthodox mysticism was given its greatest expression in the writings of Gregory Palamas in the fourteenth century. Palamas was involved in a controversy with a Greek-Italian monk, Barlaam, who argued that apophaticism led to absolute ignorance of God. In contrast, Palamas insisted that apophaticism led to genuine knowledge of God himself, and the major way he explained and defended this assertion was by using the image of divine light. On the far side of the apophatic darkness, we are brought to the uncreated light of Christ our God. We are able to see God and thus to know him in a mystical sense.

For Palamas (and for Orthodox mysticism as a whole), the two biblical events which provide the paradigm for mystical spirituality are Jesus' transfiguration (Mt. 17; Mk. 9; Lk. 9) and Paul's vision of the third heaven (2 Cor. 12). The Orthodox insist that at the transfiguration, it was not Jesus who changed, but rather Peter, James, and John. Jesus remained who he always was – the divine Son of God. But the disciples' hearts were purified so that they could see him as he really was. The light which shone forth from Jesus' clothes and his face was the uncreated light of God, the eternal radiance of the Trinity. Orthodox mystical spirituality is devoted to the purification of the mind, soul, and body, so that one can behold this eternal light. Palamas writes, 'He [Christ] was divine before, but He bestowed at the time of His Transfiguration a divine power upon the eyes of the apostles and enabled them to look up and see for themselves. This light, then, was not a hallucination but will remain for eternity, and has existed from the beginning.'[16] Similarly, Palamas takes the inexpressible things which Paul saw and heard in his vision to be a revelation of the divine light:

> This most joyful reality, which ravished Paul, and made his mind go out from every creature but yet return entirely to himself – this he beheld as a light of revelation, though not of sensible bodies; a light without limit, depth, height or lateral extension. He saw absolutely no limit to his vision and to the light which shone round about him; but rather it was as it were a sun infinitely brighter and greater than the universe, with himself standing in the midst of it, having become all eye.[17]

One should note here that as Palamas interprets Paul's vision, Paul himself is reduced to an eye, to the one who sees. He is no longer an actor in the drama, but rather he is the one who is bathed in God's light. To see this light is to be ravished, to be full of joy. This is the goal of the Eastern Orthodox mystic.

It is the mystical concept of divine light which enables one to understand the apophatic theology which I discussed in the previous section. Even though God is completely inaccessible to our minds, to our philosophical investigation, he is not pure darkness. Rather, he can be seen through the process of deification, a process which rejects the path of knowledge as a means to God and instead embraces the path of moral and spiritual purification. To say it a different way, apophaticism is not a theological method leading to utter agnosticism about God; it is a spiritual pathway which prepares one to see God. John Meyendorff explains Palamas' thought as follows:

> The major point made by Palamas in his *Triads* is precisely that the darkness of the cloud surrounding God is not an empty darkness. While eliminating all perceptions of the senses, or of the mind, it nevertheless places man before a Presence, revealed to a transfigured mind and a purified body. Thus, divine 'unknowability does not mean agnosticism, or refusal to know God,' but is a preliminary step for a 'change of heart and mind enabling us to attain to the contemplation of the reality which reveals itself to us as it raises us to God.'[18]

In fact, it is somewhat ironic that Eastern mysticism, in spite of its apophaticism, is generally a much sunnier and more optimistic spirituality than is Western Christian mysticism. The focus on the transfiguration lifts Orthodox mystics up to aspire to the divine light and to bask in God's presence, whereas the Western concentration on the cross often drives Catholic mystics to a dark spirituality focused on faithfulness to God in spite of his apparent absence. Lossky aptly summarises this difference when he writes:

> Both the heroic attitude of the great saints of Western Christendom, a prey to the sorrow of tragic separation from God, and the dark night of the soul considered as a way, as a spiritual necessity, are unknown in the spirituality of the Eastern church … The one proves its fidelity to Christ in the solitude and abandonment of the night of Gethsemane, the other gains certainty of union with God in the light of the Transfiguration.[19]

Lossky's assertions in this passage do not serve simply to point out a difference between Eastern and Western spirituality; they also serve as an oblique criticism of the West. Because Western theology is so knowledge-oriented and thus (according to the East) leads only to a philosophical concept of God, those within the Western church who have a deep spiritual hunger recognise the bankruptcy of focusing on the God of scholars and philosophers. They are thus forced into a spirituality of darkness as they grope for the absent God of the Bible (absent because he is not the one being proclaimed by the theologians). In contrast, Eastern spirituality begins with a rejection of philosophical concepts of God, confesses that the true God is inaccessible to reason, and seeks purification so as to see and be united to that God. If this implied criticism is accurate, then Orthodox mysticism constitutes a significant indictment of the theology (and the mysticism) of the Western church. But before I attempt to respond to this criticism, I will examine one other idea which is crucial for an understanding of Eastern mysticism.

God's Essence and Energies

In the section of this essay on apophaticism, I asserted that Orthodox mystics see God as being fundamentally incomprehensible in his essence. Not only are *we* unable to understand God's inner life, but there is *nothing there to understand*, nothing which is accessible to rational investigation. At that point, I raised and responded to the potential Western objection that such an approach to spirituality would lead to agnosticism. Even if one accepts the Orthodox response to this objection (namely, that although we cannot know God rationally or philosophically, we can know him mystically through *theosis* on the basis of revelation), one may still have grave reservations about the role of revelation in Orthodox mysticism. If there really is nothing to know about God's inner life, then what *does* Scripture reveal about God? What does even the incarnation reveal about God, if his essence remains absolutely hidden from us even after God the Son has lived among us on earth?

Orthodoxy responds to this question by making a distinction between the essence and energies of God, and this distinction is central to all of Orthodox mysticism.[20] The first Eastern theologians to make a marked distinction between what we can and cannot know of God were the Cappadocians[21] in the fourth century, and Pseudo-Dionysius and Maximus Confessor developed this idea further. As in the case of the concept of divine light, so also here, it was Gregory Palamas who gave the essence-energies distinction its classic formulation. During the controversy with Barlaam, Palamas repeatedly insisted that what the mystic sees in the vision of divine light is not the essence of God. For example, he writes that the human mind 'will attain to that light and will become worthy of a supernatural vision of God, not seeing the divine essence, but seeing God by a revelation appropriate and analogous to Him.'[22] Later he asserts, 'God, while remaining entirely in Himself, dwells entirely in us by His superessential power; and communicates to us not His nature, but His proper glory and splendour.'[23] And during one of his many discussions of Paul's vision in 2 Cor. 12, Palamas writes:

> But in attaining this condition, the divine Paul could not participate absolutely in the divine essence, for the essence of God goes beyond even non-being by reason of transcendence, since it is also 'more-than-God'.

> But there is also a 'not-being by transcendence' spiritually visible to the senses of the soul, which is definitely not the divine essence, but a glory and radiance inseparable from His nature, by which He unites Himself only to those who are worthy, whether angels or men.[24]

In spite of the difficult terminology Palamas uses in these passages, it is clear that he is making a distinction between God's essence and some aspect outside of his essence, in which God allows us to participate. He describes this participable element of God as an analogous revelation, as power, glory, splendour, and radiance. He insists that it is here, in this

radiance or power which is distinct from the essence and yet not separate from the essence, that people can be united to God. In Orthodox
mystical theology, this participable element is called God's energies.

In his extant writings, Palamas devotes a great deal of attention to the
energies of God. He writes:

> Neither the uncreated goodness, nor the eternal glory, nor the
> divine life nor things akin to these *are* simply the superessential
> essence of God, for God transcends them all as Cause. But we say
> He is life, goodness and so forth, and give Him these names,
> because of the revelatory energies and powers of the Superessential
> … But since God is entirely present in each of the divine energies,
> we name Him from each of them, although it is clear that He tran-
> scends all of them.[25]

And near the end of his discussion, he concludes: 'Do you not see that
these divine energies are *in* God, and remain invisible to the created faculties? Yet the saints see them, because they have transcended themselves
with the help of the Spirit.'[26] Notice that Palamas tries to do three things
in these passages. First, he wants to distinguish the essence of God from
his energies, as he has sought to do throughout his writings. Second, he
attempts to show that the essence of God is beyond his energies and is
their cause. Third, he seeks to demonstrate that although the energies are
logically secondary to God's essence, they are nevertheless uncreated and
eternal, and they exist in God. It is these energies which the mystic sees
when he or she is united to God and thus enabled to see the divine
light.

What then *are* the essence and energies of God? A Westerner would
be likely to see God's essence as that which is common to the persons
of the Trinity and to define it as the sum total of the attributes which all
three trinitarian persons possess. He or she might then be inclined to see
the energies of God as something analogous to what Westerners call
God's actions. But this does not do justice to the Eastern understanding
of essence and energies. Rather, in Eastern Orthodox thought, God's
essence is more likely to be described as his inner divine life, the life of
the trinitarian persons.[27] The energies, then, seem to include both what
Westerners would call God's attributes and things such as his will and
providence.[28] Lossky writes that one can call the energies God's attributes, as long as 'one remembers that these dynamic and concrete attributes have nothing in common with the concept-attributes with which
God is credited in the abstract and sterile theology of the manuals [that
is, systematic theology textbooks written by Westerners or influenced by

Western theology].'[29] It is clear that the purpose of the essence/energies distinction, like the purpose of apophatic theology in general, is in part to protect the Orthodox understanding of God from reduction to a philosophical idea. It is not really a relevant question whether God's energies correspond to what we would call attributes or to what we would call actions. The point is rather that God cannot be reduced to an idea which we can describe in philosophical language. But at the same time, he is not a bare existence, a featureless 'It.' Rather, he is a personal being whose inner life is thoroughly unknown to us, but who makes himself known by showing us his outward life, his glory, power, and loving communion as they are directed toward his creation. Orthodox mysticism seeks not to peer into the mystery of God's inner life, but rather to rejoice that he has granted us to share in his outward life as we are united to him in his energies.

One Evangelical's Appraisal

Now that I have briefly treated apophaticism, *theosis* as divine light, and the Orthodox distinction between God's essence and energies, we are in a somewhat better position to begin addressing the questions with which I began this essay. As I do this, I will consider the typical Western charge that Orthodox mysticism is simply a disguised form of Neoplatonic philosophy or Eastern monism. Then I will turn my attention to the Orthodox charge that Western theology leads not to the true God but to the God of philosophical speculation. Finally, I will point out two aspects of Orthodox mysticism which I believe should be of concern to evangelicals.

From what we have seen of Pseudo-Dionysius, Maximus, and especially Palamas, it should be clear that Orthodox mystical theology is very far removed from either Eastern monism or Neoplatonism in two crucial ways. First, in contrast to both monism (in which all things have an essential connection with the divine) and Neoplatonism (in which the human soul has an essential connection with the divine, even though the material realm does not), Orthodoxy insists not only that God is *distinct* from us in essence, but even that he is *incomprehensible* to us in essence. Throughout the process of *theosis*, God remains absolutely transcendent, and we do not participate in him in any essential or ontological way at all. No aspect of our being (not even the soul) is naturally or essentially divine, nor is any aspect of our being absorbed into deity so as to *become* essentially divine. Second, as I have hinted throughout this essay, in Orthodox mysticism God is understood in distinctly personal terms, which is irreconcilable with the impersonal concept of God in monism and Neoplatonism. There, God is utterly alone and cares nothing for the progress of the soul toward him.[30] But in Orthodox mysticism, God shares in personal communion within himself between the persons of the Trinity, and he longs to share this communion with us. He has made the path of deification possible through the incarnation, and he is deeply concerned about the quest of the mystic to see his divine light.[31] In light of these two differences, there is no basis for the Western charge that Orthodox mystical theology is monistic or pagan. If it ever does happen that Eastern Orthodox mystics understand deification in an absorption-istic way, that understanding is an aberration from the intent of Orthodox mysticism. The best of Orthodox mystical theology is clearly theistic and in fact trinitarian, with no blurring of the line between God and his creatures.

The Orthodox accusation that Western kataphatic theology leads to a philosophical idea of God, rather than to the true God, is a very serious one. How often do we allow philosophical (or even scientific) notions of the way God should be to lead us astray from the biblical depiction of God? How often is our theology characterised by intellectual rigour and logical consistency, but at the same time by a lack of awe and won-der as we bow before our God? How often are we content with simply knowing things about God, rather than seeking to know God deeply and personally? When I study Orthodox mystical theology, questions such as these haunt me, and perhaps they *should haunt* all of us. In fact, one of the most valuable lessons which an evangelical can take away from the study of Orthodox mysticism is the reminder that our quest is not ultimately for knowledge (be it philosophically-based or even bibli-cally-based). Our quest is for God himself, and even the Bible is but a means to a greater end. The Eastern mystics hungered (and hunger) for God himself. Do we?

However, when one considers the charge itself, I have to disagree that kataphatic theology leads to philosophical ideas, rather than to the true God of Scripture. It doubtless *can* lead away from God, and we should certainly be on our guard so as not to long more for philosophical con-sistency than for the truth. But I do not believe that kataphaticism and knowledge-based approaches to theology *necessarily* fail to lead believers to the true God. As we have seen, apophaticism seeks to prostrate the believer before the God who is beyond his or her comprehension. But I suggest that kataphaticism, if carried out with a spirit of humility and reverence, will accomplish the same purpose. The more deeply we seek to probe the mysteries of God, the more we learn about his character and his ways with people. We study so as to learn so as to understand. But do we seek understanding so as to fancy that we have mastered the subject 'God'? (This, I think, is what the Orthodox fear we are doing.) No, we seek (or at least, we *should* seek) understanding so that we can marvel all the more at the vastness of our God, the vastness of the one who is far beyond our comprehension. Orthodox mysticism stands in opposition to a knowledge-based theology, but I suggest that a reverent knowledge-based theology (one which is based firmly on Scripture and which uses philosophical and scientific reasoning tools only with great care) can actually enhance personal experience of God by leading us both to a deeper appreciation for who he is and by helping us to marvel at the degree to which he transcends our comprehension.

As I conclude this essay, I now turn to two aspects of Orthodox mysticism which I believe are problematic from an evangelical perspective. The first of these is the distinction between God's essence and energies. I completely concur with the Orthodox that we must uphold both the transcendence and the immanence of God. He is and always will be distinct from the creatures he has made, and yet at the same time, he does genuinely share himself with us in grace and salvation. To be saved is not simply to receive a gift *from* God; it is to receive *God himself*. However, I do not think that the essence-energies distinction is an appropriate way to uphold God's transcendence and immanence, for two reasons. First, I believe that what God shares with us when he saves us is much more personal than the word 'energies' suggests. Most of the words which Orthodox mystics use to explain God's energies (light, radiance, power, glory, etc.) have to do with rather impersonal aspects of God's being. The use of these words gives the impression that what we can share is simply some of God's qualities. Of course, this *is* part of what God gives us when he saves us, but not the only part, and, I think, not the main part. Rather, the heart of salvation is that God grants us to share in the very love and fellowship which the Father has with the Son and the Spirit. Perhaps I am misreading the mystical sources, but this element of salvation seems to be lacking or underemphasized in Orthodox mystical literature.

My second reason for finding the essence/energies distinction problematic is that is seems to cast some doubt on the integrity of God. I agree fully with the Orthodox that we cannot have any direct knowledge of God's inner trinitarian life; we know, see, and experience only what he reveals of himself. But by making a distinction between God's outer life (energies) and his inner life (essence), Orthodox mysticism seems to imply that the two are not consistent with each other. At the very least, it implies that we cannot be *confident* that the way God reveals himself to us accurately reflects who he really is in his essence, in his inner life. In contrast, evangelicals would all assert that God's integrity demands that he reveal himself as he really is. As a result, we can be confident of his inner nature, his inner life, because we see that inner life reflected in his outer life – in the way he reveals himself and the way he interacts with his creatures. If one could not be sure that the way God reveals himself is the way he really is, then the result would be a potential crisis of confidence about the very character of God. Again, it is possible that I am misreading the sources, but I fear that the essence/energies distinction opens the door for such a crisis of confidence about God's character.

The second aspect of Orthodox mysticism which I find problematic has to do with the relation between divine and human action in the process of deification. The Orthodox insist that God's action always takes precedence: It was the incarnation, the descent of God the Son to the human sphere, which made possible the way of human ascent and union with God. It is grace which undergirds and enables the mystic's striving for deification. Nevertheless, at several points in this essay it has emerged that Orthodox mysticism places much more emphasis on the uplifting of humanity to the divine sphere than it does on the descent of God to the human sphere. The focus of spiritual life is the mystic's effort to purify himself or herself, to transform the mind, body, and soul, so as to be able to see the divine light. God's grace assists these efforts, but there is comparatively little emphasis on grace as that which *grants* union with God to the believer. One is left with the impression that union with God is the culmination of spiritual life, a climax reached substantially through the mystic's own (grace-assisted) efforts.

It seems to me that a more biblical paradigm would be one in which God initially grants both union with himself and the desire to appreciate and deepen that union. Thus grace and union with God would be the prerequisites for a life of seeking divine light, rather than the mystic's effort being a prerequisite for union with God. The resulting mysticism would be one in which the Christian seeks to experience God more deeply and thus to know more fully who he or she already is as a child of God. Perhaps this is what Orthodox mysticism does intend to do. It is possible that the Eastern mystic's quest for divine light actually represents an attempt to enjoy more fully what he or she already has in Christ, and that it merely seems (to this critical outsider) that the mystic is attempting to *gain* something he or she does not yet have. But I fear that too often Eastern mysticism operates from a paradigm of seeking a not-yet-present union with God, rather than seeking to know the God to whom one has already been united through faith. If my fears are justified, then Eastern Orthodox mysticism does stray significantly from the pattern we evangelicals find in Scripture.

This second problem points to one of the central questions about Christian mysticism, and indeed about all of Christian spirituality, Eastern or Western. Is Christian life primarily an anticipation of a future beatitude toward which one must strive, or an act of gratitude for a beatitude which God has already given? Of course, it is both, and when a Westerner criticises Eastern mysticism for failing to emphasise the 'already' dimension of Christian life, he or she must recognise that we are vulnerable to the charge that we care too little for the 'not yet' aspect of spirituality. At the same time, I do not believe it is sufficient for us simply to say that we need to stress both the 'already' and the 'not yet.' To say that union with God awaits a future time after a person has been purified through *theosis* is to place too much of the responsibility (and the credit) for Christian life in the hands of the believer, the mystic. If we really long to see God more fully, then we *do* need to seek purification, holiness, and sanctification. But more than that, we need to recognise that we are able to seek God's face only because he has already made us his own children. Only then will our focus be on the God who has saved us and is saving us, rather than on our own efforts as the prerequisite for obtaining the vision of God. When we begin to see our efforts as primary and God's grace as secondary, we have obscured what is truly Christian about Christian spirituality. Grace can never be allowed to hold an auxiliary role in Christian life; it must be primary (and thus the human response to or participation in grace must be auxiliary), from beginning to end.

Notes

[1] This writer is so-called because he adopted the persona of Dionysius the Areopagite, one of those who was converted to Christianity as a result of Paul's sermon on the Areopagus in Athens in Acts 17. Nothing is known of the writer's life, and some scholars place him as early as the third century, but his writings surfaced rather suddenly in the early sixth century in Syrian circles. His writings very quickly assumed considerable spiritual authority, partly because of his famous pseudonym.

[2] Evagrius identified eight principal vices: gluttony, fornication, covetousness, anger, dejection, weariness, vainglory, and pride. In the West, dejection and weariness were later combined into 'sloth,' thus producing the medieval list of the 'seven deadly sins'.

[3] This three-step approach to monastic life was itself based on the thought of the great third century Alexandrian theologian Origen, who saw Christian life as a progression from the active sphere of struggling with one's passions to the contemplative realm of meditation on God. Both Origen and his follower

Evagrius were condemned at the Council of Constantinople in 553 (mainly because of their cosmology, which saw all of the souls as having been eternally existent), but in spite of that condemnation, their spirituality has been immensely influential.

[4] This progression from *praktike* to *psychike* to *theologike* is clear from Evagrius' *Practicus* and *Kephalaia gnostica*, which unfortunately have not been translated into English. See A. Louth, *The Origins of the Christian Mystical Tradition* (Oxford: Clarendon, 1981), 102–9, for an excellent summary of Evagrius' approach to spirituality. See also Mark Elliot's discussion of the Desert Fathers in this volume (ch. 10).

[5] Pseudo-Dionysius, *Mystical Theology* 1.1, in *Pseudo-Dionysius: The Complete Works*, Classics of Western Spirituality (New York: Paulist, 1987), 135.

[6] Ibid.

[7] Maximus, *Chapters on Knowledge* 1.83, in *Maximus Confessor: Selected Writings*, Classics of Western Spirituality (New York: Paulist, 1985), 144.

[8] V. Lossky, *The Mystical Theology of the Eastern Church* (Cambridge: James Clark & Co., 1957), 28.

[9] V. Lossky, *Orthodox Theology: An Introduction* (Crestwood, New York: St Vladimir's Seminary Press, 1978), 24.

[10] Pseudo-Dionysius, *The Divine Names* 1.1, in *Pseudo-Dionysius: The Complete Works*, 49.

[11] Ibid. 1.2, 50–1.

[12] A. Schmemann, *For the Life of the World: Sacraments and Orthodoxy* (Crestwood, NY: St Vladimir's Seminary Press, 1973), 32 (emphasis his).

[13] Maximus, *Commentary on the* Our Father 5, 118.

[14] Maximus, *Chapters on Knowledge* 2.21, 152.

[15] J. Zizioulas, *Being as Communion: Studies in Personhood and the Church* (Crestwood, NY: St Vladimir's Seminary Press, 1985), 49–50.

[16] Palamas, *Triads* 3.1.15, in *Gregory Palamas: The Triads*, Classics of Western Spirituality (New York: Paulist, 1983), 76.

[17] Ibid. 1.3.21, 38.

[18] J. Meyendorff, 'Introduction' to *Gregory Palamas: The Triads*, 14 (In the quotations within this passage, Meyendorff is himself quoting Lossky, *Mystical Theology*, 43).

[19] Lossky, *Mystical Theology*, 226–7.

[20] See Lossky's assertion that the doctrine of the energies is the dogmatic basis for all mystical experience, in ibid., 86.

[21] That is, Basil the Great, his brother Gregory of Nyssa, and their friend Gregory of Nazianzus. The three were from the same region in Cappadocia (what is today central Turkey), and all figured prominently in the trinitarian controversy.

[22] Palamas, *Triads* 1.3.4, 32.

[23] Ibid., 1.3.23, 39.

[24] Ibid., 2.3.37, 66.

[25] Ibid., 3.2.7, 95–6.

[26] Ibid., 3.3.10, 107.

[27] When one describes the essence this way, it is easier to understand why the Orthodox insist that we can know nothing about God's essence. Do any of us really claim to know anything of God's life before he created the world, when there was nothing outside of himself with which to interact?

[28] Palamas uses the eternality of God's providence as an argument for the eternality of his energies in *Triads* 3.2.6, 94.

[29] Lossky, *Mystical Theology*, 80.

[30] The third century Neoplatonic philosopher Plotinus described the process of the soul's union with God as 'the flight of the alone to the Alone'.

[31] See Louth, *Origins*, 194–8, for a similar discussion of the differences between early Christian mysticism and Neoplatonism.

10

The Desert Fathers, Cassian and Western Monastic Spirituality

Mark W. Elliott

Whom do we mean by 'the Desert Fathers'? Are they restricted to those who lived in the real Egyptian desert? Syrian saints lived closer to towns, only in semi-desert places, yet they seemed to continue and increase the rigour of the earlier fourth century Desert Fathers of Egyptian monasticism with its three-fold classification of eremite (hermit) semi-eremite (Sunday communion, but eremitic isolation the rest of the week), and cenobitic (communal). Rigorous asceticism was not recognised as the equivalent of martyrdom until around the time of Athanasius's influential *Life of Antony* (360). However, public recognition of the *monachos* had already been received by the 330s.[1]

There is a temptation (which is to be firmly resisted!) to view the spirituality of the Desert Fathers and their Syrian successors as excessively world-denying. One thinks of Stylites like Symeon, imaginatively described by William Dalrymple:

> Standing on their pillars, they were believed to be bright beacons of transcendence, visible from afar; indeed in some cases we hear of disciples claiming to be unable to beat the effulgence of the holy man's face, so bright had it become with the uncreated life of the divine' ... St Symeon originally mounted his pillar in order to stop pilgrims attempting to pluck hairs from his cloak or person.[2]

Yet, both Eastern and Western traditions of spirituality can be defended as quite different to a Gnostic flight from creation. For the Desert Fathers of the East, as a rule,

> this making a City of the Wilderness was no mere flight, nor a rejection of matter as evil (else why did they show such aesthetic sense in placing their retreats, and such love for all God's animal

creation?). It was rooted in a stark realism of faith in God and acceptance of the battle which is not against flesh and blood, but against principalities, against powers, against the world-rulers of this darkness, against the spiritual things of wickedness in the heavenly places.[3]

Even Proclus the philosopher, near contemporary of Augustine, denied that matter was evil and therefore to be shunned. Evil is not a substance, but is rather 'a turning away from God', particularly a turning away from God as the source of the gifts. Spirituality means humility: it is about descent, not elevation. Augustine in *On the Trinity* (XV:20:39) avers: 'As far as we could, we have also used the creation which God made to remind those who ask for reasons in such matters that as far as they can they should descry his invisible things by understanding them through the things that are made.'[4] At I:1, Augustine has already said that God is no more like our spirit than he is like our body. His otherness is not to do with his immateriality so much as with his immutability.

John Cassian

The way of classic Christian spirituality is the way of shuttling between the transcendence of God in himself and the immanence of his gracious activity among his creatures. It is also about being involved in the shipping of different types of practice and discourse around the Mediterranean. Cassian, Ambrose, Rufinus and perhaps Jerome acted as conduits which allowed the East to influence the West.[5] One who spent much time considering this was John Cassian. Cassian is not only such a liminal figure, one who carried over traditions, practises and theology from the Greek and Syriac East to the Latin West; he is himself a ghostly presence about whom we know less than we should, flitting between the doors of east and west at unspecified times. As Columba Stewart puts it: 'His humility, however virtuous, is his biographer's first challenge.'[6]

It can be argued that Cassian was born sometime around 360 on the grounds that he was still young when he entered Egypt in the mid-380s, and hailed perhaps from Scythia Minor (this reinforced by his bilingualism), although places from Gaul to Kurdistan have been canvassed as possible alternatives. As a sort of roving spiritual reporter, he was marked more by his time in Egypt – fifteen years in various monastic settlements in the Nile Delta, Scetis, Nitria, Kellia. He left Egypt around 400, possibly because his sympathies lay with those monks known as the 'Tall Brothers', especially the Evagrian Amoun, who were critical of popular anthropomorphism. (In *Conferences* 10.2 Cassian refers to the problem that the simple monks sincerely thought the Almighty had a human-like figure.[7]) Cassian tried to have John Chrysostom of Constantinople vindicated when this patriarch became caught up in the fall-out of the ensuing Origenist controversy, and possibly stayed on in Rome after 405, before arriving in Gaul where he would establish a monastic network and model for the West, before dying in the mid-430s. There he wrote the *Institutes*, inescapably a critique of the native monastic tradition associated with Martin of Tours. The overwhelming tone is a moral one: the wonder-working St Martin, the local Christian hero of recent blessed memory was suspected of being somewhat *arriviste*. Concerning miraculous cures, Cassian tended to ask, 'Could not a doctor have done as much?' The *Institutes* can be read as a critique of the miracle-story emphasis of Martin of Tours and Sulpitius the reporter. Cassian laid into Gallic monasticism as lazy, and lacking in moral good works.[8] Reports of prophecies and dreams were met often with a command to go back and instruct brethren.[9] Whereas the *Institutes* are 'institutes or rules of the monasteries, and especially the origins, causes, and cures of the principal faults, which they reckon as eight', the *Conferences* are set out in a dialogical, question-and-answer format, and are perhaps for the more advanced, being more about solitude.

It is hard to deny that there is an individualising tendency at work in Cassian. If Peter Brown can speak of Augustine as the first subject for (auto)biography, and Charles Taylor locate him at the start of his 'Sources of the Self', then it must be said that the desert tradition and Cassian with it affirms a still more radical independence of the church as an institution, and is severely critical of it in a way unknown in Augustine. God can bypass the church and sacraments. After all, in semi-Pelagian circles baptism was not so all-important. The cells were collections of individuals, and one becomes 'spirit' by becoming closer to God as an anchorite. Cassian further adopted from Origen the idea of the three-stage 'ascent of the soul', but starts it two stages up – the first is the cloistered, the second is the anchoritic. However much he was an influence, we should not make the mistake of thinking Cassian's monasticism was that of the medieval Benedictines 'in community' as they became.[10] The community life was moral as a step towards the hermit's, which was much more mystical; one needed to get the passions cured first in the monastery before progressing, as John did, to the solitary life. Lust is the crossroads for sins which come from pride and sins which originate in greed; Cassian did not expect that a monk would actually be troubled by fornication.[11] Purity of soul was proved when one had quiet dreams, untroubled by sex, a corruption that is the pollution 'with which we have become infected by glutting ourselves all day long on unhealthy emotions' (*Institutes* VI:11). With the Almighty's help, one achieves sub-jectivification, which is self-knowledge, the opposite of illusion-filled pride.

Cassian wrote his only strictly theological treatise, *De Incarnatione*, at the request of a deacon, who later became Pope Leo. At VI:14 and VII:22 of this work, he claims that the Nestorian view that Christ was a strong man who received grace in return for moral progress is Pelagian.[12] He argues against this, emphasising the need to see Christ 'properly' as divine (*Conferences* X:6:1–3). It is the transfigured Christ that we must aim to see. This does not mean that he has no sympathies with Pelagius when it comes to the activity of grace in believers. Unlike what often seems the case with Evagrius, Cassian's remains a Christocentric spirituality; the aim is to see 'light in [God's] light' (Ps. 36:9), but it is the light of *Christ*. One should be able to *see Christ* to visualise God, since *his* special humanity, as a deified one, is transparent. Anthropomorphism equals idolatry; anthropomorphism is closely related to anthropopathism (as treated in *Conferences* VIII). Cassian is not saying that it is divinity which the believer should aim to see, but rather the synthesis of the human in the divine.[13] Jesus' humanity is not, for Cassian in *Conferences* X.6.4, *only* exemplary, but rather it is also the source of sanctity![14] Christ, 'being exalted by pure faith and the heights of virtue reveals the glory of his face and the image of his splendour to those who are able to look on him with pure eyes of the soul.' The visible Jesus no more than the visible Adam can be said to 'contain' God who in himself has no body. What we have then is an account of being led into the inside of the Trinitarian love (cf. *Conferences* X.7), which is the basis of continual prayer. However, one cannot do this by side-stepping Christ in favour of mental 'pure light'.

There was also the ecstatic, 'Syrian' side to Cassian. Indeed, according to Stewart, his synthesis of Evagrian (intellectual) and Syrian (more affective) spirituality prefigures that of Diodochus.[15] Thus, as Stewart observes, there is a simplifying, perhaps a de-intellectualising of Evagrius in the playing down of the *physike* ('natural contemplation') in favour of a direct exchange between *theoretike and praktike*. It is not only that Cassian seemed aware that he must cover the traces that led from him to Evagrius, and through him, to Origen. 'Evagrius was the single most important influence on Cassian's monastic theology, although Cassian never mentions him by name. Even after twenty-five years, with the fiercest of the anti-Origenists' dead and doctrinal controversy now focused on other issues, Cassian felt constrained to downplay his links with the Evagrian Origenism of Nitria and Kellia'.[16]

For Cassian, the natural contemplation is substituted by contemplation which draws on Scripture. The practical moral application from the

Bible comes first and yet is enriched by the gaining of insights of passages of Scripture through scriptural meditation. As Stewart puts it
(rather well), the anthropomorphites 'have reduced an encounter with a
divine person to an imaginative description, which for Cassian means
replacing someone with something.'[17] The way to the knowledge of God
is through contemplation of his saving deeds.

Living in the Trinity, living in the flow of love, means receiving love,
but also giving it out:

> He [Cassian] laid much stress upon our need to decide morally, and
> our need to discipline our own wills so that they decide rightly.
> Hence, he was striving against St Augustine's doctrines of predesti-
> nation and irresistible grace, and devoted one of the *Conferences*
> (XIII) to confute Augustine and explain what he took to be the
> proper doctrine of grace and free will.[18]

Spirituality involves uniting the will and the rooting out of self-will.
'The six steps that lead to chastity represent steps toward the disinvolve-
ment of the will'.[19] Fear takes the monk away from earthly things, but
love directs him to Christ. This is quite different from the Egyptian
anchorites and owes much to the psychology of Evagrian Origenism,
and along with it, a semi-Pelagian God-human synergy: '*cooperatio homin-
is cum deo*.'

Augustinianism

Stewart contends that Cassian was not so much reacting against
Augustine's *De corruptione*, but that in fact he wrote *Conference* XIII a
good time before he read the North African bishop. Of course,
Conference XIII in some respects was not written by Cassian at all, only
edited by him; its choice parts come from Abba Chaeremon whom he
met in the 390s. In other words, Augustine in his later works is the
newer 'alternative' to the catholic view, which is opposed to expecting
God always to provide the *initium fidei*.

According to Paula Fredriksen, E.P. Sanders has suggested that 'Paul's
exposition in Romans is not the way he came to faith, but the result of
the new perspective on the past provided by newness of life in Christ.
Paul moved ... not from plight to solution, but from solution to plight.'[20]
As Fredriksen comments, this Pauline anthropology became clear to
Augustine already by the time of his musings in the *Confessions*:
Augustine had tried virtue which had been popular in Ambrosian
Catholicism, but it had not altogether worked for him. However, this is
not to say that he deprecated personal responsibility. When one moves

from philosophers to Augustine, or from philosophy to the exegesis of Scripture – Frances Young insightfully reminds us that the Bible was for him *the Doctrina Christiana* – there is a change in the question: it is no longer *unde malum?* but *unde male faciemus?*

Another difference which Young notes between Augustine and the Cappadocians, as representatives of a more speculative and a more ascetic Christianity, is 'a shift from the shared search to know the unknowable God, from the shared recognition of the immense infinity of the mystery beyond the grasp of the human mind, to an experience of being *known by* God.'[21] This means that there is no place for synergy, even a synergism which gives God the greater part. Rather it means 'a spiritual participation in the redemptive process',[22] or, as Luther would have it, justification by *faith*.

Some of the differences between the ascetical and the Augustinian traditions are rather superficial. One could argue that Augustine's rule is shaped by his theology of the oneness of love.[23] Thus, spiritual renunciation is about chastity and obedience for Augustine; not about giving up people and friendship; whereas Cassian and the Benedictines are a bit more exclusive. However, the attempt to show that the rule of Augustine provided an alternative non-monastical, non-ascetical, perhaps 'humanist' canonical tradition down through the centuries is tendentious.[24] Again, regarding the body, Cassian seems to agree with Augustine in the area of sex, viewing it as a symptom of soul-sickness rather than its cause, and presumably would have joined in the great bishop's condemnation of the position of Julian of Eclanum. Also there is their shared emphasis on Scripture. Cassian saw the connection between a Pelagian human nature of Christ and Nestorianism; to that extent, in his sideswipes at both, he implicitly sides with Augustine, evinced not least in their overlapping efforts to restore Leporius to the doctrinal 'straight and narrow'.

A Brief Reading of Conference XIII

Part of the *animus* which drove Cassian was the concern that it should be remembered that there would be reward for the hard labour of chastity. It is not, as he insists in XIII:3, that humans can do without grace: 'human pride should never try to put itself on a level with the grace of God or to intermingle itself with it'. Germanus's view, reported in XIII:4, that surely Gentiles seem to show that chastity can be got without grace (*viz.* the philosophers), is answered in XIII:5 by Chaeremon, who claims that the ancient philosophers did not have inner chastity, but merely a particle of it; for example, Socrates still had the desire to abuse young boys. For Chaeremon, chastity is itself a gift;

in monastic life grace has already prevened – so there are *motus* which are opportunities for God's completing grace, and the will shares in the good preserved in the nature as created. (In other words, we should be slow to deprecate the work of the Creator.) The will can still be attracted to virtue; Cassian has no need of any distinction between operative and cooperative grace; even if free will is limited in its operation, nonetheless it operates. God looks for some effort (*conatus*), some foundation of good will (*initium bonae voluntatis*). God is in the business of overcoming unwillingness; only where there is stubborn and complete refusal does he refrain.

In XIII:7 the argument is advanced that God calls all and wills all to be saved (1 Tim. 2:4). Otherwise, there would be some (the elect) who in fact would not be 'heavy laden either with actual or original sin' (Wis. 1:13). Further, those who perish do so against his will (Matt. 23:37). Moreover, the very fact that the Psalmist prays for grace is a sign of free will (XIII:8).

Conference XIII:9–13

Proper of Aquitaine wrote *Contra Collatorem*, literally 'against the one who wrote the *Conferences*', sometime around 432. In it he singled out passages from *Conference* XIII:9–13 as offending against the, by now, orthodox Augustinian theology of grace. This was, as Columba Stewart has it, a respectful attack on the eastern idea that 'stirrings of good remain possible even to fallen mankind.'[25] The first such passage is in Chapter 9:

> But let it appear obvious in what manner the completion (*summa*) of our salvation is assigned to our own will, of which it is said: 'If you be willing, and hearken unto me, you shall eat good things of the land' (Isa. 1:19), and in what manner it is 'not of him that wills or runs, but of God that having mercy?' (Rom. 9:16) [26]

Cassian (or Chaeremon who is speaking) seems to be hedging his bets here. But it seems that the human will completes what the divine will starts. A page later and the converse is affirmed:

> But that it may be still clearer that through the excellence of nature which is granted by the goodness of the Creator, sometimes the first beginnings of a good will arise, which however cannot attain to the complete performance of what is good unless it is guided by the Lord, the Apostle bears witness and says; 'For to will is present with me, but to perform what is good I find not' (Rom. 7:18).[27]

So God and human wills take turns to start and finish.

The next offending texts are in Chapter 11, although Chapter 10 has a number of references to free will in Scripture. Overall, the position seems to be that it is still the will that works but one which needs assistance in its weakness. A carefulness to balance 'grace' and 'freewill' appears throughout the *Conference*. Piety and the rule of faith, the central message of Christian theology as handed down, demand both.

For some in their Christian experience it is 'grace' first (Paul on the road to Damascus); for others it is 'free will' (Zacchaeus). So we find the following in Chapter 11:

> What are we to say of the goodness of the thief on the cross, who by his own desires brought violence to bear on the kingdom of heaven and so prevented [in the sense of 'prevenient grace'] the special leadings of his vocation?[28] ... These two then; *viz.*, the grace of God and free will seem opposed to each other, but really are in harmony, and we gather from the system of goodness that we ought to have both alike, lest if we withdraw one of them from man, we may seem to have broken the rule of the church's faith.[29]

And then, in Chapter 12:

> For we should not hold that God made man such that he can never will or be capable of what is good: or else He has not granted him a free will, if He had suffered him only to will or be capable of evil, but neither to will or be capable of what is good of himself. And, in that case how will that first statement of the Lord made about men after the fall stand: 'Behold Adam is become one of us, knowing good and evil?' For we cannot think that before, he was such as to be altogether ignorant of the good ... Moreover as the wisest Solomon [*sic!*] says: 'God made man upright,' i.e., always to enjoy the knowledge of good only.'But they have sought out many imaginations' (Ecc. 7:29) for they came, as has been said, to know good and evil. Adam therefore after the fall conceived a knowledge of evil which he had not previously, but did not lose the knowledge of the good which he had before. [30]

> Wherefore we must take care not to refer all the merits of the saints to the Lord in such a way as to ascribe nothing but what is evil and perverse to human nature ... It cannot be doubted that there are by nature some seeds of goodness in every soul implanted by the kindness of the Creator: but unless these are quickened by the assistance of God, they will not be able to attain to an increase of perfection.[31]

'Doth Job serve thee for nought? Hast thou not hedged him in, and all his substance round about? But take away thine hand', i.e. allow him to fight with me in his own strength, 'And he will curse thee face to face' But as after the struggle the slanderous foe dare not give vent to any such murmur as this, he admitted that he was vanquished by his strength and not by that of God; although we must not hold that the grace of God was altogether wanting in him … and with the centurion whom the Lord praised (Matt. 8:7–10) For there would have been no ground for praise or merit, if Christ had only preferred in him what He himself had given.[32]

Lastly, in Chapter 13 Cassian asserts that grace is given in return for a nominal fee:

And none the less does God's grace continue to be free grace while in return for some small and trivial efforts it bestows with priceless bounty such glory of immortality, and such gifts of eternal bliss. For because the faith of the thief on the cross came as the first thing, no one would say that therefore the blessed abode of Paradise was not promised to him as a free gift …

The keyword is 'cooperation', following 1 Corinthinians 15:10. God does not tempt the saints of the Scriptures in order to test that faith which he gives them, but 'that which when called and enlightened by the Lord he could show forth by his own free will.' He adds: 'And why is it necessary for them even to be tried if He knows them to be so weak and feeble as not to be able by their own power to resist the tempter?' As we get older the nursemaid leaves us more and more to ourselves: a sort of 'taking leave of God' occurs, although not in the way the twentieth-century 'radical' theology has meant this phrase. The 'nursemaid' analogy for grace came, it would seem, from Pseudo-Macarius, the Greek spiritual writer of Syrian origin who wrote about spiritual *eros*. At these times, to transpose the metaphor, God can be like a woman who punishes her suitor for his indifference, by the withholding of affection until his passion for her returns.[33]

Continuity between the 'desert' and the 'cloister'

Cassian went on to have some influence in the East. John Climacus and John Damascene borrow from the Greek epitome of the *Institutes*, especially on the topic of *accidie*. In the West, there was something about the eschatological tone which attracted those for whom Augustine's triumphalism seemed over-relaxed. Cassiodorus claims to have been inspired by Cassian on prayer, even though he warns about 'free will'. It is part of Cassian's legacy to the Benedictine tradition that because a human being has free will there is more danger and a need to discipline.[34] Likewise, the Syriac fathers provided the tradition with a poetical style of theology, such that it is perhaps better to call them poets than theologians. This is not, as in the case of the more recent Christian poetry of such as T.S. Eliot, because the content is 'Being' rather than God, but because of the aim of their poetry, not simply to expound doctrine but also to clothe it, to create something new with it. In the strength of imagination came both inspired hymns of praise and the locus for fighting with demons. The poetry is so strong that the Marys Magdalene and Mother of Christ are often fused (cf. Ephrem's *Diatessaron* Commentary).[35] Alongside this a stark contrast, and perhaps a helpful check, is provided by the very *regularity* of the 'Western' Benedictine Rule. The latter suggests that the monastery provides needed support; obedience rather than love is the master virtue. Benedict had dealt with that master vice, lust, responding to one such temptation during his three years in a cave near Subiaco by rolling in a patch of nettles, if we are to believe Gregory the Great in his *Dialogues*. The practice of obedience required, of course, a communal life: 'hasten to obey the command of a superior as if it were a command of God.'[36]

In monastic circles the 'Rule of Cassian' was adapted from *Conferences* I–IV. In turn, the Rule of the (anonymous) Master (the *Regula Magistri*), revived by Cassian for the Gallic communities of the sixth century, promoted an unashamed 'soul–body' dualist anthropology. Among the evidences of Cassian's enduring influence are the moral theology of the seven (originally eight) deadly sins in Gregory the Great; the Rule of St Benedict of Nursia (the founding document of the major part of Western monasticism: e.g., the ten marks of humility [*Institutes* 4:39], which are the basis for the Master's twelve degrees, in turn adopted by Benedict); the Principle of purification through Scripture meditation while working (*laborare est orare*), leading into contemplation ('in cheerful silence') of pure divinity; the notion of following the path made by Jesus' humanity, which, 'post-resurrection' had been assumed into his divinity.

Perhaps the clearest link between the Desert Fathers and the Benedictines, one that was relayed through Cassian, is the placing of the Psalms at the heart of religious life: 'No matter what, all 150 psalms must be chanted during the week so that on Sunday Matins the series may start afresh ... Our spiritual fathers performed with determination in one day what we now take a whole week to do.'[37]

The rest of the Rule of Benedict shows a rigour of military style. Banning from the common table is the usual sanction (there is no mention of a liturgical eucharist, still less excommunication defined in those terms[38]), with whipping for obstinate cases.[39] After this, if no amendment, ' … the abbot must behave like a wise physician. He applies the salves and compresses of advisement, the medicine of the Holy Scriptures and the hot iron of excommunication'. The diet seems to have been vegetarian (fish perhaps included), with meat only allowed for those recovering from sickness (Chapter 36). The body may not be the enemy, rather the battlefield; yet every battlefield is by definition 'enemy territory', so that, again, the 'soul–body' dualism is unabashed. The charge of elitism made by Philip Sheldrake seems ill-founded when he observes: ' … given that the monasticism of the Rule of St Benedict originated as an essentially *lay* movement, the creation of a distinct *class* of lay-brethren from about the eighth century onwards, and refined by the Cistercian usages, is an indication of the degree to which religious life and its government had become clericalised?'[40] This would be valid only if we think that the term 'lay' meant anything other than 'not ordained for a eucharistic function'; to call a monk 'lay' surely did not mean that the monks were not seen as set apart by the nature of their vows and practice. It is a myth to think that here was a decline, between 450 and 750, from a sort of open brotherhood to a closed, exclusive clerical club.

Something that becomes clear through looking at lives of Desert Fathers is how the narrator serves as the mediator of the 'great man' (or great women): when Ephrem writes that 'if the animals in Noah's ark were chaste, how much more so Mary'.[41] This is an argument from silence no better than those who would see her as a feisty leader of the early church; it is the conception of Jesus which purifies her, rather than her own conception by Anna, and while intercourse is good, chastity is better as befitting the lifestyle of the angels and because it means one can thus, for some reason, be bold before God without the shame appropriate to creatureliness, as Mary was. Sexuality is not sin, even if abstinence is in some sense 'virtuous'. The term liminality can be overused, but the likes of Pambo and Cyrus are presented as those close to the abyss.[42] (The concept of sacred time meant that in the desert the punishments of hell seem very close.) 'Early Syriac ascetical writing appears almost entirely individualistic.'[43] Robert Murray had argued that Ephrem and Aphrahat inherit the tradition of the androgynous Adam from Jewish midrash (although he admits that the *Liber Graduum* did not see sexuality as the result of the Fall: sex will be sublimated in the religious life of the sons of the covenant). Women who heeded the call were no longer functionally subordinate, and as Lucien Regnault has shown, there were more of them than we have thought.

All this is hardly mysticism, properly defined. To speak, as Bernard McGinn does, of Macarius as a developing *Gestalt-mystik* not a *Seins-mystik* is not altogether helpful, not only because of the jargon.[44] What we have in Cassian, as well as in his teachers, is not a developed mysticism: the Desert Fathers were about obedience to God and the life of their souls was not so much intimacy with the divine as standing in the divine power in order to overcome temptations.

This means that the military-like discipline would not have been so difficult to combine. In fact, the individual spirituality and the common life become fused in the seven-stage round of the monastic daily office; as compared with the habit of daily morning and evening prayer only in non-monastic settings. There is some sort of an explanation by D. Hope and G. Woolfenden:

> Since their inception, monastic communities had normally comprised lay monks and only very much later had they come to accept the possibility of the priest-monk. Once this had happened, naturally the priest-monk wished to exercise, within the community, the office and function for which he had been ordained. The daily private Mass thus became the norm in such monasteries'.[45]

Conclusion: What the Spiritual Fathers Tell Us

What they tell us is that the spiritual life means facing up to ourselves – or the sin, anxiety, depression in all of us – and also doing this in an ordered but compassionate community. As Rowan Williams has recently put it, the classic texts of Christian spirituality are not so much about how to cope with this world, as about redrawing the environment, the imaginative world. It is about human life (according to the spirit) in a place defined by Jesus.[46] Ted Yarnold gives it a Trinitarian gloss: 'Christian tradition, following the New Testament, has identified these three coefficients as the Father who is the source of being, the Son or Word, through whom all things are made, and the Holy Spirit who unites personal beings with God as his sons and daughters.'[47] The Desert Fathers made it their business to force themselves to be confronted with the darker side of life. Cassian's spirituality was particularly regular in its expression and it touched the centre of personal life, life together and even the social-political sphere of bishops and government. It directed the heart to place itself where God's grace could be found to flow. It tries to remind us that spiritual discipline is not so very esoteric, the preserve of ordinands and of those who can afford retreats and command 'spiritual direction'. From the excerpted texts which caused controversy at the time, there is a belief that human beings can become virtuous although that is something for others to recognise. True, as the example of the thief on the cross shows, grace alone is sufficient for salvation of the willing, but with the examples of Job and even the Roman centurion one can still speak of those whose hearts are turned to God as capable of being 'good' (not 'saved'), and, conversely, that when we sin we do not deny responsibility or pretend that we had no inkling of what the good might be. Lastly, although this may sound trite, the monastic movement was always about the balance between private spiritual struggle and seeking support from one's brothers and sisters. Some form of life analogous to a monastic community is not an optional extra for Christians, who, to recast McIntyre's somewhat wistful and even romantic conclusion, find themselves in a time of 'waiting *as* St Benedict' for *Christ*.[48]

Notes

[1] Cf. the influential article by Edwin Judge: 'The Earliest Use of "Monachos" for "Monk" (P. College.Youtie 77) and the Origins of Monasticism', *Jahrbuch für Antike und Christentum* 20 (1977), 72–89.

[2] See W. Dalrymple, *From the Holy Mountain* (Flamingo, 1996), 462.

[3] D. Chitty, *The Desert a City* (Crestwood: St Vladimir's Press, 1995), xvi.

[4] E. Hill (tr.), *The Mystery of the Trinity* (London: Geoffrey Chapman, 1985), 426

[5] Although there are grounds for seeing Jerome as resolutely conservatively Western in some ways, one could argue that the insistence on the priority of the Hebrew text of the Old Testament (*Hebraica veritas*) was responsible in part for the East-West split and he had no great liking for 'Greek' speculative theology.

[6] Columba Stewart, *Cassian the Monk*, Oxford Studies in Historical Theology (Oxford: Oxford University Press, 1998), 4.

[7] Graham Gould has asserted that the monks were probably not so naïve, but were concerned to hold fast to the analogy of God and humanity. This would of course be compatible with a Christology in which divine and human were able to mix (a nascent monophysitism). See 'Doctrine of the Image: Origenism and the Monks', in R. J. Daly (ed.), *Origeniana Quinta: Papers of the 5th International Origen Congress, Boston, 1989,* (Leuven: Leuven University Press, 1992).

[8] Cf. *Conferences* XXIV:2:1.

[9] On this, see Foucault's lively account of Artemidorus in *The History of Sexuality 3: The Care of the Self* (Harmondsworth: Penguin, 1990); also Robin Lane Fox,

Pagans and Christians (London: Penguin, 1986), 155–58. All these are seen as part of nature: 'The dreams even of saints, it was held, were to be received with caution, since there (*sic*) were almost certainly the work of demons and a temptation to that last horror of the desert, loss of humility. Secondly, where a dream or vision is related and accepted as a wonder, it almost always gives focus to some dramatic turning point in the waking life of the dreamer' – taken from Benedicta Ward, 'Signs and Wonders: Miracles in the Desert Traditions', *Studia Patristica* 17 (1982), 539–42, 541.

[10] *Conference* XIX:8: 'I should absolutely maintain that one and the same man could not attain perfection in both lives unless I was hindered by the example of some few' (*Nicene and Post Nicene Fathers*, Vol. 11, 492.) All quotations from Cassian will be based on the translation in the *Nicene and Post Nicene Fathers*, Vol. 11 (Edinburgh: T. & T. Clark, 1980), with some amendments by this author.

[11] As Michel Foucault notes in 'The Battle for Chastity', in *Ethics* (London: Allen Lane/Penguin, 1997), 185–97, 189.

[12] This after attempting to oppose the Antiochenes wth their own creed (' a short word will the Lord make on the earth' – an unusual translation of Rom. 9:28.) (*Nicene and Post Nicene Fathers*, Vol. 11, 593) 'You certainly make two Christs; after the manner of that abominable error of Pelagius, which in asserting that a mere man was born of the Virgin, said that He was the teacher rather than the redeemer of mankind.. They maintain that a mere man was born of Mary; you do the same… They do not deny that He became God after His Passion: you deny Him after his ascension' (*Nicene and Post Nicene Fathers*, Vol. 11, 598f) 'For he (as Leporius his follower said) declared that our Lord was made the Christ by his baptism: you say that by his baptism he was made the temple of God by the Spirit' (*Nicene and Post Nicene Fathers*, Vol. 11, 616) The one other reference to Pelagianism as a cognate heresy is at V, ii (*Nicene and Post Nicene Fathers*, Vol. 11, 581): 'You add besides, that Jesus Christ the Lord of all should be termed a form that received God: i.e., not God, but the receiver of God, so that your view is that He is to be honoured not for his own sake, because he is God, but because he receives God into himself…that Christ was not to be worshipped for His own sake because He was God, but because owing to His good and pious actions he won this, viz., to have God dwelling in Him. You see then that you are belching out the poison of Pelagianism …'

[13] Stewart makes reference to the formula at Ephesus: 'one incarnate nature of the Word': but it is unlikely that Cassian would have been happy with this.

[14] M. Petschenig (ed.), *Corpus Scriptorum Ecclesiasticorum Latinorum (CSEL)* 13 (Vienna, 1886), 92, 5–24.

[15] Stewart, *Cassian the Monk*, 86.

[16] Ibid., 11–12.

[17] Ibid, 95, with reference to Victor Codina, *El aspecto cristologico en la espiritualidad de Juan Cassiano* (OCA 175; Rome: Ponticium Institutum Orientalium

Studiorum, 1966). When Stewart claims that the Evagrian spirituality meant for Cassian that the transfigured One (referred to in *Conferences* X.6) is not a 'floodlit human Jesus, still bound by form and time, but the divine transcendence of all limits' (98), the language needs to be checked, not least because such a stage of deification (*theôsis*) is for the end-time, not yet: '(292, 25: *ut in hoc corpore conmorantes ad similitudinem quandam illius beatitudinis, quar in futuro repromittitur sanctis, vel ex parte aliqua non aptare possimus, sitqe nobis omnia in omnibus deus)*'.

[18] Owen Chadwick, *John Cassian*, (Cambridge: Cambridge University Press, 1968²), 147.

[19] Foucault, 'Chastity', 191.

[20] E.P. Sanders, 'Beyond the Body/Soul Dichotomy: Augustine's Answer to Mani, Plotinus, and Julian', in W.S. Babcock (ed.), *Paul and the Legacies of Paul* (Dallas: Southern Methodist University Press, 1990), 227–51, 247.

[21] F. Young, *Biblical Exegesis and the Formation of Christian Culture* (Cambridge: Cambridge University Press, 1997), 274. Cf. Gal. 4: 9: 'Now, however, that you have come to know God, or rather to be known by God …'; 1 Cor. 8:3; 'anyone who loves God is known by him.'

[22] G. Florovsky, *The Byzantine Ascetic and Spiritual Fathers*, tr. R. Miller, A. Dollinger-Labriole, & H.W. Schmiedel (Vaduz: Buchervertriebsanstalt, 1987.)

[23] See G. Lawless, *Augustine of Hippo and his Monastic Rule* (Oxford: Clarendon Press, 1987).

[24] As advocated by P. Sheldrake, *Spirituality and History: Questions of Interpretation and Method* (London: SPCK, 1995), 122; cf. Carol Walker Bynum, *Jesus as Mother: Studies in the Spirituality of the High Middle Ages* (Berkeley: University of California Press, 1982). Note that the title it is the 'high' middle ages. Likewise, Dionysian anti-material influences came later, not at the start of the Benedictine tradition.

[25] Stewart, *Cassian the Monk*, 21. At the Council of Orange in 529, Caesarius of Arles would put the final hole in Cassian's reputation, yet the price was a dismissal of the old Augustine's form of the doctrine of predestination. Interestingly, Caesarius of Arles' *Rule for Nuns* depends on *Institutes* 4.

[26] *CSEL* 13, 372.

[27] Ibid., 374, 4–10.

[28] Ibid., 376, 9–11.

[29] Ibid., 377, 15–19.

[30] Ibid., 378, 3–20. Note the attribution of the passage from Sirach to 'Solomon'. After the Fall ('post praevaricationem Adae') there is some good left in humans according to Rom. 2:14–16.

[31] Ibid., 379, 24–380, 1; 380, 19–22.

[32] Ibid., 385.

[33] *CSEL* 13, 371, 13–26 (ref. Ps. 58:11).

[34] K.S. Frank, 'Zur Anthropologie der Regula Magistri', *Studia Patristica* 17 (1982), 477–90.

[35] Robert Murray, *Symbols of Church and Kingdom a Study in Early Syriac Tradition* (Cambridge: Cambridge University Press, 1975), 337. Murray notes, however, that the writers of the *Liber Graduum* seem 'systematically to reject the abundant imagery of Aphrahat'.

[36] A.Vogüé, *Histoire littéraire du mouvement monastique dans l'antiquité* (Paris: Cerf, 1991).See also his *De Saint Pachôme à Jean Cassien* (Rome: Studia Anselmia, ca 120, 1996).

[37] Rule of St Benedict, ch. 18.

[38] Cf. Cheslyn Jones (ed.), *The Study of Liturgy* (London, SPCK, 1992.) This may be explained by the semi-eremite doing without mass and priests.

[39] Compare the practice at Qumran, *The Community Rule* (1QS); however, in the Benedictine Rule there is no mention of a cut in rations.

[40] P. Sheldrake, *Spirituality and History: Questions of Interpretation and Method* (London: SPCK, 1995), 72f.The point concerns a need to resist secular control.

[41] *Hymn on the Nativity* 28, 1, in Kathleen McVey (ed.), *StEphraim* (New York: Paulist Press, 1989), 214. Cf. A. de Halleux, 'St Ephrem le Syrien', *Revue Théologique de Louvain* (1983), 320–55.

[42] 'There is nothing beyond me except darkness and the punishments that sinners are enduring' quoted in Tim Vivian (ed.), *Journeying into God : Seven Early Monastic Lives* (Minneapolis: Fortress, 1996), 33f.

[43] R. Murray, *Symbols,* 155.

[44] Bernard McGinn, *The Foundations of Mysticism* (London: SCM, 1992), 144:'It may well be, as Gilles Quispel suggests [*Makarius, das Thomasevangelium und das Lied von der Perle* (Leiden: Brill, 1967)], that we have in Macarius no "Seinsmystik," or mysticism of being in the manner of Origen, Gregory of Nyssa, and those influenced by Greek philosophical mysticism, but a "Gestaltsmystik," or a mysticism of the divine form, rooted in Jewish Christianity and analogous to such roughly contemporary Jewish mystical texts as the *Shi 'ur Qomah.'*

[45] 'The Medieval Western Rites', in Jones (ed.), *Study of Liturgy,* 282.

[46] R.D. Williams, 'To Stand Where Christ Stands', in Ralph Waller & Benedicta Ward (eds.), *An Introduction to Christian Spirituality* (London: SPCK, 1999), 1–13.

[47] E.D. Yarnold, 'Introduction', in C. Jones, G. Wainwright, E.D. Yarnold (eds.), *The Study of Spirituality* (London: SPCK, 1986).

[48] See A. McIntyre, *After Virtue: a Study in Moral Theory* (London: Duckworth, 1985²), 263.

11

Creation Mysticism in Matthew Fox and Francis of Assisi

Richard Bauckham

In this chapter we shall study and compare two examples of 'creation mysticism' in the Christian tradition. The work of Matthew Fox provides probably the best-known contemporary example, while Francis of Assisi is without doubt the greatest nature mystic in the Christian tradition, and some would say the first.[1] We shall argue that Francis' form of creation mysticism is a more authentically Christian form than that of Fox, who moves away from elements central both to the Christian tradition in general and to Francis' spirituality in particular.

Matthew Fox

Matthew Fox, former Dominican friar, is well-known as the proponent and exponent of what he calls 'creation-centered spirituality' (or, more briefly, 'creation spirituality' or, sometimes, 'creation mysticism'). We can appropriately call this a form of mysticism, partly because Fox's thought is deeply inspired by several of the medieval Christian mystics, especially Meister Eckhart, Hildegard of Bingen and Mechtild of Magdeburg, but also because he believes that 'creation spirituality liberates the mystic in us all'.[2] 'A basic teaching of all in the creation mystical tradition,' he claims, 'is this: everyone is a mystic'.[3] The mystical is the repressed shadow side of the Western personality, which only the recovery of a sense of belonging to a sacred cosmos can liberate. Thus Fox is not interested in a mysticism that is only attained by a spiritual elite, as the great mystics of the Catholic tradition have sometimes been seen, and certainly not in a mysticism which offers mystical experience only as the culmination of a long and arduous process of ascetical practice. Much as he looks to some of the great Christian mystics, those he sees as creation mystics, for inspiration, his concern is with a mysticism that can be experienced and lived by ordinary people in experience of the cosmos, in new and revitalised forms of meditation and ludic ritual, in all forms of artistic creativity and imagination, and which is inseparable from the practice of prophetic justice in relation to the earth and to the poor. When he speaks of his extensive experience that 'all kinds of persons are waking up to the mystic within them today',[4] we can easily recognise the cultural reality to which his understanding of mysticism corresponds.

Essential to mysticism as he sees it are awe and playful wonder and celebration in relation to a cosmos seen as sacred.[5] Also definitive of mysticism for him are the themes of unity and wholeness:

> Our mystical experiences are unitive experiences. They may occur on a dark night with the sparkling stars in the sky; at the ocean; in the mountains or fields; with friends or family; with ideas; in love-making; in play; with music and dance and art of all kinds; in work; in suffering and in letting go. What all mystical experiences share in common is this experience of nonseparation, of nondualism … [As] Julian of Norwich put it, 'Between God and the soul there is no between' … Here Julian is celebrating the end of the primary dualism – that between humans and divinity. The mystics promise that within each of us there is a capacity – the experience of the 'no between' – to be united and not separate. Mysticism announces the end of alienation and the beginning of communion, the end of either/or relationships (which form the essence of dualism) and the beginning of unity. Yet the unity that the mystics celebrate is not a loss of self or a dissolution of differences, but a unity of creativity, a coming together of different existences.[6]

This view of 'nondualism' is central to Fox's thought and we must return to it. Not unconnected is the definition of mysticism, borrowed from Josef Pieper, as 'an affirmation of the world as a whole'. This is 'to embrace a cosmology' which, in spite of human degradation of the world, affirms the goodness of the cosmos as a whole and therefore finds the cosmos a source of sustenance.[7]

Fox's creation spirituality can be situated both in its present cultural context and in relation to the Christian tradition of the past. While Fox writes deliberately within the Christian tradition, there are many features of his work which connect with that very diverse and characteristically postmodern religious phenomenon known as the New Age movement. There is the turn from anthropocentric thinking, focusing on the human apart from the rest of nature, to a focus on the cosmos and nature and the human in relation to nature. There is the turn from rationality to imagination, or at least an attempt to balance analytic and logical thinking with imaginative, intuitive, and mythic thinking. There is the turn from dualistic to holistic thinking, from compartmentalising reality to appreciating the interdependence and connectedness of all things. There is the turn from divine transcendence beyond the world to divine immanence within the world, even to the divinity of the world. There is the attempt to see justice and peace in human society as equivalent to harmony in nature and harmony with nature. There is the appeal, against patriarchy, to the allegedly feminine principles of intuition and imagination, connectedness and relationality, bodiliness and fertility, embodied in images of the divine as female (the divine motherliness), the Earth as female (Mother Earth), and the neologism 'birthing' as a constantly recurrent metaphor. Of course, many of these features are not confined to the New Age movement, but can be found in other contemporary trends of thought such as feminist theology and Green thinking. They express a certain kind of cultural (or perhaps one should say: counter-cultural) mood, into which Fox taps with something of the eclecticism of the New Age movement itself.

Finally, there is the common sense of the dawning of the new age itself. Fox calls this the birth of a global renaissance, or, using Christian mythical imagery, the coming of the cosmic Christ. This he envisages, much as New Age thinkers do, as an emerging paradigm shift in religious conceptuality, sensibility and world view, a paradigm shift which is at the same time a return to forgotten, ancient wisdom. In Fox's case the ancient wisdom is the so-called creation-centred tradition of spirituality within Christianity, though he is quite prepared to draw on, for example, Native American traditions and to emphasise the spiritual wisdom of traditional peoples. The global renaissance will be a move beyond the alienation of religion, science and art, to a newly holistic outlook which Fox calls a living cosmology. In this will coalesce science (in the form of the new creation story which contemporary science tells, a universal cosmological story to replace the creation stories of the various religions); mysticism (in the form of a new awakening of the human psyche's potential for unitive cosmic imagination); and art (as the new form of meditative religious practice in which our awe at creation is expressed).

A particular understanding of the history of the Christian tradition, with a resulting discernment as to what can be retrieved and what we should discard, is integral to Fox's project. This is a process of 're-visioning' history in order to allow 'the best and most often forgotten and repressed elements of our tradition ... to come to the fore'.[8] Fox presents the tradition of creation spirituality as the alternative to what he calls the fall/redemption tradition of Christian spirituality, which has been more dominant especially in the modern period. Christian theologians, mystics and spiritual writers in the Western tradition from Augustine onwards he assigns to either one or the other of these two traditions, one of which, the fall/redemption tradition, has promoted a negative view of creation, while the other, the creation spirituality tradition, has maintained that positive view of creation which Fox sees himself reviving. In Fox's now notorious family tree of creation spirituality[9] he lists a very diverse range of people he approves of and evaluates them with stars, as though they were hotels. Only Jesus gets five stars, but three people get four stars. These are Fox's favourite medieval mystics: Hildegard of Bingen, Francis of Assisi and Meister Eckhart. The other tradition, the fall/redemption tradition, stems from Augustine of Hippo, whose vast influence over the Western Christian tradition Fox seems to evaluate as indiscriminately regrettable.

Fox sometimes identifies the fundamental fault of the fall/redemption tradition as dualistic thinking – a rather slippery term in his as in other people's usage. Dualistic thinking sets up oppositions between matter and spirit, between body and soul, between humans and the rest of creation, and (apparently the most pernicious of all) between God and creation. According to Fox, the various dualisms inherent in the fall/redemption tradition promote a kind of anthropocentrism in which human beings consider themselves apart from the rest of creation and seek God not in the cosmos but introspectively within their own souls. This disastrous tendency is further promoted by Augustine's doctrine of original sin, which, according to Fox, 'grew to become the starting-point for Western religion's flight from nature, creation, and the God of creation'.[10] In place of the fundamental goodness of creation, human and non-human, the fall/redemption tradition is obsessed with the fallenness of human and non-human nature, and seeks liberation from sin and guilt in purely personal spiritual salvation, understood as redemption from this fallen, material world. A world-rejecting and body-hating asceticism is a prime characteristic of spirituality in this tradition. By contrast, the creation-centred tradition emphasises 'original blessing,' concerns itself with the people of God and the cosmos, is aesthetic rather than ascetic, emphasizes thanksgiving, praise and creativity rather than guilt, redemption and obedience.

Many critics have challenged this typology of the two traditions as a misleading view of history.[11] Of course, the Western Christian tradition is such a complex historical phenomenon, subject at many points to very varied influences, spawning many different schools of thought and traditions of spirituality, that almost any contemporary Christian thinker will be able to find precedents with which he or she can closely identify, as well as examples of what he or she thinks the most aberrant or deleterious forms Christianity can take. But the fact is that most of the thinkers and mystics of whom Fox approves lived and worked within the same broad theological framework as those of whom he disapproves, that is, a framework in which creation, fall and redemption are closely related. (We shall see later how this is true of Francis of Assisi.) The variations occur within this common framework rather than constituting two opposed traditions.

In fact, even Fox's own work throws doubt on the way he polarises the two traditions. It might seem as though Fox himself has no place for sin or salvation, but in fact he has his own definitions of sin, such as the damage humans do to creation, and of salvation, such as the healing of creation in which we help to establish cosmic harmony. Indeed, he even has a substitute for the Augustinian understanding of original sin that he rejects: dualism, 'the dualism that human, sexual, racial, economic exploitations are all about,' is 'the basis of all sin'.[12] Dualism 'is what the creation-centered tradition considers to be original sin or the sin behind sin'.[13] Another major flaw in Fox's historical typology is that he misses the extent to which the depreciation of the material world and the introspective turn to the spiritual within, real tendencies in much of the tradition of Christian spirituality, were due, not to the fall/redemption doctrine as such, but to the quite different influence of Platonism in the Christian tradition. Finally, he also leaves secularization and the loss of religious belief largely out of his account of what has gone wrong in modern Western history. He joins in a popular contemporary game of blaming on the Christian tradition, or on part of it, such things as the modern project of technological domination of the world which have in fact coincided with the progress of Western rejection of the Christian tradition.

Rather as New Testament scholars in the first half of the twentieth century tended to use first century Judaism as a foil to set off the virtues of early Christianity, attributing to Judaism precisely the faults which Christianity remedied, so Fox's account of the fall/redemption tradition is little more than a means of highlighting all the attractions of the creation-centred tradition by contrasting it with everything it was not. How else can we read, for example, Fox's exhortation 'to let the preoccupation with human sinfulness give way to attention to divine grace'?[14] – as though Augustine and the Reformers (among others), seriously as they took human sinfulness, did not give at least equal attention to divine grace! Fox's work is best read, not as the recovery of a lost tradition, but as his own eclectic creation, drawing on many sources in the tradition and the contemporary world.

Fox's work is too wide-ranging to be adequately summed up here. Instead, I shall pick out some features which seem to me of special interest for pursuing a comparison between Fox and Francis of Assisi, who is widely considered the first and the greatest 'creation mystic' in the Christian tradition. Are there aspects of Fox's thought which positively correspond, in a helpfully contemporary way, to aspects of Francis' spirituality? Are there aspects which seem more problematic from the position centrally within the Christian mainstream that Francis, for all his remarkable exceptionality, certainly occupies, as we shall see? I shall briefly discuss two themes in each of these two categories.

Creation as well as Salvation

The Christian tradition has always understood salvation as the restoration and renewal, as well as completion, of God's good creation. When Fox insists that salvation loses its meaning if creation drops out of view,[15] he is representing, not a minority tradition of creation-centred spirituality, but the mainstream of the Christian tradition, which, incidentally, has never denied that the goodness of God's creation is more fundamental than the sin that has damaged and distorted it. It may well be the case that in the modern period, Christianity of several types has taken creation for granted just at the juncture of history when it could no longer be taken for granted, and focused too exclusively on human salvation, whether in an individualistic way or in terms of a social gospel of reforming society. In the long run, the loss of a sense of creation has undermined the meaningfulness of salvation, while the understanding of God as Saviour without an equally strong sense of God as Creator has unwittingly colluded with the general loss of a sense of God in our time. It is for the sake of God and the gospel, as well as for the sake of the Earth and its non-human inhabitants, that Christian recognition of the world as God's good creation and ourselves as part of that creation is urgently needed. As Fox knows, such recognition is not a merely intellectual matter, but a deeply experiential way of relating to God and creation.

Gift and Gratitude

To such an experience, as Fox stresses, the themes of blessing, gift and gratitude are central: the blessing of creation in God's continuous and extravagant lavishing of goodness on it, the giftedness of creation, including ourselves, as given to us, and thankfulness and praise as the wellspring of life ('a thanks from the depths of the cosmos that we are for the cosmos in which we live'[16]). Fox rightly identifies 'taking for granted' as one of the peculiar afflictions of modern Western humanity and a prime source of its ills,[17] and one could add that a false estimation of achievement, rather than being given, as what matters, an unwillingness to recognise that every achievement is deeply indebted to what we are given, is a closely related failure. Though Fox does not say this, one way in which salvation is related to creation in experience is in the sense of being given oneself and the world afresh in 'grace' (which means God's generous gift) – a redemption from 'taking for granted' such that all of life becomes experience of gratuitousness. Once again, one does not have to polarise the Christian tradition in order to recover this: it runs through the whole tradition and has been lost through secularization rather than Augustinianism.

Theism, Panentheism and Dualism

One of the most important of the differences between the two traditions as Fox constructs them is the difference between theism and panentheism. This is also, in terms of Fox's key category of dualism, a difference between a dualistic understanding of the relationship of God and the world and a non-dualistic understanding of that relationship: 'The idea that God is 'out there' is probably the ultimate dualism, divorcing as it does God and humanity'.[18] Fox makes the common mistake of supposing that theism posits God's transcendence as distance between God and the world, whereas the true meaning of transcendence is difference between God and the world. This is a mistake of very considerable significance for the way Fox thinks about God. For theism he substitutes panentheism, which certainly does, as he claims, distinguish God from creation without separating God from creation: 'everything is truly in God and God is truly in everything.'[19] But what gets lost in Fox's particular version of a move from theism to panentheism is a sense of God's personal otherness and a sense of God's surpassing God's creation. The former seems to be flatly denied in the statement that panentheism 'does not relate to God as subject or object.'[20] The latter is from time to time affirmed, but generally lacks relevance to experience.

The more one reads Fox the more striking, by comparison with the whole Christian tradition, is the lack of inter-subjective relationship with God and the lack of an awareness of God in which God is distinguished from the creation. These things have been abandoned in the repudiation of dualism, but it is far from clear why they should have been. The passage quoted near the beginning of this chapter about mystical experience as unitive rather than dualistic[21] clearly states that lack of

separation does not mean denying difference, that the opposite of dualism is not identity but communion. So why may a non-dualistic experience of God not be one of intensely intimate relationship to God as
personal other? The statement that panentheism 'does not relate to God
as subject or object'[22] seems to result, by a *non sequitur*, from the claim
that all 'theisms are about subject/object relationships to God.'[23]
Dualisms in Fox are about subject/object relationships, which are ipso
facto oppressive.[24] But subject-to-subject communion of persons is not
oppressive. This has been left out of the possibilities of relationship to
God by sleight of hand, not argument.

The lack of inter-subjective relationship with God appears, for example, in what Fox does with such traditional elements of the spiritual life
as faith and forgiveness. He, quite appropriately, translates faith as 'trust'
and makes a great deal of this theme, but trust is almost always a matter
of trusting the cosmos[25] or of trusting ourselves[26] or simply of trusting
tout court,[27] almost never a matter of trusting God.[28] This must be a
deliberate avoidance of the traditional language. Similarly, forgiveness is
a matter of 'letting go,' of forgiving ourselves, and of forgiving others,
not of being forgiven by God.[29] What is operative here and elsewhere is
a fundamental assumption that relationship to God is nothing other than
relationship to oneself and the cosmos. Because God is in all things and
all things are in God, our relationships to all things certainly are relationship to God. Fox is neither an atheist nor a pantheist. But there is no
distinguishing of God from creation, such that to trust God amounts to
anything more or other than to trust the cosmos. Relationship to God
simply is the right kind of relationship (e.g. trusting rather than fearing)
to the cosmos. A curious effect is that while personal language about
God is sparse in Fox, he is not averse to personifying the cosmos.[30]

In fact, Fox is capable of saying an extraordinary amount about mysticism without mentioning God. At one point he justifies this: 'As one
grows more deeply into a panentheistic awareness, one's need to invoke
the actual name of God becomes less compelling.'[31] But in support for
this statement he can only observe that the biblical books of Esther and
the Song of Songs never name God, and that Francis of Assisi's *Canticle
of the Creatures* does not mention Jesus Christ.[32] The latter point is entirely spurious, since although the *Canticle* does not mention Jesus, it
invokes God by name in every single stanza. In fact, the idea that mystical awareness of God in creation reduces the need to refer to God has
no support from the Christian spiritual tradition at all, not even from
Fox's own favourite mystics. Those who find God in creation feel the
need to say so, because finding *God* in creation requires distinguishing
God from creation. They recognise God in the creatures precisely as the

creatures refer beyond themselves to the God who made them and surpasses them.

A section called, 'What is Creation?,' in the first chapter of Fox's book
Creation Spirituality, is instructive. From a traditional Christian perspective in which creation is distinguished (not separated!) from its Creator,
in which creation is the gift and God the giver, in which creation reflects
its Creator but in such a way as to distinguish itself as creation from its
Creator, this section of Fox's work describes creation in terms some of
which are appropriate to creation, some of which are appropriate only
to the Creator. Thus, for example, on the one hand, the cosmos is
'sacred',[33] because it is God's creation, and 'gift'[34] of the Creator, but also,
on the other hand,

> Creation is the source, the matrix, and the goal of all things —the
> beginning and the end, the alpha and the omega. Creation is our
> common parent, where 'our' stands for all things. Creation is the
> mother of all beings and the father of all beings, the birther and the
> begetter.[35]

The terms applied to 'creation' here are mostly scriptural terms which
in Scripture and tradition refer precisely to the uniqueness of the one
God who alone brought all things into being and who alone is the goal
of all things.[36] It is hard to see what Fox, who certainly knows their biblical usage, means by applying them to creation, since 'creation' is, by definition, the sum total of 'all things' created by God. What does it mean
to call *creation* the creator of all things? That Fox can speak without conscious difficulty of 'creation' both as creator of 'all things' and as itself 'all
things' that are created by God is significant. Despite a formal distinction
between the Creator and the creation, what Fox is primarily concerned
to express is the divinity of the cosmos, the cosmic whole, to which all
particular creatures relate as those who owe their existence and their
reverence to this cosmic whole. In thus relating to the cosmos, rather
than in acknowledging the cosmos to which they belong to be the creation of the transcendent one who made it, they are relating to God. It
is odd that Fox uses the term 'creation-centered spirituality' for a spirituality in which the *createdness* of the cosmos plays so negligible a role.

In such a theological context, is the 'gratitude' of which Fox so
importantly speaks (see above) directed to God or to the cosmos? In the
place Fox gives it[37] in his discussion of 'the new creation story' (i.e. the
contemporary scientific account of the origins and development of the
universe) God is unmentioned and gratitude to the cosmos seems the
appropriate meaning.[38] The distinction is clearly not significant to Fox.

Yet why should we feel the awe and gratitude of which Fox speaks simply from learning from this story 'how gratuitous our existence is'? Why should we not feel the absurdity of our existence as a meaningless accident in a cosmos without purpose or meaning? The scientific story of the universe, simply as a scientific account, is precisely *not* a 'new *creation* story,' for it does not speak of a Creator. To respond to our 'gratuitousness' with gratitude there must be intentionality and love to thank. Gratitude must be directed either to the one Creator of all things, transcendent beyond his creation (as in the whole Christian tradition), or to the universe conceived mythologically as itself a purposive, intentional being. What Fox calls 'living cosmology' is really a cosmic myth of the latter kind, with occasional support from the biblical and Christian faith in the transcendent Creator.

Jesus and the Cosmic Christ

In *The Coming of the Cosmic Christ* Fox makes a notable attempt to repristinate the notion (and experience) of 'the cosmic Christ' found in the New Testament and the theological tradition, and to give it a key role in his creation-centred spirituality: 'The coming together of the historical Jesus and the Cosmic Christ will make Christianity whole at last'.[39] As this quotation suggests, Fox is aware that in the New Testament and the theologians and mystics who have spoken about the cosmic Christ, this Christ in whom all creation coheres should not be separated from Jesus of Nazareth, the figure whose human life is narrated in the Gospels. In arguing that the modern 'quest of the historical Jesus' now needs to be supplemented by a quest for the cosmic Christ, he acknowledges that a 'theology of the Cosmic Christ must be grounded in the historical Jesus, in his words, in his liberating deeds ..., in his life and orthopraxis,' and speaks of a dialectic between the two: 'a dance between time (Jesus) and space (Christ); between the personal and the cosmic; between the prophetic and the mystical'.[40]

The relationship between the two is evidently that Jesus is one form of incarnation of the Cosmic Christ: 'Wisdom [a term for the cosmic Christ] has been made flesh not only in Jesus the Christ but in *all expressions of the Cosmic Christ*'.[41] This means that the divinity suffused throughout the cosmos (the cosmic Christ) imparts divinity to all creatures,[42] and especially comes to 'birth' in the lives of humans, who consciously mirror the divine qualities: 'A theology of the Cosmic Christ is not embarrassed by the deification of humans.'[43] One of the messages to us which Fox puts into the mouth of the cosmic Christ is: '"Be still and know that I am God" (Ps 46:10). And you are too.'[44] In this sense, Fox's use of the idea of the cosmic Christ is another expression of his wish to avoid a 'dualism' of God and creation: 'divinity' is really a quality of things, rather than a way of naming the One to whom all things owe their existence and their goodness. The purpose of the incarnation of the cosmic Christ in Jesus of Nazareth is therefore to reveal the immanence of the cosmic Christ 'in the sufferings and dignity of each creature of the Earth'.[45] Quite remarkably Fox takes the Johannine Jesus's use of the 'I am' declaration, that in the biblical tradition indicates the mysterious uniqueness of the one God, as a 'challenge to name (or claim) our lives and beings in a similar fashion'.[46] Jesus claims the unique divinity of the one God in order to encourage us all to do the same.

But Fox's most original contribution to Christology is his proposal for 'naming the paschal mystery anew for the third millennium of Christianity'.[47] The paschal mystery is the Christian story of the passion, resurrection and ascension of Jesus Christ. Fox proposes that for our age of ecological destruction 'the appropriate symbol of the Cosmic Christ who became incarnate in Jesus is that of Jesus as Mother Earth crucified and rising daily'.[48] As not infrequently, it is hard to pin down Fox's language to a precise statement. Having spoken of Mother Earth's 'crucifixion' as a 'symbol' of Jesus,[49] he goes on to speak of it as how we are to understand the paschal mystery. In his fullest summary of the new naming of the paschal mystery, he claims that,

> matricide, mysticism, and the Cosmic Christ name the Paschal story we have understood as the death, resurrection and second coming of Jesus the Christ. The death of Mother Earth (matricide) and the resurrection of the human psyche (mysticism) and the coming of the Cosmic Christ (a living cosmology) name the mystery of the divine cycle of death and rebirth and the sending of the Spirit in our time.[50]

This is how Fox conceives the 'resurrection' of Mother Earth as occurring through a worldwide renaissance of mysticism and 'living cosmology' (i.e. understanding and experience of the cosmos as sacred). It is not at all clear how this relates to the particular story of Jesus of Nazareth, other than as a more universal playing-out of the cosmic principle that was made known to us through its particular occurrence in Jesus' case.

Much as Fox wishes to retain a significant place for the human story of Jesus of Nazareth, he treads a fine line between attributing universal significance to the particular historical man Jesus and his story (as any Christology must) and dissolving that particularity of Jesus into a universal divine presence. It is a line between a spirituality which focuses on Jesus in his relationship to the whole cosmos and a spirituality which focuses on the divinity of the cosmos. Perhaps there is room to read Fox in both ways, but the overall trend of his thought pushes in the latter direction.

With a view to ways in which we shall see that the mysticism of Francis of Assisi differs significantly from Fox's creation-centred mysticism, we could summarize the last two sections by saying that there is a strong tendency in Fox for the transcendence of God to be reduced to the cosmos and for the particularity of Jesus to be dissolved in the cosmos. While retaining some qualifications from the Christian tradition that mitigate these tendencies, on the whole the trend of Fox's thought is to a spirituality of cosmic divinity, to which neither the transcendence of God as Creator nor the particularity of God's incarnation as Jesus are important.

Francis of Assisi[51]

It has become commonplace to lament that Francis' attitude to the non-human creation, remembered in some of the most attractive stories of his relationships with animals, has been sentimentalized and thereby trivialized in popular perceptions. The stories are important, because, as with the Jesus of the Gospels, much of what we know of Francis is found in the stories told about him, and it is primarily these that convey the irresistible attractiveness of Francis, a figure like few others in the history of Christianity. We cannot understand Francis' 'nature mysticism' outside its context in the extraordinary intensity, self-giving and joyousness with which Francis lived his whole life in his devotion to God and his compassionate being-with God's creatures, human and others. Leonardo Boff lists 'his innocence, his enthusiasm for nature, his gentleness with all beings, his capacity for compassion with the poor, and of confraternalization with all the elements,'[52] and considers his 'communion and confraternalization with all of reality such as has never been seen since.'[53] Though Francis was no theologian in the academic sense, his attitude and relationships with the non-human creation reflect a profoundly theological vision of the community of God's creation in relation to its Creator. They also belong to an integrated ideal of life and praxis, which included a particular vision of the ascetic life, including absolute poverty, radical humility and constant prayer. Humility and poverty were the radical alternatives to status, power, possession and domination, removing these from all of Francis' relationships with humans and other creatures. By not valuing them as objects of possession, power or gratification for himself, he was freed to treat them all 'fraternally'[54] as fellow-creatures with the value they have for God their Creator. With the poorest of the poor, such as the lepers he tended, and the lowliest of God's creatures, such as the worm and the cicada, Francis was able to be brotherly and compassionate only because of the rigorous asceticism through which he was freed from other desires. Of course, there was also the ecstatic joy in God and God's creation which has led to the view that he was the first true 'nature mystic' in the Christian tradition.

It is important, first, to recognize that Francis does not at all conform to Fox's 'two traditions' model of Christian history. Theologically, he stands unequivocally in the mainstream, with a balanced and integrated view of creation, fall, sin and redemption:

> You have created everything spiritual and corporal and, after making us in Your own image and likeness, You placed us in paradise. Through our own fault we fell. We thank you for[,] as through Your Son You created us, so through Your holy love with which You loved us You brought about his birth ... and You willed to redeem us captives through His cross and blood and death.[55]

God, for Francis, is the Trinity, 'Father, Son and Holy Spirit, Creator of all, Savior of all who believe and hope in Him, and love Him'.[56] Creation and salvation belong together in God's relationship to the world. Francis' strong sense of human sinfulness ('by our own fault, we are disgusting, miserable and opposed to good, yet prompt and inclined to evil';[57] 'nothing belongs to us except our vices and sins'[58]) by no means impedes his delight in God's good creation.[59]

One aspect that holds creation and salvation together is Francis' strong sense of God as the Giver and all good things as God's gift:

> Let us refer all good to the Lord, God Almighty and Most High, acknowledge that every good is His, and thank Him, from whom all good comes, for everything.[60]

> [L]et us all love the Lord God who has given and gives to each one of us our whole body, our whole soul and our whole life, Who has created, redeemed and will save us by His mercy alone, Who did and does everything good for us.[61]

There is no ambiguity in Francis as to whether it is to God or the cosmos that we owe creation and ourselves. All creation is gift of the transcendent and only ultimate Creator, the only ultimate source of good

(since he 'alone is good'[62] in the sense that all other good is by deriva-
tion and gift from God). The Creator alone is therefore worthy of all
thanks and praise. Francis finds God in all things, but he finds *God*, the
Creator and Saviour of all, only by at the same time distinguishing God
from all things, by finding all things the gift of the God who exceeds and
surpasses them.

We should now begin to be able to see that Francis' spirituality is
really neither creation-centred not anthropocentric, but *centred on God*.
His own writings contain remarkable passages of praise and devotion
which require the dedication of the whole person to God alone and that
God should be the only goal of human desire.[63] This does not demean
the creatures, but gives them their true dignity and worth as precisely
creatures of the one Creator. As such they are loved and honoured by
those who love God. By thus ensuring that the devotion of the whole
person is owed to the one who surpasses creation Francis rules out the
idolatry that divinizes creation and expects of it therefore what it was
never able to supply: a true object of total, all-encompassing trust and
devotion. Instead, the creatures can be for Francis truly themselves, his
creaturely brothers and sisters, forming a community of mutual dependence, assisting each other in their common praise of the Creator who
made them all and values them all, each in its own distinctive reality.

Francis and the Non-human Creation

The many stories of Francis' delight in the companionship of animals
and his loving care for animals are not at all unprecedented. There was a
long tradition of stories of saints and animals (doubtless some historical
and others legendary) reaching back to the Desert Fathers and including especially the Celtic saints.[64] We do not know whether Francis knew
any of them, but they have in common with Francis a context in the
ascetic tradition of hermits who went to live (permanently or temporarily) apart from human society in order to devote themselves entirely to God. Because they deliberately sought out places remote from
human habitation, these hermits lived amid wild nature, closer than most
people to nature unmodified by human use. Alone with the non-human
creatures they came to love them and to value them as fellow-creatures
of God. So it was with Francis, who spent long periods alone or with a
few of his friar brothers in places where they would have close experience of wild creatures. Since Francis and his friars did not *own* animals,
even as pets, relationships of mutuality with wild creatures were the easier to form. Many of the stories show Francis' care for animals in ways
that are relatively traditional, though not exactly paralleled in the stories

of other solitary saints. Like other saints, Francis fed and protected his fellow-creatures. He wanted Christmas Day, a festival of special importance to Francis, to be honoured by the provision of abundant food for birds and more than the usual amount of food for domestic animals.[65] He saw to it that bees were provided with honey or wine lest they die of cold in the winter.[66] Several stories portray him saving animals from danger or harm, freeing animals which had been caught and brought to him, returning fish to the water, even removing worms from the road lest they be trampled.[67] Many of the stories stress the reciprocity of Francis' relationships with the creatures: they are tame and friendly as he is gentle and concerned.

An aspect of many of the earlier stories of saints and animals which continues in those about Francis is the theme of the restitution of paradise. Because these saints are living closely with God their dealings with animals reflect the originally intended relationship of humans to the rest of creation. One aspect of this is that the friendly and non-violent harmony of paradise is restored. Another, closely connected, is that the saints exercise the human dominion over other creatures, given in creation, as it was originally intended. This introduces a hierarchical element into the relationship, but it is one in which the animals willingly serve and obey the saints, and in which the saints care for the animals. The hierarchy is one of mutual service and care. In the stories about Francis, he frequently acts with authority to command the animals.[68] The fierce wolf which was terrorising the town of Gubbio was tamed and became friendly under Francis's influence.[69] Animals serve him, like the falcon, which during Francis' residence in his hermitage at La Verna used to wake him in time for matins, but showed such consideration for the saint that when Francis was tired or ill it would delay waking him until dawn.[70] Like many of the stories in the earlier tradition, this one emphasizes the affectionate friendship between the saint and the bird. The creatures respect Francis's authority, but they do so lovingly and willingly, as friends rather than slaves.

Francis is reported as saying that 'every creature says and proclaims: 'God has created me for you, O man!'' Although this reflects the medieval theological commonplace that the rest of the material creation was made for humanity, the context should be noted. Francis was telling the brother gardener not to plant vegetables everywhere, but to reserve part of the garden for plants whose scent and flowers 'might invite all men who looked at them to praise God'.[71] Thus Francis refuses to limit the value of the rest of creation for humanity to its practical usefulness but sees it as consisting also in its assisting humanity's praise of God. But his principle (expressed most fully at the end of his life in the *Canticle of the Creatures)* was that because the 'creatures minister to our needs every day,' and 'without them we could not live,' therefore we should appreciate them and praise God for them.[72] Thus the theme of human dominion is understood theocentrically rather than anthropocentrically. The creatures' service of humanity is properly received only as cause for praise and thankfulness to God. Therefore the human dominion over the creatures becomes for Francis primarily a matter of dependence on the creatures, with whom humanity shares a common dependence on the Creator. The creatures on whose service we depend are not to be exploited, but to be treated with brotherly/sisterly respect and consideration.

This means that in Francis the sense in which humanity has been given a special place in creation is only to be understood in relationship to his overwhelming sense of the common creatureliness which makes all creatures his 'sisters' and 'brothers.'[73] This linguistic usage seems to be distinctive of Francis. The Celtic saints had called the animals who befriended them their brothers in the monastic sense. Francis regards all the creatures (not only animals, but also fire and water, sun and moon, and so on) as brothers and sisters, because they are fellow-creatures and fellow-members of the family of those who serve God. The terms denote affection and especially affinity. Thus, while there is a residual element of hierarchy in the relationship, this does not negate the common creatureliness of humans and other creatures. Francis was a man of the thirteenth century, not the twenty-first, and so the chivalric notion of 'courtesy,' current in his time, was one idea that helped Francis to understand the relationship of humans and other creatures in terms not of domination but of mutuality.[74] Courtesy is the magnanimous, deferential, respectful attitude which enables love to be shown up and down the social hierarchy. In the community of creation, brothers and sisters on different levels of the hierarchy can interact with mutual respect and loving deference. With the chivalric notion of courtesy Francis fused the traditional monastic virtues of obedience and humility,[75] so that he can say that obedience,

> is subject and submissive to everyone in the world, not only to people but to every beast and wild animal as well[,] that they may do whatever they want with it insofar as it has been given them from above by the Lord.[76]

Here the hierarchy is virtually subverted by mutuality: the obedience which the creatures owe to humanity is reciprocated by an obedience of humanity to the creatures. What Francis envisages, in the end, is a kind of mutual and humble deference in the common service of the creatures to their Creator. When Boff refers to Francis' view of the world as 'cosmic democracy,'[77] the description is too modern to be entirely appropriate, and it does not distinguish a 'democracy' of political rights from one of mutual service, which would be more appropriate for Francis' view. But with all due qualifications it does suggest something of the direction in which Francis characteristically developed the Christian tradition.

All Creatures' Praise of God

Francis' exceptionally positive valuation of all his fellow-creatures did not derive simply from his encounters with them. It reflected his profound sense of God as Creator and therefore also of the creatures as each valued by God. He recognised God's generous giving in his provision for all of the animate creation, following Jesus' words about the birds in the Sermon on the Mount (Matt 6:25). In relation to the birds, for example, he recognised God's special gifts to them ('noble among His creatures') as constituting their particular worth within the community of creation.[78] Another theme with strong biblical and traditional roots Francis made very much his own and fundamental for the way he related to his fellow-creatures and, with them, to God. This is the idea that all creatures praise their Creator and that human worship of God is participation in this worship of the whole creation.

In his own works Francis echoes the main biblical sources of this idea: the Benedicite (Daniel 3:52–90 in the Vulgate);[79] Psalms 69:34; 96:11–12; 103:22; 148;[80] Revelation 5:13.[81] These texts would have been very familiar to Francis, especially since the two most ample in their depiction of the praise of the creatures feature prominently in the daily offices he recited according to his breviary: Psalm 148 was to be said every morning, the Benedicite every Sunday and feast day morning.[82] Most revealing are Francis' own liturgical compositions, which often consist of a collage of texts carefully selected from Scripture, especially the Psalms. One of these ('The Praises to be Said at All the Hours') was to be used by the friars before each hour of the office. This outpouring of praise to the Trinity is based largely on the heavenly liturgy depicted in Revelation 4–5, and like that liturgy it culminates in the praise of God by every creature in the cosmos. Calls to all the creatures to praise alternate with a refrain ('Let us praise and glorify Him forever') based on that in the Benedicite. The 'Exhortation to the Praise of God' calls on all the creatures, including both general references and specific references to rivers and birds, to praise God. In these liturgies of creation there is no hierarchy, not even an order of importance in calls to praise. Before God, as his creatures, humans stand alongside other creatures, and are united with all other creatures in a harmony formed by their common praise of the one Creator. Expressed here is not only a 'living cosmology' (Fox) in which humanity finds its place, but a wholly theocentric cosmology in which the transcendent Creator is distinguished from his creation in the praise that unites his creatures. The ideal harmony and interdependence of creation are most fully realised when humans join other creatures in praise of the Creator.

Characteristically and originally, Francis also translated this liturgical usage into an actual practice of addressing the creatures themselves.[83] This began with the famous sermon to the birds,[84] which initiated a regular practice:

> From that day on, he carefully exhorted all birds, all animals, all reptiles, and also insensible creatures, to praise and love their Creator, because daily, invoking the name of the Savior, he observed their obedience in his own experience.[85]

The reference to 'the name of the Savior' is significant, because it relates creation and salvation in a way that is rarely explicit in the material about creation's praise of God,[86] but is surely often implicit. Since salvation entails the restoration of creation to its proper harmony and order in relation to God, the praise of the creatures is directed to Christ as Saviour as well as to God as Creator. This is what occurs at the end of the great cosmic liturgy in Revelation 4–5, which Francis evidently knew well: when the slaughtered Lamb is enthroned in heaven, every creature in the cosmos joins in the doxology addressed to God and the Lamb. This eschatological goal of all worship Francis anticipated whenever he invoked the name of Jesus and called on creatures to praise their Creator.

We should also remember Francis's habit of singing along with cicadas or birds in what he understood as their praise of their Creator.[87] In this way he translated the sentiments of the Benedicite into a real human solidarity with the rest of creation understood as a theocentric community existing for the praise and service of God. There is no trace in Francis of the idea that the creatures need humans to voice their praise of God for them. On the contrary, the cicadas and the birds are already singing to God's glory; Francis joins their song.

The Canticle of the Creatures

In the famous *Canticle of Brother Sun* or *Canticle of the Creatures*, written at the end of his life, Francis summed up much of his attitude to creation. It is important to appreciate fully the opening two stanzas that praise God before reference is made to the creatures:

> Most High, all-powerful, good Lord,
> Yours are the praises, the glory, and the honor, and all blessing,
> To You alone, Most High, do they belong,
> and no human is worthy to mention Your name.

That God surpasses the creatures in such a way as to be the only praise-worthy one could not be clearer. So, when the next stanza continues,

> Praised be You, my Lord, with all Your creatures

The praising of the creatures can only be a way of praising their Creator, from whom their praiseworthy features derive. This praise of God *with* the creatures (stanza 3–4) is a transition from the praise of God without the creatures (stanzas 1–2) to the praises of God *for* the creatures, which occupy stanzas 5–13. In these stanzas the various qual-ities of the creatures are lovingly detailed, so that God may be praised for them. Each of these stanzas begins (in Francis' Italian original): '*Laudato si, mi Signore, per ...*,' followed by reference to one or more of the creatures. There has been controversy over whether the meaning is 'Be praised, my Lord, by ...' "Be praised, my Lord, through ...' or 'Be praised, my Lord, for ...' Divergent interpretations of the phrase go back to soon after Francis' death,[88] and any would be consistent with his thinking about the creation. But the latest detailed study by Sorrell argues very convincingly for the translation: 'Be praised, my Lord, for ...'.[89] In that case the Canticle does not call on Sister Moon, Brother Wind, Sister Water and the rest to praise God, even though Francis, as we have seen, could well have done this. Rather the Canticle takes up Francis' conviction, which we have also noticed, that human beings should praise God for their fellow-creatures. The creatures are appreci-ated in three ways: for their practical usefulness in making human life possible and good, for their beauty, and for the way their distinctive qualities reflect the divine being (in particular 'Sir Brother Sun,' in his beauty and radiance, resembles God). This is an appreciation of the God-given value of creation which goes far beyond a purely utilitari-an, anthropocentric view. It celebrates the interdependent harmony of creation. The Canticle is designed to teach people to think of creation with gratitude, appreciation and respect.[90]

Differently from Francis' earlier hymns of liturgical praise, the clos-ing stanzas of the Canticle,[91] praising God for 'those who give pardon for your love and bear infirmity and tribulation' and 'for Sister Bodily Death, from whom no one living can escape,' make reference to negative aspects of the world and the painful reconciliation they require to make all good: forgiveness of injuries, endurance of suffering, acceptance of death. The Canticle thus moves through the ideal harmony of the creatures, reflecting God's goodness in creation, through the painful healing of the negative, reflecting God's patient and forgiving love in salvation, to the final stanza which calls on its hearers to praise:

> Praise and bless my Lord and give Him thanks
> and serve Him with great humility.

In the light of Francis' earlier compositions and practice, this is surely addressed not only to humans but to all the creatures.

Murray Bodo's comment on the Canticle is apt:

> [T]he final poem of [Francis'] life reveals what happened to that man for whom the love of God was everything. And the surprise is that when God is everything, then everything else becomes more important and holy. The whole creature world is enhanced instead of being neglected and de-emphasized for some spirit world, as so often happens in pseudo-spirituality. For Francis, whatever demeans and devalues the creature demeans the Creator, so that reverence for and joy over every thing and every person becomes *the* sign of the love of God.[92]

Thus we see in Francis that the alternative to a spirituality that despises the created world does not have to be one which divinises the created world (as Fox tends to imply). It can be one in which the created world is sacred and valued for love of its Creator who always surpasses it. Love of the Creator can include the creation without being reduced to love of the creation.

The whole Canticle is a hymn to the Creator and Saviour of all, a theocentric celebration of creation, stemming both from Francis's own intense nature mysticism and also, in the closing stanzas, from his christological mysticism of identification with Jesus Christ, that climaxed in his receiving the stigmata. It is the only text from Francis himself in which these two aspects of his mystical awareness of God and creation clearly come together, no doubt because it was written during the painful and dark days of the last two years of his life. We turn to consider each briefly.

Creation Mysticism

We have considered various aspects of Francis' attitude to and relation-ships with the non-human creation, but we have still to register the intensity of delight in the creatures that frequently raised Francis to ecstatic rejoicing in their Creator. Some comments from his early biog-raphers will illustrate this:

> He used to extol the artistry of [the bees'] work and their remark-able ingenuity, giving glory to the Lord. With such an outpouring, he often used up an entire day or more in praise of them and other creatures.[93]

> He had so much love and sympathy for [the creatures] that he was disturbed when they were treated without respect. He spoke to them with a great inner and exterior joy, as if they had been endowed by God with feeling, intelligence, and speech. Very often it was for him the occasion to become enraptured in God.[94]

> [H]e caressed and contemplated [the creatures] with delight, so much so that his spirit seemed to live in heaven and not on earth.[95]

Christ Mysticism

Equal to the intensity of Francis' glorification of God the Creator with and for the creatures was the intensity of his identification with the human Jesus, the incarnate Son of God. Just as there is no loss of tran-scendence in Francis' adoration of the Creator of all things, so there is no loss of particularity in his devotion to the Saviour in his humanity. Francis was christocentric in his praxis, following as fully as possible the humili-ty and poverty of Jesus and his confraternity with the poor and the mar-ginalized. He was christocentric also in his communion with God through intense meditation on Jesus and identification with his passion.
Cousins calls this 'the mysticism of the historical event':

> In this type of consciousness, one recalls a significant event in the past, enters into its drama and draws from it spiritual energy, even-tually moving beyond the event towards union with God.

The Christian form of this mysticism, which in Cousins' view began with Francis, consists, of course, in contemplation of the events of the story of Jesus.[96] It was to facilitate spiritual participation in such an event that Francis, famously, created the first Christmas crib (with live animals).[97] (Christmas was his best-loved festival because it recalled the humility of Christ in undergoing birth as a human being and in poverty.) But Cousins' characterization of Francis' Christ mysticism perhaps misses the intensity of his devotion to the person of Jesus which accompanies his desire to participate in Jesus' story. Again we may rely on comments from the early biographers:

> [Of the period soon after his conversion:] Every day he meditated on the humility and example of the Son of God; he experienced much compassion and much sweetness from this, and in the end, what was bitter to his body, was changed into sweetness. The sufferings and bitterness which Christ endured for us were a constant subject of affliction to him and a cause for interior and exterior mortification; consequently, he was totally unconcerned with his own sufferings.[98]

> The brothers who lived with him know that daily, constantly, talk of Jesus was always on his lips, sweet and pleasant conversations about Him, kind words full of love .... Often he sat down to dinner but on hearing or saying or even thinking 'Jesus' he forgot bodily food ... Often as he walked along a road, thinking and singing of Jesus, he would forget his destination and start inviting all the elements to praise Jesus.[99]

Francis' desire to identify with his Saviour was granted finally when he received the stigmata.

The two different aspects of Francis' mysticism – his nature mysticism and his Christ mysticism – could be said to correspond to creation and redemption. This may be broadly true, but we have already noticed that it was not characteristic of Francis to hold creation and redemption apart. The last sentence just quoted[100] illustrates how easily they could come together. Another example derives from the way Francis, following the medieval practice of seeing religious allegories in nature but as always making something characteristically his own out of it, used to be moved to praise or reflection by features of nature that recalled scriptural images of God, Christ or humanity. Especially he loved lambs, because they symbolised the humility of Jesus. In one story, Francis came upon a flock of goats:

> There was one little sheep walking humbly and grazing calmly among these many goats. When blessed Francis saw it, he stopped

in his tracks, and touched with sorrow in his heart, he groaned loudly, and said to the brother accompanying him: 'Do you see that sheep walking so meekly among those goats? I tell you, in the same way our Lord Jesus Christ, meek and humble, walked among the Pharisees and chief priests. So I ask you, my son, in your love for him to share my compassion for this little sheep. After we have paid for it, let us lead this little one from the midst of the goats'.[101]

Spontaneously compassionate though they were, incidents like this functioned as acted parables, conveying something of Francis' deepest apprehensions of God to his brothers.

Conclusion

There are aspects of Francis, such as this last example, which doubtless seem alien to our time and place. But there is much in Francis to be appreciated and retrieved. His is a creation mysticism thoroughly rooted in and coherent with the orthodox mainstream of Christian belief and life. Essentially it was the biblical understanding of creation that Francis lived more profoundly and intensely perhaps than any other Christian has done.

Notes

[1] R.D. Sorrell, *St. Francis of Assisi and Nature* (New York: Oxford University Press, 1988), ch. 4.
[2] M. Fox, *Creation Spirituality* (San Francisco: HarperSanFrancisco, 1991), 105.
[3] M. Fox, *The Coming of the Cosmic Christ* (San Francisco: Harper & Row, 1988), 48.
[4] Fox, *Cosmic Christ*, 42.
[5] Fox, *Creation Spirituality*, 29–30; cf. *Cosmic Christ*, 51.
[6] Fox, *Cosmic Christ*, 49–50.
[7] Ibid., 51–2.
[8] Fox, *Creation Spirituality*, 33.
[9] Appendix A in M. Fox, *Original Blessing* (Santa Fe: Bear & Co., 1983), 307–15.
[10] Ibid., 48.
[11] E.g. T.E. Clarke, 'Theological Trends: Creational Spirituality,' *The Way* 29 (1989), 77; B. Newman, 'Romancing the Past: A Critical Look at Matthew Fox and the Medieval "Creation Mystics",' *Touchstone* 5 (1992), 5–10 (I owe this reference to Lawrence Osborn); M. Goodall & J. Reader, 'Why Matthew Fox Fails to Change the World,' in I. Ball, M. Goodall, C. Palmer & J. Reader (ed.), *The Earth Beneath: A Critical Guide to Green Theology* (London: SPCK, 1992), 115–16.

[12] Fox, *Original Blessing*, 296.

[13] Ibid., 210.

[14] Ibid., 26.

[15] Ibid., 108.

[16] Ibid., 115.

[17] E.g. Fox, *Creation Spirituality*, 92–3.

[18] Fox, *Original Blessing*, 89.

[19] Ibid., 90.

[20] Ibid.

[21] Fox, *Cosmic Christ*, 49–50.

[22] Fox, *Original Blessing*, 90.

[23] Ibid., 89.

[24] Cf. ibid., 119.

[25] E.g. Fox, *Original Blessing*, 203; *Creation Spirituality*, 99; *Cosmic Christ*, 53.

[26] E.g. Fox, *Original Blessing*, 120, 259, 260; *Cosmic Christ*, 49.

[27] E.g. Fox, *Original Blessing*, 164.

[28] The only instance I have found is in *Original Blessing* (283), where it may well equate with trusting ourselves as God's image.

[29] Ibid., 163, 171.

[30] Fox, *Creation Spirituality*, 10.

[31] Fox, *Original Blessing*, 90–1.

[32] Oddly, Fox in his own, later exposition of the *Canticle,* takes the 'Lord' and the 'Most High' to whom the *Canticle* is addressed to be the Cosmic Christ. Fox, *Cosmic Christ*, 112.

[33] Fox, *Creation Spirituality*, 9.

[34] Ibid., 11.

[35] Ibid., 10.

[36] For 'the beginning and the end, the alpha and the omega' see Isa. 41:4; 44:6; 48:12; Rev. 1:8, 17; 21:6; 22:13.

[37] Fox, *Creation Spirituality*, 28.

[38] Ibid., 27–9.

[39] Fox, *Cosmic Christ*, 7.

[40] Ibid., 79.

[41] Ibid., 147 (original emphasis).

[42] Ibid., 145.

[43] Ibid., 109.

[44] Ibid., 142.

[45] Ibid., 155.

[46] Ibid., 154.

[47] Ibid., 162.

[48] Ibid., 145.

[49] Ibid., 145, 149.

[50] Ibid., 162–3.

[51] Significant relevant studies of Francis: E.A. Armstrong, *Saint Francis: Nature Mystic* (Berkeley: University of California Press, 1973); R.J. Armstrong & I.G. Brady (ed.), *Francis and Clare: The Complete Works*, Classics of Western Spirituality (London: SPCK, 1982); M. Bodo, *The Way of St Francis* (Glasgow: Collins, 1985); L. Boff, *Saint Francis: A Model for Human Liberation*, tr. by J.W. Diercksmeir (London: SCM Press, 1985); E.H. Cousins, 'Francis of Assisi: Christian Mysticism at the Crossroads,' in S.T. Katz (ed.), *Mysticism and Religious Traditions* (Oxford: Oxford University Press, 1983), 163–90; E. Leclerc, *Le Chant des Sources* (Paris: Editions Franciscaines, 3rd edition, 1975); J.R.H. Moorman, *Richest of Poor Men: The Spirituality of St Francis of Assisi* (London: Darton, Longman & Todd, 1977); M. Robson, *St Francis of Assisi* (London: Chapman, 1997); Sorrell, *St. Francis of Assisi and Nature*.

[52] Boff, *Saint Francis*, 18.

[53] Ibid., 19.

[54] The word is unfortunately gender-specific (at least in its etymology) and has no feminine equivalent, but I use it to refer to the way in which Francis considered all creatures as sisters and brothers.

[55] Francis, *The Earlier Rule*, in R.J. Armstrong, J.A.W. Hellmann & W.J. Short (eds.), *Francis of Assisi: Early Documents*, Vol. 1: *The Saint* (New York: New City Press, 1999), 23:1.

[56] Ibid., 23:11.

[57] Ibid., 21:6.

[58] Ibid., 17:7.

[59] Fox in *Original Blessing* (275) blames Bonaventure's Life of Francis for conforming him to the fall/redemption theological tradition, but the quotations in the above paragraph are all from Francis' own writing. Fox is here probably following L. White, 'The Historical Roots of our Ecologic Crisis,' *Science* 155 (1967), 1203–7 (and subsequently reprinted in several edited collections). Against White's claim that Bonaventure suppressed Francis' views on creation, see Sorrell, *St. Francis of Assisi,* 148.

[60] *Earlier Rule*, 17:17.

[61] Ibid.; cf. also Francis, *Second Letter to the Faithful*, in Armstrong, Hellmann & Short, *Early Documents*, 61.

[62] Francis, *Second Letter*, 62; *Earlier Rule*, 23:9.

[63] Francis, *Earlier Rule*, 23:8–11; Francis, *The Praises of God*, in Armstrong, Hellmann & Short, *Early Documents*; Francis, *A Prayer Inspired by the Our Father*, in Armstrong, Hellmann & Short, *Early Documents*, 5; Francis, *A Letter to the Entire Order*, in Armstrong, Hellmann & Short, *Early Documents*, 50.

[64] H. Waddell, *Beasts and Saints* (London: Constable, 1934) is a collection of some of the best of the Latin stories in translation. Many of the stories about the desert fathers can be found in translation in N. Russell and B. Ward, *The*

Lives of the Desert Fathers (London: Mowbray/Kalamazoo: Cistercian Publications, 1981). Some of the stories of the Celtic saints are retold in R. Van de Weyer, *Celtic Fire: An Anthology of Celtic Christian Literature* (London: Darton, Longman & Todd, 1990). Studies of the stories include S.P. Bratton, 'The Original Desert Solitaire: Early Christian Monasticism and Wilderness,' *Environmental Ethics* 10 (1988), 31–53; R.D. Sorrell, *St. Francis of Assisi and Nature* (New York: Oxford University Press, 1988), 19–27; and especially W.J. Short, *Saints in the World of Nature: The Animal Story as Spiritual Parable in Medieval Hagiography (900–1200)* (Rome: Gregorian University, 1983) (I am grateful to Dr Short for providing me with a photocopy of this book, which is unobtainable in Britain).

[65] *The Remembrance of a Desire of a Soul*, in M.A. Habig (ed.), *St. Francis of Assisi: Writings and Early Biographies: English Omnibus of the Sources for the Life of St. Francis* (Chicago: Franciscan Herald press, 1983), 200.

[66] *The Life of St. Francis by Thomas of Celano*, in Armstrong, Hellmann & Short, *Early Documents*, 80.

[67] Listed in Sorrell, *St. Francis*, 44.

[68] Examples listed in ibid., 43.

[69] *The Little Flowers of St. Francis*, in Habig, *Writings and Early Biographies*, 1:21.

[70] *The Remembrance of a Desire of a Soul*, in ibid., 168.

[71] *The Anonymous of Perugia*, in ibid., 51.

[72] Ibid., 43.

[73] Sorrell, *St. Francis*, 66, 127–8.

[74] See ibid., 69–75.

[75] On the relationship of humility (and poverty) to Francis's confraternity with creatures, see Boff, *Saint Francis*, 38–40.

[76] Francis, *A Salutation of Virtues*, in Armstrong, Hellmann & Short, *Early Documents*, 14.

[77] Boff, *Saint Francis*, 34.

[78] *The Life of St. Francis by Thomas of Celano*, 58.

[79] The *Benedicite* is the canticle which appears in the Greek version of the book of Daniel as Daniel 3:52–90. This makes it part of the canonical book of Daniel for the Orthodox and Roman Catholic churches, but since it is absent from the Hebrew and Aramaic text of Daniel, the Protestant churches assigned it to the Apocrypha, where it occurs among the Additions to Daniel, as the Song of the Three. But White, who remarks that it 'contradicts the historically dominant Judeo-Christian anthropocentrism,' is quite wrong in supposing that it shows the influence of Hellenism or was ever thought in the least heretical. On the contrary, it merely develops at length the theme of nature's praise of God to be found in the Psalms (especially Ps 148). See L. White, 'Continuing the Conversation,' in I.G. Barbour (ed.), *Western Man and Environmental Ethics* (Reading, Massachusetts: Addison-Wesley, 1973), 61–2.

[80] For a valuable study of this theme in the Psalms, see T.E. Fretheim, 'Creation's Praise of God in the Psalms,' *Ex Auditu* 3 (1987), 16–30.

[81] The allusions are in *Exhortation to the Praise of God*, in Armstrong, Hellmann & Short, *Early Documents*, 138 (Ps. 69:35; Dan. 3:78; Ps. 103:22; Dan. 3:80); *Second Letter to the Faithful*, 61 (Rev. 5:13); *Praises to be Said at All the Hours* (Dan. 3:57; Ps. 69:35; Rev 5:13); *The Office of the Passion*, in Armstrong, Hellmann & Short, *Early Documents*, 7:4 (Ps. 96:10–11); *The Canticle of the Creatures*, in Armstrong, Hellmann & Short, *Early Documents*, 113–4 (Ps. 148; Benedicite). On the relationship of *Canticle of the Creatures* to Psalm 148 and the Benedicite, see Sorrell, *St. Francis,* 99, 102–5.

[82] Sorrell, *St. Francis,* 99.

[83] It is typical of Francis to put biblical passages into practice in a way that might seem naively literal, but really constituted a particularly potent expression of a biblical theme.

[84] *The Life of St. Francis by Thomas of Celano*, 58; *Little Flowers*, 1:16.

[85] *The Life of St. Francis by Thomas of Celano*, 58; cf. 81.

[86] See also ibid., 115 – quoted below.

[87] *Remembrance of a Desire of a Soul*, 171; *The Major Legend by Bonaventura*, in Habig, *Writings and Early Biographies*, 8:9. See also (for the nightingale) J.R.H. Moorman, 'A New Fioretti' 57, in Habig, *Writings and Early Biographies*, 1881–1882.

[88] Sorrell, *St. Francis,* 116–17, 119.

[89] Ibid., 118–22.

[90] Ibid., 124.

[91] These sections were added later, the one on Sister Death shortly before his death.

[92] M. Bodo, *The Way of St Francis* (Glasgow: Collins, 1985), 150.

[93] *The Life of St. Francis by Thomas of Celano*, 80.

[94] *Anonymous of Perugia*, 49.

[95] Ibid., 51.

[96] E.H. Cousins, 'Francis of Assisi: Christian Mysticism at the Crossroads,' in S.T. Katz (ed.), *Mysticism and Religious Traditions* (Oxford: Oxford University Press, 1983), 166.

[97] *The Life of St. Francis by Thomas of Celano*, 84–6.

[98] *Anonymous of Perugia*, 37.

[99] *The Life of St. Francis by Thomas of Celano*, 115.

[100] From ibid.

[101] Ibid., 77.

12

St John of The Cross

Helen Marshall

Many people are familiar with the phrase 'dark night of the soul' and it is used in many different contexts, but far fewer people are acquainted with the writings of St John of the Cross from which this phrase is derived. John was a sixteenth century Spanish mystic whose writings on the spiritual life are exceptionally profound and challenging. His concern was not to commend strange or ecstatic 'mystical' experiences; on the contrary he warns against setting too much store on extraordinary phenomena. His aim was rather to reflect on how we can grow in a union of love with God, a union that will involve the whole of our lives. Along with St Paul he urges that we need 'to grasp how wide and long and high and deep is the love of Christ, and to know this love that surpasses knowledge – that [we] may be filled to the measure of all the fullness of God' (Eph. 3:18–9).

This chapter will provide a brief sketch of the life of St John of the Cross, after which there will be a short discussion of his principal teachings, and finally some reflections on the relevance of his writings for the church today.

Life and Character

Juan de Yepes (later to be known as St John of the Cross) was born in 1542 in the small town of Fontiveros, midway between Madrid and Salamanca on the rocky plateau of Castile. His father, Gonzalo de Yepes, belonged to a wealthy family of silk merchants from Toledo. His mother, Catalina, was a poor orphaned girl who struggled to make a living by her weaving. The two fell in love and married in 1529. To a very status-conscious society, this was seen as profoundly shocking and Gonzalo was disinherited by his family for betraying his roots.

The couple had three sons: Franscisco, Luis and Juan (John). John was only two years old when his father died, worn out by drudgery and poverty. Catalina had to manage as best she could, receiving no support from Gonzalo's family. After the death of her second son, she moved with her two remaining sons to Medina, the major market town of Castile. John was then nine years old and attended a school for disadvantaged children. Later, in his teens, he began to work as a nurse in one of the city's hospitals, specifically for those suffering from syphilis, where he was noted for his gentleness and his patience. He was also obviously very intelligent and the administrator of the hospital provided for John to attend the Jesuit school, where he studied Latin and Greek, grammar and rhetoric.

After finishing his studies, at the age of twenty-one, John entered the Carmelite novitiate recently founded in Medina. It was perhaps surprising that he did not join the Jesuits, but he was probably attracted to the more contemplative tradition of the Carmelites. As part of his Carmelite training he was sent to Salamanca University, which ranked at the time with the universities of Oxford, Bologna and Paris, to study philosophy and theology. After three years he was ordained. But he had become dissatisfied with the Carmelite Order and the ambitious, point-scoring competitiveness of the university world. He was seeking something else, and was on the point of leaving the Carmelites for a more solitary, disciplined life (possibly with the Carthusians) when he met Teresa de Jesus (later known as Teresa of Avila).

Teresa had begun a reform movement among the women of the Carmelite Order in Avila, and this movement was beginning to spread. She wanted to set up small communities which were committed to poverty, simplicity and contemplation, and which were independent of rich benefactors. The obsession with status and hierarchy in the wider society of the time was also found within Carmelite communities. Teresa was determined to resist this and to create communities where all the members were equal whatever their social status. The reformed Carmelite communities, the 'Discalced Carmelites', were named after their tendency to wear sandals rather than shoes. These communities dedicated much more time to individual silent prayer in addition to the communal worship.

Teresa was an inspirational figure and John, drawn to her vision of reform, agreed to join her. The two shared much in their understanding of prayer and their ideals of community life, although they were very different personalities. When they first met, Teresa was 52 and John 25. He had much to learn from her, but she also immediately perceived his wisdom. She was later to comment: 'though he is small in stature, I believe he is huge in God's eyes.'

In 1568, John founded the first discalced monastery at Duruelo, where he took the name John of the Cross. A few years afterwards, Teresa asked him to go to Avila to act as spiritual director to the convent of nuns there, including Teresa herself. While in Avila, John also offered spiritual counsel to others in the city, including to professors, but also to simple people and to well-known 'sinners'. He gave time to teaching the children of the poor, remembering his own deprived childhood.

The most formative experience of John's life happened in 1577, when he was kidnapped by unreformed elements of the Order, becoming the target for their opposition to reform. On the night of 2 December 1577, a group of Carmelites and armed men broke into the chaplain's quarters in Avila and seized John. He was taken to the monastery in Toledo and when he refused to renounce the way of the discalced friars he was imprisoned. For most of the next nine months he was kept in a small room measuring six feet by ten feet in which the only light came from a narrow slit in the roof. John remained alone in this room through the extremely cold winter months and the suffocating heat of the summer months. He was given nothing but bread and water, was not able to wash and was flogged regularly. He also suffered psychological torture from his captors.

However, it was in these circumstances that John wrote much of his poetry, including a major portion of 'The Spiritual Canticle'. He experienced being stripped bare in himself and he knew the agonising darkness of God's seeming absence. Yet this produced in him a far sharper yearning for God and a deeper openness to God's grace. In one sense, this experience coloured all of his writings.

After nine months of imprisonment, John escaped. He was emaciated and barely alive, but had enough nerve and ingenuity to loosen the screws on the lock on his door while his jailer was absent and lower himself though a tiny window with the aid of some knotted strips of sheet. He found refuge with the Teresian nuns in Toledo.

When he had recovered, John was appointed Vicar of El Calvario, a monastery near Beas in Andalusia, where he enjoyed the spectacular natural scenery. Less than a year later he moved yet again to the university city of Baeza to be Rector of a new Carmelite college where he remained until 1582. Then he was elected Prior of a monastery in the city of Granada. During these years much of his time was spent in the ministry of spiritual direction, again not only to friars and nuns, but also to university professors and uneducated lay people.

In 1585, John was elected Vicar-Provincial of Andalusia. This involved travelling around all the houses of friars and nuns in Andalusia. He also founded seven new monasteries. In 1588, John was elected councillor to the Vicar-General for the Discalced Carmelites, Father Nicolas Doria. But when, at the General Chapter of 1591, Doria expressed his intention to make changes to the Teresian Constitution of 1581, John spoke against this move. As a result, John was removed from office and sent to the isolated friary of La Penuela.

In September 1591 he became ill with a fever caused by an inflammation of the leg which he at first ignored. When it became obvious he needed medical attention, he journeyed to the monastery at Ubeda. However, not only was he virtually unknown at Ubeda, but he was also not very warmly welcomed. It was here that he died, after much suffering. He died repeating the words of the psalmist, 'into your hands I commend my spirit.'

John's life was marked by suffering. His childhood was spent in poverty and deprivation, and he ended his life in great physical pain surrounded by people who were more or less indifferent towards him. He knew what it meant to be in positions of leadership, but he also experienced torture and rejection. He was the target of the anger of the unreformed Carmelites who kidnapped and imprisoned him; later, towards the end of his life, he was cast off by members of the Reform itself.

The different kinds of suffering that John experienced could have produced a bitter and cynical person. Instead, no doubt partly because of his suffering, John was a man of deep insight and compassion. Throughout his life he took a particular interest in the poor and the sick. When visiting a monastery, he always went first to the infirmary to ensure the sick were well looked after. He was concerned with people's physical and practical needs, but also with their deeper spiritual needs. He had a special concern for those whose spiritual journey was marked by trial and suffering, and much of his writing seeks to guide those who found themselves in this way.

John was highly intelligent and singularly gifted, but he was also truly humble. He never claimed any kind of special treatment for himself, and he took his turn cleaning the floors even when he was Prior. In a society which emphasised hierarchy this must have been very striking. Many witnesses comment on John's sense of humour and his letters testify to his personal warmth. Indeed, it is important to note this warmth, humour and compassion in the context of the depth of his personal suffering, because when one studies his writings it often seems that he is commending such a hard and uncompromising spirituality that it is easy to question whether he was really human! John was indeed very human, but along with his patience and compassion there is a spiritual rigour informed by a remarkably single-minded desire for God and a profound insight into the capacity of human beings for self-deception.

Teaching[1]

John was first and foremost a poet. He wrote most of his poetry first and only later wrote his great prose works, 'The Ascent of Mount Carmel' and 'The Dark Night'. Much of his poetry speaks of the love between God and the soul in terms of the love between the bridegroom and the bride, echoing the Song of Songs in the Old Testament. His prose works seek to explain how this love of God impacts our lives and what it demands of us if we are to grow in love ourselves.

John's writings are deeply scriptural. There are biblical references on almost every page. More importantly, his thinking is moulded by the scriptural witness to a self-giving God who demands our all in return. When we read his most uncompromising passages we need to recognise that they merely echo or interpret the radical challenges found in the New Testament.

Union with God

For John the goal of the spiritual journey is union with God. Human beings were made for such a union: 'After all, this love is the end for which we were created.'[2] John grieves that so many people are not interested in this goal: 'O souls, created for these grandeurs and called to them! What are you doing? How are you spending your time? Your aims are base and your possessions miseries!'[3] John is convinced of the great potential human beings have to love even as God loves: 'the soul's aim is a love equal to God's'; just as the soul will one day know 'as she is known by God (1 Cor. 13:12), so she will also love God as she is loved by him.'[4] John is aware, however, of the depths of sin which hinder such a transformation in love; he seeks in his writings to show us how we can cooperate with the grace of God in removing these blockages to union with him.

What does John mean by 'union with God'? This phrase can easily be misunderstood. *Firstly*, John does not imply that we will in the end become of one substance with God, or that individuals will be absorbed into an undifferentiated Absolute Oneness in the sense envisaged by some Eastern mystics. John is speaking of a union of love and likeness in which our wills are united to God's will. He comments on Jesus' prayer for his disciples in John 17: '... that they may be one as we are one, I in them and you in me' saying: 'it should not be thought that the Son desires here to ask the Father that the saints be one with him essentially and naturally as the Son is with the Father, but that they may be so through the union of love, just as the Father and the Son are one in unity of love.'[5] We are invited to share in the relationship of love which flows between Father, Son and Holy Spirit.

Secondly, the 'union' John is talking about is not primarily a transient, ecstatic experience in prayer, but a fundamental union of the will of the whole person with God, 'for the two wills are so united that there is only one will and love, which is God's.'[6] Union with God may indeed include direct and joyful experiences of God (as we will see), but these experiences in themselves do not constitute union with God. What matters is the complete giving of one's whole self to God, whatever profound experiences we do or do not receive.[7]

Thirdly, John emphasises that it is by the work of God's fiery love that we are transformed into his likeness and united with him. We can, and indeed must, cooperate by removing those things in us that hinder the work of God's grace in our lives, but it is primarily *his* work. John expresses this powerfully in his poem 'The Living Flame of Love':

> Flame, alive, compelling,
> yet tender past all telling,
> reaching the secret centre of my soul!
> Since now evasion's over,
> finish your work, my Lover,
> break the last thread, wound me and make me whole!
>
> Burn that is for my healing!
> Wound of delight past feeling!
> Ah, gentle hand whose touch is a caress,
> foretaste of heaven conveying
> and every debt repaying:
> slaying, you give me life for death's distress.
>
> O lamps of fire bright-burning
> with splendid brilliance, turning
> deep caverns of my soul to pools of light!
> Once shadowed, dim, unknowing,
> now their strange new-found glowing
> gives warmth and radiance for my Love's delight.
>
> Ah! gentle and so loving
> you wake within me, proving
> that you are there in secret and alone;
> your fragrant breathing stills me,
> your grace, your glory fills me
> so tenderly your love becomes my own.[8]

As Iain Matthew points out, the poem is all about what *God* is doing: he is piercing, repaying, slaying, giving life, waking, breathing. John's God 'anticipates, initiates, gives, transforms; like a flame entering till it engages the "deepest centre". John's universe is drenched in a self-outpouring God.'[9]

In his commentary on the poem, John states that 'the soul now feels that it is all inflamed in the divine union … that in the intimate part of its substance it is flooded with no less than rivers of glory.'[10] The poem describes union with God here as an overwhelming experience of the active, fiery love of God and the radiant love it evokes in the soul. However, this experience cannot be separated from the union of wills outlined above; union with God is never to be conceived of as a 'mystical experience' which is unrelated to the total giving of oneself to God. John emphasises throughout his writings that we should never seek 'experiences' for their own sake, but seek only God himself.

Fourthly, John does believe that it is possible, though rare, for a person to attain to this union of love with God in this life, a state sometimes called the 'spiritual marriage'. But he says of such a soul: 'even though there is a true union of will in this high state she now enjoys, she cannot attain the excellence and power of love that she will possess in the strong union of glory.'[11] The union with God attainable in this life is a foretaste of that deeper and fuller union in heaven.

It needs to be emphasised that for John the goal of the spiritual journey is union with God, rather than our own self-realisation and perfection. Our gaze is to be on God rather than ourselves. The love of God is both that towards which we move, and also the way in which we travel. There is never any sense in John's writings that union with God is something we reach through our own achievements; rather it is only through God's grace that any spiritual growth happens. However, what we are required to do is to open ourselves up to that grace of God, realise our need of it and let go of those things which frustrate its work in our lives.

In reflecting first on John's teaching on union with God, I have begun at the end of the spiritual journey rather than the beginning. This is because it helps us to understand John's writings if we bear in mind always the goal towards which we are moving. As John describes the darkness, the suffering, the sacrifices of spiritual growth, we need to realise he is not presenting these as ends in themselves, but as part of a process by which we are prepared for union with God. 'St John of the Cross is normally associated with an almost inhumanly negative and comfortless view of the spiritual life; and it is true that he sets out the human cost of faith with more pitiless candour than almost any

comparable writer (even Luther). Yet it is a movement towards fulfilment, not emptiness, towards beauty and life, not annihilation.'[12]

A Radical Stripping of Self

What is the ultimate direction of our lives? This is the question John puts
to us. If our deepest desire is union with God, we will need to discipline
ourselves to seek God above everything else and this will involve a radical stripping of self. God must become greater and we must become
less; in John's terms we must become Nothing (*nada*) and God must
become All (*tada*):

> To reach satisfaction in all
> desire satisfaction in nothing.
> To come to the knowledge of all
> desire the knowledge of nothing.
> To come to possess all
> desire the possession of nothing.
> To arrive at being all
> desire to be nothing.[13]

John wrote these words on a sketch at the beginning of 'The Ascent of
Mount Carmel'. The sketch depicts a mountain leading up to God, with
several wide paths leading to dead ends. The central narrow path leads
up to the top of the mountain, and along this path is written several
times the word '*nada*'. This is repeated all the way up – '*nada, nada, nada,
nada, nada, nada.*'

John is not implying that Christian growth involves a negation of joy
and life, but he is emphasising that Christian progress involves a 'dying
to self', a self-emptying rather than a possessive spirit. It is as we divest
ourselves of the desire to grasp and possess, and create what Matthew
calls the 'right kind of emptiness',[14] that we become more open to
receiving the fullness of love which God has for us. John's words seem
frighteningly radical and uncompromising, but in this he merely echoes
the challenge of Jesus: 'If anyone would come after me, he must deny
himself and take up his cross and follow me. For whoever wants to save
his life will lose it, but whoever loses his life for me and for the gospel
will save it' (Mk. 8:34–5). Following this way of '*nada*', of self-emptying,
we are in fact following the way of Christ himself, 'who, being in very
nature God, did not consider equality with God something to be
grasped, but made himself nothing, taking the very nature of a servant,
being made in human likeness' (Phil. 2:6–7).

As we learn to let go of our need to grasp and possess, we are learning what John and other spiritual writers call 'detachment'. We are to develop the attitude of detachment towards the gifts of creation, our relationships with other people and our own gifts and achievements. This term 'detachment' is very often misunderstood. It does not imply 'indifference'; we are not required to become indifferent to other people and the world around us, nor to develop an attitude that despises the created order. But we do not seek our final good in these things; we look beyond them to the God who created them. 'John echoes Augustine's attitude to the beauties of creation. God has passed by and touched them ('The Spiritual Canticle' 5), yet his clothing of creation with loveliness serves only to intensify the sense of his own unique, total and inimitable beauty.'[15] If we can learn to seek God above all things, and let go of our desire to possess anything else, we will paradoxically learn to appreciate the gifts of creation much more deeply and freely. John refers to 2 Corinthians 6:10, where Paul speaks of 'having nothing, yet possessing everything', and comments that 'those, then, whose joy is not possessive of things rejoice in them all as though they possessed them all; those others, beholding them with a possessive mind, lose all the delight of them all in general.'[16]

John encourages us to discipline ourselves to learn the inner freedom of being empty and poor before God, so that he can fill us. In the first book of 'The Ascent of Mount Carmel', Chapter 13, he offers 'some immediate remedy'[17] to help us to learn to 'die to self':

> Endeavour to be inclined always:
> not to the easiest, but to the most difficult;
> not to the most delightful, but to the most distasteful;
> not to the most gratifying, but to the least pleasant;
> not to what means rest for you, but to hard work;
> not to the consoling, but to the unconsoling;
> not to the most, but to the least;
> not to the highest and most precious, but to the lowest and most
>   despised;
> not to wanting something, but to wanting nothing.
> Do not go about looking for the best of temporal things, but for
> the worst, and, for Christ, desire to enter into complete naked-
> ness, emptiness, and poverty in everything in the world.[18]

These words may sound alarming, but John does advise that we 'put them into practice with order and discretion'.[19] He does not say we should 'always do' that which is most unpleasant or difficult, but that we should 'endeavour to be inclined always to [do so]'; we are to learn to resist the natural human instinct for our own self-gratification and see the value of being little, empty, poor, in order that we may be filled with God.[20] John's words are designed to shock us into realising how often in reality we are seeking our own gratification and importance, rather than embracing emptiness and poverty for Christ's sake. As Ruth Burrows comments, 'it is easy to say we want God, that we hand ourselves over to him. John reveals that we scarcely know what we are talking about. He exposes our deepest selfishness and shows us just what true spirituality really is ... The appetite for self-gratification must be replaced with an appetite for Christ, for living our human lives as he lived his.'[21]

The Dark Night

John uses the image of the 'dark night' to describe the radical stripping of self outlined above. His main systematic teaching about the dark night is found in 'The Ascent of Mount Carmel' and 'The Dark Night'. These two prose works are commentaries on his poem 'The Dark Night', although 'The Ascent of Mount Carmel' has a much looser relationship to the poem. Doctrinally, the two prose works belong together although they are very different in style. 'The Ascent of Mount Carmel' needs to be read first, for 'The Dark Night' is in a sense a continuation of 'The Ascent', which was never finished.

John's use of the image 'the dark night' is rather complex. He talks of the active night of the senses and the passive night of the senses and the active night of the spirit and the passive night of the spirit. Before examining these distinctions it is worth emphasising that 'there is in fact only *one* night, properly speaking ... Night is simply the saint's term for "privation", eradication of attachment to all that is not God ...'[22]

So what does John mean by his different descriptions of the night? The first distinction John makes is between the night of the senses and the night of the spirit. The night of the senses (sometimes called the 'first night') is described in Book 1 of 'The Ascent of Mount Carmel' and involves our detachment from all worldly ambitions, pleasures and comforts. This is the stage of 'beginners' in the spiritual life. The night of the spirit (the 'second night') is the purification of 'those who are already proficients, at the time God desires to lead them into the state of divine union.'[23] This night involves us learning detachment from spiritual experiences, supernatural gifts and pleasures. This night is described in Books 2 and 3 of 'The Ascent of Mount Carmel'.

The further distinction John makes is between 'active' and 'passive' stages within both the night of the senses and the night of the spirit. By 'active' he means that we are disciplining ourselves (with God's help) to learn detachment, whether towards things of the senses or towards things of the spirit. Our own active involvement in this purification process is essential. 'No one will insist more than John that the mountain cannot be scaled by ourselves. Nevertheless he is equally emphatic that unless we do undertake a thorough asceticism we cannot even begin the ascent.'[24] But John was aware that the soul could never achieve complete detachment by its own efforts; therefore he teaches that, once a person has shown a determination to persevere in seeking God above all things, God completes the process solely by his own activity. 'Hence the soul by its own effort (though aided by the grace of God) enters each night actively before God completes the process "passively" (i.e. by his activity, unassisted by the soul).'[25] 'The Ascent of Mount Carmel' ends abruptly and does not describe the passive night of the spirit – this is the focus of the second book of 'The Dark Night'.

John is relentlessly thorough in his description of the dark night and the depth of purification which we need in order to be free to seek God fully. He is particularly sharp and perceptive concerning our need to learn detachment in spiritual matters as well as worldly matters. He criticises those who think that self-denial only concerns the latter. These people, he says, 'still feed and clothe their natural selves with spiritual feelings and consolations instead of divesting and denying themselves of these for God's sake … they wander about in search only of sweetness and delightful communications from God. Such an attitude is not the hallmark of self-denial and nakedness of spirit but the indication of a spiritual sweet tooth.'[26] We are not to seek spiritual experiences but God himself.

God may indeed feed the beginner in faith with a sweet sense of his presence, but as we mature in faith we need to learn not to be dependent on these experiences but rather to trust in God even when he appears to be absent. John compares the way God deals with us to that of a loving mother:

> … God nurtures and caresses the soul, after it has been resolutely converted to his service, like a loving mother who warms her child with the heat of her bosom, nurses it with good milk and tender food, and carries and caresses it in her arms. But as the child grows older the mother withholds her caresses and hides her tender love…and sets the child down from her arms, letting it walk on its own feet so that it might put aside the habits of childhood and grow accustomed to greater and more important things.[27]

These 'more important things' are not spectacular paranormal experiences, but rather constitute naked faith in God, even in the deepest darkness. However, John does seem to expect that Christians will from time to time receive visions, words from God and other supernatural gifts. These experiences were very common in the Spain of John's day. As Burrows comments regarding the religious culture of the time: 'All around are false notions, spurious spiritualities, paranormal experiences so abounding as to be almost normal, a craving for the sensational, sensual indulgence in the name of divine love.'[28] John was insistent that we need to learn to be detached from such spectacular experiences even when they are given by God, otherwise we will become proud. He comments that those who receive visions 'go about feeling pleased and somewhat satisfied with themselves, which is against humility.'[29] Again he emphasises that we should not desire such spiritual favours from God and, even when we receive them, we should not focus on the experience itself but on God. 'The Christian will make the greatest spiritual gain from such favours by detaching himself from all desire for them.'[30]

In John's scheme, we enter the dark night when we begin to detach ourselves from the things of the senses, and we move deeper into the night as we learn to free ourselves (and allow God to free us) from our dependence on spiritual experiences and walk only by faith, but we need to remember that we are heading always for the day and complete union with God. John compares the journey to that of a natural night which has three phases: 'The first part, the night of the senses, resembles early evening, that time of twilight when things begin to fade from sight. The second part, faith, is completely dark, like midnight. The third part, representing God, is like the very early dawn just before the break of day.'[31] These three phases correspond to the three phases of the spiritual journey outlined by many spiritual writers: the 'Purgative Way' (the active and passive night of the senses), the 'Illuminative Way' (the active and passive night of the spirit) and the 'Unitive Way' (union with God).

One thing that needs to be clarified is that the Illuminative Way (the night of the spirit) describes, in fact, the *darkest* period of the night; it is the way of faith which is 'completely dark, like midnight'. This night of the spirit is a deeper and more painful experience than the night of the senses, 'striking harder at the very roots of illusion and systematically reducing human spiritual activity to the one act of faith and longing'.[32] But when all is stripped from us except faith and longing we begin to see more truly, both ourselves and God. In this sense, the way of darkness can be called 'illuminating'.

The most painful experience of all is the passive night of the spirit. 'The Dark Night' deals with this passive night, which John describes as being much more costly than the active night alone. In the passive night of the spirit the soul experiences God as absent, even as hostile. The soul experiences the direct purifying activity of God, and because the light of God is too bright and powerful for us, the soul experiences it as darkness. The purifying activity of God, John maintains, is loving, but it is fearful in its thoroughness and it brings all kinds of ugliness in the soul to the surface. He compares the effect the divine light has on a soul to the effect that fire has on a damp log of wood. The fire

> first dehumidifies it...then it gradually turns the wood black, makes it dark and ugly, and even causes it to emit a bad odour. By drying out the wood, the fire brings to light and expels all those ugly and dark accidents that are contrary to fire. Finally, by heating and enkindling it from without, the fire transforms the wood into itself and makes it as beautiful as it is itself.[33]

In a similar way the soul is transformed by the fiery love of God, and just as the wood turns black and gives off a bad odour before it glows and becomes beautiful, so the darkness deep within the soul is brought to the surface. 'The divine purge stirs up all the foul and vicious humours of which the soul was never before aware; never did it realise there was so much evil in itself, since these humours were so deeply rooted.'[34]

As we reflect upon John's teaching on the 'dark night' we must continually remind ourselves that 'the night' is a process by which we are prepared for 'the day', which is union with God. He also teaches that when we go through the dark night (particularly the dark night of the spirit) we are identifying with Christ and, as we do so, his spirit is being formed within us. We will consider this more fully below.

Contemplative Prayer

John does not set out to offer a systematic theology of prayer, but he does seek to describe the nature of contemplative prayer and how we might know if God is calling us to this. Prayer is always but one part of our growth in love; John has no interest in prayer experiences which bear no fruit in our daily lives.

What is contemplative prayer? Whilst the term is used today for a wide variety of activities and experiences, as Trueman Dicken points out, when John speaks of contemplation he is not referring to the kind of contemplation achieved by the techniques of Zen, Transcendental Meditation or Yoga, and he means something very different from the imaginative contemplation which is so important in the 'Spiritual Exercises' of St Ignatius.[35]

For John, contemplative prayer is part of the general process of the stripping, the simplification, of the self. In contemplation we come before God naked, not thinking or doing anything, but simply waiting with loving attentiveness for God. In contemplation, we cease to think and meditate with our minds on God's greatness and his acts of salvation; rather we are simply present to meet with God himself. This encounter with God may often seem like meeting with darkness or, in the words of the anonymous fourteenth century English mystic, a 'cloud of unknowing'.[36] The experience can at first be alarming and bewildering, and leave the person praying feeling confused and distressed. However, if God leads one into such kind of prayer, it is important not to give up, but to persevere; gradually it becomes clear that there is a more profound meeting with God in such simple darkness than in all one's previous rewarding meditations and thoughts about God.

John makes clear that such prayer is not for 'beginners' and it cannot be self-induced but is a gift from God. John outlines the signs by which we may recognise we are being called to this contemplation in 'The Ascent of Mount Carmel' (II:13). He assumes here that up to this point Christians will have been practising what he calls 'discursive meditation'; meditation on scripture, on the passion of Christ and other Christian truths using our minds and our imagination. Indeed, these practices are essential for us to grow in knowledge of our faith and what God has done for us. But, John insists, there may come a time when God is calling us to leave such practices of prayer behind (not necessarily completely but at least for certain periods in our prayer) and we need to recognise this when it happens. He outlines the harm done by spiritual directors who insist their directees continue in their old styles of prayer when God is leading them into something new.

The signs that John describes here to help us to recognise the beginning of contemplation are as follows. The first sign is that we cease to be able to meditate profitably – instead of such meditation bringing insight and encouragement it simply produces a sense of dryness and dissatisfaction. The second sign is that we find we have no desire to fix our minds or imagination on any particular object or thought. 'The third and surest sign is that a person likes to remain alone in loving awareness of God, without particular considerations, in interior peace and quiet and repose … Such a one prefers to remain only in the general loving awareness and knowledge we mentioned, without any particular knowledge or understanding.'[37] Rather than our prayers focusing on a *particular* thought about God or the Christian life, we have a deep but general loving awareness of God.

John wisely counsels that 'to leave the state of meditation and sense and enter that of contemplation and spirit, spiritual persons must observe within themselves at least these three signs together.'[38] The occurrence of the first two signs without the third could simply mean the person is ill or suffering from 'melancholia'.

Burrows makes a helpful distinction about the kind of knowledge we gain from contemplation as compared to meditation. In meditation we 'use our minds to discover more and more about God so as to discern his will with greater clarity. But there is another kind of knowledge, secret, obscure, non-conceptual, for which we have the potential and which needs a divine impulse to activate it. This is what John calls infused or mystical contemplation.'[39] She then goes on to give an example, comparing the knowledge the 'beginner' gains from meditation with the knowledge of the contemplative: 'Two persons could be dwelling on the same passage of scripture and have basically the same ideas. In the case of the beginner the ideas would be the sum total, whereas "behind", around, permeating the ideas of the other would be the obscure, divine "knowing".'[40] This is the knowledge that comes from loving attentiveness to God; doing and thinking nothing but single-mindedly concentrating one's will towards him and allowing him to work deeply within the soul.

The temptation of those who are beginning to experience contemplation and of those who observe from the outside is to think that contemplation is a waste of time, for we are not accomplishing anything. Indeed, John does describe contemplation as 'holy idleness'.[41] (This phrase is remarkably similar to that of the fourteenth century English mystic, Walter Hilton, who calls contemplation 'a holy inactivity and a most active rest'.[42]) However, he sees this 'holy idleness' as of the greatest value to God. Concerning the account of Martha and Mary in Luke 10:39–42, he makes the following comment: 'Martha thought that she herself was doing all the work and Mary, because she was enjoying the Lord's presence, was doing nothing. Yet, since there is no greater or more necessary work than love, the contrary is true.'[43] John does emphasise that we need to practice love both in action and in contemplation,[44] but he is critical of those who give little time to prayer and think the active life accomplishes more for God. 'They would profit the church and please God much more ... were they to spend at least half of this time with God in praye ... However much they may appear to achieve externally, they will in substance be accomplishing nothing; it is beyond doubt that good works can be performed only by the power of God.'[45]

The Centrality of Christ

One criticism that is often made of John of the Cross is that he makes remarkably few specific references to Jesus. Are his works in fact 'theocentric', but not 'Christocentric'? On the contrary, John's works make no sense without a profound understanding of Christ crucified, and his whole scheme of self-emptying, growing in faith through the darkness, and being brought at last into union with God rests fundamentally on Christ.

As Matthew points out, a key passage to understanding the centrality of Christ comes in the second book of 'The Ascent of Mount Carmel' (Ch. 22). The first twenty-one chapters emphasise that neither in meditation, nor feelings, nor visions and spiritual experiences do we truly meet God, and that we meet God only in dark faith. In the twenty-second chapter, John makes the point that in the Old Testament people did rely on supernatural experiences and signs, but that we should not rely on such things. All that has been said in 'The Ascent of Mount Carmel' so far 'rises to this question: What should we seek, if we don't seek all of that? Put otherwise, the author says: not this, nor that, nor that, nor this, nor – and we say, "Well what!? We have to look somewhere!" Again, John says, faith, faith, faith, faith – and we say, "What *is* this faith for which we sacrifice everything else?" The answer: Jesus Christ.'[46]

John emphasises that, since God has given us his Son, we need nothing else and we should seek nothing else. 'In giving us his Son, his only Word (for he possesses no other), he spoke everything to us at once in this sole Word – and he has no more to say.'[47] He tells us that those who seek from God some other kind of vision are guilty 'of offending him by not fixing their eyes entirely on Christ and by living with the desire for some other novelty.'[48] At best, supernatural experiences and gifts can point us to Christ, but at worst they can be a dangerous distraction and, as John makes clear, they are never necessary, for all we need is to be found in Christ.

It is not simply that Christ is the only person in whom we should put our faith, but also that he is 'the way' of our spiritual journey towards union with God. The radical stripping of self involved in this journey is a living out in ourselves of the total self-giving of Christ. We must take up our cross and follow Christ crucified – John makes this very clear in 'The Ascent of Mount Carmel' (II:7). Because this chapter is crucial in understanding John of the Cross, I quote here a substantial section from it:

> A person makes progress only by imitating Christ, who is the Way, the Truth, and the Life. No one goes to the Father but through him … Accordingly, I would not consider any spirituality worthwhile that wants to walk in sweetness and ease and run from the imitation of Christ.
>
> Because I have said that Christ is the way and that this way is a death to our natural selves in the sensory and spiritual parts of the

soul, I would like to demonstrate how this death is patterned on Christ's for he is our model and light.

First, during his life he certainly dies spiritually to the sensitive part [that is the things of the senses] and at his death he died naturally. He proclaimed during his life that he had no place whereon to lay his head (Mt. 8:20). And at his death he had less.

Second, at the moment of his death he was certainly annihilated in his soul, without any consolation or relief, since the Father had left him that way in innermost aridity in the lower part. He was thereby compelled to cry out: 'My God, my God, why have you forsaken me?' (Mt. 27:46). This was the most extreme abandonment, sensitively, that he had suffered in his life. And by it he accomplished the most marvellous work of his whole life, surpassing all the works and deeds and miracles that he had ever performed on earth or in heaven. That is, he brought about the reconciliation and union of the human race with God through grace. The Lord achieved this, as I say, at the moment in which he was most annihilated in all things: in his reputation before people, since in watching him die they mocked him instead of esteeming him; in his human nature, by dying; and in spiritual help and consolation from his Father, for he was forsaken by his Father at that time, annihilated and reduced to nothing, so as to pay the debt fully and bring people to union with God.[49]

Jesus himself went through the dark night of the senses and the dark night of the spirit, for love of the Father and love of us. We are called to follow his way. 'John of the Cross's doctrine (how aptly he is named!) is thoroughly Christocentric. It would make no sense whatever without this vision of Christ crucified ... He would have us lay aside our own desires, our own ideas and visions, our own will, and abide "blindfolded" in Jesus; content to be ignorant and helpless, trusting ourselves to Jesus who sees the Father, who truly knows him as he is in himself ... Jesus crucified is the dark night into which we must enter so as to be one with God.'[50]

John emphasises that we are not merely called to trust in what Jesus has done for us: 'he brought about the reconciliation and union of the human race with God through grace.'[51] But we are called also to allow him to live his way of total self-emptying and self-giving within us. As Paul states: 'I have been crucified with Christ and I no longer live, but Christ lives in me' (Gal. 2:20). Our spiritual journey must be a living out of the truth that we are crucified with Christ. 'The journey, then, does not consist in consolations, delights, and spiritual feelings, but in the living death of the cross, sensory and spiritual, exterior and interior.'[52] Hence, as Matthew rightly points out, 'John's vision commits believers, not simply to acknowledging formulae about Jesus, or to following a benign ethic; it commits them to allowing Jesus to work out his dying and rising in their lives.'[53]

John's Message for Today: Personal Reflections

Although John wrote mainly for those living in religious communities, the main thrust of his teaching is relevant for anyone who is earnest about spiritual growth. He offers both a challenge and a hope.

A Profound Challenge

John's writings are not easy to read; neither is the message 'easy'. If we want a spirituality which is soothing, encouraging, and which will cost us little, we must look elsewhere. As Allison Peers says, 'His medicine is never emollient or sedative but tonic and astringent.'[54]

John challenges a comfortable spirituality which leaves untouched the depth of our self-centredness and self-deception. His mystical thought requires a person to undergo an utter and costly transformation by God's love. In different ways, he asks again and again how much we want God; not a spiritual experience or a saintly self-image, but God himself. He emphasises that the goal of our spiritual journey is a relationship with God, 'union with God'; rather than our own self-fulfilment (which often seems to be the goal of so much contemporary popular spirituality).

At a time when there is, within the church, a temptation to seek spiritual 'experiences', and a danger of Christians developing what John calls a 'spiritual sweet tooth', John's voice offers a powerful corrective. Whilst not denying that charismatic gifts should be exercised in the church, John calls Christians to question their attitudes towards such gifts and experiences.

Christians need to hear John's voice about single-mindedness and detachment. We are urged to yearn for God first and let go of our possessive desire for anything else, even our own spiritual experiences and achievements. John encourages us to trust God when there seems nothing but darkness and to allow his grace to work in us to transform us. This process will involve facing the depths of ourselves which we would rather not see; we need to face reality. Indeed, one of the effects of reading John is to feel we are being led beyond our illusions to the reality of who God is and who we are before him. 'The impact of John in his works is painful, unforgettable and decisive. Very few writers have so plainly set out what it means to allow God to *be* God when we pray, and how this entails for us both total cost and total transformation.'[55]

John's works may at times seem ruthless and frightening, but at their heart lies the challenge to hear afresh the radical call of Jesus: 'if anyone would come after me, he must deny himself and take up his cross and follow me. For whoever wants to save his life will lose it, but whoever loses his life for me and for the gospel will save it' (Mk. 8:34–5).

A Glorious Hope

John's message may be deeply challenging, but it is also full of hope. John is not 'optimistic' about human nature in a superficial sense; he sees clearly the depth of self-deception and sin of which human beings are capable. However, he also holds out the vision that we can be utterly transformed; human beings have the capacity to be filled with the love of God. John challenges those of us who feel human beings are 'not that bad', but he also challenges us not to have too low expectations of what we can become. John leads us to face head on the reality of who we are, not who we would like to think we are, yet he urges us never to lose our vision of our destiny. We need his ruthless perception and vision today.

John speaks powerfully to those who suffer great darkness and suffering, externally or internally. Whatever depths we may experience Jesus has been through those depths before us. If we can hold fast to God through these times we will discover that God may in fact give himself to us more deeply through the darkness than through all our times of comfortable spirituality. There is an authenticity and an authority in John's writings that come out of his own experience of suffering. We are encouraged to commit ourselves in dark faith to the God whose love is all-consuming and wonderful beyond our comprehension.

The God John urges us to trust, and to whom we are to commit ourselves wholeheartedly, is holy and transcendent, yet lovingly intimate at the same time. John never loses the sense of God's infinite greatness and the power and awesomeness of his love. God is not a 'tame' God; he is not a 'friendly chum' whom we can simply draw into our lives on our own terms. He is majestic, holy, even terrifying in his love; he draws us into *his* life on *his* terms. Reading the writings of St John of the Cross can restore a sense of perspective that some streams of contemporary Christianity may be in danger of losing.

Notes

[1] On the sources of John's teaching, see K. Kavanaugh & O. Rodriguez, *The Collected Works of St John of the Cross* (Washington: ICS Publications, 1991),

35–7, and E.W. Trueman Dicken, *The Crucible of Love: A Study of the Mysticism of St Teresa of Jesus and St John of the Cross* (London: Darton, Longman & Todd, 1963), 318–26.

[2] Kavanaugh & Rodriguez, *Collected Works*, 588; quotation from 'The Spiritual Canticle' 29.3.

[3] Ibid, 624.; quotation from idem. 39.7.

[4] Ibid, 618–9.; quotation from idem. 38.3.

[5] Ibid, 624.; quotation from idem. 39.5.

[6] Ibid, 619.; quotation from idem. 38.3.

[7] Teresa of Avila was not always so clear in her use of the term 'union'; she was happy to describe short-lived, ecstatic states of prayer as a 'delectable union' and she was certainly rather fascinated by these subjective experiences. However, she does make clear that these experiences mean little in comparison to the fundamental union 'in which we resign our wills to the will of God.' See E. Allison Peers (ed.), *The Complete Works of Saint Teresa of Jesus*, Vol. 2 (London: Sheed & Ward, 1946), 259–60.

[8] Quoted in Iain Matthew, *The Impact of God: Soundings from St John of the Cross* (London: Hodder & Stoughton, 1995), 23–4.

[9] Ibid., 24.

[10] Kavanaugh & Rodriguez, *Collected Works*, 641; quotation from 'The Living Flame of Love' 1.1.

[11] Ibid., 618; quotaton from 'The Spiritual Canticle' 38.3.

[12] Rowan Williams, *The Wound of Knowledge: Christian Spirituality from the New Testament to St John of the Cross* (London: Darton, Longman & Todd, 1979), 164.

[13] Kavanaugh & Rodriguez, *Collected Works*, 111; cf. 150.

[14] Matthew, *The Impact of God*, 35ff.

[15] Williams, *The Wound of Knowledge*, 163.

[16] Kavanaugh & Rodriguez, *Collected Works*, 302; quotation from 'The Ascent of Mount Carmel', Book 3, 20.3.

[17] Ibid., 148; quotation from idem., Book 1, 13.1.

[18] Ibid., 149; quotation from idem., 13.6.

[19] Ibid., 149; quotation from idem., 13.7.

[20] See Matthew, *The Impact of God*, 46–7.

[21] Ruth Burrows, *Ascent to Love: The Spiritual Teaching of St John of the Cross* (London: Darton, Longman & Todd, 1987), 23.

[22] Dicken, *The Crucible of Love*, 223.

[23] Kavanaugh & Rodriguez, *Collected Works*, 119; quotaion from 'The Ascent of Mount Carmel', Book 1, 1.3

[24] Burrows, *Ascent to Love*, 24.

[25] Dicken, *The Crucible of Love*, 229.

[26] Kavanaugh & Rodriguez, *Collected Works*, 170; quotation from 'The Ascent of Mount Carmel', Book 2, 7.5.

[27] Ibid., 361; quotation from 'The Dark Night', Book 1, 1.2.

[28] Burrows, *Ascent to Love*, 16.

[29] Kavanaugh & Rodriguez, *Collected Works*, 211 quotation from 'The Ascent of Mount Carmel', Book 2, 18.3.

[30] Dicken, *The Crucible of Love*, 378.

[31] Kavanaugh & Rodriguez, *Collected Works*, 121; quotation from 'The Ascent of Mount Carmel', Book 1, 2.5.

[32] Williams, *The Wound of Knowledge*, 166.

[33] Kavanaugh & Rodriguez, *Collected Works*, 416; quotation from 'The Dark Night', Book 2, 10.1.

[34] Ibid., 417; quotation from idem., 10.2.

[35] See E. W. Trueman Dicken, 'Teresa of Avila and John of the Cross', in C. Jones, G. Wainwright, & E. Yarnold (eds), *The Study of Spirituality* (London: SPCK, 1986), 372.

[36] On *The Cloud of Unknowing*, see W. Johnston, *The Mysticism of the Cloud of Unknowing* (Wheathampstead: Anthony Clark, 1978).

[37] Kavanaugh & Rodriguez, *Collected Works*, 189–90; quotation from 'The Acent of Mount Carmel', 2, 13.4.

[38] Ibid., 190.

[39] Burrows, *Ascent to Love*, 55.

[40] Ibid.

[41] Kavanaugh & Rodriguez, *Collected Works*, 588 quotation from 'The Spiritual Canticle', 29.4.

[42] W. Hilton, *The Ladder of Perfection* (Harmondsworth: Penguin, 1957), 224.

[43] Kavanaugh & Rodriguez, *Collected Works*, 587; quotation from 'The Spiritual Canticle', 29.1.

[44] Ibid; 58.9, referring to idem 29.2.

[45] Ibid., 588.

[46] Matthew, *The Impact of God*, 124.

[47] Kavanaugh & Rodriguez, *Collected Works*, 230; quotation fro 'The Ascent of Mount Carmel', Book 2, 22.3.

[48] Ibid, 230; quotation from idem, 22.5.

[49] Ibid., 172; quotation from idem, Book 2, 7.8–11.

[50] Burrows, *Ascent to Love*, 83.

[51] Kavanaugh & Rodriguez, *Collected Works*, 172; quotation from 'The Ascent of Mount Carmel', book 2, 7.11.

[52] Ibid., 172; quotation from idem, Book 2, 7.11.

[53] Matthew, *The Impact of God*, 133.

[54] E. Allison Peers, *Spirit of Flame: A Study of St John of the Cross* (London: SCM, 1943), 118.

[55] R. Williams, 'The Stars of the Millennium: St John of the Cross (1542–1591)', *The Tablet* (17 June 2000), 842.

13

Mysticism and Fantasy in Lewis, Williams, Tolkien and Barfield

Colin Duriez

Introducing The Inklings

On almost any Tuesday morning for many years a group of writers and friends, many of them Oxford dons, could be observed congregating in a snug room in the Eagle and Child public house, near the city centre. Among thick tobacco smoke, tables laden with beer or cider mugs, subjects discussed (often loudly, and always wittily) included theology and books, poetry and stories, and issues as diverse as whether or not dogs have souls or transferring stories to film. Two of the group's members, C.S. Lewis and J.R.R. Tolkien, were honing ideas that were in later years to capture a vast audience across the globe. Like most in the group, they were Christians, committed to an orthodox expression of faith owing much to G.K. Chesterton, Arthur Balfour and John Henry Newman.

The same group also met once a week for over fifteen years in Lewis's rooms in Magdalen College, and occasionally in Tolkien's in Exeter, with a specifically literary purpose. They read to each other for pleasure and criticism pieces they were writing, and usually enjoyed a good Thursday evening of 'the cut and parry of prolonged, fierce, masculine argument'. The Inklings embodied Lewis's ideals of life and pleasure. The literary group of friends was held together by his zest and enthusiasm. Tolkien was also a central figure in the Inklings, who cast them fictionally in his unfinished 'The Notion Club Papers'. Their important years as a literary group were from around 1933 to about 1949. Charles Williams, another member, wrote poetry, novels, plays, literary criticism, and imaginative theology. He powerfully influenced Lewis, though Tolkien was not so taken with him. Tolkien played a vital role in Lewis's conversion to Christianity – the latter was for many years an atheist, then a pantheist.

Other key members of the informal group making up the Inklings included Lewis's brother (Major W.H. 'Warnie' Lewis), Owen Barfield (a brilliant thinker, follower of Rudolf Steiner's anthroposophism, and author of a key book in Lewis's and Tolkien's thinking, *Poetic Diction*,[1]) H.V.D. 'Hugo' Dyson, and others. It is generally agreed by Inklings scholars that the four key members are Lewis, Tolkien, Williams and Barfield.

Barfield, interestingly, felt that the Inkling's represented a stage in the evolution of Romanticism, pointing the way for modern people, increasingly alienated from nature, to return to a harmonious relationship with the divine.

An Approach to Mysticism and Fantasy in the Inklings

I had better now lay out my assumptions that will provide the context for exploring religious fantasy in the Inklings. It seems to me that to speak of mysticism is to step where angels fear to tread.

My first assumption is that it is possible to distinguish Christian and theistic (or pagan) mysticism – though of course there are many mysticisms. Theistic mysticism (most notably in the form of Neoplatonism, as shaped by Plotinus) of course had a profound effect on the medieval West and also on Islam. Of the Inklings I would place Owen Barfield as a theistic mystic. He was philosophically an idealist, and it seems to me that idealism (as it flowered in the nineteenth century) lends itself to a theistic mysticism. Christian mysticism (for example, Christian Platonism) has to struggle to be consonant with orthodox theology. I would therefore place Tolkien, Williams and Lewis, of the central figures of the Inklings, as Christian mystics to various degrees – with Williams as the most, and Lewis as the least, with Tolkien in the middle.

My second assumption is that a phenomenological description of the relevant human experiences that are mystical, and have theological implications, is not of course adequate in itself to account for the mystical. There are ontological, moral and epistemological issues that are essential, even though the experiences may be phenomenologically friendly.

If the core members of the Inklings represent mysticism, then it is likely that an individual Inklings' vision will affect all his life, thought and experience. One could start almost anywhere in expounding that individual's mysticism, not just in a theme like say a preoccupation with the numinous. To give an example from Lewis's characteristic literary criticism in one place, he speaks of the humble act of reading a book, which in his vision becomes sacramental. In *An Experiment in Criticism* (1961), he points out that good reading has something in common with love, moral action, and the growth of knowledge. Like all these it involves a surrender, in this case by the reader to the work being read. A good reader is concerned less with altering his or her opinion than in entering fully into the opinions and worlds of others.

Defining mysticism

What is the mystical, the religiously attractive mystery? Here are a couple of definitions from two authors of about the same period. Mysticism is linked with the idea of mystery and secrecy, with initiation. Thus mystics are viewed as people with special insight into the nature of God and reality. Their words and pictures are considered to be revelation.

According to Caroline F.E. Spurgeon, in *Mysticism in English Literature* (1913), the mystic makes 'one passionate assertion, that unity underlies diversity. This, their starting point and their goal, is the basic fact of mysticism, which, in its widest sense, may be described as an attitude of mind founded upon an intuitive or experienced conviction of unity, of oneness, of alikeness in all things.'[3] She continues that, for the mystic, 'All things about us are but forms and manifestations of the one divine life, and that these phenomena are fleeting and impermanent, although the spirit which informs them is immortal and endures.'[4]

Caroline Spurgeon points out that mystics sense that human beings share the nature of God, carrying the spark of the divine within them. She points out the influence of Plotinus, vividly suggesting that the story of the Prodigal Son is in fact the history of the universe, according to the mystic. There is a three-fold way, of originating with God, emanating away from the divine, and returning as one lost to him.

Evelyn Underhill, an important influence on Charles Williams, wrote in the same period as Spurgeon: 'The mystics ... know a spiritual order, penetrating, and everywhere conditioning though transcending the world of sense. They declare to us a Reality most rich and living, which is not a reality of time and space; which is something other than everything we mean by "nature", and for which no merely pantheistic explanation will suffice.'[5]

Central Themes in Lewis, Williams, Tolkien and Barfield

Speaking in America in 1969, Owen Barfield reflected on the attitude of the literary group[6]. He wondered if something was not happening to 'the Romantic Impulse' during its life. He could discern four important strands, each mainly identified with Lewis, Tolkien, Williams, or himself: (a) the yearning for the infinite and unattainable – Lewis' *sehnsucht* or joy; (b) in Barfield's own words, 'The conviction of the dignity of man and his part in the future history of the world conceived as a kind of progress towards increasing immanence of the divine in the human'[7] (Barfield's own position); (c) the idealization of love between the sexes, as in Charles Williams' thought and writings; and (d) the opposite of tragedy, the 'happy ending', Tolkien's idea of the eucatastrophe. These are convenient themes to explore in this paper, even though there are other relevant themes (such as the numinous).

Lewis tells us in his preface to the third edition of *The Pilgrim's Regress* that, when he wrote that book in the early 1930s, he meant 'romanticism' to mean the special experience of inconsolable longing, or joy.[8] He certainly was not in revolt against reason or classicism, which romanticism is sometimes taken to mean. He was not a subjectivist, seeing art as the expression of its maker's soul.

In English literature, the Romantic Movement is often taken to begin with the publication of *Lyrical Ballads* in 1798 by Wordsworth and Coleridge. This was part of a wide reaction against deism and a mechanistic view of nature and mankind. Romanticism gave rise to the Gothic genre, and its offspring, Mary Shelley's remarkable *Frankenstein* (1818) and the rise of science-fiction. It also created a vogue for historical romance, as in the novels of Sir Walter Scott. In Germany Romanticism was connected with the rise of a modernist theology, in reaction to rationalism. George MacDonald's rejection of his native Calvinism was part of the same trend.

The Inklings of course also influenced each other, a subject explored by Diane Pavlac in her doctorate, 'The Company They Keep: Assessing the Mutual Influence of Lewis, Tolkien and Williams.'[9] As literary artists, Lewis, Tolkien and Williams certainly seemed to try to redeem the romantic tradition which had been distorted by the Romantic Movement and its predecessors in the eighteenth century. Reaching back to the periods before the Enlightenment, they were premodernist in orientation. In their attempt, they rehabilitate an understanding that has almost been lost by modern people. Lewis, Tolkien, and Williams, following Owen Barfield's *Poetic Diction*, saw that there is a rightness or correctness in the imagination itself. Furthermore, without the enrichment of proper imagining, thought is impoverished, and eventually becomes meaningless. Paradoxically, therefore, through fantasy or the play of imagination, thought makes true contact with reality.[10]

The four men attempted, in their fiction and poetry, to provide what they saw as true or objective images that had a place in the contemporary world. While a novel, a play, or a poem is not meant primarily to put over Christian or even moral truths, or to be 'about life' – imagination has a different function from theoretical thinking – images embodied in such works of literature can enrich and liberate our thinking by enriching and defining our concepts, and can enhance our experience of the world by enlarging our perception of, and sensitivity to, existence. Imagination helps to inculcate a symbolic perception of reality – what may have been a natural way of viewing the world in the ancient and medieval periods.

Introduction: A Theology of Romance

Like his friends J.R.R. Tolkien and Charles Williams, C.S. Lewis worked in his fiction according to a theology of romanticism which owed much to the nineteenth century writer who was Lewis's mentor, George MacDonald. The term 'romantic theologian,' Lewis tells us in his Introduction to *Essays Presented to Charles Williams*, was invented by Charles Williams.[11] What Lewis says about Williams applies also to himself. 'A romantic theologian,' he points out,

> does not mean one who is romantic about theology but one who is theological about romance, one who considers the theological implica-tions of those experiences which are called romantic. The belief that the most serious and ecstatic experiences either of human love or of imag-inative literature have such theological implications and that they can be healthy and fruitful only if the implications are diligently thought out and severely lived, is the root principle of all his [Williams'] work.[12]

Whereas a key preoccupation of Charles Williams was romantic love, Lewis was 'theological' about romantic longing or joy, and Tolkien reflected deeply on the theological implications of fairy tale and myth, particularly the aspect of sub-creation. Implied in Tolkien's reflection was the importance of eucatastrophe or happy ending. Barfield, from a different perspective, was interested in changes in human consciousness in history, in which he traced a positive evolution.

Joy and C.S. Lewis

C.S. Lewis's autobiography up to his conversion at the age of thirty-one is recorded in *Surprised By Joy* (1955),[13] and somewhat in his long alle-gory, *The Pilgrim's Regress*. These tell us that his lengthy, varied, and reluc-tant pilgrimage to truth was greatly influenced by a certain distinct tone of feeling which he discovered in early childhood, and which stayed with him on and off throughout his adolescence and early manhood.

There is a relationship between love and zest for life and the desire for beauty that constantly fascinated Lewis. The stories of George MacDonald, which shaped Lewis's imagination, are dominated by a joyful quality of holiness or goodness in life. MacDonald's stories (including his novels) concern the homely and ordinary, transformed by a new light. Lewis captured this exactly when he wrote: 'The quality which had enchanted me in his imaginative works turned out to be the quality of the real universe, the divine, magical, terrifying and ecstatic reality in which we all live.'[14]

Lewis's own imaginative creations such as *The Chronicles of Narnia*[15] sprang from this love of life. He seems to have been very preoccupied with 'joy', as he called it, throughout the 1940s and early 1950s. The last chapter of *The Problem of Pain* (1940)[16] speaks of it; a sermon, 'The Weight of Glory' (1941), tries to define the desire; *The Voyage of the Dawn Treader* (1952)[17] is about the Narnian mouse Reepicheep's quest for Aslan's Country at the World's End; *Surprised By Joy* traces the twin threads of Lewis's thinking and his longing for beauty up to his conversion; and in *Till We Have Faces* (1956)[18] the princess Psyche has a love of this beauty that is stronger than death.

Such joy, thought Lewis, inspired the writer to create fantasy. In fact, *Sehnsucht*, seen as a yearning or longing that is a pointer to joy, was for Lewis a defining characteristic of fantasy. The creation of 'Another World' is an attempt to reconcile human beings and the world, to embody the fulfilment of our imaginative longing. Imaginative worlds, wonderlands, are 'regions of the spirit'. Such worlds of the numinous may be found in some science fiction, some poetry, some fairy stories, some novels, some myths, even in a phrase or sentence. Lewis claimed in *Of This and Other Worlds*: 'To construct plausible and moving "other worlds" you must draw on the only real "other world" we know, that of the spirit.'[19]

Lewis saw this unquenchable longing as a sure sign that no part of the created world, and thus no aspect of human experience, is capable of fulfilling fallen mankind. We are dominated by a homelessness, and yet by a keen sense of what home means. This view is imaginatively akin to Plotinus's Neoplatonism.

In *Surprised by Joy* Lewis reported his sensations of joy, some of which were responses to natural beauty and others of which were literary or artistic responses, in the belief that other people would recognize similar experiences of their own. Even some who cannot through Lewis's autobiographical account, however, respond to this experience when reading his fiction. He claimed that distant hills, seen from his nursery window, taught him longing, and made him for good or ill a votary of the 'blue flower' before he was six years old. The blue flower is the symbol of *sehnsucht* or inconsolable longing in German literature and Scandinavian ballads, dating back to the Middle Ages.

For Lewis, joy was a foretaste of ultimate reality, heaven itself, or, the same thing, our world as it was meant to be, unspoilt by the fall of mankind, and one day to be remade. 'Joy,' wrote Lewis, 'is the serious business of Heaven.'[20] Lewis's portrayal of joy can be seen as providing valuable data of a key human experience, data which has philosophical and religious importance. It also lends itself to phenomenological enquires into mysticism. It was central to his apologetics for the Christian faith.

Tolkien and Eucatastrophe

Tolkien was fascinated by several structural features of fairy tales and other stories that embodied myths. These features are all related to a sense of imaginative decorum, a sense that imagining can, in itself, be good or bad, as rules or norms apply strictly in fantasy, as they do in thought. Meaning can only be created by skill or art, and play an essentially part in human thought and language. As Tolkien said, 'The incarnate mind, the tongue, and the tale are in our world coeval.'[21] As Barfield has shown in his introduction to the second edition of *Poetic Diction*, the ideal in logical positivism and related types of modern linguistic philosophy is, strictly, absurd; it systematically eliminates meanings from the framing of truths, expecting thereby to guarantee their validity. In Tolkien's view, the opposite is the case. The richer the meanings involved in the framing of truths, the more guarantee is there of their validity.

G.K. Chesterton once wrote that we should sometimes take our tea in the top of a tree, as our perceptions tend to get dulled. One of the essential features of the fairy tale or mythopoeic fantasy is the sense of 'recovery' – the regaining of health or a clear view of things. Tolkien pointed out that we too often get caught in the specific corridor of daily, mundane life, and lose a view of 'things as we are (or were) meant to see them'. Entry into an imaginary world 'shocks us more fully awake than we are for most of our lives'. Lewis said the latter of myth, but it applies to this feature of recovery. Part of this recovery is a sense of imaginative unity, a survey of the depths of space and time. The essential patterns of reality are seen in a fresh way.

Related to recovery, Tolkien believed that consolation was a central quality of good fantasy or fairy tale – the kind of story he wrote in *The Lord of the Rings*[22] or the tale of Beren and Luthien.[23] The quality is related to that of escape (but not escapism). There are things 'grim and terrible to fly from', says Tolkien. 'These are hunger, thirst, poverty, pain, sorrow, injustice, death.' But even when people are fortunate enough not to face such extremes 'there are ancient limitations from which fairy stories offer a sort of escape, and old ambitions and desires (touching the very root of fantasy) to which they offer a kind of satisfaction and consolation'. Some include the desire 'to visit, free as a fish, the deep sea' or to fly among the clouds.[24] There is also primordial desires to survey the depths of space and time and to converse with animals. The desire for talking animals comes from a sense of separation from nature, from the fall.

Lewis tried to define such a desire. In 'The Weight of Glory' (1949) he wrote: 'We do not want merely to see beauty … We want something else which can hardly be put into words – to be united with the beauty we see, to pass into it, to receive it into ourselves, to bathe in it, to become part of it. That is why we have peopled air and earth and water with gods and goddesses and nymphs and elves.'[25]

The oldest desire of course, Tolkien points out, is to escape death. This desire is a common characteristic of the fairy stories of human beings. Elves would be concerned to escape deathlessness. Tolkien feels however that the consolation of fairy stories has a more important aspect than 'the imaginative satisfaction of ancient desires'. This is the consolation of the happy ending. He coins the term 'eucatastrophe' for this ending – the theme isolated by Barfield as central to Tolkien's romanticism.[26]

Just as tragedy is the true form of drama, its highest function, eucatastrophe is the true form of the fairy tale. Such eucatastrophe, the sudden 'turn' in the story, 'is not essentially "escapist" or "fugitive". In its fairy tale – or otherworld – setting, it is a sudden and miraculous grace: never to be counted on to return.' This is not to deny or make light of sorrow and failure, for their possibility 'is necessary to the joy of deliverance'.[27]

What is denied, says Tolkien, is 'universal final defeat'. This denial is 'evangelium, giving a fleeting glimpse of Joy, Joy beyond the walls of the world, poignant as grief.'[28] This joy 'rends indeed the very web of story, and lets a gleam come though'.[29] The source of joy and consolation is objective (as it was for Tolkien's friend C.S. Lewis). Reality itself is the grounding of the meaning of such stories. In his essay on fairy stories, Tolkien explicitly links consolation with the Christian gospel.

Related to the capture of the quality of eucatastrophe is Tolkien's emphasis on sub-creation. He believed that the art of true fantasy or fairy story writing is sub-creation: creating another or secondary world with such skill that it has an 'inner consistency of reality'.[30] This inner consistency is so potent that it compels Secondary belief or Primary belief (the belief we give to the Primary or real world) on the part of the reader. Tolkien calls the skills to compel these two degrees of belief 'fantasy' and 'enchantment' respectively. A clue to the concept of sub-creation lies in the fact that word 'fairy', or more properly 'faery', etmologically means 'the realm or state where faeries have their being'.[31] A faery story is not thus a story which simply concerns faery beings. They are in some sense other-worldly, having a geography and history surrounding them. Tolkien's key idea is that faery, the realm or state where faeries have their being, contains a whole cosmos. It contains the moon, the sun, the sky, trees and mountains, rivers, water and stones, as well as dragons, trolls, elves, dwarves, goblins, elves, talking animals, and even a mortal person when he or she is enchanted (through giving Primary belief to that other world). Faery is sub-creation rather than either mimetic representation or allegorical interpretation of the 'beauties and terrors of the world'.[32]

Sub-creation comes, says Tolkien, as a result of a twofold urge in human beings: (1) the wish to survey the depths of space and time, and (2) the urge to communicate with living beasts other than mankind, to escape from hunger, poverty, death, and to end the separation between mankind and nature. Just as the reason wishes for a unified theory to cover all phenomena in the universe, the imagination also constantly seeks a unity of meaning appropriate to itself.

Holding such an attitude to invention in fantasy Tolkien belongs to the tradition of romanticism, but with important differences, the important one being that the imagination is not for him the organ of truth. But as with the romantics, symbols play an integrating part in his fiction. His symbolism helps to make his work a lamp as well as a mirror; depicting reality, but also illuminating it. His characteristic symbols or symbolic themes include death, an Elven quality, healing, light, music, the numinous, the quest, the Rings of Power, the Road, the tree and underground places and journeys. On a greater scale, the geography and history is Middle-Earth is symbolic, enriching the stories that come from the various Ages. Further enrichment is obtained from invented beings such as the Valar, the Maiar, Balrogs, Elves, dwarves and Hobbits.

The process of invention that Tolkien calls sub-creation allows the imagination to employ both unconscious and conscious resources of the mind. This is particularly so with regard to language, which is intimately connected to the whole self, and not just theoretical thought. Sub-creation allows powerful archetypes to became an effective part of an art-work. This accounts for the universal appeal of deeply imaginative writing like Tolkien's. Like the other Inklings, Tolkien above all values myth and story.

Romantic Love and Charles Williams

Charles Williams' 'romantic religion', though concerned with romantic love, took the form of what he characteristically called 'the Way of the Affirmation of Images'.[33] In *The Allegory of Love*, much admired by Williams, Lewis pointed out that there are basically two ways in which the mind may develop an essential equivalence between material and immaterial, natural and spiritual. When a person begins with immaterial fact – such as qualities like beauty or joy – and invents visibilia to express them, he is allegorising. It is possible, however, to reverse this process, and to view the material world as itself a copy of the invisible world. When a person attempts to read something else through the sensible – to discover the idea or meaning in the copy – he is engaged in symbolism or sacramentalism. 'The allegorist,' argues Lewis, 'leaves the given – his passions – to talk of that which is confessedly less real, which is a fiction. The symbolist leaves the given to find that which is more real.'[34] Later, Lewis was to write that allegory in its highest form approaches myth. The idea of sacramentalism applies to Charles Williams; except that when he leaves behind the given to find its meaning he retains the importance of the given. It has a greater reality which can now be seen. Thus in romantic love (as when Dante saw Beatrice) the Beloved is both an image of Divine Beauty and important in him or herself. To care for Divine Beauty is to care for the ordinary yet transfigured mortal before you. This is Philip's experience in Williams' novel,[35]

> Now, suddenly, he understood Rosamond's arm when she leant forward to pass a plate to her sister; somehow that arm always made him think of the Downs against the sky. There was a line, a curved beauty, a thing that spoke to both mind and heart; a thing that was there for ever. And Rosamond? Rosamond was like them, she was there for ever. It occurred to him that, if she was, then her occasional slowness when he was trying to explain something was there for ever. Well, after all, Rosamond was only human; she couldn't be absolutely perfect. And then as she stretched out her arm again he cried out that she was perfect, she was more than perfect; the movement of her arm was something frightfully important, and now it was gone.

This interplay between the reality of the image (here the image of perfection) and the reality pictured by the image is captured in Williams' distinctive doctrine of the twofold Way of the Affirmation and Rejection of Images. Here we say of any created person or thing in reference to the Creator: 'This also is Thou; neither is this Thou.' In his *The Descent of the Dove*, Williams described the principle like this:

> The one Way was to affirm all things orderly until the universe throbbed with vitality; the other to reject all things until there was nothing anywhere but He. The Way of Affirmation was to develop great art and romantic love and marriage and philosophy and social justice; the Way of Rejection was to break out continually in the profound mystical documents of the soul, the records of the great psychological masters of Christendom. All was involved in Christendom ...[36]

The validity of both aspects of the twofold Way was connected in Williams' thinking with another key doctrine of Christianity, namely 'co-inherence'. This doctrine was captured for him, characteristically, in the beautiful image of the city. This social image brings out, for Williams, the dependence of each of us upon others' labours and gifts, and the necessity of bearing one another's burdens.

Williams argues that romantic love between men and women can help us to understand better the ways of God. Theologians have tended to overlook romantic love as expository source material, though they have often used natural phenomena, ethical issues and human reasoning. But why ignore the experience that human beings universally share?

Barfield and Evolution of Human Consciousness

Evolution of human consciousness
Barfield believed that, corresponding to stellar and biological evolution, there has been an evolution of consciousness. Evolution has been guided by a telos, design or purpose, and not by chance or chaos. The emergence of the human mind is at the very centre of evolution. In holding to such a view, Barfield admired the teaching of Pierre Teilhard de Chardin.

The evolution of consciousness is reflected precisely in changes in language and perception, from a primitive unity of consciousness to a future achievement of a greater human consciousness. In this the subject–object dichotomy is overcome in a harmonious human participation with nature.

Participation
The Inklings sometimes discussed primitive human beings, and pre-Christian paganism is explored as a central theme in Tolkien's tales of

Middle-Earth. Enlightened paganism is also a common theme in Lewis, as in *Till We Have Faces*. Barfield's thinking is constantly captured by a vision of an ancient unity, by definition embodied both in perception and language, a unity we have lost. Central to this vision was a sense of what Barfield called 'original participation', a sense we can glimpse at times through dreams, poetry and myth. He believed that this primitive awareness was 'pre-logical' and 'pre-mythical'.

Barfield defines original participation in a philosophically idealistic way as the belief that 'there stands behind the phenomena, and on the other side of them from me, a represented which is of the same nature as me...of the same nature as the perceiving self, inasmuch as it is not mechanical or accidental, but psychic and voluntary.'[37] He explained that human beings, in this primitive state, feel themselves to be 'a functioning member of the natural world, as a finger is a member of the physical body.'[38]

Barfield's concept inspired Lewis particularly, but also Tolkien.[39] Lewis shows how animal consciousness presents a hint of this original human participation in his affectionate portrayal of Mr Bultitude the bear in *That Hideous Strength*:

> Mr. Bultitude's mind was as furry and as unhuman in shape as his body ... Indeed he did not know that he existed at all: everything that is represented by the words *I* and *Me* and *Thou* was absent from his mind. When Mrs. Maggs gave him a tin of golden syrup, as she did every Sunday morning, he did not recognise either a giver or a recipient. Goodness occurred and he tasted it. And that was all ... He was no more like a human egoist than he was like a human altruist. There was no prose in his life. The appetencies which a human mind might disdain as cupboard loves were *for* him quivering and ecstatic aspirations which absorbed his whole being, infinite yearnings, stabbed with the threat of tragedy and shot through with the colours of Paradise. One of our race, if plunged back for a moment in the warm, trembling, iridescent pool of that pre-Adamite consciousness, would have emerged believing that he had grasped the absolute for the states below reason and the states above it have, by their common contrast to the life we know, a certain superficial resemblance. Sometimes there returns to us from infancy the memory of a nameless delight or terror, unattached to any delightful or dreadful thing, a potent adjective floating in a nounless void, a pure quality. At such moments we have experience of the shallows of that pool. But fathoms deeper than any memory can take us, right down in the central warmth and dimness, the bear lived all its *life*.[40]

Participation is one of Barfield's central concepts, closely tied to his belief in an original state of unified perception. It had many consequences for our understanding of the nature of language and metaphor. Participation, according to Barfield, is a 'predominately perceptual relation between observer and observed, between man and nature...nearer to unity than dichotomy.'[41] In this relation mind is not yet detached from its representations; the subject and the object not divorced. Barfield believes that some of this ancient participation endures in medieval art and thought, the four elements theory, the four humours, and in astrology.[42] There are some parallels with Barfield in Michael Polanyi's exposition of a tacit dimension to knowledge[43] and in Herman Dooyeweerd's idea of naïve or common experience.[44]

History, Guilt and Habit (1979)

Barfield explored the ideas of participation and evolution of consciousness in many writings. *History, Guilt and Habit* is an excellent introduction to Barfield's thought which is lucid and distils his earlier work of over 50 years.[45] Chapter One draws on his lifelong interest in history, as in *History in English Words* (1926).[46] For Barfield, language itself records the history of, and changes in, human consciousness. Chapter Two focuses upon idolatry, the theme of *Saving the Appearances* (1957).[47] He employs this concept to highlight the main heresy of the modern world of scientism and technocracy. He points out a serious one-sidedness in contemporary knowledge and virtue, a theme that compliments Lewis's *The Abolition of Man*.[48] Chapter Three reflects Barfield's belief that a 'Romanticism come of age' gives hope for a future reconciliation between humanity, nature and God. The imagination has a key role to play in restoring a perception of the inside of things as well as their surfaces. In an older age perceptions were images – symbolically portraying the actual world. The modern mistakenly worships the image. This idolatry misplaces the image, thus the surface, for the reality. This leads to a reduced reality, stripped of qualities like beauty and love. Paradoxically it denies the very human consciousness that is able to make such a truth claim. (In Lewis's parallel analysis in *Miracles*, this is the problem of naturalism.)

Whereas for Lewis and Tolkien, a critique of the modern world is based upon Christian orthodoxy, Barfield finds an affinity with his approach in anthroposophy. There is, however, considerable overlap between Barfield, Lewis and Tolkien. In their core ideas not only do they share a deep preoccupation with language, but also a profound sense of great loss in the modern consciousness. They all sought to rehabilitate insights from an older world, in the belief that such values constitute the irreplaceable character of our humanity.

In *History, Guilt and Habit* Barfield argues that, though we can distinguish between thinking and perception, we are not to divide them. This is because consciousness includes perception as well as thinking. Knowledge is both subjective and objective. Our ordinary perception is of the actual world – the world of molecules and particles disclosed by science is not more real.

Barfield points out that changes in human consciousness are therefore also changes in the actual world. Consciousness is not on the 'outside', but rather on the 'inside' of the world. But perception is not as such based on a particular philosophy. Rather, it is founded on historically infixed habits of thought – habits that are to us unconscious. For this reason the study of changes in consciousness in history is different from a history of ideas. Barfield's analysis has therefore parallels with sociology of knowledge.

This interpenetration of thinking and perceiving is a fact of consciousness. It is easier to see the interpenetration in language than in consciousness itself, for it is impossible of course for consciousness to stand outside of its consciousness. Language, according to Barfield, reveals a varying proportion of thinking and perceiving – for instance, poetic language is more perceptual than prose, and prose more conceptual than poetry.

History in English Words (1926)

This, Barfield's second book, is a meditation into the etymology of key words, tracing changes in human consciousness, changes Barfield regarded as an 'evolution of consciousness'.[49] For Barfield, a history of consciousness must be very different from a history of ideas, as he points out in *History, Guilt and Habit*. Consciousness is intimately related to perception as well as to the products of thinking. Once upon a time, there was a feeling thinking and a perceiving word. The etymology of words often gives a glimpse of an ancient unity of consciousness, as Barfield tries to show. Cultural and historical changes might be better explained by shifts in consciousness than by changes in intellectual ideas.

Barfield found that by tracing the changes of meanings of words, he could get an insight into the very different kind of consciousness that our ancestors had. He was anxious to show that it was not just that people in the past think like us but have different ideas; rather, they have a different way of thinking. In particular, the separation of objective from subjective – even the seemingly fundamental distinction between the self and the world – is a relative newcomer in human consciousness.[50]

Poetic Diction (1928)

Along with an intoxicating freedom from the invisible presuppositions of one's age, in rejecting chronological snobbery, Lewis also inherited Barfield's highly original insights into the nature of poetic language. Tolkien also incorporated them into his thinking. These insights were embodied in Barfield's perhaps most important book *Poetic Diction*.

Barfield had gone up to Oxford in October 1919, and after graduation began a B.Litt., the thesis of which became *Poetic Diction*. As undergraduates Lewis and Barfield had often walked together or asked each other to lunch, but did not really see a lot of each other until after graduation, when the 'great war' started between them.

Barfield drew inspiration from anthroposophism and Rudolf Steiner for his many writings, and his adherence to this view formed the basis for that 'great war' between Lewis and himself. His influence on Lewis and Tolkien was mainly through *Poetic Diction*, though later ideas of Barfield sometimes appear in Lewis's writings. This book concerns the nature of poetic language and his theory of an ancient semantic unity, which require no commitment to anthroposophical interpretations of Christianity. The 'great war' of ideas in fact helped to prepare Lewis for accepting orthodox Christianity, rather than any anthroposophist ideas. Significant differences remained between Lewis and Barfield until the end of his life, even they held an enormous amount in common.

Poetic Diction offers a theory of knowledge as well as a theory of poetry. At its heart is a philosophy of language. Barfield's view is that 'the individual imagination is the medium of all knowledge from perception upward.'[51] The poetic impulse is linked to individual freedom: 'the act of the imagination is the individual mind exercising its sovereign unity.'[52] The alternative, argues Barfield, is to *see* knowledge as power, to 'mistake efficiency for meaning', leading to a relish for compulsion. He speaks of those who 'reduce the specifically human to a mechanical or animal regularity' as being likely to be 'increasingly irritated by the nature of the mother tongue and make it their point of attack'.[53]

Characteristically he writes:

> Language is the storehouse of imagination; it cannot continue to be itself without performing its function. But its function is, to mediate transition from the unindividualized, dreaming spirit that carried the infancy of the world to the individualised human spirit, which has the future in its charge. If therefore they succeed in expunging from language all the substance of its past, in which it is naturally so rich, and finally converting it into the species of algebra that is best adapted to the uses of indoctrination and empirical

science, a long and important step ... will have been taken in the...liquidation of the human spirit.[54]

This fighting talk anticipates much of Lewis, as in his *The Abolition of Man*. Indeed many of Lewis's preoccupations, and those of the Inklings, are anticipated in Barfield's book. Some are undoubtedly the fruit of the many conversations and letters between the two men.

Knowledge as power is contrasted with knowledge by participation (as we saw, a key word in Barfield). One kind of knowledge 'consists of seeing what happens and getting used to it' and the other involves 'consciously participating in what is.'[55] The proper activity of the imagination is 'concrete thinking' – this is 'the perception of resemblance, the demand for unity' (the influence of Coleridge can be seen here).[56] There is, therefore, a poetic element in all meaningful language. Lewis elaborates this same point about the poetic condition of meaning in thought in *Selected Literary Essays*, and in the chapter 'Horrid Red Things', in *Miracles* – a chapter which tries to capture the core of Barfield's ideas in *Poetic Diction*.

Christian Mysticism and the Inklings: a Medieval Synthesis?

Christian mysticism has to reckon with the *Logos*/Word. It seems to me that the Prologue of John's Gospel is increasingly relevant to a postmodernist culture, where mysticism and spirituality is more acceptable than it was under modernism. According to Scripture God in relation to his creation is not in principle ineffable, but 'the Word'. His lordship of the Word extends over all possible human experience and every part of the universe. Even in the visual, relating to dreams and visions, as well as the visual arts, there is a linguistic parallel in the iconic[57]. There is a visual language which covers for instance the apocalyptic visions of Ezekiel, Daniel and the Book of Revelation, where there is visual inter-reference, as when John draws on Daniel and Ezekiel in describing the vision of the glorified Christ. In creation also, as presented to our senses, there is a coherent visual language:

> The heavens are telling the glory of God;
> and the firmament proclaims his handiwork.
> Day to day pours forth speech,
> and night to night declares knowledge. (Psalm 19)

An important element in the Inklings, deserving much study, is mythopoeia – the making of myth. Their view of myth and story brings them under the lordship of Christ, the Logos – the epitome of myth, in their view, is the Gospels, where myth becomes fact. It is entirely in keeping that, in the context of Gnostic mystery religions, St Paul declares: 'Behold *I tell you* a mystery' (1 Cor. 15:51 – italics mine). In Christian mysticism, mystery is relative. It is our knowledge that is incomplete – the vastness of reality is not a wordless mystery to the Lord who is the Word. It can be told.

For Lewis and Tolkien particularly, all pagan insights are unfinished and incomplete, anticipating the greatest story, God's spell, or the Gospel. As Christian mystics, what they did was grapple with pagan insights, exploring how far the pagan imagination could go without the light of Scripture, God's special revelation. In grappling with and affirming pagan insights, their attitude belongs to the thought patterns of the Middle Ages, to a pre-modernist world. They re-establish (or, more accurately, pick up on a continuity with) a premodernist understanding and vision of reality to which they give contemporary form. The same is largely true of Charles Williams. As for Barfield, though he enormously influenced Lewis, and left his mark on Tolkien, he is, I believe, a theistic more than a Christian mystic.

Because of time limits, I'll confine myself to a brief examination of how Tolkien's Christian mysticism expressed itself in relation to the challenge of pagan insights (in his case, pre-Christian paganism of the type which was such a challenge and stimulus in the Middle Ages).[58]

Tolkien's Christian Exploration of Paganism

Tolkien, by confession, is a Roman Catholic. His natural theology is unusual in that his stress is with the imagination, rather than with reason. It is by imagination that there can be genuine insight into God and reality independently of the specific revelation of scripture. However, he emphasises in his essay, 'On Fairy Stories',[59] that any such insights are acts of grace from 'the Father of Lights.' They are a kind of pre-revelation, opening the way to receiving the special revelation of the Gospel. They are not rival or superior revelations.

Whereas traditional Roman Catholic thought emphasizes the rat-ional and cognitive in natural theology, Tolkien links it with imaginative meaning. It is a complimentary revelation to that of the propositional. The story, like language, is evidence of the image of God still remaining in fallen humankind. 'The tongue and the tale,' believed Tolkien, 'are coeval'. He also spoke of the seamless 'web of story', the interrelationship of all storytelling.[60] Tolkien, like Lewis, believed that, in a sense, it was natural to believe in Christ our saviour.[61]

For Tolkien, monotheism is natural religion, and is the faith of the Three Ages of Middle-Earth (the pre-Christian era, highlighting the best of such a situation). He writes that *The Lord of the Rings* depicts 'a monotheistic world of "natural theology".'[62] The Edain, willing to learn from the Elves, had turned to the West and towards Ilúvatar. In so doing their nature was enhanced and fulfilled. They were rewarded with the gift of the island of Numenor.

Sub-creation, nature and grace

Tolkien's conception of sub-creation, which was mentioned above, has important consequences for epistemology. Tolkien seems to be saying that in sub-creation stories take on an inevitable structure, anticipating or referring to the *evangelium*. Grace thus intervenes in the activity of sub-creation, leading to insight into and contact with reality.

The medieval concept of mankind was that we are a microcosm. According to Tolkien, secondary worlds of the imagination – the fruit of sub-creation – are miniature worlds, focussing primary reality on their limited scale, providing an imaginative survey of space and time. This parallels the view of humans as a miniature universe.

Vico taught that people can best know what they make themselves, namely history.[63] Similarly, Leonardo earlier had a concept of operational knowledge, where man redesigns the world in creating, and thus uncovers its hidden structures.[64] The early scientists (perhaps like some modern cosmologists) believed that they were thinking God's thoughts after him. In a similar way, for Tolkien, his imaginative making, or sub-creation, unlocks the meaning of God's primary creation, even discovering hints of his plan to redeem mankind and set a spoiled world right. This is why Tolkien disliked allegory. Allegory as invention is too conscious, with not enough imaginative making. Successful sub-creation can achieve myth. Pre-eminently the gospel story makes myth that is also true in the actual, primary world rather than only in a 'secondary world.' In that story God casts his spell over us, a spell stronger than any human-made myth.

Paganism

In exploring the pattern of nature and grace in Tolkien a consideration of paganism is inevitable. It seems that, for Tolkien, paganism was a central case study for the intervention and integration of grace in nature. Tolkien's tales of Middle-earth are thoroughly set in a pagan context. It is a pagan world, like the setting of his model, *Beowulf*, the great Early English poem. In *Beowulf*, according to Tolkien, there is a fusion of the Christian and the ancient north, the old and the new. Yet the imagination of the *Beowulf* author had not developed into an allegorical one. Allegory was a later development. His dragon, as a symbol of evil, retains the ancient force of the pagan northern imagination; it is not an allegory of evil in reference to the individual soul's redemption or damnation. He is concerned with 'man on earth' rather than the journey to the celestial city. 'Each man and all men, and all their works shall die … The shadow of its despair, if only as a mood, as an intense emotion of regret, is still there. The worth of defeated valour in this world is deeply felt.'[65] The poet feels this theme imaginatively or poetically rather than literally, yet with a sense of the ultimate defeat of darkness.

The *Beowulf* poet indicates for Tolkien the good that may be found in the pagan imagination, a theme also powerfully explored by Lewis in *Till We Have Faces*. In sharing such a view of what may be called enlightened paganism, Lewis was heavily influenced by Tolkien.

There are a number of parallels between the author of *Beowulf*, as understood by Tolkien, and Tolkien himself. Tolkien is a Christian scholar looking back to an imagined Northern European past. The *Beowulf* author was a Christian looking to the imaginative resources of a pagan past. Both made use of dragons and other potent symbols, symbols which unified their work. Both are concerned more with symbolism than allegory. As with the *Beowulf* author, what is important is not so much the sources, but what Tolkien did with them. Like the ancient author, also, Tolkien, at his most successful, created an illusion of history and a sense of depths of the past.

Tolkien's world in general is replete with Christian heroes and yet, like *Beowulf's*, it is a pagan world. Ultimately, grace successfully spiritualises nature. The fading of the elves is sad for the elves. Aragorn however stands at the end of the Third Age with Arwen at his side, a reminder of Lúthien in her grace and beauty. The future ages are full of the promise of the *evangelium*. The White Tree had at last flowered, a sign of permanent and ultimate victory over evil.

Tolkien's treatment of paganism has the same potency that he found in *Beowulf*. The potency is there also in Lewis's *Till We Have Faces*. In it, Princess Psyche represents a Christ-likeness, though she is not intended as an allegory of Christ. Lewis wrote in explanation to Clyde S. Kilby:

> Psyche is an instance of the *anima naturaliter Christiana* making the best of the pagan religion she is brought up in and thus being guided (but always 'under the cloud', always in terms of her own imagination or that of her people) towards the true God. She is in some ways like Christ because every good man or woman is like Christ.[66]

Tolkien as a Christian artist

Tolkien is a pre-modern rather than postmodern author who has outstanding contemporary appeal. This appeal transcends the universal attraction of a good story. The qualities of what he considered authentic sub-creation are there in his work – consolation, joy, recovery and myth – what Tolkien might describe as the presence of grace derived from the *evangelium*, God's story or 'the Godspell.'

Tolkien has an important place as a Christian artist because his fiction successfully embodies Christian meaning in artistic form, suitable for a contemporary readership that generally doesn't share his Christian beliefs. In this sense, Tolkien is a twentieth century Christian apologist. We are perhaps used to thinking of Lewis's fiction and popular theology as of a piece as apologetics. Tolkien's fiction is in the same apologetic framework, recovering and restoring a Christian way of seeing reality.

In a letter to W.H. Auden (in 1965), Tolkien commented on *The Lord of the Rings* in relation to Christian theology: 'I don't feel under any obligation to make my story fit with formalized Christian theology, though I actually intended it to be consonant with Christian thought and belief.'[67] Tolkien's words are the heartbeat of a Christian mysticism.

Tolkien has also contributed to a Christian understanding of imagination, in association with Lewis and Barfield. Though Tolkien and Lewis are in a tradition of romanticism, they are distinctive in not identifying imagination and truth. In the terms of C.S. Lewis, imagination is the organ of meaning, not truth.

Imagination perceives reality. In a sense, reality is meaning, in being a dependent creation of God's, referring to him as its source, and not having meaning in itself. These are familiar Christian ideas of meaning, found for example in such diverse thinkers as Michael Polanyi and Herman Dooyeweerd, yet dramatically applied to the imagination.

Conclusion

To summarise: Tolkien's view of sub-creation expresses a kind of natural theology, while his notion of the seamless 'web of story' has story alive with God's presence, through the intervention of the Gospel narrative. Central to Tolkien's fiction is the creation of Elves. These are representative of human spirituality and culture, and human spirituality itself has an Elven quality. He portrayed a pre-Christian, pagan world, with *Beowulf* as his model. His preoccupation with paganism has a strong affinity with Lewis's *Till We Have Faces*. If nature and grace can be integrated, as Tolkien desired, the position of the pre-Christian world is highly significant. Indeed, most of Tolkien's fiction is set in such a world.

Ultimately, I believe, Tolkien is successful in integrating nature and grace in *The Lord of the Rings*. Tolkien is a Christian artist.

The Heart of the Inklings' Vision: A Symbolic Perception of Reality

Their view of fantasy, and its harmonious relation with the intellect, illuminates the nature of the Bible as a pre-modernist book. Barfield, echoed by Lewis and Tolkien, suggests that comparatively recently we have lost an ancient unity between the poetic and the prosaic, the symbolic and the literal. In the Bible, to give an example, 'spirit', is equally 'spirit' and 'breath' and 'wind'. Again, the *Logos* of John's Gospel is a profound unity integrating many meanings which we today have to separate out. The same would be true of early Genesis; the common dichotomy of facticity and poetry in reading these chapters is misleading.

Seen as a whole, if we follow their logic, the Bible encourages, in a very basic, straight-forward and ordinary way, what might be called a symbolic perception of reality – looking *at* reality *through* the frame of narrative, story, image, and other symbolic elements. The Bible begins symbolically with seven-day creation and the events in the Garden of Eden and ends with the visions of the Book of Revelation and the denouement of the Holy City, within which is the Tree of Life introduced in Genesis. The hero of heroes of Scripture is the lamb which was slain from the creation of the world. In a profound sense, such symbols are not merely poetic, but solidly real. The lamb which was slain, for instance, is linked in a myriad ways to actual events in documented history, such as the crucifixion and resurrection of Christ.

By saturating ourselves in the Scriptures a healing of this division, a restoration of a basic human unity of consciousness, can begin to take place. We find this far harder than, for instance, a seventeenth century English, German or Dutch reader of the Bible. For this reason Lewis advocated a diet of old books, i.e. books belonging to the period he called the 'Old West'. He would favour all educated people reading Boethius' *The Consolation of Philosophy* (one of the most influential and widely read books in the Middle Ages). Scripture blatantly appeals to our human taste for a story, and to our delight in other unifying symbolic elements such as archetypes. Tolkien and Lewis instanced this integration in the meeting of myth and fact in the Gospels.

The imaginative work of Lewis, Tolkien and Williams reinforces such a biblical emphasis upon a symbolic perception of reality. Their symbolic worlds, even though fictional, are in some sense solidly real. For this reason they take us back to the ordinary world which is an inevitable part of our human living and experience, deepening both the wonders and the terrors of our world. Our awareness of the meaning of God's creation and his intentions for us is enlarged. Lewis, Tolkien and Williams guide us in seeing this world with a thoroughly Christian understanding. They also illuminate what is revealed of God in the natural order.

Perhaps the dominance of realistic literature has coincided with the reign of modernism – the pattern of the Enlightenment – that squeezed fantasy on to the periphery of the canon of literature. Now that we are in a postmodern culture, the character and social role of fantasy might change and become more central, as it was before the Enlightenment became dominant. The continued popularity and thus cultural relevance of the fantasy fiction of Lewis and Tolkien – both avowedly anti-modernist – is surely significant. They might be called pre-modernist rather than postmodernist authors who have outstanding contemporary appeal, an appeal that continues to grow. It may well be that the neglected writings of Williams will find a new readership in a changed culture. Barfield's influence as an innovative thinker continues to grow, mainly in the USA.[68]

Lewis and Tolkien saw the symbolic appeal of the Bible most focussed in the Gospels. These, in form and in substance, have an extraordinary imaginative draw. Indeed, Auden points out, in *Secondary Worlds* that they subverted classical ideas about the imagination. The incarnation of Christ and the other events of the Gospel story locate the imagination in the ordinary world of creation, or nature.[69]

Tolkien and Lewis both were convinced that the events documented in the Gospels, located in the real world of first century Palestine, nevertheless retain the quality of myth – that is, they are the epitome of human storytelling. But just as they retain the quality of myth, they equally are true history. Though this combination was alien to a Greco-Roman mentality, it was fully consistent with the logic and imagination of a theology steeped in the Bible. The Gospels thus require an imaginative as well as an intellectual response. The Gospels, if Lewis and Tolkien are right, satisfy the mystical longings of the human heart and the persistent desire for intellectual unity of the human mind. In their narratives they reconcile what otherwise seem intractable paradoxes: Jesus as fully God and fully human, the relationship between human free agency and divine providence, the reality of evil and suffering and the goodness of God's purpose for his creation, and, not least, the human and divine authorship of the written words of the Gospels.

The view of Lewis, Tolkien and their friends may be summed up by Tolkien's observation in his essay, 'On Fairy-Stories': 'God is the Lord, of angels, and of man – and of Elves. Legend and history have met and fused ... Art has been verified.'[70]

Notes

This article draws upon material that appeared in Colin Duriez & David Porter, *The Inklings Handbook: The Lives, Thought and Writings of C.S. Lewis, J.R.R. Tolkien, Charles Williams and Their Friends* (London: Azure/SPCK, 2001), Colin Duriez, *Tolkien and The Lord of the Rings* (London: Azure/SPCK, 2001) and Colin Duriez, *The C.S. Lewis Encyclopedia* (London: Azure/SPCK, 2002), and is used with permission of the publishers.

[1] Owen Barfield, *Poetic Diction: A Study in Meaning* (London: Faber and Faber, 1962[2] – originally published 1928).

[2] Humphrey Carpenter, *The Inklings: C.S. Lewis, J.R.R. Tolkien, Charles Williams and their Friends* (London: George Allen & Unwin, 1978); John Wain, *Sprightly Running: Part of an Autobiography* (London: Macmillan, 1962); Rand Kuhl, 'Barfield in Southern California', *Mythlore* 1:4 (1969), 8–10. Diana Pavlac 'The Company They Keep: Assessing the Mutual Influence of C.S. Lewis , J.R.R. Tolkien, and Charles Williams', (unpublished Ph.D. thesis, University of Illinois at Chicago, 1993); Gareth Knight, *The Magical World of the Inklings* (Longmead: Element Books, 1990).

[3] Caroline F.E. Spurgeon, *Mysticism in English Literature* (Cambridge: Cambridge University Press, 1913), 3.

[4] Ibid., 3.

[5] Lumsden Barkway & Lucy Menzies (eds.), *An Anthology of the Love of God: From the Writings of Evelyn Underhill* (London: Mowbray, 1953), 116, 117.

[6] Rand Kuhl, 'Barfield in Southern California', *Mythlore* 1.4 (1969), 8–10.

[7] Quoted in ibid.

[8] C.S. Lewis, *The Pilgrim's Regress* (London: Fount, 1977[3]), 11–12.

[9] Pavlac, 'The Company They Keep'.

[10] See C.S. Lewis, 'Bluspels and Flalansferes: A Semantic Nightmare,' in *Selected Literary Essays* (Cambridge: Cambridge University Press, 1969), especially 265.

[11] C.S. Lewis, 'Introduction', in C.S. Lewis (ed.), *Essays Presented to Charles Williams* (Oxford University Press, 1947), vi.

[12] Ibid.

[13] C.S. Lewis, *Surprised by Joy: The Shape of My Early Life* (London: Geoffrey Bles, 1955).

[14] C.S. Lewis (ed.), *George MacDonald: An Anthology* (London: Geoffrey Bles, 1946), 21.

[15] Published in seven volumes between 1950–56.

[16] C.S. Lewis, *The Problem of Pain* (London: Geoffrey Bles, 1940).

[17] C.S. Lewis, *The Voyage of the Dawn Treader* (London: Geoffrey Bles, 1952).

[18] C.S. Lewis, *Till We Have Faces* (London: Geoffrey Bles, 1956).

[19] C.S. Lewis, *Of This and Other Worlds* (London: Collins, 1982), 35–6.

[20] C S. Lewis, *Letters to Malcolm* (London: Geoffrey Bles, 1964), 122.

[21] Lewis (ed.), *Essays Presented to Charles Williams*, 50.

[22] J.R.R. Tolkien, *The Lord of the Rings* (London: George Allen & Unwin, 1954–55).

[23] 'Of Beren and Luthien', in J.R.R. Tolkien, *The Silmarillion* (London: George Allen and Unwin, 1977), 162–87.

[24] J.R.R. Tolkien, 'On Fairy-Stories,' in Lewis (ed.), *Essays Presented to Charles Williams*, 79.

[25] 'The Weight of glory,' reproduced in C.S. Lewis, *Essay Collection and Other Short Pieces* (London: HarperCollins, 2000), 104.

[26] Tolkien, 'On Fairy-Stories', 81, 83; Kuhl, 'Barfield in Southern California.'

[27] Tolkien, ibid., 81.

[28] Ibid.

[29] Ibid., 82.

[30] This is a central theme of Tolkien's seminal essay, 'On Fairy-Stories'.

[31] Ibid, 42.

[32] Ibid., 51.

[33] See, for example, Charles Williams, *The Descent of the Dove: A Short History of the Holy Spirit in the Church* (London: Collins Fontana, 1963), 124; see also, Duriez & Porter, *Inklings Handbook*, 49–50.

[34] C.S. Lewis, *The Allegory of Love: A Study in Mediaeval Tradition* (Oxford University Press, 1936), 45.

[35] Charles Williams, *Shadows of Ecstasy* (London: Victor Gollancz, 1933).

[36] Williams, *Descent of the Dove*, 59.

[37] O. Barfield, *Saving the Appearances* (New York: Harcourt, Brace Jovanovich, 1957), 42.

[38] O. Barfield, *Romanticism Comes of Age* (Middletown: Wesleyan University Press, 1944²), 230.

[39] This influence is argued in Verlyn Flieger, *Splintered Light: Logos and Language in Tolkien's World* (Grand Rapids: Eerdmans, 1983).

[40] C.S. Lewis, *That Hideous Strength* (London: Bodley Head, 1945), 378–9.

[41] O. Barfield, *History, Guilt, and Habit* (Middletown: Wesleyan University Press, 1979), 26.

[42] O. Barfield, *The Rediscovery of Meaning and Other Essays* (Middletown: Wesleyan University Press, 1977), 18.

[43] See Polanyi's *Personal Knowledge: Towards a Post-Critical Philosophy* (Chicago: Chicago University Press, 1958).

[44] See Herman Dooyeweerd, *A New Critique of Theoretical Thought*, originally published in Dutch in three volumes between 1935–36; the English edition in two volumes, tr. David H. Freeman and William S. Young (Phillipsburg: Presbyterian & Reformed Publishing Company, 1969).

[45] Barfield, *History, Guilt and Habit*.

[46] Owen Barfield, *History in English Words* (London: Faber and Faber, 1926).

[47] Owen Barfield, *Saving the Appearances: A Study in Idolatry* (New York: Harcourt, Brace Jovanovich, 1957).

[48] C.S. Lewis, *The Abolition of Man: Reflections on Education with Special Reference to the Teaching of English in the Upper Forms of Schools* (London: Oxford University Press, 1943).

[49] Barfield, *History in English Words*.

[50] See Barfield, *Poetic Diction*, 206.

[51] Ibid., 22.

[52] Ibid.

[53] Ibid., 23.

[54] Ibid.

[55] Ibid., 24.

[56] This insight is fundamental in Samuel Taylor Coleridge's *Biographia Literaria*. See also Owen Barfield, *What Coleridge Thought* (Middletown: Wesleyan University Press, 1977).

[57] See H.R. Rookmaaker, *Gauguin and Ninth Century Art Theory*, in *Art, Artists and Gauguin: The Complete Works of Hans Rookmaaker*, Vol. 1 (Carlisle: Piquant, 2002), 169–75.

[58] For a fuller examination see Colin Duriez, 'The Theology of Fantasy in Lewis and Tolkien', *Themelios* 23:2 (1998), 35–51.

[59] J.R.R. Tolkien, 'On Fairy Stories', in *Tree and Leaf* (London: Unwin Hyman, 1988²).

[60] Ibid., 82.

[61] See especially Tolkien's 'Epilogue,' in ibid., 82–4.

[62] Humphrey Carpenter (ed.), *The Letters of J.R.R. Tolkien* (London: George Allen & Unwin, 1981), 220.

[63] David A. Fraser & Tony Campolo, *Sociology Through the Eyes of Faith* (Leicester: Apollos, 1992), 17f.

[64] See G. de Santillana, *The Age of Adventure* (New York: Mentor Books, 1956), 69.

[65] J.R.R. Tolkien, *The Monsters and the Critics and Other Essays* (London: George Allen & Unwin, 1983), 23.

[66] W.H. Lewis (ed.), *Letters of C.S. Lewis* (London: Geoffrey Bles, 1966), 274.

[67] Carpenter (ed.), *Letters of J.R.R. Tolkien*, 355.

[68] For insights into the nature of his thinking see Duriez & Porter, *Inklings Handbook*.

[69] See W.H. Auden, *Secondary Worlds: the T.S. Eliot Memorial Lectures Delivered at Eliot College in the University of Kent at Canterbury, October 1967* (London: Faber & Faber, 1967), 120, 121.

[70] Tolkien, 'On Fairy-Stories', 84.

14

Save the Name

Mysticism and Modern French Thought

Arthur Bradley

In his essay '*Sauf le nom: (Post-Scriptum)*' (1993), the contemporary French philosopher Jacques Derrida speaks of a desire to 'save the name' of Christian mysticism.[1] Mysticism, it seems, is alive and well in post-modernity. The last few years have witnessed a sudden explosion of interest in the relationship between the work of Christian mystical theologians like Pseudo-Dionysius and continental philosophers like Jacques Derrida.[2] This interest has gradually widened to encompass the larger questions of the relationship between continental philosophy, Christian, Jewish, Islamic and Pagan mysticisms more generally.[3] Developments like these provoke enthusiasm, ambivalence and unease in equal measures amongst contemporary theologians but they also prompt a series of critical questions which form the backdrop to this paper. What exactly *is* the relationship between mysticism and continental philosophy? Is there anything to be gained by this unlikely *rapprochement* between the sacred and the secular, the pre-modern and the postmodern? And does the work of philosophers like Derrida have anything constructive to say to Christians, in particular, about the role of mysticism today, here, now? In this paper, I would like to offer a brief survey of some current critical thinking on Christian mysticism and modern French thought.

Christian Mysticism

I would like to begin by saying something about the term 'Christian mysticism'. Christian mysticism, as the contributions to this book show, is an extremely difficult term to define. Popular definitions still speak of an intensely personal experience of God. Modern theologians, however, appear to agree neither about the meaning of the term nor even about the terms by which its meaning might ultim-ately be determined. Bernard McGinn decisively rejects the experiential defi-nition by describing the mystical element in Christianity as 'that part of its belief or practices that concerns the preparation, the conscious-ness of, and the reaction to what can be described as the immediate or direct presence of God'.[4] Michel de Certeau goes further than McGinn when he defines '*mystics*' as the expression of a divine *absence* rather than a real presence: 'its literature, therefore, has all the traits of what it both opposes and posits … it is the trial, by language, of all the ambiguous passage from presence to absence'.[5] More disarmingly still, Denys Turner blithely admits that 'he does not know of any discussions which shed less light on the subject of "mysticism" than those which attempt definitional answers to the question "what is mysticism?" '[6] The absence of any critical consensus on the term leads many theolo-gians to set aside definitional approaches to 'mysticism' in favour of a more pragmatic and descriptive focus on particular theologians or the-ological idioms that are commonly identified as 'mystic'. This strategy of focusing on what mystics *do* rather than what mystics *are* is adopt-ed to a greater or lesser degree by McGinn, Certeau, Turner and other influential theologians and it is one that I would like to borrow here for my own purposes. In this section, then, I would like to concentrate on the particular but exemplary mystical theology of Pseudo-Dionysius the Areopagite.

Pseudo-Dionysius was a fifth-century Christian theologian who adopted the name of an Athenian convert of St Paul. Dionysius's deci-sion to write under the name of an Athenian is now thought to be a strategic move which advertises his audacious attempt to synthesise Judaeo-Christian theology and Greek philosophy. He specifically attempts a synthesis between the Judaeo-Christian tradition of biblical revelation and liturgical practice and the Neoplatonic and Plotinian concept of emanation from the One. The stitching together of Greek and Christian thought in this way enables Dionysius's theology to strike a balance between the revealed and transcendent nature of God. God is knowable through revelation in Scripture and liturgy but he simultane-ously transcends all knowledge. This theology is generally agreed to have been massively influential upon the reception and development of mys-tical theology within Western Christianity from the twelfth to the six-teenth centuries. In Turner's view, Dionysius practically 'invented the genre' of mystical theology for the Latin church.[7]

Let us examine Dionysius's theology in a little more detail. In *The Divine Names*, *The Mystical Theology* and other texts, Dionysius gives a systematic account of the names of God. Dionysius's theology is generally agreed to fall into three distinct phases and I would like to briefly summarise these.

(1) *The Kataphatic*. Kataphatic theology is a product of the believer's desire to gain account of God by representing him through a series of positive, human images that are perceived to be 'like' him. Dionysius affirms, in strict hierarchical order, the Unity and Trinity (*The Theological Representations*), the conceptual names (*The Divine Names*) and the perceptible and multiple symbols of God via the Platonic concept of emanation (*The Symbolic Theology*).

(2) *The Apophatic*. Apophatic theology follows on from kataphatic theology. The apophatic stresses the infinite transcendence of God from all human images of him by attaching negative prefixes or suffixes to their positive images or by using a series of obviously incongruous images which are clearly 'unlike' him (*The Celestial Hierarchies*). Thus Dionysius also works backwards, according to the Platonic concept of return, negating all the hierarchical names he has previously attributed to God before he arrives back once again at the Unity and the Trinity (*The Divine Names* and *The Mystical Theology*).

What is the relationship between the kataphatic and the apophatic ways? The two forms of theology are equally necessary and it would be a mistake to prioritise one at the expense of the other. Kataphatics without apophatics would reduce God to human images of him and thus risk idolatry. Apophatics without kataphatics would find nothing secure to say about God in the first place and would thus fall into agnosticism or atheism. These are mutually complimentary theologies, in other words, and the relationship between them is commonly seen in dialectical terms. Kataphatics provides the root affirmation of God without which apophatics could not take place. Apophatics corrects and refines kataphatics by checking that it *really* does refer to God and not just some human image of him. This dialectical process of affirmation and negation or verification and falsification enables mystical theology to arrive at a more accurate image of God. Dionysius himself adapts the famous Plotinian image of the sculptor to show how negations can be used to progressively elicit what God is by chipping away at everything that He is not.[8] But this is not the whole story. There is, according to many theologians, a third form of theology in Dionysius's texts which supersedes both the kataphatic and the apophatic. In recent years, this theology has been given various names including mystical theology, hyper-negation and negative (mystical) theology but I would like to follow the phenomenologist Jean-Luc Marion here and simply call it 'the third way'.[9]

(3) *The Third Way*. Dionysius argues that there is a third form of theology which insists that God is subject to *neither* kataphatic *nor*

apophatic theologies because e infinitely transcends both: 'Think not that affirmations and denials are opposed but rather that, long before, is that – which is beyond all position and denial – beyond privation' (*Mystical Theology*).[10] Now the first thing to be said about the third way is that it not only transcends the kataphatic and apophatic ways but also the dialectical truth-game of affirmation and negation or verification and falsification that these two theologies play out. If kataphatics and apophatics share a common desire to speak the truth about God, then the theology that transcends them must also transcend the metaphysical and more specifically Aristotelian value of truth as *adequatio* to which they are committed. Marion insists that it is no longer a question of saying the true or the false: 'one can no longer claim that it means to affirm a predicate of a subject, not even beneath the absurd dissimulation of a negative, nor that it has the least bit of interest in doing so'.[11] This is because the third way is no longer a predicative discourse which attempts to speak *of* God, but a more pragmatic use of language which attempts, however imperfectly, to speak *to* God.

Let me summarise. Dionysius's third mystical way offers praise to God because he is infinitely beyond all knowledge and comprehension: 'God is not known, not spoken, not named, not something among beings, and not known in something among beings'.[12] It is very important to stress that when Dionysius talks about the incomprehensibility and unknowability of God here, he is not bemoaning a failure or absence of knowledge of God but a different and better way of knowing him that he calls 'unknowing'. The 'unknowing' he is referring to here is not the consequence of a *lack* of God, in other words, but of a *fullness* or excess of him that hyperbolically exceeds all conceptuality. In Marion's phenomenological terms, God is a 'saturated phenomenon'[13] or a phenomenological intuition so powerful and bedazzling that it fills and overflows all intention.

Modern French Thought

I would now like to put Dionysius to one side for a moment and turn to the diverse set of contemporary texts, signatures and gestures that Geoffrey Bennington has recently gathered together under the title of 'modern French thought'.[14] 'Modern French thought' is no more accurate a term than 'continental philosophy' or 'literary theory' to describe what I am going to be talking about here. The very inadequacy of the term does, however, help to advertise the *singularity* of the thing it signifies and for that reason it is probably the least worst of its kind currently available. This is because 'modern French thought' signifies something that that is not quite modern, not necessarily French, nor even paradoxically, a form of thought. There is within it, as we will see in a few moments, a willingness to consider critically the concept of modernity, to engage with philosophical traditions outside France (most notably German ones) and to open itself to what might quite literally be unthinkable as such. In other words, the defining characteristic of modern French thought is precisely its openness to what is *other* than modernity, Frenchness and even thought itself.[15]

What, then, is the relation between Christian mysticism and modern French thought? It is important to start by stressing the basic and irreconcilable differences between the two. Modern French thought is emphatically *not* 'mystical'. Whilst Derrida, Foucault, Lacan and many other continental philosophers had more or less rigorous religious educations, most, if by no means all, call themselves atheists. The heterodox direction of continental philosophy, as we will see, often brings it into direct conflict with the doctrinal orthodoxies of theologians and particularly the ontotheological God of the philosophers. These basic and fundamental differences must be the starting point of our discussion but it is not necessarily the last word on the subject. For modern French thought's defining interest in what is other than itself does occasionally take it in recognisably theological directions even if it can never be identified with theology. This is not to claim that Christian mysticism gives us any unique or privileged access into the workings of continental philosophy that could not be gained by any secular discourse, but merely to say that it offers an interesting, valid and (until recently) neglected way of reading Derrida and his contemporaries. In the particular context of this discussion, I would identify four obvious lines that a theological reading of modern French thought might pursue:

(1) *Modernity*. Modern French thought is, very crudely speaking, an attempt to think the limits of modernity. It is almost a cliché to say that the work of post-structuralist or 'postmodern' philosophers is defined by a critical attitude to certain enlightenment ideas. Lyotard defines 'postmodernity' as an incredulity towards the grand narratives of enlightenment progress.[16] Foucault demonstrates the totalitarian implications of the Enlightenment concepts of individual reason, liberty and equality.[17] Derrida locates aspects of the mystical, apocalyptic thought that enlightenment rationality defines itself against within the enlightenment itself.[18] This critique of enlightenment thinking has meant that the philosophers mentioned above have faced predictable accusations of obscurity, irrationalism, and even a certain *recherché* mysticism. There are, however, good reasons for thinking that this identification of pre-modern mystics with postmodern philosophers is nothing more than a misrepresentation of

both. Contemporary French philosophy's critique of the Enlightenment is emphatically not an attempt to return to some mystical pre-modernity but to reinvent or reaffirm the concept of modernity differently. Lyotard, Foucault, Derrida and other thinkers re-read aspects of Kant, Descartes et al which do not fit conventional definitions of modernity in an effort to reimagine the enlightenment as less a timeless set of values or a period concept but an ongoing attitude, mood or project. They are not closet mystics hankering after a pre-modern theocracy, in other words, but modern *Aufklärers* in search of what Derrida revealingly calls 'the Enlightenment of today or tomorrow'.[19]

If we put these crucial differences in parentheses, however, we can still note a number of important similarities between Christian mysticism and modern French thought. This is not to say that mystics and moderns oppose the Enlightenment for the same reasons but that, despite coming from very different directions, they arrive at uncannily similar conclusions about the limitations of secular modernity. In their respective ways, Christian mystics and contemporary French philosophers both look askance at the pretensions of reason to total domination, the concept of religion within the limits of reason alone and the secular disdain for faith as an alternative source of knowledge. Nowhere is this more apparent than in their approach to the question of the Enlightenment subject.

(2) *The Subject*. Modern French thought is also an attempt to rethink the concept of the subject. The concept of the individual or autonomous subject has dominated philosophical thinking from Cartesian rationality to Sartrean existentialism. This concept is criticised in different ways by different continental thinkers, but what they all share is a concept of subjectivity as originally split or decentred by philosophical, psychoanalytic, historico-political and other forces. Lévinas, for example, sees the subject as something called into being by a pre-subjective ethical responsibility to the other person or *autrui*.[20] Lacan sites the subject within the lack of an Imaginary psychological unity or completeness.[21] Foucault situates it as the effect of certain historico-political discourses or *epistemes*.[22] Derrida, Nancy and others locate it at the site of certain textual differences.[23] Irigaray, Kristeva and Cixous criticise the positioning of the female subject within phallogocentric hierarchies and insist that 'she' actually resists singular definition or nomination.[24] In each case, the Cartesian transcendental *Cogito* is fissured, demythologised, or deconstructed by a dependence upon what is other than itself.

Now the post-Cartesian definition of the subject as dependent upon the other again recalls the pre-Cartesian mystical definition of the self as dependent upon the otherness of God. It is impossible to understand the mystical concept of subjectivity in Cartesian terms.[25] The concept of *individual* consciousness or experience would, for instance, make little sense to a group of theologians steeped in the *collective* experience of liturgy, ecclesiastical practice or monastic orders. This assertion of a fundamental non-contradiction or identity between self and other is always present in Christian mysticism but I would argue that it reaches its apex with the so-called 'experiential' mysticism of the medieval and renaissance mystics. Julian of Norwich, Teresa of Avila and John of the Cross describe how the self must be negated, detached or annihilated in order to reach its true centre or ground as a soul which exists in a non-differentiated union with God. Michel de Certeau writes of St Teresa: '"I is an other" [*Je est un autre*] – that is the secret told by the mystic long before the poetic experience of Rimbaud, Rilke or Nietzsche'.[26] The concept of the self's ground *being* an other is absolutely central to Christian mysticism but it is one that could only appear paradoxical or contradictory to a concept of individual subjectivity, so here is another area in which the continental critique of the *Cogito* might be of use to theologians of mysticism. This is not to imply that there is any necessary corollary between the contemporary concept of the split subject and the wounded or annihilated subject of mysticism but to recognise again that their very different analyses can occasionally confirm each other. In an increasingly secularised climate, modern French thought's approach to subjectivity helps to sustain and lend credence to a mystical account of subjectivity as split that might otherwise appear vulnerable to philosophical ridicule or crude psychological reductivism.

(3) *The negative way*. Modern French thought often takes the form of a *via negativa*. It is consistently interested in thinking or exploring what is unthinkable or unpresentable as such. Derrida, for instance, consistently denies deconstruction is a form of method, analysis, critique, a Kantian idea, X,Y nor Z.[27] Foucault defines his archaeology of knowledge in negative terms insisting ultimately that his historical archive is not an object of knowledge.[28] Lyotard insists on judgements without pre-determined criteria and rewrites the event via the Kantian concept of the sublime.[29] This consistent reliance on negative formulations often leads these thinker to articulate their ideas in unmistakably negative theological or Christian mystical idioms and this may be another reason why they are sometimes accused of being mystics *manqué*. Indeed, Derrida, Foucault, Irigaray and others have admitted that there are certain stylistic, structural and thematic parallels between their work and that of negative theologians like Pseudo-Dionysius.

What, though, are the theological implications of modern French thought's interest in negative theology? The crucial difference between the modern and mystical approach concerns exactly *how* negative they are. There is no doubt that contemporary philosophy is committed to a thoroughgoing negativity but, as we will see later on, mysticism is sometimes criticised for concealing within it a hidden positivity. But this defining difference does not mean that they do not share certain ideas and premises about negativity before they go their separate ways. Modern French thought and Christian mysticism share a scepticism about the ability of language to represent the particular kind of alterity they want to address. They are equally sceptical of the credibility of metaphysical concepts which simply assume a transparent relationship between signifier and signified, name and thing, *logos* and *theos* and so on. For all their differences, I will argue later on that Dionysius and Derrida's discourses offer a similar kind of negative check upon the positive, ontotheological claims of rationalist theology from Aquinas to Hegel. Just as Dionysius uses a pragmatic rather than a predicative, metaphysical language to speak *to* God rather than *about* him, Derrida, Lyotard and other contemporary French philosophers employ a performative rather than constative mode of discourse which works perfectly in singular contexts but could never be mistaken for a universal description of a prior 'real'.

(4) *The absolutely other.* Modern French thought is a thought of the other as absolutely other. 'Western philosophy', Rodophe Gasché argues, 'is in essence the attempt to domesticate otherness, since what we understand by thought is nothing but such a project'.[30] Plato's *eidos*, Aristotle's *ousia*, Kant's Categories, even Heidegger's *Dasein* can be interpreted as examples of the domestication of alterity, multiplicity, and singularity into sameness, oneness, unity. Contemporary French philosophy is not another attempt to domesticate otherness but rather to respect the absolute alterity of an other that is irreducible to thought. The absolute other is something unforeseen, singular or irregular that shatters our horizons of expectation and exceeds our attempts to understand it. This absolute other takes different names and forms in the work of different thinkers but more celebrated examples include the *Autre* or *le Dire* (Lévinas) the Real (Lacan), the Event (Lyotard and Foucault), difference (Deleuze) and the impossible (Derrida). Lévinas famously argues how ethics begins with the face of an other (*l'Autre*) who exceeds 'the idea of the other in me'[31]. Foucault defends the alterity of madness against its domestication by enlightenment rationalism as merely the other side of reason.[32] Derrida's critique of structuralism ratchets the attempt to think the other as absolutely other up another notch. In his reading of Levinas, Foucault and other contemporaries, Derrida critic-ises them for unwittingly contributing to a further domestication of the other by opposing

it *too* absolutely to a given same, and seeks to open up both same and other to a still more radical *tout autre*.[33]

Now the relationship between the modern respect for the other as absolutely other and the mystical thought of a God who transcends all knowledge and can only be known through unknowing has been the subject of great theological debate. The debate encompasses those on one extremity who argue that philosophy is simply appropriating theological resources to those on the other who object that it is in fact theology that is co-opting philosophy. On the one hand, John Milbank's polemical Radical Orthodoxy group sees the continental approach to the other as a Gnostic, Zen or even nihilistic denial of immanence in favour of an anonymous transcendent emptied of all theological content.[34] On the other hand, Dominique Janicaud sees the so-called 'theological turn' in recent French phenomenology as a distortion of recent philosophical history that would have Husserl and Merleau-Ponty spinning in their graves.[35]

What possibility is there of mediating between these two approaches? The relationship between the two thoughts of the other does not have to be seen as a battle between philosophical nihilism on the one extreme and theological dogmatism on the other. There are some philosophers who detect certain parallels between mystical and modern approaches to otherness and I would identify Marion and Derrida as exemplars of this point. Jean-Luc Marion attempts to square the circle between philosophical and theological alterity by thinking God as a phenomenon of saturating *givenness* that paradoxically exceeds all ideas, intentions, and concepts.[36] But perhaps the most interesting example of this potential chiasmus between the 'holy other' and the 'wholly other' is the work of Jacques Derrida. Derrida suggests, as we will see later on, a number of intriguing comparisons between deconstruction's desire for the absolute other and the mystical desire for God. The arrival of the *tout autre* is described by Derrida in quasi-religious language as a form of messianism, a form of promise, an act of saying or praying 'come' or 'yes'. There is, in Derrida's account, no need to choose between respecting the absolute other of philosophy and the divine other of theology because they belong to the *same* structure.

Let me conclude this section by mapping some general trends in critical work on Christian mysticism and modern French thought. What will be the relationship between Christian mysticism and contemporary French philosophy in the foreseeable future? Critics suggest many different answers to these questions but I would identify two more or less obvious works-in-progress. (1) *The re-evaluation of the mystical tradition.* The first major trend in recent critical work is the re-evaluation of certain key theological figures in the light of contemporary philosophical developments. This re-evaluation sometimes takes the form of reassessing neglected or repressed aspects within the mystical corpus which anticipate certain modern developments.[37] Alternatively, it leads to a critique of aspects of the mystical tradition from modern historical, political or gender standpoints.[38] Finally, it defends the church's difference from, or resistance, to contemporary criticisms.[39] (2) *The re-enchantment or re-mystification of modernity*. The second major trend is the rereading of contemporary French thought in the light of theology and mysticism. Graham Ward has recently borrowed Zygmunt Bauman's concept of 're-enchantment' to call for a rediscovery of 'ambivalence, mystery, excess and *aporia*' in a modernity where orthodox faith is seemingly on the decline and theology's status as a credible academic discipline is increasingly under attack.[40] This re-enchantment often takes the form of revisionary readings of continental thinkers whose earliest reception and reputation in the anglophone world was as late-enlightenment 'death of God' secularists.[41] Perhaps another area of future re-enchantment would be the re-extension of mystic theology into areas from which modern-ity has long since expelled it like ethics, politics and anthropology: John D. Caputo, Thomas Carlson and others have begun to chart this almost unthinkably large territory.[42] Now the majority of contemporary work by philosophers and theologians on mysticism tends to fall into one or other of these categories but they are obviously not mutually exclusive projects. There is no need to choose between respecting the theological tradition of Christian mysticism and the philosophical conditions of modernity. The re-assessment of what we take to be the tradition will always lead to the reassessment of what we understand as modernity and vice versa so the two projects are really different sides of the same coin. This point of chiasmus can be most effectively seen if we move from the general to the particular and focus in on one specific example of the relationship between Christian mysticism and modern French thought.

Deconstruction and Negative Theology

I want to continue, then, by looking in more detail at the relation between Dionysius and Derrida.

Derrida's interest in the *via negativa* is long-standing. It is mentioned repeatedly if somewhat briefly in key early texts like 'Violence and Metaphysics' (1964) and 'From Restricted to General Economy: A Hegelianism without Reserve' (1967). The references here are largely negative in character because Derrida is less interested in negative theology per se than in differentiating it from his own discourse of deconstruction. But more recent texts like 'How to Avoid Speaking: Denegations' (1987), *The Gift of Death* (1992) and '*Sauf le nom: (Post-Scriptum)*' (1993) return to the topic in more detail. If the earlier treatment of the subject is largely negative, these texts go on to explore negative theology in remarkably patient, grateful and affirmative terms. The meaning of this 'affirmation' has been pondered by many theologians and philosophers in recent years and this is something I, too, would like to consider in a little more detail. Deconstruction has been criticised and congratulated for being everything from a closet mysticism to a 'death of God' atheism or nihilism over the last thirty years or so but my opinion is that both interpretations are misjudged. In my view, deconstruction's relationship to Christian mysticism should be construed as neither a critique nor an apologia but as a potentially more complex attempt to *repeat mysticism differently*, or as Derrida puts it, to 'save the name' of the *via negativa*.

First, a few words about the term 'deconstruction' itself. Derrida famously argues that the western philosophical tradition is what he calls a metaphysics of presence in *Of Grammatology* (1967).[43] Presence, he argues, takes various forms: presence of thought or consciousness, present being of the subject, presence as substance, essence or existence, the temporal presence of the present moment and so on. The philosophical tradition reveals its dependence upon the value of presence in different ways but its most consistent form is to oppose and hierarchise philosophical values by identifying a 'superior' value with presence and an 'inferior' value with the negation, mediation or complication of that presence. This has historically meant that speech is privileged over writing, the intelligible over the sensible, the transcendental over the empirical and so on *ad infinitum*. Now these hierarchies are usually presented as natural, objective or scientific by the philosophies that are responsible for erecting them but Derrida's argument is that they are actually the result of a series of contingent decisions that are anything but neutral.

The contingency of these philosophical hierarchies can be demonstrated by a patient, rigorous reading which follows no pre-determined method but, in Derrida's earlier texts at least, characteristically involves two stages. First, the hierarchy is reversed to show that the supposedly 'superior' values actually depend upon their 'inferior' equivalents rather than presence for their value. Secondly, the opposition *itself* is displaced to reveal that *both* the 'superior' *and* the 'inferior' values depend for their value upon a prior ground which is not presence in any of the senses indicated earlier but a kind of constitutive incompleteness or dispersion that Derrida nicknames '*arche*-writing' or, more famously, *différance*.

'*Différance*' is (1) the real 'ground' of all philosophical hierarchies what-soever (2) their condition of possibility because it is the only thing that can get them going in the first place (3) paradoxically their condition of impossibility as well because it is never firm enough to allow them to absolutely establish themselves, and (4) both possible *and* impossible for us to name, think or describe (hence the real need for those otherwise rather pedantic nick-names and scare-quotes).

Derrida pursues this quasi-concept of *différance* across a vast number of readings of almost every major thinker in the philosophical canon from Plato to Heidegger. These readings are necessarily surprising but it is possible to identify at least two consistent lines of argument within them. (1) Derrida is concerned to argue that the metaphysical tradition remains impossible to absolutely establish because it relies on a set of demonstrably inaccurate assumptions about presence. Transcendental philosophers like Husserl, for instance, are shown to be indebted to the realm of the empirical, material and contingent even when they claim to transcend it. (2) Derrida is also at pains to demonstrate that this does not mean that the metaphysical tradition can simply be dispensed with and that some complicity with it is unavoidable even or especially when we think we have avoided it. Linguists like Saussure and historians like Foucault are unable to reduce philosophy to empirical or material ques-tions of language, history or power because they, like the rest of us, can-not help but use the terms the tradition supplies us with. For Derrida – *pace* Heidegger – the belief that we have avoided, circumnavigated or otherwise transcended metaphysics is perhaps the metaphysical gesture *par excellence*.

So what is the logical conclusion of Derrida's argument? Derrida's analysis is much misunderstood at this point and is worth considering in a little detail. It is first important to be clear about what Derrida is and is not arguing here. The argument does not claim that talking about the other, difference and Nietzsche is in some way 'better' than talking about metaphysics, presence and Rousseau. There is no question of choosing one approach over the other because what Derrida is describing here is, of course, the *same* system in its constitutive quasi-state of semi-com-pleteness or *différance*. 'If deconstruction maintains that we are always in a *tension* between the metaphysical and its undoing', Geoffrey Bennington writes, 'it cannot predict *a priori* what the best adjustment of that tension might be in a given case'.[44] This emphasis on an essential unpredictability or undecidability at the heart of philosophical thinking is a defining theme in Derrida's thought and has prompted quite mis-taken allegations of relativism and even nihilism. Undecidability is not an attempt to say that everything is 'equally valid', nor to reduce everything to nothing, but rather an attempt to respect the singularity, uniqueness and alterity of the other. Deconstruction does not defend or attack metaphysics, then, but simply *repeats* it in such a way as to let its essential instability and openness to what lies outside it emerge. In Derrida's words, it is 'not an enclosure in nothingness but an openness towards the other.'[45]

Let me now turn to Derrida's early readings of negative theology. In 1968, Derrida was asked whether or not deconstruction was a form of negative theology. He somewhat equivocally replied: 'it is and it is not. Above all it is not'.[46] What exactly *is* the relationship between deconstruction and the *via negativa* then? Derrida begins by admitting that deconstruction and negative theology share certain superficial similarities. Deconstruction, as we have already seen, has a predilection for negative predicates. *Différance* is neither this nor that, neither one thing nor another, *epekeina tes ousia, tout autre*, in some sense beyond the ontological categories of being and essence. This refusal to play by the ontotheological rules results, Derrida has noted, in a similar fate to that of many negative theologians. Their shared interest in what transcends or exceeds speech has led to accusations that they both conceal a crude political elitism. Just as negative theologians were suspected of being cultists, charlatans or heretics in the early church so deconstructionists endure the same suspicions in the modern University.

Yet this is where the similarities between deconstruction and mystical theology would seem to come to an end. Negative theology, Derrida argues, is not *actually* negative at all. Dionysius and other mystics deny the being or essence of God only in order to affirm it. If Dionysius's third way claims that God is beyond all position and negation, Derrida argues that this is simply because the mystic theologian wants to *re-establish* the transcendence of God all the more completely.[47] The *via negativa* remains, rightly and emphatically, a theology but this means that in Derrida's analysis it *forecloses* the question of the other by constantly identifying that other with God. So negative theology remains committed to the metaphysical tradition of presence that Derrida is concerned to deconstruct. Deconstruction, in this context, is more radically negative than negative theology. *Différance* is not God, not even the *deus absconditus* of mystical theology. The reason we cannot address it is not because it is the mystical Godhead that grounds the universe, but because it is the foundational incoherence that ensures everything remains open to the other. In this strict and technical sense, Derrida is absolutely right to insist that deconstruction is not, above all, a negative theology.

Now Derrida's remarks on negative theology have been the subject of an extended debate. It is again important to be clear about what he is and is not saying here. To begin with, Derrida clearly isn't attacking negative theology or belief in God more generally. He is simply and correctly asserting that deconstruction is *different* from negative theology. It would be wrong, then, to attach any first-order philosophical claims to what is simply a statement of formal differences. If we bracket off these differences, moreover, I think it again becomes possible to observe certain syntactical, historic and structural parallels between them. Deconstruction and negative theology may not be the same thing, but deconstruction does borrow some of the resources of negative theology while negative theology can be seen as a theological mode of deconstruction.

But what might this mean in practice? Take, for example, the classic philosophical distinction between faith and reason or knowledge. Christian mysticism has historically taken the role of a negative, theological check upon positive, philosophical claims about God. Apophatic or negative theology has never questioned the *existence* of God, of course, but it has frequently called into question the philosophical idea of God as *presence* in the Derridaean sense. Mysticism is an attempt to defend the God of Scripture, the God of Abraham, Isaac and Jacob, the God whom none shall see and live, over and against the God of the philosophers, the God of Aquinas, Descartes and Hegel, the God who is simply the best example of certain Greek concepts. Now a number of recent critics have observed a certain chiasmus between the Dionysian project of dehellenizing theology and the Derridaean project of de-constructing philosophy. Just as Derrida deconstructs metaphysics in the name of absolute alterity, the argument goes, so Dionysius's third way criticises theological discourse in the name of the absolute alterity of God. Kevin Hart takes issue with Derrida's claim that negative theology always contains a hidden positivity by arguing that Dionysius's third way stresses how God is absolutely other than all affirmations of presence.[48] Jean-Luc Marion endorses and refines this position by arguing that Derrida overlooks the pragmatic nature of the third way which bypasses all positive or negative attempts to predicate God.[49] Far from deconstruction undermining negative theology, Marion argues, it is actually negative theology that pre-empts and trumps deconstruction.[50] The re-evaluation of the tradition in the light of deconstruction has, then, produced a more rigorous understanding of mystical procedures than the predictable vocabulary of experience, paradox and so on. This does not mean that deconstruction and negative theology are the same thing but that perhaps they haunt one another in a certain uncanniness, a certain ghostly anachrony that Derrida has recently analysed under the figure of the specter.[51] Negative theology might be a mode of deconstruction *avant la lettre* whereas deconstruction can be read as a repetition of the negative theological project by other means.

Finally, let me consider this possibility in a little more detail by turning to Derrida's most recent texts on Christian mysticism. In '*Sauf le nom: (Post-Scriptum)*' (1993), Derrida offers a more affirmative reading of negative theology than he has ever done before. The *via negativa*, he admits, is a more varied body of work than he has previously allowed for. There are many possibilities within it, many different voices to listen to. They do not all fall under the category of the 'metaphysics-of-presence-to-be-deconstructed' and perhaps some of them still have something to say to us today. Negative theology, in summary, might be a name worth saving. In my view, Derrida's reading of negative theology takes the typical form of a double reading, indeed what we might call a double salvation.

(1) *On the one hand*, Derrida wants to save the *nomen innominabile* of negative theology in all its rich, neo-Platonic, Judaeo-Christian glory. Negative theology is 'a rich and very diverse corpus',[52] he writes, 'a memory, an institution, a history, a discipline'[53]. Its rich and diverse history means, however, that it has also been subject to the kind of contingent ethico-political decisions we mentioned earlier. Derrida's reading of negative theology is thus concerned to trace the decisions, the motivations and the hierarchisations that have gradually determined the fate of the *via negativa* today. The relationship between the *via negativa*, Christian ontotheology and the concept of Christian democracy is something that particularly concerns and worries him. This recondite theological tradition has become insuperable not simply from the ecclesiastical structure of the Christian church, he believes, but the geo-political formation of western civilisation itself. For Derrida, this theology of silence, solitude and secrecy also gives rise to a tradition of pedagogy, community, the *polis*, the nation state and the super-state: 'the one that gives rise to the State, the nation, more generally to the philosophical community as rational and logocentric community'.[54] These political communities, however secular, 'enlightened' or technological they may consider themselves, continue to bear the traces of their origin in a very specific – not to say exclusive – theological context as they grow bigger. Now Derrida thinks this politico-theological tradition comes to a head in the last decade with the rise and rise of Christian fundamentalism, Pope John Paul II's call for a new Holy Alliance in the aftermath of the Cold War, and perhaps most disturbingly of all, the Christian and crusading rhetoric of the Allies during the Gulf War.[55] In the 1990s, the 'rich and very diverse' corpus of negative theology has been honed into a 'smart' bomb aimed at Baghdad.

This is the point at which someone who is a self-confessed man of the Left, an enlightenment man –, not to mention a man who describes his childhood self as 'a little black and Arab Jew'[56] – begins to part company with the negative theology he respects so much. Derrida's respect for the massive resources and traditions of the *via negativa* convince him that it could not and should not be dispensed with altogether. But it could and should perhaps be saved from the particular history, tradition and interpretation to which it has been subjected. Negative theology needs to be rescued from the ideological decision-makers who have determined its current politico-theological destiny: from Christian ontotheology, from those disturbingly neo-conservative examples of repetition in alterity John Paul II and President(s) Bush, from the more or less disguised hegemonies of the USA, the UN and NATO. There are other resources within negative theology which its historic Greco-Christian filiation has left untapped, other voices which are as yet unheard.

(2) *On the other hand*, then, saving the name of negative theology involves rescuing it *from* its politico-theological context and preserving it *for* other contexts, other politics, other theologies yet to be written:

> How would what still comes to us under the domestic, Greek and Christian name of negative theology, of negative way, of apophatic discourse be the chance of an incomparable translatability in principle without limit? Not of a universal tongue, of an ecumenism or of some consensus, but of a tongue to come that can be more shared than ever?[57]

The second form of saving negative theology's name is by identifying another voice within it which goes beyond its particular Greco-Christian context into something that could certainly be called more universal, more democratic, more fraternal even if it never totally coincides with Greco-Christian definitions of those terms either. This voice saves negative theology from simply being a politico-theological discourse which respects the otherness of God – as important as that mission is – and gives it the chance to be a discourse which respects the otherness of every other:

> Once more, one should say of no matter what or no matter whom what one says of God or some other thing: the thought of whom-ever concerning whomever or whatever, it doesn't matter, [*n'importe*].[58]

Now it is important to stress that Derrida is not using negative theology to 're-Christianise' philosophy but rather to show that Christian orthodoxy does not exhaust the theological and philosophical possibilities of negative theology. Negative theology, as a discourse whose very purpose and duty is to go beyond itself, can also go beyond its specifically Christian mission. 'Smart' bombs, as any Iraqi civilian knows, don't necessarily hit their targets.

In summary, Derrida's double salvation of negative theology is an attempt to save it *for* Christian orthodoxy and an attempt to save it *from* Christian orthodoxy.

What does all this say to Christians about the role of Christian mysticism today? It's unlikely, on the face of it, that this reading of Christianity would satisfy anyone. Derrida's account could be accused of being far too religious on the one hand and never quite religious enough on the other. Christians may object to what looks like the wilful distortion of negative theology to the point where it becomes an almost meaningless term for Derrida to use and abuse as he likes. Atheists may be equally disturbed by what they perceive to be Derrida's attempt to generalise an out-of-date set of dogmas on to a literally global scale. '*Sauf le nom*' is neither simply a repetition nor a distortion of Christian mysticism, however, but what I have called an attempt to *repeat* it *differently*. The essay certainly does not express a preference for *less* negative theology, less Christianity, less Eurocentric politics over and against *more* negative theology, more Christianity, more Eurocentricism. There is no question of choosing between the two modes of saving negative theology because, as we saw earlier, the point is that they are two sides of the *same* system in its permanent state of de-construction. This means that the second, non-traditional form of saving negative theology is neither a distortion nor a generalisation of the traditional form of the first but the faithful *repetition* of the first from a *different* perspective. Perhaps, as Derrida ponders, it is only possible to repeat a tradition when we do not view it as a passive inheritance but a work in progress, an ongoing project, a task.[59] Nothing, after all, could be more faithful to negative theology's original mission of salvation through sacrifice than its own sacrificial salvation. Negative theology's historic purpose has been to go beyond itself into the *hyperousios* so it could never be wholly surprised by its own re-inscription in new contexts: 'Isn't it what, in essence, exceeds language, so that the "essence" of negative theology would carry itself outside language?'.[60]

Now it is this, ultimately, that I think Derrida has to say to us about the relevance of Christian mysticism today. Far from distorting Christian mysticism beyond all recognition, or generalising it to a massive extent, I would argue that deconstruction can, in certain contexts, be read as a *re-extension* by other means of the Christian mystical tradition into areas from which it has long since been forcibly ejected.[61] Christian mysticism's respect for the otherness of God also contains within it an ethico-political message for all of us – Christian and non-Christian – about respecting every other as absolutely other: '*tout autre est tout autre*'.[62] Pseudo-Dionysius's ancient discourse on respecting the alterity of God still speaks to us today in the modern Europe of Kosovo, of attacks on immigrants and of the internment without trial of 'bogus' asylum seekers.[63] Let us listen to what he has to say.

Conclusion

My argument, then, is that Christian mysticism and modern French thought can engage in a dialogue that is constructive, beneficial and, perhaps most importantly, ongoing. The cross-fertilisation of ideas between mystics and moderns can be witnessed in many ways but for the purposes of economy I have focused on Dionysius and Derrida. There are irreconcilable differences between Dionysius and Derrida and deconstruction and negative theology which cannot be surmounted but these should not be allowed to obscure the parallels between them. If we suspend the fundamental differences between them, however, it becomes clear that negative theology and deconstruction share a number of mutually clarifying features. Negative theology's historical project of de-hellenizing Christian ontotheology can now be seen as a form of deconstruction *avant la lettre*. Deconstruction's interest in a generalised ethics and politics of negativity can be seen as an continuation and extension by different means of negative theology's hyperbolic desire for the beyond. Thus the re-evaluation of the tradition goes hand in hand with the re-enchantment of modernity because, as Derrida argues, the former is nothing less than the repetition by other means of the latter. Far from being the enemy of Christianity, then, modern French thought offers a different way of perpetuating the role of Christian mysticism within the church and extending mysticism's influence outside it. In Derrida's words, modern French thought 'saves the name' of Christian mysticism.

Notes

[1] Jacques Derrida, '*Sauf le nom: (Post-Scriptum)*', tr. John P. Leavey Jr., in Thomas Dutoit (ed.), *On the Name* (Stanford: Stanford University Press, 1995), 35–88.

[2] Harold Coward & Toby Foshay (eds.), *Derrida and Negative Theology* (Albany: SUNY, 1992).

[3] Susan Handelman, *The Slayer of Moses: The Emergence of Rabbinic Interpretation in Modern Literary Theory* (Albany: State University of New York Press, 1982);

Harold Coward, *Derrida and Indian Philosophy* (Albany: State University of New York Press, 1990); Akbar S. Ahmed, *Postmodernism and Islam: Predicament and Promise* (London: Routledge, 1992); David Loy, *Deconstruction and Healing: Postmodern Thought in Buddhism and Christianity* (Atlanta: Scholars Press, 1996).

[4] Bernard McGinn, *The Foundations of Mysticism*, Vol. 1. *The Presence of God* (New York: Crossroads, 1992), xvii.

[5] Michel de Certeau, *The Mystic Fable*, vol. 1. *The Sixteenth and Seventeenth Centuries*, tr. Michael B. Smith (Chicago & London: Chicago University Press, 1991), 5.

[6] Denys Turner, *The Darkness of God: Negativity in Christian Mysticism* (Cambridge: Cambridge University Press, 1995), 2.

[7] Turner, *Darkness*, 13.

[8] Pseudo-Dionysius the Areopagite, *The Divine Names and The Mystical Theology*, tr. John D. Jones (Wisconsin: Marquette University Press, 1980), 215.

[9] Jean-Luc Marion, 'In the Name: How to Avoid Speaking of "Negative Theology"', in *God, the Gift and Postmodernism*, tr. Jeffrey L. Kosky (Bloomington: Indiana University Press, 1999), 24.

[10] Pseudo-Dionysius, *The Divine Names and The Mystical Theology*, 212.

[11] Marion, 'In the Name', 26.

[12] Pseudo-Dionysius, *The Divine Names and the Mystical Theology*, 178.

[13] Jean-Luc Marion, 'The Saturated Phenomenon', tr. Thomas A. Carlson, in Leonore Langsdorf & John D. Caputo (eds.), *Philosophy Today: Studies in Phenomenology and Existential Philosophy*, vol. 21 (Spring, 1996), 103–24.

[14] Geoffrey Bennington, 'The Very Idea of a Centre for Modern French Thought', <www.sussex.ac.uk/Units/frenchthought>. The Centre for Modern French Thought is a research centre at the University of Sussex.

[15] In this respect, the following comments on 'modern French thought' are necessarily selective, simplistic and sometimes brutally reductive. I particularly regret the absence of any substantial comments on indispensable precursors to contemporary French philosophy like Husserl, Heidegger and Blanchot; on those critics whose work has done so much to shape the reception of that philosophy like de Man, Hillis Miller, Spivak and Weber, and on those philosophers whose work has, for various reasons, still not received the attention it deserves in the anglophone world like Badiou, Janicaud, Serres and Steigler.

[16] Jean-François Lyotard, *The Postmodern Condition: A Report on Knowledge*, tr. Geoff Bennington & Brian Massumi (Manchester: Manchester University Press, 1984).

[17] Michel Foucault, *Discipline and Punish: The Birth of the Prison*, tr. Alan Sheridan (New York: Pantheon, 1977).

[18] Jacques Derrida, 'Of an Apocalyptic Tone Recently Adopted in Philosophy', tr. John P. Leavey, Jr, *The Oxford Literary Review* 6.2 (1984) 3–37.

[19] Jacques Derrida, 'Honoris Causa: "This is *also* extremely funny"', tr. Marion Hobson & Christopher Johnson, in Elisabeth Weber (ed.), *Points ... Interviews 1974–1994* (Stanford, CA: Stanford University Press, 1995), 400.

[20] Emmanuel Lévinas, *Totality and Infinity*, tr. Alphonse Lingis (Pittsburgh: Duquesque University Press, 1969).

[21] Jacques Lacan, *Écrits: A Selection*, tr. Alan Sheridan (London: Routledge, 1977).

[22] Michel Foucault, *The Order of Things: An Archaeology of the Human Sciences*, tr. Alan Sheridan (London: Routledge, 1991).

[23] Jacques Derrida, *Of Grammatology*, tr. Gayatri Chakravorty Spivak (Baltimore & London: Johns Hopkins University Press, 1976); Jean-Luc Nancy, *The Inoperative Community*, tr. Peter Connor *et al* (Minneapolis: University of Minnesota Press, 1991), *The Birth to Presence*, tr. Brian Holmes *et al* (Stanford: Stanford University Press, 1993).

[24] L. Irigaray, *This Sex Which is Not One*, tr. Catherine Porter (New York: Cornell University Press, 1985); Julie Kristeva, *In the Beginning was Love: Psychoanalysis and Faith*, tr. Arthur Goldhammer (New York: Columbia University Press, 1988); Hélène Cixous, 'The Laugh of the Medusa', tr. Keith & Paula Cohen, in Isabelle Courtivron (ed.), *New French Feminisms* (Brighton: Harvester Press, 1981), 245–64.

[25] Jean-Luc Marion's readings of Descartes have, however, unsettled the notion of the autonomy of the *Cogito* by locating an 'grey' or ambiguous ontology and a 'white' or blank theology within Cartesian epistemology. Jean-Luc Marion, *Sur l'ontologie grise de Descartes: Science cartesienne et savoir aristotelicien dans les regulae* (Paris: Vrin, 1975); *Sur la théologie blanche de Descartes: Analogie, creation des verites eternelles, fondemont* (Paris: Vrin, 1981).

[26] Michel de Certeau, 'Mystic Speech', in *Heterologies: Discourse on the Other*, tr. Brian Massumi (Minneapolis: University of Minnesota Press, 1986), 96.

[27] Jacques Derrida, 'Letter to a Japanese Friend', tr. David Wood & Andrew Benjamin, in Peggy Kamuf (ed.), *A Derrida Reader: Between the Blinds* (New York: Columbia University Press, 1991), 269–76.

[28] Michel Foucault, *The Archaeology of Knowledge*, tr. A. M. Sheridan Smith (London: Tavistock, 1972), 130–1.

[29] Jean-François Lyotard (with Jean-Loup Thébaud), *Just Gaming*, tr. Wlad Godzich (Minneapolis: University of Minnesota Press, 1985), *Lessons on the Analytic of the Sublime*, tr. Elizabeth Rottenberg (Stanford, CA: Stanford University Press, 1994).

[30] Rodolphe Gasché, *The Tain of the Mirror: Derrida and the Philosophy of Reflection* (Cambridge, MA: Harvard University Press, 1986), 101.

[31] Lévinas, *Totality and Infinity*, 50.

[32] Michel Foucault, *Folie et deraison: Histoire de la folie à l'âge classique* (Paris: Plon, 1961).

[33] Jacques Derrida, 'Violence and Metaphysics: an Essay on the Thought of Emmanuel Lévinas', in *Writing and Difference*, tr. Alan Bass (London and New York: Routledge and Kegan Paul, 1978), 79–154.

[34] Phillip Blond, 'Introduction: Theology before Philosophy', in Phillip Blond (ed.), *Post-Secular Philosophy: Between Philosophy and Theology* (London: Routledge, 1998), 1–66. Radical Orthodoxy's readings of continental philosophy and, in particular, Lévinas and Derrida have been the subject of numerous critiques.

[35] Dominique Janicaud, *Le tournant théologique de la phénoménologie française* (Paris: L'éclat, 1991). Janicaud objects to what he sees as the theological appropriation of the phenomenology of perception by Levinas, Marion and Henry.

[36] Jean-Luc Marion, *L'idole et la distance: Cinq etudes* (Paris: Grasset, 1977); *God without Being: Hors-Texte*, tr. Thomas A. Carlson (Chicago and London: Chicago University Press, 1991), *Reduction and Givenness: Investigations of Husserl, Heidegger and Phenomenology*, tr. Thomas A. Carlson (Evanston, Ill.: Northwestern University Press, 1998) and *Etant donné: Essai d'úne phénoménologie de la donation* (Paris: Presses universitaires de France, 1997). Marion re-states his argument in *Etant donné* that his work is a more radical version of phenomenology and has no ulterior theological motive.

[37] John D. Caputo, *Radical Hermeneutics: Repetition, Deconstruction and the Hermeneutic Project* (Bloomington: Indiana University Press, 1987); Edith Wyschogrod, *Saints and Postmodernism: Revisioning Moral Philosophy* (Chicago: University of Chicago Press, 1990).

[38] Grace Jantzen, *Power, Gender and Christian Mysticism* (Cambridge: Cambridge University Press, 1991; *Becoming Divine: Towards a Feminist Philosophy of Religion* (Manchester: Manchester University Press, 1998); Pamela Sue Anderson, *A Feminist Philosophy of Religion* (Oxford: Blackwell, 1998).

[39] John Milbank, Catherine Pickstock & Graham Ward (eds.), *Radical Orthodoxy* (London: Routledge, 1998).

[40] Graham Ward, *Theology and Contemporary Critical Theory* (Manchester: Manchester University Press, 2000), 161.

[41] Mark C. Taylor, *Deconstructing Theology* (New York: Crossroad, 1982); Kevin Hart, *The Trespass of the Sign: Deconstruction, Theology and Philosophy* (Cambridge: Cambridge University Press, 1989); John D. Caputo, *The Prayers and Tears of Jacques Derrida: Religion without Religion* (Bloomington: Indiana University Press, 1998) and James Bernauer, *Michel Foucault's Force of Flight: Towards an Ethics for Thought* (Atlantic Highlands, NJ: Humanities Press, 1990). Taylor, Hart and Caputo re-assess the overwhelmingly atheistic interpretation of Derrida advanced by early anglophone commentators like Spivak.

[42] John D. Caputo, *Against Ethics: Contributions to a Poetics of Obligation with Constant Reference to Deconstruction* (Bloomington: Indiana University Press, 1993); Thomas A. Carlson, *Indiscretion: Finitude and the Naming of God* (Chicago: Chicago University Press, 1998).

[43] Jacques Derrida, *Of Grammatology*, tr. Gayatri Chakravorty Spivak (Baltimore and London: The Johns Hopkins University Press, 1976), 12.

[44] Geoffrey Bennington, 'Jacques Derrida', in *Interrupting Derrida* (London and New York: Routledge, 2000), 15.

[45] Richard Kearney, *Dialogues with Contemporary Continental Thinkers* (Manchester: Manchester University Press, 1984), 124.

[46] Jacques Derrida, 'The Original Discussion of Différance', in David Wood and Robert Bernsaconi (eds.), *Derrida and Différance* (Evantson, Ill: Northwestern University Press, 1988), 84.

[47] Jacques Derrida, '*Différance*', in *Margins of Philosophy*, tr. Alan Bass (Chicago: University of Chicago Press, 1982), 6.

[48] Hart, *The Trespass of the Sign*, 201–2.

[49] Marion, 'In the Name', 20–39. See my 'God *sans* Being: Derrida, Marion and "a paradoxical writing of the word *without*"', *Literature and Theology* 14 (2000), 299–313, for an attempt to mediate between Derrida's critique of negative theology and Marion's objections to it.

[50] In his essay 'In the Name: How to Avoid Speaking of "Negative Theology"' (1997), Marion argues that negative theology constitutes 'first a rivalry (presence can be deconstructed without it), then a marginalisation (deconstruction would not forbid access to God, outside presence and without Being)' of deconstruction (22). Marion's reading of negative theology is formidable, but I would want to take issue with his interpretation of deconstruction here. First, I do not agree that negative theology can be a 'rival' to deconstruction (in the sense that it pre-empts and challenges deconstruction) because, as we have seen, deconstruction cannot be understood as a period-based concept which comes 'after' negative theology and 'before' something else but as the grounding incoherence upon which the western philosophical tradition in its entirety depends. The *via negativa* thus cannot pre-empt or challenge deconstruction because it is already *in* deconstruction and any resemblance between the two can be accounted for by this simple fact. Secondly, I am not convinced that negative theology can marginalise deconstruction (in the sense that it foils deconstruction's supposed prohibition on God-talk) either for the simple reason that deconstruction *never* forbids access to God, outside presence or being. Deconstruction certainly calls into question the ability to gain access to God *within* presence or being but, as we have seen, it is concerned with *nothing other* than that which is outside being. Whether or not that *tout autre* could be described in religious terms is a question that Derrida, at least, seems to leave suspended. This, presumably, is why Derrida does not find negative theology's adoption of deconstructive strategies quite as devastating a blow to deconstruction as Marion seems to think he should: 'that is not surprising' (47).

[51] Jacques Derrida, *Specters of Marx: The State of the Debt, the Work of Mourning and the New International*, tr. Peggy Kamuf (London: Routledge, 1994).

[52] Jacques Derrida, 'Letter to John P. Leavey, Jr.', in 'Derrida and Biblical Studies', Robert Detweiler (ed.), *Semeia* (23) (Chico, California: Scholars Press, 1982), 61.

[53] Derrida, '*Sauf le nom*', 54.

[54] Ibid., 67.

[55] Ibid., 78.

[56] Jacques Derrida, 'Circumfession: Fifty-nine Periods and Periphrases', in Geoffrey Bennington & Jacques Derrida, *Jacques Derrida* (Chicago: University of Chicago Press, 1993), 58.

[57] Derrida, '*Sauf le nom*', 47.

[58] Ibid., 73.

[59] Derrida, *Specters of Marx*, 54.

[60] Derrida, '*Sauf le nom*', 48.

[61] See my 'Without Negative Theology: Deconstruction and the Politics of Negative Theology', *The Heythrop Journal* 42 (2001), 133–48 for a more detailed examination of the political implications of negative theology from the perspective of deconstruction.

[62] Jacques Derrida, *The Gift of Death*, tr. David Wills (Chicago: Chicago University Press, 1995), 82–115.

[63] In the British general election campaign of 2001, the Labour and Conservative parties both advocated policies of imprisoning asylum seekers in so-called 'secure detention centres' whilst their individual cases were being considered.

15

Dispensing with Christian Mysticism

L. Philip Barnes

In recent decades there has been a revival of interest in Christian mysticism. It is as though the West, long exposed and attracted to the spirituality of the East, has turned at last homeward and now seeks in more familiar places for spiritual riches. Theologians and philosophers of a religious bent are clamouring to recover the ancient wisdom of Christian mysticism and put it to evangelistic or apologetic use.[1] Interest in mysticism is not just scholarly but also practical and popular.[2] For some Christians, mysticism suggests itself to be a form of spirituality ideally suited to the (post)modern age: experiential, individualistic and progressive. But is the Christian heritage of Western mysticism worth reviving? Is there a rich tradition of faith and devotion within mysticism that is overlooked to the detriment of our spiritual nourishment and growth? Against expectations and in disregard of the received wisdom of the Christian tradition, I shall argue that nothing of significance to the truth or validity of Christian existence and experience turns on the matter of Christian mysticism. Christian discipleship, without a knowledge or an experience of Christian mysticism, can legitimately aspire to be genuinely biblical and devoutly Christian.

My case for dispensing with Christian mysticism is structured along the following lines. I shall begin by defining mystical experience over against other types of religious experience. This initial definition is then developed and refined in the context of a detailed discussion of the relationship between mystical experience and the doctrinal interpretations that are frequently placed upon experience and which are integrated into reports of mystical experience. Following this, I develop a series of arguments for the conclusion that the same mystical experience is common to different religions and cultures. This amounts to a denial of the existence of a distinctively Christian mystical experience. Christian mysticism does not differ in kind or substance from Theravada mysticism, Sufi mysticism, or *Advaita Vedanta* mysticism. In other words, mystical experience is the same in the different religions. Such a conclusion is widely disparaged by Christian theologians and philosophers, even though it is, in my opinion, consistent with Christian orthodoxy. Finally, in order to press home the case for the phenomenological unity of mystical experiences, I consider the writings of the medieval Christian mystic, St John of the Cross, as representative of the primary literature to which an appeal is often made by commentators in substantiation of the existence of a distinctively Christian form of mysticism. I find this appeal unconvincing. Integrated into my critique of the Christian character of Sanjuanist mysticism are some considerations that are suggestive of the incompatibility of mysticism with Christian discipleship. These considerations are not systematically pursued but when conjoined with the conclusion that there is no distinctively Christian mystical experience they are sufficient, I believe, to caution Christians against embarking upon the mystical path in the quest for mystical experience.

Defining Mystical Experience

Those familiar with the subject of mysticism will be aware of the debate that surrounds definitions of mysticism. Towards the end of the nineteenth century the Christian theologian and philosopher W.R. Inge could note twenty-eight different definitions.[3] This was added to in the twentieth century, with magical, cosmic, and occult (basically all preternatural) experiences often regarded as mystical. For some popular writers and not a few theologians the whole domain of religious experience is to be equated with mysticism. Thus Karl Rahner can affirm that 'the devout Christian of the future will either be a "mystic", one who has experienced something, or he will be nothing at all.'[4] Here the mystic is equated with someone who has experienced God, as opposed to someone who accepts what the church teaches or what other people report about God. On Rahner's usage, charismatic experiences, conversion experiences, and numinous encounters are all properly classified as mystical. But such a wide application of the term mystic (and its cognates) is not helpful, for it obviously conflates experiences that are better distinguished for the purposes of interpretation and of assessment.[5]

Recent philosophers of religion and professional scholars of the literature who are alert to methodological and interpretative issues have been much more restrictive in their definitions, and the following would be widely accepted: *mystical experiences are 'unitary' or 'unitive' states which are noetic or perception like, but lack specific empirical content.*[6] This definition will initially serve our purposes, though it will be further developed and refined below. It has the virtue of being both sufficiently broad to admit experiences from a wide variety of different religions, as well as experiences not taken by their subjects as religious, and sufficiently specific to exclude other types of religious and secular experience, such as visions or charismatic experiences.[7]

It is also common among scholars of the literature to distinguish between two forms of mystical experience (two species of a single genus, as it were): one in which union or identity is experienced with the external world of the senses; and the other in which union is achieved within the human self, when the mind of the mystic is emptied of sensory and (ordinary) conceptual content.[8] One example of each should be sufficient to illustrate the difference:

> I was alone upon the seashore as all these thoughts flowed over me, liberating and reconciling; and now again, as once before in distant days in the Alps of Dauphine, I was impelled to kneel down, this time before the illimitable ocean, symbol of the Infinite. I felt that I prayed as I had never prayed before, and knew now what prayer really is: to return from the solitude of individuation into the consciousness of unity with all that is, to kneel down as one that passes away, and to rise up as one imperishable. Earth, heaven and sea resounded as in one vast world-encircling harmony. It was as if the chorus of all the great who had ever lived were about me. I felt myself one of them, and it appeared as if I heard their greeting: 'Thou too belongest to the company of those who have overcome.'[9]

> Suddenly at church, or in company, or when I am reading ... I felt the approach of the mood. Irresistibly it took possession of my mind and will, lasted what seemed an eternity and disappeared in a series of rapid sensations which resembled the awakening from an anaesthetic influence. One reason why I disliked this kind of trance was that I could not describe it to myself. I cannot even now find words to render it intelligible. It consisted in a gradual but swiftly progressive obliteration of space, time, sensation, and the multifarious factors of experience which seem to qualify what we are pleased to call our Self. In proportion as these conditions of ordinary consciousness were subtracted, the sense of an underlying or essential consciousness acquired intensity. At last nothing remained but a pure, absolute, abstract Self. The universe became without form and devoid of content.[10]

Both accounts exhibit the sense of (experienced) unity and overcoming of separation that is essential to mysticism, yet the first report differs significantly from the second: the experience of union with the world and the objects of the world contrasts with an experience of pure consciousness, an experience from which the world of sense experience and ordinary conceptual thought is excluded. Walter Stace refers to the distinction as that between extrovertive and introvertive mystical experiences;[11] Ninian Smart speaks of exterior and interior mysticism.[12] Although the terminology may differ, the distinction itself, as James Horne has remarked, 'is beyond dispute.'[13] There is mystical union with the world, and the objects of the world (often referred to as nature mysticism),[14] and there is mystical union *without* the world and its objects – an inner experience of direct, unitive consciousness. Although both types of experience are usually interpreted religiously by mystics, the latter is more consistently so interpreted; the latter is also regarded by mystics as more important in terms of religious and philosophical significance. As Stace remarks, 'The extrovertive type of mystical consciousness is ... vastly less important than the introvertive, both as regards practical influence on human life and history and as regards philosophical implication.'[15]

In what follows mystical experience will be equated with *introvertive* or *interior* mysticism, except where the context requires that both forms of mysticism be distinguished. When Christian mystics maintain that their experience is distinctive it is invariably interior mysticism to which they are referring. This is because exterior or nature mysticism does not naturally suggest itself as amenable to the task of distinguishing *Christian* mystical experiences from all other varieties of mystical experience. The focus of union in exterior mysticism is the world and its objects, experienced in some form of unifying vision. Mystics from different religious traditions necessarily enjoy the same unitive experience of the world, precisely because there is only one world to be experienced. They differ over the proper interpretation of the experience. For the Christian, union with nature may be interpreted as union with God; for the Hindu, union is achieved with Brahman. It could be maintained that because mystics believe themselves to be experiencing a different spiritual object, albeit experienced in and through the objects of sense perception, that the experiences do differ. There is some plausibility to this claim, but as we shall see the same contention also arises in connection with interior mysticism and its significance is best considered there.

At this point a division arises among those equally well acquainted with the literature of interior mysticism. One group holds that all such experiences are essentially the same, this is the view of Walter Stace and

Ninian Smart, for example. The other group holds that there are a number of different mystical experiences. Quite obviously this latter group, unlike the former, admits a diversity of opinion. Some like R.C. Zaehner believe in two distinctive forms, which he calls monistic and theistic mysticism,[16] and some admitting many more forms. In point of fact it is currently fashionable to believe that there are as many forms of mysticism as there are religious and conceptual frameworks used to interpret the experience; or if we want to be more circumspect in our use of language, there are as many forms of mysticism as there are different beliefs *incorporated* into the experience. This is the view of Steven T. Katz. According to him, mystical precepts are shaped and constructed by the religious *a priori* structures of the understanding into the definite (and different) objects of mystical experience: the prior religious beliefs of the mystic shapes his or her experience in such a way as to conform the experience to existing religious and theological beliefs. Thus he speaks of 'the conservative character of mysticism'.[17] Mystical experiences conform to what is already believed.[18] While acknowledging the importance of Katz's account and its relevance to our concerns, I do not intend reviewing or developing the criticisms to which I believe it is susceptible.[19] Instead we shall pursue an alternative line of enquiry that supports a different interpretation of the evidence of mysticism.

Mystical Experience and Doctrinal Interpretation

In this section I shall argue that some kind of distinction between mystical experience and doctrinal interpretations of that experience can and should be drawn.[20] The limited nature of this endeavour needs to be appreciated, for although a distinction between experience and interpretation (within the terms specified below) undoubtedly enjoys an application beyond the realm of mystical perception, it is not my intention to delineate its limits. Our focus will fall on the distinction as it has come to be both applied and criticised by scholars of mysticism.

A distinction between experience and interpretation has been central to the case for a common mystical experience that transcends cultural and religious boundaries. Obviously, at face value mystical experiences are not all the same, for mystics do not unanimously speak of encountering the same spiritual object. The response of those who believe that mystical experiences are essentially alike (for reasons that are considered below) is to distinguish between the experience and its interpretation and to argue that mystical experiences are the same, whereas the interpretations differ. This is the view of Walter T. Stace, one of the chief advocates of the 'unanimity thesis'. According to him, the distinction between mystical experience and conceptual interpretation expresses the difference between what is actually experienced (what is called the phenomenological content of experience), and the interpretation added to, or incorporated into, the report of the experience, on the basis of some religious or philosophical commitment. Mystical experiences are all the same, but they are subject to different interpretations: 'the interpretation will as a rule largely depend on the cultural environment and the prior beliefs of the individual mystic'.[21] Thus the *same* experience can be interpreted by one mystic as experience of God and by another as experience of Brahman. But how plausible is this distinction between mystical experience and conceptual interpretation? Without it Stace's case for a common cross-cultural and cross-religious mystical experience collapses. To answer this I shall begin by noting some weaknesses in Stace's presentation of the distinction between experience and interpretation, restate it using a different vocabulary, which in turn raises difficulties of its own, and then conclude by noting that even though both sets of terminology are not without their problems, a distinction, however made, between what mystics experience and what they add to experience by way of doctrinal interpretation requires to be drawn.

Stace defines interpretation as 'anything which the conceptual intellect adds to the experience for the purpose of understanding it'.[22] This, some would contend, is unsatisfactory, because it seems to suggest that in normal cognition ('raw') experience occurs independently of conceptual interpretation. Recent work in the philosophy and psychology of mind challenges this notion. According to it, normal experience is always interpreted experience. The material of the senses is organised, interpreted and conceptualised in quite complex ways by the mind. There is no meaningful experience without conceptual interpretation.

The distinction, however, could be restated and reinterpreted in a way that escapes the type of criticism we have noted. Interestingly, at one point, Stace expresses the distinction between experience and interpretation in terms of the difference between a low-level interpretation and a high-level interpretation of a mystical experience.[23] This terminology (which is more characteristic of Ninian Smart's interpretation of mysticism) may be better suited to the point he is attempting to make, namely, to distinguish between what is experienced and what is added to experience on the basis of some previously held doctrinal commitment. Equally, it would also give expression to the interpretative element in all human experience. (In addition it removes a dubious correlated distinction drawn by Stace between indubitable experience and dubitable interpretation.[24]) This new terminology, however, has been criticised by some commentators for precisely the opposite reason as the distinction between experience and interpretation has been criticised, namely, that to speak of higher and lower interpretations of mystical apprehension (effectively) falsifies the experience of union by compromising its felt immediacy and directness; an immediacy that is believed to contrast with the mediated and interpretative character of all other human experiences.[25] On this view the essence of mystical union is a direct experience of *pure* ('raw'?) consciousness that bypasses the normal processes of linguistic and conceptual mediation: a proper distinction should be drawn between mystical experience and conceptual interpretation. As a result of this disagreement much effort has been expended by philosophers and scholars of mysticism in attempts to identify and uncover the theoretical commitments that underlie particular choices of terminology and the implications that are presumed to follow for the nature of mystical experience as a result of these commitments.

The problem with this debate, however, is that it distracts attention away from the very real issue that the use of the terminology is meant to clarify and identify in the first place, that is, the need to draw some kind of distinction between what is experienced in mystical union (its phenomenological content) and what is added to the report of the experience on the basis of some previously held doctrinal commitment. The relevance of this distinction to our concerns should be obvious: comparisons between reports of mystical experiences from different religious and cultural contexts should be made on the basis of what is actually experienced by mystics and no on the basis of highly ramified doctrinal interpretations that are read into the experience and which incorporate beliefs and assumptions that are strictly speaking extraneous to it. Extra-experiential content should not be used to distinguish between mystical experiences. A proper appreciation of the nature of mystical experience requires that attention is given to the actual contents of experience and not to the doctrinal content of religious systems which are (frequently) used to interpret and report the experience.

Is it possible to distinguish experiential from extra-experiential content in mystical reports? To answer this we will focus on one particular group of mystical experiences and review the reasons why such a distinction can and should be made.[26]

Let us consider the Christian mystic's claim to experience God. Now God as traditionally understood by Christians is a most unusual entity: an omniscient, omnipotent, omnipresent, omni-benevolent, trinitarian, moral agent who created everything external to himself.[27] This is the spiritual object Christian mystics profess to encounter. But can the traditional predicates of God, of the kind to which we have just referred, be substantiated by an appeal to mystical experience alone? Quite obviously not, for how can one (mystic or otherwise) experience omniscience or omnipotence? Finite creatures, such as we are, cannot experience infinite qualities. Or again one may ask how could the mystic know on the basis of experience alone that God created the world – a belief essential to any orthodox Christian doctrine of the divine.[28] The answer of course is that mystical experience does not provide such knowledge, nor do mystics suggest it does. If the description of God as creator is appropriate, it is believed on grounds other than experience; usually it is accepted on the authority of a verbal revelation from God in the Bible, or on the basis of natural theology. Consequently, if Christian mystics, in describing their experience, refer to God, by which they mean something like the God of traditional theism, then they would appear to be over-describing it. Over-describing it in the sense that the subject of the experience, on the basis of the experience alone, could not know (given human finitude and the nature of the experience) that the object experienced possessed all of the perfections traditionally ascribed to God, that is, that God is omniscient, omnipotent, the maker of heaven and earth, and so on. There is a gap between what was actually experienced and the report of the experience. Let me illustrate the nature of this gap by reference to a mundane experience.

I take you to view a particular house. It is a chalet bungalow of modern style, with a double garage. From your vantage point you are able to familiarise yourself with the external features of the house. In response to questions about the house you should be able to provide appropriate and accurate answers. There are ten windows; there are two doors; there is a double garage. On what basis can you accurately describe the house? Presumably on the basis of your experience. You see the house and you are able to count the number of doors and windows, and to ascertain the type of garage. The phenomenological content of your visual experience enables you to reach justified conclusions on the nature of the external features of the house. Now suppose you are asked to name the owner of the house and to this you respond correctly. The owner/occupier of the house is p. How did you know this? In fact you noted the house number and the address; and you remembered that p, a colleague of yours from work, lives at this address. Although your identification of the owner is correct, it is not an item of knowledge that is vouchsafed by your visual experience of the house. Your answer goes beyond what you are entitled to know on the basis of your present experience. Your external view of the house does not warrant this conclusion. There is a gap between what you know about the house on the basis of your current visual experience and your wider knowledge of the house and its owner from past experience (moreover, your past experience need not necessarily be visual). The nature of this gap necessitates some kind of distinction in this situation between experiential and extra-experiential content.

The same distinction requires to be drawn in reports of mystical experience when they go beyond phenomenological description and incorporate beliefs and doctrines that are strictly speaking external to the experience, in that they go beyond what could conceivably be known on the basis of mystical experience. When a subject accredits to an experience content which the form of the experience appears to exclude then we should bracket out such content when attempting to provide a straightforward (phenomenological) account of what was actually experienced. Accordingly, speaking of God, or Allah, or Brahman, as the object of mystical experience is an interpretation that goes beyond the experienced content. Such interpretations should not be used to distinguish between mystical experiences. To take account of this some kind of distinction is necessary, hence Stace's distinction between experience and interpretation.

What results when a proper distinction between experience and doctrinal interpretation is applied to reports and descriptions of mystical union?

The Unanimity Thesis

The application of a distinction between experience and interpretation to reports of mystical experience from different cultures and religions has yielded different results. It is not uncommon for theistic and Christian theologians to distinguish between a theistic and a monistic form of mystical experience. Moreover, some Christian writers identify further a peculiarly Christian form of mystical experience. Thus Christian mysticism should be properly distinguished from theistic mysticism. This is the contention of Stephen Payne and William Wainwright. Other writers, such as Walter Stace and Ninian Smart, maintain that application of the distinction between experience and interpretation to mystical reports, and the resultant differentiation of phenomenological content from non-phenomenological content, reveals that there is a single cross-cultural, cross-religious mystical experience. This is the conclusion that I will seek to justify in this section. In the next section I will meet some common objections that are intended to undermine the case for the essential similarity of mystical experiences and to establish the positive case for a distinctively Christian form of mystical experience.

The chief reason that is adduced for the existence of a single cross-cultural, cross religious mystical experience is that there is a remarkable agreement between descriptions of the experience. This is the reason explored by Stace in considerable detail and implicit in Smart. According to Stace (interior) mystical experiences share the following characteristics/content: unitary consciousness, a sense of the transcendence of space and time, a feeling of objectivity, blessedness, awareness of the divine, paradoxicality, and (with some reservation) ineffability.[29] Whether his list of common features is sufficiently accurate or not is a controversial question and can only be settled by an extended and close analysis of reports of mystical experience. This cannot be attempted here. The crucial question to ask is whether the agreement Stace finds between descriptions of mystical experiences glosses over differences (as opposed to interpretations) that lend support to an alternative reading of the evidence that would identify a number of distinctive forms of interior mysticism. This is precisely what some Christian mystics and Christian commentators upon mysticism claim: that there are descriptive elements within reports of mysticism that justify the positing of a distinctively Christian form of mysticism. This contention will be the focus of discussion in the next section. It may be that Stace claims too much agreement between mystical experiences, but this does not greatly detract from his overall argument. In other words, even if he has an inflated view of the content common to mystical experiences, this does not necessarily detract from his central contention that mystical experiences are essentially the same. One answer to the question how we ordinarily know that two or more people have enjoyed the same experience is if their descriptions of the experience are the same. This is what we find with regard to (interior) mystical experiences: there is a striking similarity of description (with no disagreement). That is, once the highly ramified interpretations are bracketed out, similar descriptions of the experience remain, therefore we should conclude that all such experiences are the same.

Although I have provided only a sketch of Stace's argument, I hope I have said enough to indicate both its nature and its plausibility. The appeal to common content is the reason normally adduced for the conclusion that mystical experiences are essentially the same. This focus upon phenomenological content is understandable and entirely proper: it is in terms of content that judgements can and should be made when addressing the question of whether mystics of different traditions enjoy not just similar but the same experience. But is this preoccupation with content (within the parameters set by Stace) the only relevant consideration? Certainly if we are guided by the professional and philosophical literature on the subject, content would appear to be the only relevant consideration. There are grounds, however, for believing that the parameters of academic discussion of this issue have been too narrowly drawn. There are additional considerations apart from content that lend support to the unanimity thesis.

The first consideration focuses on the means by which mystical experiences are facilitated and expedited. Mystics are broadly agreed on the path which has to be followed if mystical experience is to be gained. Commentators upon mysticism have long recognised that whereas nature mysticism typically occurs spontaneously, interior mystical experience occurs, with very few exceptions, only after a long period of spiritual training and mental preparation; and interior mystics, of whichever religious tradition, follow the same spiritual exercises. These include adopting certain bodily postures, breathing exercises, meditation on a particular object, meditation without an object, repetition of a sacred word or phrase, and so on. Usually these exercises are divided into stages, so that there is a programme of structured and progressive learning with proximate goals (experiences) appropriate to each stage until mystical union is consummated. In addition asceticism and submission to a spiritual director are normal components of the mystical path.[30]

It would be misleading to suggest that every mystic agrees on the details of the mystical path. We can readily acknowledge that they do not all identify the same number of stages, prescribe the same proximate goals, or recommend the same spiritual exercises. But recognition of this is relatively unimportant. This is because there is an accepted diversity of practice and procedure within each of the (mystical) religious traditions, and this diversity within each religion is sufficiently broad to bring each into agreement with the accepted range of diversity in other (mystical) religious traditions. For example, many Hindu mystics, but not all, recommend the repetition of a sacred word or phrase; most Christian mystics do not, but some do. Most Christian mystics identify either three or five distinct stages towards mystical union, but some can speak of four, seven, and even nine stages; in the main, Indian mystics (Hindu and Buddhist) identify eight stages, but some can speak of more and some less. The point is that there is cross-religious agreement between mystics. Each religious tradition allows for a variety of steps on the mystical path, and this same variety is paralleled in other religious traditions.

The full range of spiritual exercises can be classified as methods of detachment. Each exercise and technique is intended to detach (or withdraw) the practitioner from the external world of sense experience and the inner world of discursive thought.[31] As one progresses through the prescribed stages so one progresses further toward the goal of pure consciousness.

What is the relevance of this to the case for the essential similarity of mystical experiences? Let me explain by means of an example. If I presently arise, leave my room, turn right, and proceed down the corridor for about twenty paces, and then turn right again, I will have entered the common room. Someone else beginning from the same place, and following the same directions (path), will likewise arrive at the common room, and upon entering will have the same experience of a smoke filled room, faded easy chairs and decor, and see the same seated individuals. This is normally true of sense experience: if the same directions are followed (i.e. the same conditions fulfilled) the same experience results. It is also true of, what we can call for convenience, subjective experience. If one is deprived of sleep a headache naturally follows, if one goes without food for long enough hunger pangs result; anyone who fulfils the same conditions gains the same experience. Of course for each of us there is a group of experiences which we cannot have, e.g. I will never run one hundred meters in less than ten seconds, but this is because, for one reason or another, we cannot fulfil the necessary conditions. Where the same conditions are fulfilled by different persons the same experience will normally result.

What advice do mystics give to others who wish to experience mystical union? The directions are straightforward, if difficult to follow: commitment to the mystical path with its associated spiritual exercises and techniques. Mystics of whichever tradition devote themselves to the way of detachment, and urge others to do likewise: mystical union is facilitated and gained by spiritual training. Indeed such is the relationship between mystical experience and spiritual training that some commentators make reference to it in their definition of mysticism.[32] The implication of our earlier discussion on the (cross-religious) agreement between mystics on the nature of the mystical path should be obvious: because mystics recommend the same practices (i.e. they interpret the mystical path in the same way), it follows that the same conditions are met, and if the same conditions are met, then it seems reasonable to conclude that the same experience results. The critical observation that mystics aim for different experiences, in the sense that they are directed in their practice by different concepts of the divine, does little to diminish the force of this argument. This is because the various spiritual exercises are specifically intended to empty the mind of both sensory and conceptual content in preparation for mystical union (this point is further developed below). Once the principle is accepted that fulfilment of the same conditions by different people normally results in the same experience, then it is entirely to be expected that Christians practising techniques, *a*, *b*, and *c* will achieve the same experience as Buddhists practising techniques, *a*, *b* and *c*.

The next consideration in favour of the unanimity thesis is best introduced by quoting some typical accounts of mystical experience. Representative examples are taken from different mystical traditions: Christian, Greek philosophical (not usually thought of as religious), Mahayana Buddhist, and Hindu (*Advaita*) reports respectively.

> For leaving behind everything that is observed, not only what sense comprehends but also what the intelligence thinks it sees, it keeps on penetrating deeper until by the intelligence's yearning for understanding it gains access to the invisible and the incomprehensible, and there it sees God.
>
> Gregory of Nyssa (c. 330–95 CE)[33]

> There were not two; beholder was one with beheld; it was not a vision compassed but a unity apprehended. The man formed by this mingling with the Supreme must – if he only remember – carry its image: he is beyond the Unity, nothing within or without inducing diversity; no movement now, no passion, no outlooking desire, once the ascent is achieved; reasoning is in abeyance and all Intellection and even, to dare the word, the very self; caught away, filled with God, he has in perfect stillness attained isolation; all the being calmed, he turns neither to this side nor to that, not even inwards to himself; utterly resting he has become very rest.
>
> Plotinus (c. 205–270 CE)[34]

> But when [the objective world which is] the basis of conditioning as well as the wisdom [which does the conditioning]
> Are both eliminated,
> The state of mind-only is realized,
> Since the six sense organs and their objects are no longer present...
> This is the realm of passionlessness or purity.
>
> Vasubandhu (c. 596–664 CE)[35]

> That which is the hearing of the ear, the thought of the mind,
> The voice of speech, as also the breathing of the breath,
> And the sight of the eye! Past these escaping, the wise,
> On departing from this world, became immortal.
> There the eyes go not;
> Speech goes not, nor the mind.
> We know not, we understand not
> How one would teach It.
>
> (Unknown Hindu seer)[36]

These examples are uncontroversial. They are all clearly descriptions of mystical experience. More controversial is the judgement that they are all reports of the same experience. In their original settings they are presented by their subjects as of different spiritual objects, and on the basis of this presumed distinction between objects some urge a distinction between experiences. This kind of appeal is unconvincing because the terms in which the experiences are reported, such as God, the One, or Brahman, should in the light of our earlier discussion be regarded as (high-level) interpretations and not descriptions; interpretations that strictly speaking fall outside the realm of phenomenological content. The situation is analogous to the same motor vehicle being interpreted by different observers as the property of different owners. The descriptions of the vehicle agree, but there is disagreement on the identity of the owner. As with mystical experience the descriptions of the experience agree but the identifications of the object experienced differ.

A closer look at the actual mystical reports suggests a further reason for concluding that they are all the same, and by extension that all mystical experiences are the same. It is commonplace to note that interior mystical experiences are devoid of sensory content; it is precisely this feature that identifies them as interior experiences. But it is not just that the experiences are devoid of sensory content, attention to reports of interior mystical experiences also indicates that the experiences are in an important sense devoid of conceptual content. We have already noted that the aim of the different spiritual exercises is to detach the mind from ordinary consciousness, that is to detach the mind from all sensations, images, and concepts along with their attendant desires, emotions, and volitions. It is only when the mind is empty and devoid of all distractions that union is achieved. Mystics inform us that the experience of mystical union lies beyond sensory experience and discursive reason. Walter Stace has remarked that mystical union 'is not a sensory–intellectual consciousness at all'.[37] When the mind is successfully purged of all images, mystical union is gained. More precisely, mystical union is experience without images. The significance of this, however, has uniformly not been appreciated by some mystics and by commentators on mysticism alike. The nature of mystical experience as pure consciousness effectively excludes the possibility that there is, or can be, more than one form of interior mysticism.

Let me explain by posing the question how we normally distinguish between experiences. At this minute how do I know that your (external) experience differs from mine? Quite obviously because our descriptions of the experiences differ. I am seated alone, in my room, with particular books in front of me. This is the barest possible description, and the more I would specify the details, the more it would be recognised that our present experiences differ. Let us take another example, this time an internal experience. I am thinking of the work I would like to complete this week, you are probably thinking of something different, yet even if by chance you are thinking of the same subject, our experiences will still be different, because the tasks I have set myself for this week will be quite different from yours (it would be nice to think that you will redecorate our family room, but I doubt that it is included in your tasks!). The point is that we distinguish between experiences on the basis of sense and conceptual content. Where sense and/or conceptual content is the same, the experiences are the same (I have already developed this point with regard to mystical experience). Where the content differs, the experiences differ.

Mystics report a unitive experience that transcends sensory and conceptual content. But as we have recognized it is only in terms of sensory and conceptual content that experiences can be distinguished; it follows from this that all interior mystical experiences must be the same. They necessarily must be the same because the only features which could distinguish between them, i.e., sensory and conceptual content, are excluded by the very nature of the experience. Where there is no sensory content and no conceptual content, what remains to distinguish between experiences? A Christian experience of pure consciousness is exactly the same as a Buddhist experience of pure consciousness. How could it be otherwise?

There is one final consideration that lends support to the unanimity thesis, and that is the testimony of mystics who have entered into dialogue with mystics of other religious traditions. Christian writers like Thomas Merton,[38] Bede Griffiths,[39] and William Johnston[40] have spoken eloquently of the agreement in experience they have identified with mystics of other religious traditions. On this basis they have called for a new positive relationship between Christianity and the other great world religions. How seriously should we take such testimony? Certainly to make the point convincingly a much longer discussion and analysis of their positions is required than is possible here. It also has to be acknowledged that in the end there is no simple way of assessing this claimed agreement in experience between mystics of different religions that bypasses the controversial and complex philosophical issues that we have already considered. Modestly, we may conclude that the appeal to shared experience by mystics themselves gives some limited support to the unanimity thesis. The weight of argument overall, however, is a different matter. The considerations adduced provide convincing reason for believing that the same mystical experience is common to different religions.

Is Sanjuanist Mysticism Distinctively Christian?

The contention that all mystical experiences are phenomenologically the same has not gone unchallenged. One accusation is that the unanimity thesis glosses over differences between experiences (as opposed to interpretations) that lend support to the case for a distinctively Christian form of mysticism. The view that Christian mysticism is unique is naturally attractive to Christian theologians and apologists, and to some commentators on mysticism. The most extended and philosophically sophisticated presentation of this position is that of Stephen Payne.[41] He argues that there are descriptive elements within reports of mystical experience that provide compelling grounds for concluding that Christian mysticism is different from other varieties of mysticism, theistic and otherwise. We will examine his position in some detail as it poses a direct challenge to the unanimity thesis.

The point of departure for Professor Payne's justification of Christian mysticism is his conviction that most commentators are insufficiently attentive to the original literature with its detailed descriptions of mystical experience. He boldly declares that 'most Anglo-American philosophers seem to have little acquaintance with classic mystical texts, and therefore tend to base their evaluations of mysticism on the facile and sometimes misleading generalisations found in the secondary literature on the subject'.[42] It cannot be doubted that there are studies of mysticism to which this criticism is apt, even if it is unlikely that all those whose interpretation of mysticism differs from Payne's can be dismissed so summarily. In any case the import of Payne's remark is that he intends to justify the existence of a distinctively Christian form of mystical experience by reference to a very detailed, critical and rigorous examination of a narrow and circumscribed range of mystical reports, namely the reports of mystical experience contained in the writings of the Spanish Carmelite St John of the Cross (1542–1591).[43]

Of course Payne believes that reports of such experience are not confined to the Sanjuanist corpus, for he speaks of St John of the Cross as providing a 'standard' and 'reliable' account of orthodox Western mysticism.[44] But he is astute enough to realise that it takes only one convincing example to establish the case for a uniquely Christian and theistic mystical experience, provided of course that this one example is accepted by all parties as representative of the tradition under discussion;

once this is conceded, and I see no reason to challenge the representative nature of St John of the Cross' *Christian* mysticism, one example is necessary and one example is sufficient for his purpose.

Although Payne's positive case for regarding Christian mystical experiences as phenomenologically Christian is not easily summarised, there are two major planks in his argument. First, he contends that Christian mystics generally, and St John of the Cross in particular, witness to a mystical experience that is gained as a result of grace, rather than achieved through human effort. This feeling of receiving favour points back to a personal giver of grace and therefore distinguishes Christian and theistic mysticism from other varieties, where the attainment of mystical awareness is regarded as a human achievement. Secondly, and more importantly, he argues, by reference chiefly to St John of the Cross's writings, that Christian mystical experiences are properly distinguished from others on the basis of their distinctive Christian content.

In his discussion of the limitations of defining mysticism in terms of common essential characteristics, Professor Payne refers to William James's claim that a feeling of passivity is one such characteristic: 'the mystic feels as if his own will were in abeyance'.[45] Payne acknowledges that this claim is difficult to evaluate, 'since passivity can be given so many meanings',[46] yet he does feel that James has hit on something important. He notes how James' analysis of mystical experience at this point contrasts with Stace's contention that mystical experiences are normally gained through strenuous self-effort and are accompanied by a sense of human achievement.[47] According to Payne, passivity is an appropriate description of St John of the Cross's understanding of how mystical experiences are achieved. Positively it means that there is a gift-like quality about the experience, a feeling that it results from someone-else's favour and initiative, and negatively that the experience is not achieved by human self-effort: 'mystical experiences are gratuitous, not earned'.[48] The passive nature of Christian mystical experience correlates to the creative and gracious action of God within the experiencing self.

How plausible is Payne's suggestion that mystical experiences are passive in nature (possibly contrasting with a group of other mystical experiences that are acquired by self-effort), and that this feature points back to a personal and creative, external source of the experience, in the form of the Christian God? Payne recognises, and attempts to meet, the obvious criticism, set out some time ago by Walter Stace: that Christian talk of the passive nature of mystical experience is required by the demands of Christian theology. According to Stace, the insistence that mystical experiences are passive in character is merely an attempt to conform mystical reports to Christian orthodoxy. Christian theology requires that

God is experienced only when he chooses to be experienced: God must take the initiative and any talk of gaining the experience by one's own efforts must be excluded. Payne counters this by simply inverting the argument. He claims that a denial of the passive quality of mystical experience and the attribution of mystical experience to one's own self-effort simply reflects an anti-Christian or theistic bias.[49] Stalemate, not quite, for Payne has also suggested, and I accept that it can be established, that there are some non-theistic mystical reports which unambiguously assert the passive quality of mystical experience. In other words, there are mystics from non-theistic traditions who speak of their experience as having a kind of gracious character and of a feeling of being acted upon. These features, Payne suggests, point to a personal God, in the sense that they provide evidence for a spiritual object who is gracious and personal. Has Payne clinched the argument? Does the passive character of some, chiefly Christian and theistic, mystical experiences require them to be distinguished from at least some other mystical experiences, which are achieved by human self-effort, and does this feature provide some evidence for the personal nature of the source of mystical experience? I think not.

In the first place, mystics of whichever religious persuasion, Christians included, have long recognised that mystical experiences occur, with very few exceptions, only after a long period of spiritual training and mental preparation. The notion of a mystical path or discipline, in the sense of an ordered and structured series of spiritual exercises to be followed, is common to all religious traditions. We have already discussed the mystical path in some detail. A long period of intensive spiritual training and discipline is expected by those who embark on the quest for enlightenment, and there is no assurance of success. But if great effort and strenuous discipline are common to all mystics, where does the notion of grace come in?

If it were the case that Christian mystical experiences invariably occurred spontaneously, and non-Christian mystical experiences invariably occurred only after a long and arduous period of spiritual training, then one might conceivably conclude (and even this would be a shaky argument) that Christian experience was distinctive and that the passive and spontaneous character of Christian mystical experience provided some evidence for a personal God who takes the initiative in revealing himself. This is not the case. The same effort is required by aspirant Christian mystics as by other mystics and presumably there is the same failure rate among Christians as there is for among mystics of all other religious traditions. How then is talk of grace justified in this context? There is no difference in the arduous and disciplined spiritual training of the Christian mystic and the would-be mystic of any other religious traditions, whether he or she belongs to a theistic or to a non-theistic religious tradition. The use of the term 'grace' and 'being acted upon' seem strangely inappropriate to a situation in which one has devoted, not infrequently, the greater part of one's life to rigorous self-discipline of both a physical and mental form. It is self-effort in the form of practising spiritual exercises which the mystic recommends to others and it is self-effort which gains the prize – mystical union.

One possible response to this might be to maintain that Christian mystical experiences really do result from God's initiative and grace – hence the feeling of passivity – but only after great personal effort and self-sacrifice. Is it not possible that positive, active steps initiated by the individual prepare the way for a passive experience of mystical union with God? Perhaps, but to reiterate the point just made: it seems inappropriate to speak of gaining an experience by grace, and thus the experience is passive, when one has devoted perhaps the greater period of one's life engaging in rigorous and often mechanical spiritual exercises which are explicitly intended to facilitate the experience. In addition, as Walter Stace noted, 'once achieved [mystical experience] can as a rule be there-after induced almost at will at least over long periods of life'.[50] This factual point supports the contention that the achievement of mystical experience is better explained as a matter of technique and human effort rather than as resulting from divine grace. But perhaps an even firmer objection is to be found within the theological system of Christianity itself.

The term 'grace' in the Christian Scriptures has a number of uses, none of which can be extended uncontroversially to refer to the mystic's achievement of union with God. The natural theological context for the language of grace in the New Testament (the use of the word group is characteristically Pauline) is that of referring to the historical manifestation of God's salvation in Christ, and more particularly to God's act of justifying or declaring the sinner righteous. God's final verdict over the individual (for justification is an eschatological term) is brought forward into time, when by grace God acquits the guilty, by virtue of a profession of faith in Christ and the efficacy of his death. Interestingly, commenting on this usage, Hans Conzelmann, in Kittel-Friedrich's *Theological Dictionary of the New Testament*, concludes that it is to be understood 'in a wholly non-mystical sense'.[51] Conzelmann is making the point that justification, i.e. God's declaration of not guilty over the sinner, is strictly something which is external to the individual and does not depend upon or reflect one's moral standing or the effort and determination with which one has pursued the religious life. In Paul faith and grace are set in opposition to works/self-effort and Law (Rom. 3:20–26; 4:1–5).[52] It could even be argued that the kind of rigorous quest for direct union with God which characterises the mystical path both compromises the radical character of Christian grace and obscures the essential union with God which the justified sinner already possesses by virtue of his or her faith union with Christ. Now I admit that Paul can conceive of grace as having an enduring quality, in the sense that Christians are in a 'state of grace'. But the gift-like character and Christological focus of grace remain to the fore (Rom. 5:2). The church member's continued standing in God's favour depends upon the constancy of God's love and mercy and not upon religious achievement and proficiency. The New Testament, and this is the crucial point, does not link grace to human religious experience, rather grace is publicly manifest in God's gift of his Son, and in accepting this gift we experience grace. It is not at all obvious that the Christian mystic's insistence on the gracious character of mystical experience is in keeping with New Testament usage or whether the use of such language by Christian mystics to describe their experience contributes anything to the case for distinguishing Christian mystical experiences from all other or at least some other mystical experiences. Certainly in the biblical scheme of things it makes sense to speak of our growing in grace, and thus becoming more like Christ in exhibiting the theological virtues of faith, hope and love. It may even make sense to speak of our moral achievements as gained through grace, and clearly some kind of self-effort is required here, but the New Testament is strangely silent on the notion that we specifically gain or expedite certain Christian *experiences* for ourselves through rigorous self-effort. At the all-important level of religious experience, self-effort of the form recommended by Christian mystics seems to be antithetical to God's gracious activity.

What then of the reported experience of passivity, and the related feeling of a sense of gratitude, which often attends mystical union, and which is even expressed by mystics of non-theistic traditions who deny the existence of any object to whom such feelings would be appropriate? An answer to this is not difficult to find. Surely it is a praiseworthy human attribute, and not only a religious attribute, to speak humbly of one's own achievements and successes. We normally admire the person who is charitable in his estimate of the abilities of others and reticent in speaking of his own abilities. And we may note that each of the great religions, whether theistic or otherwise, commends humility over self-aggrandisement. For this reason alone, it is quite natural for those who have achieved most in the spiritual life to diminish their own importance and contribution. We may compare the mystic's sense of gratitude and humility with the lover's similar feelings upon winning the affections of the beloved. At one level, perhaps the rational level, he has gained this affection and her love for him can be interpreted properly as his achievement, and yet at another level, say the emotional level, her love for him is experienced as a gift, something he does not deserve.

This brings me to the second argument in Payne's positive case for the existence of a uniquely Christian form of mystical experience, namely, some Christian mystics, such as St John of the Cross, describe their experience in distinctively Christian terms.[53] Payne acknowledges that a proper distinction between experience and interpretation should be drawn in reports of mystical experience, but in his opinion when this is done there are recalcitrant elements in descriptions of some experiences that warrant the conclusion that there is a distinctively Christian form of mysticism.

According to Payne, certain mystics, and St John of the Cross in particular, 'enjoy states of contemplative awareness in which they feel themselves to be united with something which cannot be tasted, touched, smelled, seen or heard, but which seems personal, loving, powerful, creative and perhaps even triune'.[54] That is to say, there are mystical experiences 'which are in some sense intrinsically theistic (and even Christian) in their implications, and not merely interpreted as such'.[55] Now I think this is a rather idealised summary of St John's experience, but there is no need to debate the point. Let us simply accept that some Christians profess to enjoy union with a spiritual being who is per-sonal, loving and creative.[56] The terms employed here, initially at least, sound as if they are straightforwardly descriptive. Granted, they provide only a minimum description of God, but if they are rooted in experience, as Payne contends, then there would appear to be good grounds for concluding that there is a distinctively Christian, or at least a distinctively theistic, mystical experience.

Is Payne's suggestion that there are low-level descriptions of mystical experience that preserve a minimally Christian character convincing? The issue to be addressed is whether the mystic, in Payne's case, the Christian mystic, is in a position to know if the object experienced is loving, creative and personal.

The first thing to be said is that mystical experiences seem unlikely candidates for providing knowledge of a personal spirit who is clearly distinct from the human self, in that mystical experiences are unitive experiences: experiences in which the distinction between subject and object is overcome, or at least blurred. A mystical experience, by virtue of being a mystical experience, and not some other type of experience (say *numinous* for example), is an experience of union with some higher power, in which one's normal feeling of individuality and distinctiveness is transcended and removed. I'm not quite sure whether it actually makes sense to talk of an experience as simultaneously unitive (mystical) while preserving ... some sense ... of separateness from the object of the experience (being non-unitive!); and some degree of separateness would seem necessary if the object of mystical experience is to be regarded in any meaningful sense as a person or personal.

Let us approach the issue from another direction; this time focusing more on epistemic concerns. Christian and theistic mystics claim to experience God, or at least, according to Payne, they characteristically claim to experience a personal being distinct from the human self; thus providing a minimum content for Christian theism. Such a claim can be broken down into two parts (1) that mystical experience provides knowledge of a spiritual reality distinct from the self, and (2) this spiritual power or reality is personal in nature. Both issues are closely related and it is somewhat artificial to address one and not the other. However, for our purposes (2) is the crucial proposition. Let us simply grant that mystical experiences are cognitively meaningful, i.e. they provide knowledge of an objective sort of some super-sensible reality. But how do mystics know on the basis of their experience that this super-sensible reality is personal? When an experience is not clearly felt as external, and the usual criteria which determine whether one is in the company of another person (who is external) are not fulfilled, in that the object cannot be seen, touched, etc, how then do theistic mystics know that the object experienced is personal?

Mystical experience is within the self, not just in the sense that other persons similarly situated do not have the same experience, but in the additional sense that the professed object of mystical union is experienced as mystic's say 'in the deepest part of the soul'. In mystical rapture there is no sense of difference or distance between the human self and the divine self. Yet surely the notion of experiencing something as personal presupposes and requires some sense of distance and difference. Furthermore, mystical experience is quite unlike some other types of religious experience that could conceivably provide grounds for concluding that the divine is a person or is personal in some sense. For example, if a spiritual being delivered a verbal message to an individual, that individual might reason along the lines that only a person can communicate in this way, thus a person or a personal being has been experienced. (There is more to the identification of persons than this but what I have said is sufficient for illustrative purposes.) But mystical experiences are most certainly not like this: the deity remains mute. The peculiar nature of mystical experience effectively excludes the possibility that the mystic knows on the basis of the experience alone that the object experienced is personal or not.

This line of criticism can be extended to include other characteristics of the divine that some Christian mystics profess to know on the basis of mystical experience, for example that God is creative or loving. It is chiefly on the basis of such reports by mystics that Professor Payne concludes that Christian mysticism should be distinguished from other varieties of varieties. How could one know on the basis of mystical union that the experienced object was creative or loving? As St John of the Cross tells us, in common with all other mystics, mystical union is only possible when one has risen above discursive prayer, when there is absolute stillness within the self. Only when the mind is 'stripped of all knowledge', 'cleansed and emptied' of all 'distinct ideas and images' is the fullness/emptiness of mystical union achieved. St John describes this as 'imageless communion'. In a moment in time the infinite touches the finite; abstracted from the normal categories of though and mental discrimination the self is one with the divine; not two but one. The belief that God is personal and creative is based on other, less immediate sources than mystical experience.

Payne's appeal to the writings of St John of the Cross to establish the case for a distinctively Christian form of mystical experience is unsuccessful. Christian mystical experience is not distinguished in any phenomenological or philosophically important way from the mystical experiences of adherents of other religions.

Some writers may choose to view this negative conclusion with regard to *Christian* mystical experience in a positive light. It might be argued that mysticism witnesses to the existence of a spiritual presence in the universe. Such a position is compatible both with the truth of Christian theism and with the argument I have developed. The suspicion remains, however, that in achieving mystical union with God by one's own efforts, the realm of true religion has been forsaken in favour of 'another gospel'. The Christian gospel's elevation of what God has graciously done for us in Christ 'while we were yet sinners' stands in sharp contrast to the disciplined and rigorous following of the mystical path in order to gain an encounter with God. Moreover, if there is nothing distinctively *Christian* about Christian mysticism, then its denial as a form of Christian discipleship would not seem to deny anything that is distinctively Christian. We may simply dispense with Christian mysticism, at least in so far as it has a religious purpose or application.[57]

Notes

[1] Some writers maintain that mysticism provides the foundation for a new global, ecologically sensitive Christian ethic, e.g. Sean McDonagh, *To Care for*

the Earth (London: Geoffrey Chapman, 1986), who draws on Teilhard de Chardin's 'Christic' mysticism. Other writers maintain that mysticism provides the point of departure for a pluralist theology of religion that recognises God's grace and embrace within all the great religions, e.g. Eckard Wolz-Gottwald, 'Mysticism and Ecumenism: On the Question of Religious Identity in the Religious Dialogue,' *Journal of Ecumenical Studies* 32 (1995), 25–34; Wayne Teasdale, 'The Inter-Spiritual Age: Practical Mysticism for the Third Millennium,' *Journal of Ecumenical Studies* 34 (1997), 74–91.

[2] As witnessed by widespread interest in New Age mysticism.

[3] W.R. Inge, *Christian Mysticism* (London: Methuen & Co., 1899), 335–48.

[4] Karl Rahner, *Theological Investigations*, vol. 7 (London: Darton, Longman and Todd, 1971), 15.

[5] Richard Swinburne, *The Existence of God* (Oxford: Clarendon Press, 1979), 244–53; Rodney Stark, 'A Taxonomy of Religious Experience', in Bernard Spilka and Daniel N. McIntosh (eds.), *The Psychology of Religion* (Boulder, Colorado: Westview Press, 1997), 209–21; the former distinguishes religious experiences on a philosophical basis, the latter on a psychological basis.

[6] Cf. William J. Wainwright, *Mysticism* (London: Harvaster Press, 1981), 1.

[7] In some feminist circles it is currently fashionable to criticise interpretations of mysticism as covertly patriarchal; see Grace Jantzen, *Power, Gender and Christian Mysticism* (Cambridge: Cambridge University Press, 1995). No doubt there is evidence of this, and such bias is regrettable. My own definition and the interpretation of mysticism that follows is intended to be descriptive and neutral; I make no assumptions of male gender or Western superiority; on the latter see Richard King, *Orientalism and Religion: Postcolonial Theory, India and 'The Mystic East'* (London: Routledge, 1999), 7–34.

[8] This distinction was made in the early decades of this century by both G.J. Blewett and also Evelyn Underhill: G.J. Blewett, *The Study of Nature and the Vision of God* (Toronto: William Briggs, 1907), vii; Evelyn Underhill, *Mysticism* (London: Methuen, 1918), 83 and 149–77. It was taken up and developed in a much more systematic way by Rudolf Otto, *Mysticism East and West: A Comparative Analysis of the Nature of Mysticism* (New York: Macmillan, 1932).

[9] Quoted in William James, *The Varieties of Religious Experience* (London: Collins, 1960), 381.

[10] Ibid., 371.

[11] Stace, *Mysticism and Philosophy* (London: Macmillan, 1961), 55–62.

[12] Ninian Smart, 'Interpretation and Mystical Experience', *Religious Studies* 1 (1965), 75–87, particularly 76.

[13] James Horne, *Beyond Mysticism*, Canadian Corporation for Studies in Religion, Supplement 6 (Ontario: Wilfrid Laurier University Press, 1978), 24.

[14] The experienced unity with the world and the objects of the world that characterises extrovertive or exterior mystical experiences is frequently interpreted

by mystics as giving support to pantheism; see Nils Bjorn Kvastad, *Problems of Mysticism* (Oslo: Scintilla Press, 1980), 282–305. One can appreciate the force of this contention even if one remains sceptical regarding the (metaphysical) truth of pantheism.

[15] Stace, *Mysticism and Philosophy*, 62–3. Cf. Ninian Smart in *The Yogi and the Devotee* (London: Allen and Unwin, 1968) remarks that he wishes to reserve the term 'mystical' only for cases of introvertive (what he calls interior) mysticism, thus depreciating the importance of extrovertive experience, 66.

[16] R.C. Zaehner, *Mysticism: Sacred and Profane* (London: Oxford University Press, 1961), 153–74, et passim.

[17] This is the title of Katz's contribution to *Mysticism and Religious Traditions* (Oxford: Oxford University Press, 1983), 3–60, a collection of essays he also edited. His earlier essay 'Language, Epistemology and Mysticism', in Steven T. Katz (ed.), *Mysticism and Philosophical Analysis* (London: Sheldon Press, 1978), 22–74, has been equally influential.

[18] There are clearly difficulties with this conclusion, for it seems to exclude the possibility of novelty in religion on the basis of mystical experience. Are there not occasions when mystical experiences challenge an individual's existing religious framework of beliefs? The example of the Buddha would be relevant here. On the basis of mystical experience he concluded that there is no enduring self or substance underlying appearances that persists through time. This doctrine of *anatta* (literally 'no-self'), which is distinctive of Buddhism, owes its origin to Gautama's Enlightenment experience.

[19] Substantial and sophisticated philosophical objections to Katz's 'hyper-Kantian' account of mysticism have been pursued by J. William Forgie, 'Hyper-Kantianism in Recent Discussions of Mystical Expereince,' *Religious Studies* 21 (1985), 205–18; William J. Wainwright, *Mysticism* (Brighton: Harvester Press, 1981), 19–22; Sallie B. King, 'Two Epistemological Models for the Interpretation of Mysticism,' *Journal of the American Academy of Religion* 56 (1988), 257–79; and Nelson Pike, *Mystic Union* (Ithaca: Cornell University Press, 1992), 194–207.

[20] The denial that such a distinction can be drawn is at the heart of Katz's interpretation of mysticism.

[21] Ibid., 66.

[22] Ibid., 37.

[23] Stace, *Mysticism and Philosophy*, 37.

[24] According to Stace, what is experienced, because it is free from interpretation, can be known with certainty, whereas interpretations, being one step removed from direct experience, are 'always liable to be mistaken'. This manner of speaking was common among empiricist philosophers (of whom Stace is one) up to the late 1950s, who held that the straight-forward description of experience in terms of sensory impressions could attain the character of knowledge in a way

excluded to the object judgement (as interpretation) based upon such sensory impressions. This distinction, as generally applicable to human perception and experiencing, can no longer be sustained, chiefly for reasons set out by the Oxford philosopher, John Austin, in his *Sense and Sensibilia* (Oxford: Clarendon Press, 1962). If mystical experience has a privileged epistemic position it is not to be found in some kind of appeal to indubitable experience over against dubitable conceptual interpretation.

[25] Donald Evans, 'Can Philosophers limit what Mystics can do? A Critique of Stephen Katz', *Religious Studies* 25 (1989), 53–60; Robert K.C. Forman (ed.), *The Problem of Pure Consciousness* (New York: Oxford University Press, 1990), and the same author's *Mysticism, Mind, Consciousness* (New York: State University of New York Press, 1999).

[26] From this point on I shall employ both the terminology of experience and interpretation, and of low-level and high-level interpretations in order to express the distinction between experiential and extra-experiential content. In other words my use of terms is not meant to indicate any particular epistemological commitment, be it Kantian or otherwise, or to foreclose discussion on the precise nature of mystical experience, whether it be pure consciousness, or mediated consciousness, or whatever. Use of the terms is simply a convenient shorthand for a distinction between experiential or phenomenological content and extra-experiential content.

[27] The use of masculine pronouns in referring to God should not be interpreted to mean that God is of the male gender and that 'maleness' can be attributed to him. Equally my use of masculine pronouns is intended to be neutral with regard to the roles and functions of either sex both in the church and in society.

[28] Cf. Diogenes Allen, *Philosophy for Understanding Theology* (London: SCM Press, 1985), 1–14.

[29] Stace, *Mysticism and Philosophy*, 41–133.

[30] The best single source on the essential similarity of the various mystical paths is Daniel Goleman, *The Varieties of Meditative Experience* (New York: Irvington Publishers, 1977).

[31] This is sometimes called the enstatic method or technique; 'enstasy' in its precise etymological sense means 'standing within' or 'withdrawal'; see Mircea Eliade, *Yoga: Immortality and Freedom*, Princeton, Princeton University, 1969, 79–85; 162–99; and 395–8.

[32] As does Smart, in 'Interpretation and Mystical Experience', 75, and W.L. Reese, in *Dictionary of Philosophy and Religion* (New Jersey: Humanities Press, 1980), 374.

[33] *The Life of Moses*, tr. A. Malherbe & E. Ferguson (New York: Paulist Press, 1978), 95.

[34] Enneads, Bk. 6.9.11, tr. S. MacKenna (London: Faber & Faber 1956).

[35] Sarvepalli Radhakrishnan & Charles A. Moore (eds.), *A Source Book in Indian Philosophy* (Princeton, Princeton University Press, 1957), 337.

[36] Ibid., 42.

[37] W.T. Stace, *The Teaching of the Mystics* (New York: New American Library, 1960), 13.

[38] See N. Burton, et al, (eds.), *The Asian Journal of Thomas Merton* (New York: New Directions, 1973), 143–4, for example.

[39] B. Griffiths, *The Marriage of East and West* (London: Collins, 1982), and *Return to the Centre* (London: Collins, 1976).

[40] W. Johnston, *Silent Music* (London: Collins, 1974), and *The Inner Eye of Love* (London: Collins, 1978).

[41] S. Payne, *John of the Cross and the Cognitive Value of Mysticism: An Analysis of Sanjuanist Teaching and its Philosophical Implications for Contemporary Discussions of Mystical Experience* (Dordrecht: Kluwer Academic Publishers, 1990).

[42] Ibid., 91.

[43] This approach of basing one's interpretation of mysticism on a very detailed and close analysis of a small body of mystical literature or of confining one's attention to a single text or author is not entirely novel. Some years ago, the British philosophical theologian, H.P. Owen, reached conclusions very similar to Payne's on the basis of a study of Walter Hilton's mysticism; see H.P. Owen's 'Christian Mysticism: A Study in Walter Hilton's *The Ladder of Perfection*', *Religious Studies* 7 (1971), 31–42. Further back still, in the 1930s, Rudolf Otto based his interpretation of mysticism on a systematic comparison of the writings of the Hindu mystic Shankara and the Christian mystic Meister Eckhart, *Mysticism East and West* (New York: Macmillan, 1932).

[44] Payne, *John of the Cross*, xiii.

[45] James, *Varieties*, 372.

[46] Payne, *John of the Cross*, 104.

[47] Ibid., 105–6.

[48] Ibid., 106.

[49] Ibid., 105.

[50] Stace, *Teaching of the Mystics*, 61.

[51] Vol. 9 (Grand Rapids, Michigan: Eerdmans, 1974), 359, n.180.

[52] A reliable guide both to Paul's doctrine of justification by grace through faith in Christ and to the relevant secondary literature is Mark A. Seifrid, *Justification by Faith: The Origin and Development of a Central Pauline Theme* (Leiden: E.J. Brill, 1992).

[53] Relevant quotations from St John's works are included by Payne on 27, 28, 32, et passim.

[54] Payne, *John of the Cross*, 115.

[55] Ibid.

[56] I do not intend taking seriously Payne's suggestion, no doubt accepted on the word of certain mystics, that in some forms of mystical union all three Persons of the 'Most Blessed Trinity' are experienced (114). In the first place this is a high level-interpretation which clearly goes beyond any kind of knowledge mystical experience could provide. Secondly, does it make sense to speak of experiencing each member of the Godhead? Can God the Father be experienced in isolation from the Son and the Spirit, so that one can claim knowledge of him alone. Surely the Patristic doctrine of *Perichoresis* excludes such a possibility.

[57] I would like to thank Professor John Gaskin for written comments on an earlier version of this essay.

16

Mysticism

The Perennial Philosophy?

Dewi Arwel Hughes

Defining mysticism is not an easy task. Already at the end of the nineteenth century Dean Inge listed twenty-six definitions.[1] A century later the number of definitions has multiplied as mysticism has become a popular subject on the information super highway with over seventeen thousand references in a basic search and well over a million in a more detailed search on the world wide web. Rufus Jones writing early in the twentieth century in his introductory article in the *Encyclopaedia of Religion and Ethics* distinguished mysticism as a metaphysical teaching from 'mystical experience'. He argued that the term mysticism should be confined to the 'historic *doctrine* of the relationship and potential union of the human soul with Ultimate Reality.' 'Mystical experience' on the other hand refers to the claim of many religious people to a direct experience of Ultimate Reality. The article in the more recent *Encyclopedia of Religion* edited by Mircea Eliade, while approving William James' description of mysticism as a religious experience that is ineffable, noetic, passive and transient, views mysticism in the more general terms of Jones' 'mystical experience'.[2] On reflection it seems difficult to draw a hard line between any claim to direct experience of Ultimate Reality and the doctrine that an individual and Ultimate Reality are one reality. The two definitions seem to be different points on the same continuum. It is safer, therefore, to understand 'mysticism' as including both the doctrine of union and what Jones calls 'mystical experience'.

More fundamental to this paper than the issue of definition is the issue of *why* mysticism has come to be seen as the essence of religion. This is the main theme of the chapter.

Ever since the pioneers of the Enlightenment declared that they were free from any external religious authority the nature of freedom has become problematic in modern thought. The problem is twofold. On the one hand, the models of nature created by modern science has a tendency to capture the human in a deterministic system and, on the other, the resistance to this threat creates problems with regard to the content of human freedom.

The ground rules as to how to cope with this Enlightenment dilemma were laid down by Kant. He believed that he had created an unassailable defence against determinism by reducing nature to a phenomenon. In the realm of pure reason what can be known of nature is defined by the categories of the understanding which are human constructs. Then as a second tier he defined the nature of freedom by means of the practical reason where human beings are free to follow the moral imperative which will ultimately lead them to God. Freedom was ensured by Kant's idealism which made science a free creation of the human mind and which ensured that human beings are free to make moral choices.

Kant's concept of the practical reason was the most sophisticated statement of the deistic idea of rational religion that originated with Herbert of Cherbury in seventeenth-century England. Dogmatically minimalist and devoid of emotion it was *par excellence* a religion of the will. As such it was at the opposite end of the religious spectrum from mysticism with its emphasis on direct experience of the transcendent.

Kant typifies the postmodern view of modernity at its source in the Enlightenment. His seemingly unbounded confidence in the power of reason to master nature for the good of humanity, free from the constraint of ecclesiastical authority, and his optimism that, despite his recognition of the reality of evil, human beings can freely choose to do what is right by each other, witness to his commitment to the metanarrative of modernity. But he was not the only voice of the Enlightenment period. In fact there is a tension inherent within the Enlightenment idea of nature and freedom which makes it impossible for Kant's rationalism to be its only voice.[3] My thesis is that the attraction to mysticism as the perennial philosophy is characteristic of this other voice of the Enlightenment or modernity. Interestingly, the 'mystical' voice also seems to be something of the voice of postmodernity which suggests that postmodernity may be just another phase in the tension between nature and freedom that is endemic to Western thought since the Enlightenment.

For Kant the application of his analysis of the natural world by means of the categories of the pure reason meant a mechanistic view of nature. This is because at that time Isaac Newton was the dominant figure and physics the dominant science.[4] As stated above, Kant's genius was to formulate a powerful argument for the non-inclusion of human beings in the machine of nature – something which Boyle, Newton and other great pioneers of the scientific revolution had taken for granted. However, both his defence of human freedom from the threat of determinism and his rational religion meant that the door was left open for his successors to be more mystical in their approach to nature and the life of the spirit.

Already in Kant's lifetime the mechanistic model of nature was coming under attack from Romanticism. As reflected back into life and art, nature as machine made life very linear, structured, disciplined, and cold. The emphasis was on analysis and mastery. While accepting that this approach had a place, and rejoicing in its technological benefits, the Romantics believed that nature should be experienced as well as analysed. Herder, a contemporary and acquaintance of Kant, saw nature as an organism developing through history and reaching its apex in human self-consciousness – and the climax of human self-consciousness is to respond with warmth to the glory of the totality of things. His approach, which is typical of the Romantics is expressed in one of his poems:

> 'I   am   not   here   to   think!   –   To   be!   To   feel!
> To live! And to rejoice!⁵

Reflecting his Pietistic upbringing and the influence of Romantic aesthetics Schleiermacher, 'the father of modern theology,' found the original religious impulse, not in the will (morality) or the reason (doctrine) but in the emotions. He believed that human beings in reflecting on their individual lives in relation to everything that is other than themselves, experience a feeling of absolute dependence. According to Schleiermacher,

> there are three grades of self-consciousness: the confused animal
> grade, in which the antithesis cannot arise, as the lowest; the sensi-
> ble self-consciousness, which rests entirely upon the antithesis, as
> the middle; and the feeling of absolute dependence, in which the
> antithesis again disappears and the subject unites and identifies itself
> with everything which, in the middle grade, was set over against it,
> as the highest.⁶

In this quote from the introductory section of *The Christian Faith*, Schleiermacher describes the core religious impulse, that is at the root of all historical religions, as an experience of unity – of the One or the All. This is unquestionably a mystical conception of religion.⁷ So, at the fountainhead of modern liberal theology, mysticism is central. As an aside it may also be seen as rather ironic that the place where human beings are free from the tyranny of deterministic nature is a feeling of absolute dependence!

In England, Samuel Taylor Coleridge was responsible for turning theology in a mystical direction. As a student he had rejected the Christianity of his youth, but his friendship with Wordsworth with whom he spent fourteen months in Germany in 1798–9, where be became acquainted with Kant and German romantic literature, brought him back eventually into the bosom of the Church of England. Wordsworth re-awakened in him 'a sense of God in all and all in God, a faith in the divine spiritual activity as the ground of all existence.' He now made it his aim 'to elevate the imagination and set the affections in right tune by the beauty of the inanimate impregnated as with a living soul by the presence of life.' What impressed him in Wordsworth was 'above all the original gift of spreading the tone, the *atmosphere* and with it the depth and height of the ideal world around forms, incidents and situations, of which... custom had bedimmed all the lustre, had dried up the sparkle and the dewdrops.'[8] So much for Wordsworth's nature mysticism.[9]

Coleridge then encountered Kant and embraced his idealism. The empirically directed aspect of Kant's pure reason becomes the Understanding while the intuitive apprehension of abstract truth such as the truths of mathematics becomes speculative Reason. As for Kant the practical Reason is the source of religion. This Reason, with a capital R, is for Coleridge that of the divine, the *Logos*, that dwells in every human being. It is 'the Power of Universal and necessary Convictions, the Source and Substance of Truths above Sense.'[10] Coleridge is very glad to embrace Kant's emphasis on the freedom of the will in this realm of the Reason because of his almost pathological hatred of scientific determinism, but his ideas owe more to Platonic mysticism than to Kant. His interpretation of the fall of Adam and Eve illustrates this.

Adam represents the will as enlightened by the Reason which is the higher element in a human being. Eve represents the desire for the sensuous, the animal nature. The Serpent is the Understanding, '... the wily tempter to evil by counterfeit good: the pander and advocate of the passions and appetites; ever in league with and always first applying to the *Desire* as the inferior nature in man, the *woman* in our humanity and through the Desire prevailing on the WILL, the Man-hood, *Virtus*, against the command of the universal reason and against the light of reason in the WILL itself.' He does, however, draw back from a fully gnostic position:

> It is the same Adam that falls in every man, and from the same
> reluctance to abandon the too dear and undivorceable Eve, and
> the same Eve tempted by the same serpentine and perverted

understanding, which, framed originally to be the interpreter of the
reason and the ministering angel of the Spirit, is henceforth sen-
tenced and bound over to the service of the Animal Nature, its
needs and its cravings, dependent on the senses for all its materials,
with the World of Sense for its appointed sphere.[11]

Coleridge follows Schleiermacher in his belief that words belong to the
realm of the Understanding. Language belongs to the world of differentiation and can only point to the unity that is intuitively grasped by the
Reason. So, the Bible is a special revelation only to the extent that it
answers to the inward light of the Word or *Logos*:

> And what though my reason be to the power and splendour of the
> Scriptures but as the reflected and secondary shine of the moon as
> compared with the solar radiance: and yet the sun endures the
> occasional co-presence of the unsteady orb, and leaving it visible
> seems to sanction the comparison. There is a Light higher than all,
> even the Word that was in the beginning ... the Word that is light
> for every man, and life for as many as give heed to it.[12]

The primary reality is the indwelling Word or Reason which can only
be discovered by intuition. The biblical authors were no exception to
this rule. Their genius is that they experienced the Word more than others. The Bible's value is as a rich collection of evocations of the
Word/Reason. Its value is its ability to evoke similar experiences.
'Whatever *finds* me,' says Coleridge, 'bears witness for itself that it has
proceeded from a Holy Spirit, even from the same Spirit *which remaining in itself, yet regenerateth all other powers, and in all ages entering into holy
souls maketh them friends of God and prophets*.'[13]

   The core of religion is the mystical contemplation of the One.
However, this experience necessarily externalises itself so Religion in all
ages has an objective, historic or ecclesiastical pole. The objective aspect
of the Christian expression of this Religion is found in the Bible,
Christian dogma and tradition. Other historic religions contain different
evocations of the same Religion. For Coleridge, and Schleiermacher
before him, and many after both, the difference between the Christian
and other evocations of Religion is not a matter of essence, but of quality. For the purposes of this paper the significant fact is that Religion as
defined by Coleridge is a form of unitive mysticism:

> Revealed Religion (and I know of no religion not revealed) is
> in its highest contemplation the unity, that is, the identity or

co-inherence, of Subjective and Objective. It is in itself, and irreli-
tively, at once inward Life and Truth, and outward Fact and
Luminary. But as all Power manifests itself in the harmony of
correspondent Opposites, each supposing and supporting the other
– so has Religion its objective, or historic and ecclesiastical pole,
and its subjective, or spiritual and individual pole.[14]

Kant's location of the primordial religious impulse in the conscience
made his view of religion antipathetic to mysticism but his idealism left
the door open for Schleiermacher to resort to feeling as the door to
freedom. Coleridge attempted to combine Kant's moral emphasis and
the Romantic emphasis on feeling. Both their views of religion are
essentially mystical. Hegel, on the other hand, attempted a comprehensive synthesis with the emphasis on mind rather than emotion or will.
He did find a place for feeling in his delineation of the development of
the consciousness of spirit but at the primary level. Commenting on
Schleiermacher's view that the feeling of absolute dependence is the
heart of religion – and Schleiermacher was a fellow Professor at the
University of Berlin at the time – he said that if that was the case then
his dog was the most religious creature known to him![15]

Hegel saw the whole history of the human race as the history of the
development of the notion of the Absolute. What the Absolute is, is the
meaning of the whole process of history. First, there is the Absolute in
itself – the Absolute as subject. Secondly, the Absolute empties itself and
becomes the other – the Absolute as object. Finally, the Absolute returns
to itself – the Absolute as the unity of Subject–Object. Applied to the
development of religion, given the all-pervasive triadic form of his
thought, there are two main types or stages in the process of actualising
the notion of religion before it reaches its climax and fulfilment in what
he calls 'The Revelatory or Consummate Religion'. The two prepara-
tory stages are 'Natural Religion' and 'The Religion of Spiritual
Individuality.'

To the stage of *natural religion* belongs the belief that all things are
immediately indwelt by spirits. Included in this category are magic or
shamanism, Chinese state religion, Buddhism, Hinduism, Persian
(Zoroastrian) and Egyptian religion. What is common here is that there
is no clear distinction between Spirit and nature with the result that no
clear notion of 'God' develops. However, the belief that the spiritual per-
vades nature proves that even natural religion is a moment in the process
of the actualisation of the notion of religion.

At the level of 'The Religion of Spiritual Individuality' we have
Jewish, Greek and Roman religion. It is with the Jews that the idea of

'God' first becomes actual, though the emphasis here is on the otherness or transcendence and independence of God – the sublime Subject before whom men bow. In Greek religion, on the other hand, the emphasis is very much on the immanence of the Spirit. That said, whereas in 'Natural Religion' this immanence of Spirit develops into the amorphous pantheism of Hinduism and Buddhism, in Greek religion we have an anthropomorphous polytheism. Whereas in the Eastern traditions the Spirit has no definite shape, in ancient Greece the gods were given very definite human shapes. These gods in human form, argued Hegel, are 'projections or representations of the *implicit* divinity of the human spirit.' Thus we come to the 'Revelatory or Consummate Religion' which is Christianity, as interpreted by Hegel. The notion of Christianity, which is also the notion of religion as such, is that the Spirit which is Absolute love divests itself of its transcendence and becomes actual in human experience and so, enriched, it returns to itself.[16]

Hegel's philosophy was described as 'higher pantheism' in the nineteenth century because it clearly implies that the story of all human ideas and thought is equivalent to the story of the Absolute. The sum total of human thought in all its cultural expression is 'God'. Notionally this philosophy approximates to unitive mysticism. Because the system is intellectual the unitive experience was not a matter of emotion, but a matter of knowledge – *gnosis*. In this sense it is nearer to Rufus Jones' limited definition of mysticism as the doctrine of the individual soul's unity with Absolute Reality.

Friedrich Max Müller, who is generally regarded as one of the founding fathers of what we now call 'Religious Studies' or 'the Study of Religion', brings together the themes that we have seen in Kant, Schleiermacher, Coleridge and Hegel in his four series of Gifford Lectures delivered in Glasgow between 1888 and 1892. They were published as four volumes entitled *Natural Religion*, *Physical Religion*, *Anthropological Religion* and *Theosophy or Psychological Religion*.

In *Natural Religion*, as the title suggests, Müller examines religion as an essential aspect of human life. First of all, he attempts to define it before going on to argue for its development through history. His final definition is that 'religion consists in the perception of the infinite under such manifestations as are able to influence the moral character of man.'[17] This is a 'romantic' definition of religion with which Schleiermacher and Coleridge would have been well pleased. It is also a 'mystical' definition with a dash of Kantian moralism.[18] It asserts that simply in the act of perceiving diversity human beings have the capacity to see beyond into an infinite unity. Obviously 'seeing' or 'perceiving' the infinite is not the same as 'seeing' or 'perceiving' the trees and hedgerows of the Wye valley – it is more like seeing its beauty, the experience or feeling that is engendered by the total effect.

Human beings have also attempted to communicate their perception of the infinite. The best record of this communication, according to Müller, is found in the scriptures of the world's religions. Since there can only be one infinite and since everything is subject to the law of progressive development or evolution then a comparison of the content of the scriptures will expose the essence of religion. This is what Müller attempted in the following three series of Gifford Lectures.

The title of the second series was *Physical Religion*.[19] Here he developed in detail the idea that in perceiving the world around them human beings sense that its meaning is not exhausted by what is apparent to the senses. Historically this sense has taken human beings in two directions. First, they have conceived of the infinite as immanent in nature and second as transcendent above nature. So what was under review in this series was the development of the idea of 'God' as Object. The third series was entitled *Anthropological Religion*.[20] Here he explored the idea of the divine as immanent within human beings, the idea of the soul or self. This is the development of the idea of 'God' as Subject.

In the final series called *Theosophy or Psychological Religion*[21] he brought the themes of the previous two series together and attempted to show how the two currents described in them meet in the end in 'the perception of the essential unity of the soul with God.' It is interesting that when he arrives at the pinnacle of his theory, it is to the *Logos* theology of the early church and to mediaeval Christian mysticism that he turns as the most satisfactory expression of this unity. He believed that it was the application of the Greek concept of the *Logos* to the undeveloped ideas of early Christianity by Clement and Origen that gave to Christianity its high position among the religions. As the Greeks had developed it the *Logos* came to mean the Reason of God manifested in the phenomenal world. In Plato's idea of the origin of species this Reason or *Logos* became the universal idea in the mind of the Infinite which is realised in individual phenomena. Plato's idea was fulfilled when transplanted by Alexandrian theologians into Christian soil and the idea of the *Logos* or Reason became personalised in Jesus of Nazareth. Jesus' significance is that he is a living embodiment of the unity of the human and the divine. According to Müller the Alexandrian tradition reached its fulfilment in the German mystical tradition as exemplified by Meister Eckhart. His conclusion is that mysticism is the perennial philosophy, but that Christian mysticism is the best example of it.

Müller's star soon waned after he had delivered his Gifford Lectures. No one who dared to raise a protest, as he did, against the evolutionary theory of the social Darwinists in late nineteenth-century Britain had any hope of survival. As far as the study of the world's religions are concerned, the positivist anthropologists were now in the ascendancy. It is one of those strange episodes in the story of Religious Studies when the study of religion came to be dominated by those who believed that religion had no future because it belonged to a more primitive stage of human development. In the wider context of the break with Christian tradition that had been made in the Enlightenment, positivism represents the radical humanistic end of the spectrum. Here 'man' really is the measure of all things. There is no need to bring God, the Absolute or Spirit into the picture at all. In fact history witnesses to the gradual disappearance of these unnecessary props from the human drama. But as the pendulum was swinging very strongly in the direction of materialistic determinism there was a spate of interest in factors that pulled it in the other direction.

We are now in the period when the Theosophical Society and the Society for Psychical Research were flourishing. It was also a period of intense interest in magic as exemplified by Aleister Crowley and his associates. On a more academic plane Rudolf Otto was defending the integrity of religious experience against materialistic scientism by reapplying and refining the arguments of Kant and Schleiermacher. Not surprisingly there was also a spate of works on mysticism, the most significant being W.R. Inge's *Christian Mysticism* (1899), von Hügel's *The Mystical Element of Religion* (1908), Rufus Jones' *Studies in Mystical Religion* (1908) and Evelyn Underhill's *Mysticism* (1911). More surprising is the interest shown in mysticism by those who on the face of it belonged to the positivist camp.

R.R. Marett, the pupil and successor of the positivist founder of anthropology E.B. Tylor, was a pioneer of Social Anthropology in England. But in proposing pre-animism as a more primordial stage in the evolution of religion than Tylor's animism, he deliberately set out to undermine the positivist approach of his mentor. He thought that the 'the problem of freedom versus necessity is the most fundamental of philosophical difficulties.'[22] The solution is found in religion because it is there that it becomes apparent that human beings find some power which is greater than themselves that enables them to transcend necessity and do what is right. This power is drawn upon not through a process of reasoning, but through the emotions especially as stirred in communal activity. This is what he means in his famous statement that 'savage religion is not so much thought out as danced out.'[23] Like Otto he recognises that the religious emotion is inevitably expressed in thought, but he questions 'whether it be but a form of idolatry to deem "the peace of God" reducible to any system of thought symbols; since just as the invisible does not lend itself to picturing, so the ineffable is not containable in any construction of words.'[24] Marett, the social anthropologist, here expresses clearly a mystical view of religion so it is not surprising that Evans-Pritchard called him a classical philosopher.[25] In fact it was as a philosopher that he had become a fellow of Exeter College, Oxford and he did not forget what he had absorbed as a student of the Hegelian idealist philosopher Edward Caird when his focus moved to anthropology.

More significant than that of the anthropologists is the interest of psychologists in mysticism during this period.[26] Most impressive in this context is William James' *The Varieties of Religious Experience* which was first published in 1902 and which has been in print throughout this century.[27] James classed himself with those of his contemporary American psychologists such as Leuba, Starbuck and Coe who were seeking to apply scientific methods of research to religious experience. He regarded himself as a radical empiricist and this is apparent, for example, in his acceptance of Starbuck's conclusion that 'conversion is in its essence a normal adolescent phenomenon', or in his suggestion that 'the whole phenomenon of regeneration (may)... possibly be a strictly natural process'. He accepts Coe's conclusion in *The Spiritual Life* that scientific predictability is valid for religious conversion.[28]

However, James is at pains even from his first lecture to deny that he is a materialist even to the extent of ridiculing the type of materialism which 'finishes up Saint Paul by calling his vision on the road to Damascus a discharging lesion of the occipital cortex, he being an epileptic.'[29] His escape route from the inevitable pressure of materialism on one committed to radical empiricism is the subliminal mind – what is now called the unconscious. James believed that the publication of an article by F.W.H. Myers entitled 'The Subliminal Self' in the *Proceedings of the Society for Psychical Research* (1886) marked the discovery of the subliminal realm of the human personality. It was Myers' interest in survival after death that led him to the study of paranormal phenomena such as telepathy and clairvoyance and eventually to a subliminal self.[30] James is nervous about welcoming wholeheartedly Myers' supernatural concept of the subliminal. He is prepared to declare that, 'Psychology and religion are thus in perfect harmony ... since both admit that there are forces seemingly outside of the conscious individual that bring redemption to his life', but he goes on to say that, 'Nevertheless psychology, defining these forces as 'subconscious' ... implies that they do not transcend the individual's personality.'[31] Even so he is prepared to admit that if there is a window in the human personality looking out on

to a spiritual world that that window must be located in the unconscious. 'Just as our primary wide-awake consciousness throws open our
senses to the touch of things material,' he says, 'so it is logically conceivable that if there be higher spiritual agencies that can directly touch us,
the psychological condition of their doing so might be our possession
of an unconscious region which alone should yield access to them.'[32]

If the existence of the unconscious is established through the study of
irrational or supra-rational human experiences such as telepathy and
clairvoyance, or the fantasies and hallucinations of insane people, the evidence of its impact in the context of religion will be found in those
religious practises that lay claim to direct experience of that which lies
beyond the individual self. According to James there are clear intimations
of this in the experience of conversion and saintliness. But the clearest
evidence is found in mysticism. He lists four marks of a mystical experience. First, *ineffability*. 'Mystical states are more like states of feeling than
like states of intellect.' Secondly, they have a *noetic* quality. Mystics claim
to have passed beyond theory to knowledge. Mystical states are 'illuminations, revelations, full of significance and importance, all inarticulate
though they remain.' Thirdly, *transiency*. Mystic states do not last for long
but a memory of them persists which can be built on from one state to
the next. Fourthly, is *passivity*. Once the mystic consciousness has set in
'the mystic feels as if his own will were in abeyance, and indeed sometimes as if he were grasped and held by a superior power.'[33] James is
agnostic about the nature of the 'superior power' but is emphatic about
the subliminal as the door to experiencing it and it is the mystics who
have the best access. Because they are 'persons deep in the religious life
... the door into this region seems unusually wide open' to them.[34]

In his view of the source of religion in emotional experience James is
very much in the tradition of Schleiermacher. Even his motivation of preserving a place for religion from the threat of rationalism is the same. In a
letter to Miss F.R. Morse he stated that his aim in *The Varieties of Religious
Experience* was, 'first, to defend "experience" against "philosophy" as being
the real backbone of the world's religious life ... and second, to make the
hearer or reader believe, that I myself invincibly believed that, although all
the special manifestations of religion may have been absurd (I mean its
creeds and theories), yet the life of it as a whole is mankind's most important function.'[35] The innovation is that he locates the access to mystical
states in the subliminal or unconscious strata of the human personality.
Others have been very happy to follow him along this path.

C.G. Jung not only thought that the unconscious is the source of
mystical experience, but claimed to know this as a fact because of his
own personal experiences and what he considered scientific research. As

a therapist his route to the issue was dictated by his interest in ESP inherited from his mother and his experience with his patients which he supplemented with extensive study of various religious traditions. When asked in a television interview towards the end of his life whether he believed in God he answered, 'I know that God exists. I don't need to believe, I *know*.'[36]

It may be an example of the perverse Western desire for ratiocination to ask what Jung meant when he said that he knew God exists, but it is a fair question. In the context of Jung's understanding of the structure of human personality 'God' or the 'God-image' appears in his list of archetypes of the collective unconscious. He believed that the human personality is made up of three levels – the conscious mind, the personal unconscious and the collective unconscious. The collective unconscious which is the psychic residual of human evolutionary development as a whole is the most powerful and influential part of the system. The archetypes arise from this realm and impact the personal unconscious and the conscious mind for good or ill. An individual's mental health depends on the way the upsurge of these archetypes are handled.

Jung became conscious of the collective unconscious after he had broken with Freud in 1913. For almost four years he was in what can only be described as a very neurotic state. During that time a visionary figure called Philemon appeared to him. He described him later in Indian mystical terms as a sort of spirit guru. It was Philemon who convinced him that there are things in the psyche (the human personality) which are not produced by the individual. 'Philemon,' Jung says, 'represented a force which was not myself.'[37] During this time he also encountered the *anima* archetype, which was the feminine in him, who tempted him to forsake science. However, he resisted her because, 'In the final analysis the decisive factor is always consciousness, which can understand the manifestations of the unconscious, and take up a position towards them.'[38] He came out of the darkness when he broke with the *anima* and understood the significance of the *mandala* drawings.

The *mandala* is a circular drawing that is divided into quarters by a cross which passes through the centre of the circle and was used in the ritual and meditation of tantric Hinduism and Buddhism. Jung came to a mystical understanding that it represents the archetype of the Self – which is the ultimate archetype. What Jung meant by knowing that God exists in his television interview was probably his personal experience of the Self. 'I knew,' he says in his autobiography, 'that in finding the *mandala* as an expression of the self I had attained what was for me the ultimate.'[39] What the archetype of the self means is total integration of the psyche a wholeness that integrates good and evil, light and darkness.[40]

Jung ranges far and wide through the world of mysticism, the esoteric and the occult but throughout he presents his material in term of 'scientific facts' – a phrase which appears regularly in his works. The collective unconscious is not some ideal realm but the biological inheritance of the race. So the 'archetypes are the unconscious images of the instincts... they are the patterns of instinctual behaviour.' 'The concept of the collective unconscious,' he claims, 'is neither speculative nor philosophical but an empirical matter.'[41] Whether Jung can be taken seriously as an empirical scientist or not is not relevant here. What is relevant is his conviction that what he believed to be empirical research led to the discovery in the collective unconscious of that realm that transcends individual limitations which had always been expressed in the world's mythologies and mystical traditions.

It is interesting that Jung saw his discovery as a return to myth and mystery which had been suppressed since the onset of the Enlightenment. He saw the ascendancy of Hitler (I presume) in 1933 as a critical year in the re-emergence of myth and mystery:

> until 1933 only lunatics would have been found in possession of living fragments of mythology. After this date the world of heroes and monsters spread like devastating fire over whole nations, proving that the strange world of myth had suffered no loss of vitality during the centuries of reason and enlightenment. If metaphysical ideas no longer have such a fascinating effect as before, this is certainly not due to any lack of primitivity in the European psyche, but simply and solely to the fact that the erstwhile symbols no longer express what is now welling up from the unconscious as the end-result of the development of Christian consciousness through the centuries. This end-result is a true. ... false spirit of arrogance, hysteria, woolly-mindedness, criminal amorality, and doctrinaire fanaticism, a purveyor of shoddy spiritual goods, spurious art, philosophical stutterings, and Utopian humbug fit only to be fed wholesale to the mass man of today. That is what the post-Christian spirit looks like.'[42]

In the light of the emergence of the New Age this passage sounds prophetic. Where Jung himself is concerned the need to rediscover the significance of pre-enlightenment mystical symbolism was clearly a messianic crusade.

To complete our brief study of the fascination with the 'perennial philosophy' in the context of psychology we turn to Abraham Maslow. His major contribution to psychology was to shift its focus from the sick to the healthy personality. His hierarchy of needs is still used, particularly in education and management theory,[43] even though his definition of the pinnacle of the hierarchy, self-actualisation, has been called into question. That he placed the fulfilment of the self at the apex of human needs makes him one of the prophets of our time.

Like Jung he saw his work in messianic term. He was a typical post-Enlightenment person in seeing science as the saviour of humanity. In a paper delivered in Nebraska in 1955 he said that 'he was concerned with man's fate, with his ends and goals and with his future. I would like to help improve him,' he went on. 'I hope to help teach him how to be brotherly, co-operative, peaceful, courageous and just. I think science is the best hope for achieving this, and of all the sciences, I consider psychology most important to this end. Indeed, I sometimes think that the world will either be saved by psychologists – in the very broadest sense – or else it will not be saved at all.'[44]

It is intriguing that this atheistic psychologist became fascinated by mysticism as he developed his theory of self-actualisation. He noticed that the most self-actualised people were those who had most, what he called, 'peak experiences'. These experiences could only be described in terms of transcendence – they lifted the individual to a sense of time-lessness and intense joy and peace which was way above normal existence. He noticed that mystics were good at these experiences. So the atheist psychologist took to reading authors like Krishnamurti, Alan Watts and Mircea Eliade and gathering testimonies of mystical experiences in a way similar to William James. He became friendly with Timothy Leary, although he rejected his route to mystical/peak experiences through using drugs. He got involved with Esalen which was an institute founded to work out practically the conviction that a synthesis of Maslow's humanistic psychology and Eastern thought would lead to world transformation and peace. He lectured with great acclaim to liberal clergy. However, he was very reluctant to let go of his atheistic moorings and towards the end of his life he distanced himself from Esalen and emphasised the need to verify any claim to peak experiences by reason. When he died he had not resolved the dilemma he faced in greatly valuing mystical experiences but rejecting the religious baggage which seems so essential to producing them. But his dallying witnesses to the magnetic power of the perennial philosophy for a rational atheist devoted to the well-being of humanity.

Having taken a brief look at a post-Enlightenment theologian, poet, philologist, anthropologist, psychiatrist and a brace of philosophers and psychologists we will finish the survey with a physicist – Fritjof Capra. I will not pretend that I have an adequate understanding of the concepts that now dominate physics – relativity and quantum theory – or that I can grasp properly how these theories have drastically undermined the Newtonian view of the universe. Interestingly there are Christian physicists who see no contradiction between these current theories and the belief in a personal Creator, while others see them as undermining any possibility of a belief in God. Capra believes that they are consistent with a mystical view of the universe. In his *Tao of Physics*[45] he set out to show that the vision of the universe of contemporary physics is consistent with the ancient mystical teaching of Lao Tzu the founder of the Taoist tradition of Chinese religion. In *The Turning Point: Science, Society and the Rising Culture*[46] he attempts to show how what he calls the system-based theory of the universe, that he believes is consistent with contemporary physics, applies to various areas of life such as medicine, psychology, economics, political science and ecology.

For Capra the systems view of life is ultimately a mystical view of life. Take his discussion of free will which is particularly interesting in view of the starting point of this paper in the endemic tension between *nature* and *freedom* in Enlightenment thought:

> From the systems point of view, both determinism and freedom are relative concepts. To the extent that a system is autonomous from its environment it is free; to the extent that it depends on it through continuous interaction its activity will be shaped by environmental influences … This relative concept of free will seems to be consistent with the views of mystical traditions that exhort their followers to transcend the notion of an isolated self and become aware that we are inseparable parts of the cosmos in which we are embedded. The goal of these traditions is to shed all ego sensations completely and, in mystical experience, merge with the totality of the cosmos. Once such a state is reached, the question of free will seems to lose its meaning. If I am the universe, there can be no 'outside' influences and all my actions will be spontaneous and free.[47]

Apart from the particular type of mysticism eschewed this is not that far from Schleiermacher's escape route from the mechanistic view of nature at the end of the eighteenth century by means of a feeling of absolute dependence on the Universe which is really the One, the totality of things.

As I understand it what Capra is saying is that the new physics is driving scientists in the direction of a systems view of nature which emphasises the interrelatedness of everything. It accepts the more mechanistic view of the universe of Newtonian physics, but relativises it by placing it into a bigger more holistic picture of the universe. Since mysticism breathes the air of the bigger picture, Capra believes that the systems approach can 'provide the ideal framework for unifying' the 'scientific' and mystical view of the universe. So, the door is open for what might be considered to be typical New Age teaching – Gaia, the earth mother, cosmic unity, the Self and so on.

In New Age thinking, the notion that mysticism is the perennial philosophy is axiomatic. The following quotation from Freke and Gandy's recent book on mysticism will have to suffice as proof of this point: 'It is now becoming clear that there may be many mystical paths but there is essentially only one tradition, with a common content and history: a perennial mystical philosophy expressing itself in different words and concepts according to the culture of its origins; one timeless truth.'[48]

What I have attempted to show in this paper is not so much that the belief in mysticism as the perennial philosophy has been common since the Enlightenment – although I think that that is the case – but that the resort to mysticism is a consequence of the tension that has been inherent in Enlightenment thinking from the beginning. That tension is between a deterministic view of nature and a view of freedom which is based on the rejection of any external or dogmatic view of its foundation. The interest in mysticism which is becoming more and more pervasive today is not so much a rejection of modernism as the inevitable consequence of it. It is the other face of modernism. Really all we have done in our Western post-Enlightenment thinking since Kant and Schleiermacher is move the furniture around in the same room. There does not seem to be anything in postmodernism to suggest that anything more drastic than a swing of the pendulum from nature to freedom is happening today.

Notes

[1] W.R. Inge, *Christian Mysticism* (London: Methuen & Co., 1899.
[2] There is a separate article on 'Mystical Union' which focuses on Rufus Jones' narrower definition.
[3] My attention was drawn to this tension by Herman Dooyweerd's article entitled 'The Secularization of Science'. I acquired a photocopied translation by Robert D. Knudsen which was circulating in Reformed circles some years ago. The original entitled 'La Sécularisation de la Science' was published in *La Revue Réformée* 5 (1954), 138–55.
[4] As Alexander Pope eulogised:
> Nature and Nature's laws lay hid in night:
> God said, Let Newton be! And all was light.

[5] Taken from Karl Barth, *Protestant Theology in the Nineteenth Century* (London: SCM, 1972), 319.

[6] F.D.E. Schleiermacher, *The Christian Faith*, tr. H.R. Mackintosh & J.S. Stewart (Edinburgh: T. & T. Clark, 1928), 19–20.

[7] For a discussion of Schleiermacher's mysticism see R. Otto, *Mysticism East and West*, tr. B.L. Bracey & R.C. Payne (Oxford: Oxford University Press, 1923).

[8] Basil Willey, *Nineteenth Century Studies* (London: Chatto & Windus, 1969), 4, 10, 12.

[9] The following from Wordsworth's 'Lines Composed a Few Miles Above Tintern Abbey' is a fine example of his mysticism. To his memory of a previous visit to the Wye Valley he owes,

> … that blessed mood,
> In which the burthen of the mystery,
> In which the heavy and the weary weight
> Of all this unintelligible world,
> Is lightened – that serene and blessed mood,
> In which the affections gently lead us on,
> Until the breath of this corporeal frame
> And even the motion of our human blood
> Almost suspended, we are laid asleep
> In body, and become a living soul:
> While with an eye made quiet by the power
> Of harmony, and the deep power of joy,
> We see into the life of things.

J. Wain (ed.), *The Oxford Library of English Poetry*, Vol 2, (London: BCA, 1993), 251.

[10] S.T. Coleridge, *Aids to Reflection* (London: G. Bell & Sons, 1904), 143.

[11] Ibid., 171–2.

[12] S.T. Coleridge, *Confessions of an Inquiring Spirit* (London: 1840; Philadelphia: Fortress, 1988), 9.

[13] Ibid., 10. The quotation includes a quote from the apocryphal Wisdom of Solomon 7:27.

[14] Ibid., 91–2. Interestingly he makes the same point in his *Constitution of Church and State* when discussing the relationship between what he calls the national church and the Christian church: see J. Colmer (ed.), *The Collected Works of Samuel Taylor Coleridge*, Vol. 10 (Princeton: Princeton University Press, 1976), 55–6.

[15] See H.R. Mackintosh, *Types of Modern Theology* (London: Nisbet, 1937), 102.

[16] See my discussion of Hegel in D.A. Hughes, *Has God Many Names?* (Leicester: Apollos, 1996), 30–4.

[17] F. Max Müller, *Natural Religion* (London: Longman, 1892²), 188.

[18] The moral emphasis in this definition probably reflects Müller's return to Kant in the 1880s – he even published a new two-volume translation of Kant's

Critique of Pure Reason in 1882. Ritschl was also influential by that time and he, while starting from Schleiermacher's position, also emphasised the moral aspect of Christianity very heavily.

[19] London: Longman, 1891.

[20] London: Longman, 1892.

[21] London: Longman, 1893.

[22] R.R. Marett, *Psychology and Folklore* (London: Methuen, 1920), 154.

[23] R.R. Marett, *The Threshold of Religion* (London: Methuen, 1914[2]), xxxi; cf. 150, 181.

[24] R.R. Marett, *Head, Heart and Hands in Human Evolution* (London: Hutchinson, 1935), 118.

[25] The phrase he uses to describe Marett is 'this genial and ebullient classical philosopher'. E.E. Evans-Pritchard, *Theories of Primitive Religion* (Oxford: Oxford University Press, 1965), 35. In the same paragraph he records Marett's comment in conversation 'that to understand primitive mentality there was no need to go and live among savages, the experience of an Oxford Common Room being sufficient'.

[26] William Brown is another good example. In his chapter on 'Religion and Psychology', in J. Needham (ed.), *Science, Religion and Reality* (London: Sheldon Press, 1926), 320. He states that mystical experience is 'the most important form of religious experience ... to which all other religious feelings seem to lead'.

[27] This volume was originally delivered as a series of Gifford Lectures at Edinburgh 1901–2.

[28] W. James, *The Varieties of Religious Experience* (London: Longman, Green & Co, 1907), 199, 230, 241.

[29] Ibid., 13.

[30] In his *Human Personality and its Survival of Bodily Death*, Vol. 1 (London: Longman, Green & Co, 1903), F.W.H. Myers describes the subliminal self as follows: 'The conscious self of each of us ... the empirical, the supraliminal self as I should prefer to call it – does not comprise the whole of consciousness ... There exists a more comprehensive consciousness, a profounder faculty, which for the most part remains potential only so far as regards the life of earth but from which the consciousness and the faculty of earth life are mere selections, and which reasserts itself in its plenitude after the liberating change of death' (12).

[31] William James, *Varieties*, 211.

[32] Ibid., 242.

[33] Ibid., 380–1.

[34] Ibid., 484.

[35] Quoted in R.B. Perry, *The Thought and Character of William James*, Vol. 2 (Oxford: Oxford University Press, 1936), 326–7.

[36] T. Freke & P. Gandy, *The Complete Guide to World Mysticism* (London: Piatkus, 1997), 9.

[37] C.G. Jung, *Memories, Dreams, Reflections* (Glasgow: Fontana, 1973), 207.

[38] Ibid., 212.

[39] Ibid., 222.

[40] For an extensive discussion of Jung's idea of the self, see *Aion* in *The Collected Works*, Vol. 9, Pt.2, tr. R.F.C. Hull (London: Routledge & Kegan Paul, 1968²), 34ff.

[41] C.G. Jung, *The Archetypes of the Collective Unconscious,* in *The Collected Works*, Vol. 9, Pt.1, tr. R.F.C. Hull (London: Routledge & Kegan Paul, 1968²), 44.

[42] *Aion*, in *Collected Works*, 35.

[43] E.g. John Adair, *Effective Leadership* (London: Pan Books, 1983), 36.

[44] Edward Hoffman, *The Right to be Human: A Biography of Abraham Maslow* (Los Angeles: Crucible, 1988), 207.

[45] London: Wildwood House, 1975.

[46] London: Wildhood House, 1982; also published by Fontana, 1983 – reprinted five times by 1989.

[47] F. Capra, *The Turning Point* (London: Flamingo, 1983), 290–1.

[48] Freke & Gandy, *Complete Guide*, 19.

17

Fathoming the Unfathomable
Mysticism and Philosophy

Peter Hicks

Mysticism raises a number of philosophical issues. I shall discuss three key ones. The first is the relationship between the experiences of the mystic and the object of those experiences. In particular I shall explore whether mystical experience has any evidential value for the objective existence of God. I shall call this the evidential issue. The second issue concerns mystical awareness as a way of knowing, and its possible implications for our understanding of the concepts of knowledge and truth. This can be called the epistemological issue. Thirdly, there is the linguistic issue. Mysticism has always raised questions about our use of language. Recent discussions have particularly focused on the relationship between pre-existing cognitive structures and mystical experiences: to what extent do mystical experiences shape our descriptions of them, and to what extent do the concepts and terminology we inherit from our culture (religious or otherwise) shape our mystical experiences?

I need to make a preliminary declaration and a choice, both of which I shall briefly defend.

The declaration is that the empiricists' veto, which has dominated so much twentieth-century philosophical discussion of religious topics, can now be left behind as irrelevant. Its claim, that philosophy may involve itself only in what can be shown to be true logically or scientifically, effectively dismissed the whole of religion, along with ethics, metaphysics and various other things to the pit of meaninglessness.[1]

There is no need in this article to go into the philosophical refutations of this veto, which are, to my mind, conclusive.[2] It is sufficient to say that, until the twentieth century, the huge majority of philosophers saw all the issues that the veto rejected as proper and fruitful objects of philosophical enquiry. Virtue, freedom, beauty, goodness, God, and a whole range of issues involved in perception, experience and knowledge, have been key issues of philosophical discussion from Plato onwards. And a strong case can be made that it is these issues, and not logic and scientific verification, that most cry out for thorough and constructive philosophical consideration in the twenty-first century.

The choice concerns the concept of mystical experience I shall use as the basis for my discussion. Philosophers have used a range of concepts when talking about mystical experiences. Here are four of them:

(1) *Mystical experience as something that is wholly subjective.* By this they mean something parallel to a dream. It is an experience that is very real to the person who experiences it, but it is not in any sense caused by or immediately related to an external objective reality. Most twentieth-century critiques of mysticism assumed this concept as their starting point. Very few mystics would agree with them.

(2) *Mystical experience as something to be explained in terms of its immediate cause.* This concept is very close to (1), and equally subjective, but the emphasis is on understanding (and explaining away) the experience in terms of some non-mysterious objective reality that gives rise to it. The parallel here is a dream caused by eating too much Stilton just before going to bed. Thus mystical experience is to be understood in terms of the effect on the mystic's body of certain practices such as ritual, dance, asceticism, or the taking of drugs. Again, quite contrary to the claims of the mystics, it has been common for psychologically and philosophically based discussions to use this concept for their critiques.

It's worth noting that, quite apart from the religious mystics, many of those who have claimed mystical experiences as a result of taking drugs would not agree with this concept. For them their resulting experience is not just subjective. It is very definitely an awareness of objective reality.[3] It is, sadly, a very common blunder of psychologists and philosophers to assume that locating the immediate cause of a mystical experience in something like drugs *necessarily* removes any objective element from its content. Such an assumption is as foolish as saying that looking through a pair of binoculars necessarily removes objective reality from what we see.[4]

(3) *Mystical experience that has (or claims to have) a passive objective reality as its object.* The parallel here is my experience of a table or a tree. The table and tree exist independently of me. They would continue to exist even if neither I nor anyone observed them. And my observing them is irrelevant to them. They play no part in it. It doesn't affect them or change them in any way. Perhaps a good deal of monistic mysticism belongs in this category.

(4) *Mystical experience that claims to be two-way, or relational.* Its object is not passive. Instead it plays a part. The parallel here is personal relationships

– Martin Buber's '*I–Thou*'.[5] It is exemplified in Christian mystical writings by the preoccupation with the imagery of the lover and his bride, pictured throughout the Scriptures and especially in the Song of Solomon. The mystic may conceive of God as the initiator of the experience or relationship, or may appear to picture him as responding to the mystic's approach. Either way, he is not passive; the relationship is two-way.

To choose just one of these concepts inevitably begs questions and limits the range of discussion. On the other hand, failure to distinguish which concept is being discussed, or, worse still, to move from one concept to another without warning, is bad philosophising. A sympathetic discussion of the first of the three issues I've listed above, the evidential, would seem to require that I choose (3) or (4). Similarly, most mystics would opt for (3) or (4) as a description of their experience. These two considerations are sufficient to remove (1) and (2) from my list of options. But a choice between (3) and (4) needs a little further discussion.

Philosophically speaking, it's tempting to select (3), because philosophy has traditionally found it easier to discuss and understand one-way experiences of objects than two-way relationships between persons. Indeed, personhood itself has seemed almost a taboo subject since David Hume found such difficulty locating his self. Much easier, then, to discuss mysticism as an experience of the whole, or reality, or a part of reality, than to venture into the murky waters of personal relationships.

On the other hand, Christian mystics in particular have tended to opt for (4). And, whatever the twentieth century may have said, relationships and personhood and love are among the exciting new issues that twenty-first century philosophy is going to be exploring. So there's a lot to be said for opting for (4). Further, holding as I do a trinitarian and evangelical position, I'm much more interested in a direct experience of God than in one mediated by flowers or chair legs, and find it hard to summon up much enthusiasm for any such experience which is not personal and relational. Even if I, like John, am so overwhelmed by his glory that I fall at his feet as though dead, I cannot conceive of him being uninterested or unaffected. I'd extend this point even to those mystics who claim an experience not so much of God but of some profound and glorious Christian doctrine or truth. Truth about God, in my understanding, cannot be separated from God himself. A Christian mystic's experience of love, or grace, or Trinity, is not an exercise in systematic theology. It is being transported into the glory of the love of Christ, the grace of God, or the mystery of the person and relationships in the Trinity. Divine truth at this level cannot be separated from the divine persons. Jesus is the truth. God is love.

But I have to concede that much non-Christian mystical experience lacks this deep relational aspect. So I'm going to opt for (4) as my paradigm mystical experience while allowing the validity of (3) as well. As for mysticism's relationship to religious experience in general, my belief, shared by most philosophical discussions, is that mystical experience, though distinctive, is to be seen as a variety of general religious experience, and thus that many of the considerations that apply to religious experience also apply to mystical experience.

The Evidential Issue

Mystics believe they are experiencing objective reality. Such reality they picture in various ways. They may state it is ineffable, or they may spend a long time seeking to describe it. They may feel it is wholly other, or they may claim that they are encountering more ordinary things as they truly are. But they are sure that what they experience exists objectively. Their experience is not just subjective. They are encountering reality; in particular they are encountering the objectively existing God.

Questions immediately arise. If mystics encounter objective reality why do their experiences vary so much? Why does Huxley encounter 'is-ness', Shankara encounter Brahman, Castaneda encounter the demon Mescalito, and Julian of Norwich encounter Christ? Are we not back with Hume's argument against miracles that such divergence immediately destroys any evidential value of the accounts? Three things may be said in answer. First, a conflicting range of claims does not falsify all of them. It could be that all but one are counterfeit, but one is genuine. Alternatively, it is perfectly possible that all accounts are to be accepted as encounters with differing objective realities. Huxley really encountered 'is-ness.' There really is a god Mescalito that Castaneda knelt before. There is ultimate reality that Shankara called Brahman. Or, thirdly, all experiences may be of the same reality, but each mystic uses distinctive symbols and terminology to describe it.

A second question that arises concerns the relation between the subjective and the objective. Does a claim to objectivity exclude subjectivity? And if it doesn't, how are we to know which elements of a mystic's account are subjective and which objective? My answer is that a claim to objectivity in no way excludes subjectivity. No experience, not even that of the most 'objective' scientific observer, is totally free of subjectivity. Most experiences contain a considerable amount of subjectivity. And some experiences, mystical ones among them, contain a huge amount of subjectivity. But a huge amount of subjectivity does not have to exclude objectivity. John, Jane and Joan are playing the game where bagged objects are passed round and each person has to guess what they are, using only touch. For one object John writes 'a potato'; Jane goes for 'a pebble'; and Joan 'a bar of soap'. Jean, who has prepared the game, smiles to herself. They are all wrong; it's a large unripe kiwi fruit. But their wrong answers in no way detract from the objective reality of the kiwi fruit, or, indeed of their experience of it. They are only wrong because they have moved from the objective reality of the thing in the bag to their subjective interpretation of exactly what it is. Had they each limited themselves to saying, 'It's a round, firm object, about two inches measured one way and an inch and a half measured another way ...' they would all have been right. And the fact of the matter is that none of them would have had any difficulty distinguishing between these objective facts and their subjective interpretations of precisely what it was.

So experience in general contains both subjective and objective elements, and we don't find this a problem. The existence of subjectivity does not mean that we are unable to make claims to objectivity.

Now to the specific point. Can we validly use a mystical experience to establish belief in the object experienced? Is a mystical experience of God proof that he exists?

Perhaps we ought to digress for a moment to deal with that word 'proof', which has bedevilled much discussion over the existence of God. During the Enlightenment, maths was looked on as the paradigm rational activity, and a mathematical proof as the paradigm for all proof. Proofs of a mathematical theorem are so neat, so conclusive, so convincing. Anyone (or so they thought) who hears them will be forced to accept their conclusions. So all the arguments for the existence of God had to take the form of a mathematical proof. And none of them worked that way. It was always possible for the sceptic to say 'Yes, I've heard your argument, but it doesn't force me to believe in God. I accept, for example, that something must have started the universe off, and that God is the best candidate. But you've not proved that he's the only candidate. So I reject your argument.'

Contemporary philosophy has come a long way from such extreme rationalism. Long since we have realised that mathematical proof belongs to maths and to very little else. We don't need mathematical proof to bring in a verdict in a law court. In the real world our beliefs are based on things like the balance of probabilities, not on totally watertight arguments. Even ordinary perception and scientific theories lack total proof in the mathematical sense. I am totally convinced that what I'm experiencing is a tree, but I fully accept the sceptic's argument that I may be hallucinating or dreaming. Scientists take their theories as 'facts' fully aware that they can never be conclusively established, and, indeed, may be overturned in the next generation.

So in real life we no longer seek to build our beliefs on things that can be indubitably proved. We adopt beliefs for all sorts of reasons. Mary, for example, believes that the sun is 93,000,000 miles away, that John loves her, that she has a sore toe, that Arsenal is the best football team in the world, that she lives in Burnley, Lancashire, and that life is good. She believes these things for a whole range of often complex reasons, including authority, personal relationship, direct awareness, commitment, accumulation of evidence, and so on. And all of these are valid for her. She is sure of them all. She lives by them all. And I think we'd accept that she's fully justified in holding them all. But that's not to say that her beliefs are rigid, set in concrete. Like everything else about her they are alive, dynamic, and open to development and change. If the papers announce tomorrow that scientists have done some more accurate measuring and have decided the sun is 94,000,000 miles away, she would adjust her belief without turning a hair. Such is the authority of science, even today. And if lots of counter evidence to the supremacy of Arsenal or the name of her home town built up she would, rather more reluctantly, change her beliefs there too.

So the issue is no longer 'Do mystical experiences prove in a mathematical sense that God exists?' but rather 'Given that Mary has had a mystical experience of God, is she justified in believing that God is objectively real?' William James was quite certain she is:

> Mystical states, when well developed, usually are, and have the right to be, absolutely authoritative over the individuals to whom they come ... Our own more 'rational' beliefs are based on evidence exactly similar in nature to that which mystics quote for theirs. Our senses, namely, have assured us of certain states of fact; but mystical experiences are as direct perceptions of fact for those who have them as any sensations ever were for us.[6]

If we are justified in any belief that arises as a result of experience in general, then we are justified in a belief in God that arises from religious experience.

Richard Swinburne has explored this argument in some detail in his discussion of the evidential value of religious experience in general. He argues that, faced with any experience, we necessarily adopt a 'principle of credulity', which he describes as 'a very fundamental and very simple principle for the interpretation of experience'. This principle states that 'apparent perceptions ought to be taken at their face value in the absence of positive reasons for challenge'.[7] Not only is Mary justified in using her experience of God as evidence for belief in God; she would in fact be acting irrationally if she failed to do so. William Alston has developed an even more detailed case justifying Mary's belief in his book *Perceiving God*.[8]

But then comes the Great Pumpkin argument. Doesn't the last paragraph allow anyone to believe anything? Suppose Gustaw has a mystical experience of the Great Pumpkin. Is he justified in believing in the Great Pumpkin's objective existence? In answer we might try and point out that we've never heard of anyone in real life having a mystical experience of the Great Pumpkin, so we'd hardly be justified in abandoning our case over such a quaint possibility. But, if pushed, we might have to concede that if he should have such a mystical experience, given the last paragraph, our answer would have to be yes – at the time he has the experience. But, as with all experiences, his new belief has to be open to testing and the possibility of development and change.

Back to Mary. We've said she's convinced that John loves her. But suppose she discovers he's having an affair. And she finds a letter in which he says he's only pretended to love her for the last year. And so on. Her belief in his love will change. Maybe she won't abandon it straight away. 'I can't believe he doesn't love me any more. He must love me deep down. It's just that he's infatuated with this girl at the office.' But as the evidence piles up she eventually decides he doesn't love her after all.

The same is true of her belief in God. She doesn't hold it simply as a result of her mystical experience. Even if the experience has been the immediate cause of her holding it, she will be continually checking and testing it, consciously or unconsciously, and, if necessary, developing and changing it. One of the major tests is whether or not it fits with her other beliefs and experiences. It's for this reason that, even if Bertrand Russell had had a mystical experience, it's highly unlikely he'd have accepted it as evidence for the existence of God. His whole philosophy was so committed to atheism that it would have taken more than just one mystical experience to overthrow it. But Mary already has beliefs that fit well with the conclusion that her experience is of God. She's sure the world could not have created itself. She accepts the teaching of the Bible. She's read the accounts of other mystics. And so on. Further, as time goes by, she finds that her experience makes her a better person – more loving, more holy, more Christ-like. All this fits well with and confirms her understanding of her experience.

But when Gustaw has a mystical experience of the Great Pumpkin, it's fairly certain that he will soon find difficulty in verifying and fitting a belief in its objective reality into the rest of his experience. For a start, his whole worldview, like Russell's, has up to that point excluded the Great Pumpkin. And while Mary finds that lots of others have had parallel experiences to hers, Gustaw is strangely isolated. People look askance at him and suggest he takes a holiday. And Great Pumpkinness just doesn't sit happily alongside his other beliefs. So, perhaps after trying for a time to make it work, he reluctantly adapts his belief. 'I thought it was a mystical encounter with the Great Pumpkin, but now I realise it was something else. I thought it was the Great Pumpkin because I'd been reading *Peanuts* just before. But now I've decided it must have been Ultimate Reality that I experienced. I just interpreted it as the Great Pumpkin.'

The evidential value, then, of mystical experience is rightly very high for the mystic, provided it is checked and tested and coheres with the rest of life. But does such experience have any evidential value for the rest of us? My answer is undoubtedly yes. Unless we are particularly narrow minded and dogmatic we must say that such a meaningful and significant experience for Mary must have some bearing on our own assessment of the case for God.[9] I need to add four comments.

First, evidence can, of course, be positive or negative. If I wish to assess the evidential value of Mary's experience of God, I will also have to take into account the possibility of Gustaw's experience being evidence that Ultimate Reality is pumpkin shaped, or Castaneda's that Mescalito is green and warty and with a strawberry shaped head. Or Mary may report that Christ spoke to her words that ultimately turn out to be false.

Secondly, the evidential value of Mary's mystical experience will be different for me than for Mary, simply because the piece of evidence is different. For Mary the piece of evidence is an experience of direct awareness. For me it is (in the first place) a second hand report. We assess the evidential value of a second hand report quite differently from that of a direct experience. That is not to say that the value will necessarily be less. I accept that the sun is 93,000,000 miles away on the basis of a second-hand report, and I am totally convinced of the objective fact of that distance. In the case of Mary, my assessment of her report will have to take into account her dependability as a reporter. Is she prone to hallucinations? Is she gullible? Does she habitually fantasise or tell lies? Does the report fit with what I know of her as a person? And so on.

I've said that Mary's experience is 'in the first place' a second-hand report, and needs to be assessed as such. But there are also further more direct ways I might assess its evidential value. I'd keep an eye on her to see what effect the experience has on her life; a marked increase in godliness, for instance, might well be very significant. And, like Mary, I'd seek to work through the implications of this experience and see how it fits into the rest of life.

Thirdly, it is quite possible that I will find Mary's experience sufficiently strong evidence on its own to convince me of the existence of God. The dependability of her reporting, the impact of the experience on her life, and so on, may persuade me that there is an objective God. Alternatively, it may provide one piece of evidence among many, forming part of a cumulative case which eventually tips the balance.

Fourthly, the evidential value of Mary's experience will be different for me than for another person. We each start at different points. Some would not even bother to listen to Mary's story, so convinced are they that there is no God and all mystics are either deluded or liars. Others will already be almost at the point where they move over from atheism to belief in God, and Mary's account will be the last straw. Some know Mary well, so the weight given to her sanity and dependability and the subsequent change in her life will be considerable. For others she's an unknown quantity, so there's much more room for uncertainty and doubt.

The Epistemological Issue

Despite the many differences among mystics, it is possible to argue that all mystical experience is in some sense a way of knowing. It can be seen as a way of coming to know truth, of obtaining knowledge, a feature I focused on in the previous section. Additionally, and for most mystics much more significantly, it is a way of personally knowing reality or God, a knowledge that becomes so intimate that in many cases it can be described in terms of the mystic and the object of knowledge becoming one.

In this section I want to suggest that mystical experience has a significant contribution to make to our understanding of the concepts of knowledge and truth. I approach the discussion with the conviction that we should build our epistemology not on some doctrinaire philosophical principle, but on the way we actually find things in the real world. I thus reject the rationalistic concepts that we can't claim to know something or to have truth unless we are able to produce a rationally convincing argument for it, or that truth only operates in the sphere of scientific fact and not in the field of values. In real life knowledge and truth are both broad and rich. We know in all sorts of ways; truth takes many forms.[10] The basic intellectual stimulus towards postmodern relativism (and I'm not at all sure the intellectual stimulus is the basic one) is the pitiful inadequacy of a rationalistic epistemology. If we are to climb out of the despair of epistemological anarchy we need to develop an account of knowing and relating to truth that is much richer and able to embrace the whole of life. In this the mystical way of knowing can help us.

William James gave four marks of mystical experiences,[11] but stated that two of them, transience and passivity are 'less sharply marked' while the other two are sufficient to 'entitle any state to be called mystical'. Though they are by no means universally accepted, we will use these two as a starting point.

His first mark is ineffability. 'No adequate report' of the contents of the mystical experience 'can be given in words'. From this James concluded 'that its quality must be directly experienced; it cannot be imparted or transferred to others'.[12]

At first sight ineffability may seem to be a very distinctive quality of mystical experience, setting it apart from all other experience. However, I question this, and would like to challenge James' choice of the word.[13] Granted, it is a term that is often attached to mystical experience. But James clearly does not believe mystical experiences are truly ineffable, that is, totally unable to be described in words. They are only unable to be described 'adequately'. He doesn't tell us what he means by 'adequately', but its obvious sense is 'fully' or 'such that others grasp it clearly'.

However, as James is quick to acknowledge, this sort of ineffability is by no means limited to the mystical. He specifically cites the experiences of listening to a symphony or being in love. Indeed, it could be argued that his inclusion of the word 'adequately' in his definition allows any experience to be defined as ineffable, inasmuch as no person can ever fully express any given experience in words. So, rather than saying that mystical ineffability is such that it sets mystical experience apart from all other experiences, I suggest that mystical ineffability is no different in kind from the ineffability of all our personal experiences. I cannot adequately describe my toothache, or my reaction to Mahler's Third, or my encounter with God. This 'ineffability' arises, I suggest, not so much from the nature of the experience, as from a combination of the inadequacy of language and the lack of a parallel experience in the person to whom I'm speaking. James actually says 'One must have been in love one's self to understand a lover's state of mind', thus implying that ineffability is not a problem when there is a degree of common experience. Two mystics can talk about their experiences to each other. Nor need the degree of common experience be great. A mystic can surely communicate at least something to those who have read Wordsworth, or have had their hearts strangely warmed, or who believe in God, or who know love, or joy, and so on.

So here we find a continuum rather than a stark contrast between mystical knowing and other forms of knowing. It is not the case that other experiences give us knowledge which we can readily communicate with others, while mystical experiences are incommunicable. Rather, there are elements of ineffability about all personal experiences; words always fall short; but in most cases there is at least some common ground which allows some communication to take place.

In discussing ineffability, James comments that mystical experience is 'more like states of feeling than like states of intellect'. If mysticism is a way of knowing, he seems to say, it is a non-intellectual way. It goes beyond the confines of what can be understood as well as what can be expressed.

For some, to be beyond the reach of the intellect or inexpressible in words, is to be unreal or non-existent. But here again we do not have to take James as implying that mystical experiences are anti-intellectual or irrational. Rather they are something, like the concept of infinity, or what lies beyond the edge of the universe, that we can think about, but which goes beyond what we can totally wrap up in our minds.

We know grief. We know remorse. We know a loved one. We know intimacy. We know peace. None of these ways of knowing are intellectual. And in many cases we may be unable to put our grief or peace or whatever into words. But in a sense these things are more real than the objects of intellectual knowing. 'You may know facts about John, but I really know him'; 'You may talk about grief, but I know the real thing'. So it is with the mystic. 'You make your theological propositions about God, but I know him'; 'You talk about love, but I am overwhelmed by it'.

This brings us to James' second mark of mystical experiences, what he calls their noetic quality.[14] This, he says, enables them to be described as 'states of knowledge', 'states of insight into depths of truth unplumbed by the discursive intellect', 'illuminations, revelations', carrying with them 'a curious sense of authority for aftertime'. I shall focus on three of the terms he uses here. First, knowledge gained through mystical experience is 'deeper' than that gained by the rationalist or the empiricist. Secondly, this knowledge is not so much attained by mystics as given to them; they are 'illuminated'; there is a 'revelation'. Thirdly, there is something particularly 'authoritative' about the knowledge that is gained through mystical experience.

There are perhaps two ways of developing James' statement that mystical knowledge is 'deeper' than other knowledge. The most straightforward is to say that mystical knowledge is deeper in the sense that it deals with deeper, more profound topics. Empirical knowledge deals with comparatively superficial things like tables and trees; mystical knowledge plumbs the depths of God and reality and ultimate truth. But it is worth considering for a moment the further application of the concept, and asking whether we might suggest that mystical knowledge can be looked on as deeper in the sense of being basic, or foundational to other forms of knowing. Where the Enlightenment made intellectual knowing the paradigm for all knowing, and rationally established truth the touchstone for all truth, mysticism might suggest that its immediate awareness of overwhelming reality should be taken as the ideal or the model for all forms of knowing, knowledge at its highest peak, truth at its greatest intensity; all other concepts of knowing and of truth will then be derivative or dependent upon it, approximating to a greater or lesser degree to the ideal.

Such a suggestion is arguable, and has its attractions, though it's not quite the position I would adopt. My own view is that there is both a wide range of types of truth, and a range of ways of knowing, and that they are all equally valid in their place. Truths range through analytic, contingent, empirical, immediate, intuitive, moral, axiological, personal, 'mystical', to God himself who is the truth. Knowing also ranges, principally on the two axes of rational awareness and personal involvement. Mathematical knowledge, for example, would seem to be high on the first axis and low on the second. So would my knowledge of Tokyo. But my knowledge that witches were burnt in the sixteenth century or that Pen-y-fan is the highest mountain in Southern Wales, though still rational and factual, is beginning to move up the scale of personal involvement. These two pieces of knowledge affect me, upset me or excite me; there is a relationship between them and me. At this level the relationship is one way; I don't affect the witches or Pen-y-fan. But, further up the scale, there are ways of knowing that have two-way involvement, principally, of course, my knowledge of other people, my friends, my loved ones. It is interesting that the writer of Genesis could use *yada*, the main Hebrew word for 'know', to describe sexual intercourse between man and wife, described elsewhere in Genesis as two becoming one,[15] a theme familiar in many mystical writings.

Mystical knowing and truth are thus at the end of a spectrum. While this fact emphasises the range of the spectrum and the richness of the concepts, I'm not sure I'd wish to say they provide the paradigm for all-knowing and truth. Perhaps I'm just reacting against the old rationalistic imperialism which insisted *its* definition was the paradigm; but I'm happier saying that each type of truth and each way of knowing has its specific criteria, though, and here I reject Wittgensteinian

segregation, each is related to all the others on the scale, and each com-
plements the others. I have argued elsewhere that since we are holistic
beings, and in no way separated into rational, moral, volitional, religious,
etc. segments, *all* our knowing must include each part of us, though, in
some knowing, some aspects of us may be more or less dormant.[16] In this
sense I can accept that mystical experience is non-rational or non-intellectual, on the understanding that we see the intellect as largely dormant
during the experience. But, as I have argued above, after the experience
the intellect has every right to get to work on it, testing its validity and
significance, and so on. In this sense, I have reservations over the suggestion that in mystical experience all traces of the rational element have
been in some way been excluded; non-rational personal involvement has
taken over totally. On the grounds that the mystic does not cease to be
a holistic and so rational being, even at the height of the mystical experience, I'd prefer to speak of the rational element being inactive or
dormant rather than totally excluded.

James' use of 'illumination' and 'revelation' picks up a significant
element of mystical knowing. It is present not just in the two-way or
relational form of mysticism I mentioned above, but also in the more
monistic form where the object of knowing is more passive. The experience is one of being illuminated, of having something revealed. The
object does something to us; we are affected, even changed by it. It is
perhaps parallel to Ian Ramsey's concept of 'disclosure situations'.[17] We
emerge from the experience different people.

Without wishing to minimise the dramatic effect that their experiences have on mystics, I would suggest that here again we are not talking
about something that is unique to mysticism. In a very loose sense, I suggest that all experiences at least have the potential to affect and change
us. The sad fact is that in our contemporary culture we are subjected to
experience overload just as much as we are subjected to information
overload, so we tend to rush from one experience to the next without
allowing it to have its full effect on us. We watch a violent film, we study
a work of art, we walk in the countryside, some one expresses love or
anger towards us, we suffer pain – and all that in a few hours. But any one
of them can be a 'disclosure' experience, an illumination, a revelation.
Something comes to us from outside and changes us.

This brings us to the third significant word James uses in his discussion of the noetic quality of mystical experiences – their 'authority'.
Despite the contemporary antipathy to any concept of authority, it
would be a very bold philosopher who would dare to deny the authority of personal experience as a means of authenticating knowledge and
truth. 'I *know* it was raining; I was out in it and got soaked'; 'However

fine *you* may be feeling there's no doubt that *I've* got toothache'; 'I'm certain Bridlington is on the coast; I live there'. James' use of the word 'curious' in describing this sense of authority perhaps betrays Enlightenment scepticism. Why shouldn't a powerfully graphic and immediate personal experience carry with it a sense of authority? Here perhaps we can link back with Descartes' 'Whatever I perceive very clearly and distinctly is true'.[18] What is thus presented to us is such that we cannot doubt; we accept it as authoritative.

There are many valid aspects of our culture's rejection of authority. But complete rejection of authority means the loss of all structures, and so the disintegration of society. Each time an authority is rejected it has to be replaced by another authority. The authority of the Roman Catholic Church to pronounce on matters of astronomy was replaced by the authority of the astronomers. The authority of tradition was replaced by that of reason. The authority of God was replaced by that of the scientist. Now that these new authorities are being challenged the authority of personal experience must surely be taken very seriously, whether it is personal experience of a tree, or a pain, or of God. Again, in keeping with what I have said above, I would reject the kind of dichotomy we've been faced with all too often in recent discussions: either the authority of reason, or the authority of personal experience. The fact is that in real life it is impossible to keep the two apart. However powerful they may be, all our personal experiences will be tested by our reason, just as the dictates of reason should be assessed by what we know from personal experience. And it is the same across the board. There are many authorities whose voices we must hear and integrate into our total worldview.

Here, then, we have a number of issues raised by mystical experience which provide insights into the whole range of experience and knowledge. Once we admit that the mystical way of knowing is not unique but has parallels with other ways of knowing, and are prepared to concede that no one way of knowing has the right to oust all the others, we can allow the specific emphases of the mystical way of knowing to enrich the whole spectrum of what we take knowledge to be.

The Linguistic Issue

I have already touched on some of the issues raised by the inadequacy of language to describe the mystic's experience, and suggested that it is a mistake to see these as unique to mysticism or in any way insurmountable. Indeed, anyone who reads the writings of the mystics cannot fail to be impressed by the skilful use of language by many of them to convey at least part of what they have experienced. So, in this section, I'm not going to discuss whether or not words can be used to describe the 'indescribable'; rather, I will focus on the issue of the relationship between mystical experiences and the words used to express them.

Most of the philosophical discussions about knowledge and truth and meaning have tended to assume that words are foundational. The focus of interest is the proposition 'The cat is on the mat', not the experience of seeing Felix in front of the fire. This has meant that the key to meaning and truth is seen to lie either in the proposition, in the words used (what they refer to, how the sentence is constructed, and so on), or in the mind or intention of the proposition's speaker, why she or he is saying these particular words in a particular way in this context. This focus has led to useful insights on how we use words to describe the things in the world and to communicate. It has also led to a widespread assumption that our use of words in some way shapes reality; that the world around us is somehow formless until we impose shape and form on it by our use of language.

This assumption is typical of the overreaction that characterises so much philosophical discussion, and, indeed, the discussion of issues in many other fields. Just as the behaviourist overreacts against Freud's claim that our attitudes and actions are caused by internal factors, by insisting that all causes must be external, so philosophers like Steven Katz, in rejecting the concept that the mystics' descriptions of their experiences are totally shaped by external reality, swing to the opposite extreme and assume that they are totally shaped by pre-existing concepts and language.[19] The wise course would seem to reject such a crude either/or, and accept that both external reality and subjective interpretation play a part in the forming of descriptions of mystical experiences, just as is the case with other types of experience. When I claim to see a tree, or experience toothache, or encounter another person, both the tree, or the decay, or the person are externally objectively real and give rise to my experience. But to make sense of the experience I need to have a conceptual framework, and maybe a language, to fit the experience into, and, in particular, to be able to talk about it with others.

Mystics claim that what they experience is as objectively real as trees and other minds. Indeed, they often claim greater reality for it. They may accept that subjective elements are inevitably introduced at the point where they try to put the experience into words; descriptions are influenced by concepts and terminology that are available to them. But these things do not control the description. Mystics who experience, say, vastness, are free to select from a range of words and images such as oceans, galaxies, or infinity, according to their conceptual framework. But they are not at liberty to use words like 'small' or 'petty'.

Mystics insist that their experience is primary and foundational. We may or may not be able to put it into words. When we do put it into words our description will fall short of the reality. But the experience remains unchanged. It is the real; the language we use to describe it is the shadow.

I would like to suggest that words play a far smaller part in our living and thinking than contemporary philosophers tend to assume. We do not normally think in sentences or propositions. When I enter the room and see Felix in front of the fire I do not say or even subconsciously think the proposition 'The cat is on the mat'. Words are not involved at all; I simply have an experience of Felix in front of the fire. We've all been in the situation where a friend glances at her watch; we then ask the time, and she has to look again in order to be able to verbalise 'Half past six'. Her first glance almost certainly entailed no verbalising; she didn't need to work through a logical progression from 'It's half past six; I'm due at John's at seven. That means I've got half an hour', to 'I needn't rush'. She simply felt temporal okayness. To be more explicit, she moved from a non-verbalised feeling that time was going and she ought to be moving to a non-verbalised feeling that she could relax for a bit yet. No words were needed for this; words are only needed when she has to communicate, to tell us the time.

The huge majority of our thoughts are non-verbal. I decide I'd like a cup of coffee; nowhere, not even in my subconscious, is the framing of a proposition 'I am deciding I'd like a cup of coffee' involved. Nor is the verbal concept 'A cup of coffee', or even the word 'coffee'. All there is a feeling, an awareness, to which coffee is the answer. I see a tree, I think of my wife, I remember what a dull day it was yesterday, I decide to cut the lawn, I feel hungry or excited – all without any words being involved at all. We can think even abstract concepts, I suggest, like freedom or infinity, which may seem to need words to have any shape at all, without verbalising them. This is illustrated by the way we sometimes have to search for a word when trying to communicate an idea we have in our mind. We are thinking of the concept to which we would attach the words *joie de vivre* or sophistry. We know exactly what we are thinking, but we've forgotten the word. 'What's that word that means so and so?', we ask. Up to that point the lack of the word doesn't matter; our thought is unhindered; we don't need the word to think the idea. We only need it when we have to communicate the idea to others.

Mysticism, with its stress on experience as foundational, thus provides us with a model which counters the excessive stress on the role of language in shaping reality. Words are not primary; indeed, in a sense they are tertiary. Reality is primary; next comes our experience of reality; and only thirdly comes our attempts to put our experience into words.

So at this point we can return to the issue of the diversity of mystical experience. If mystics encounter objective reality, why, we asked, does Huxley encounter 'is-ness', Shankara encounter Brahman, Castaneda encounter the demon Mescalito, and Julian of Norwich encounter Christ? Can we say that all mystical experiences are of the same reality, but each mystic uses distinctive symbols and terminology to describe it? I would like to suggest we can, with two provisos. The first is that mysticism, like politics, philosophy, religion and life in general, has its fair share of cranks and charlatans. A claim that mystics do have experiences of reality must not be taken as saying that every mystical experience is an experience of reality. But it is a claim that many mystical experiences may well be of genuine reality. At the very least we should approach them with the assumption that they are innocent until proved guilty, following Swinburne's principle of credulity or what Donald Davidson more attractively calls the principle of charity. The second proviso is that we are to expect reality to be complex and varied. It contains both chair legs and God. If Julian experiences spiritual reality as glorious, and Castaneda experiences it as grotesque, then we can accept that spiritual reality is both grotesque and glorious. The evangelical worldview has no problem in accepting both the existence of God and the existence of a demonic force that lies behind Castaneda's drug taking, and which he actually encountered and described.

Stace suggests that though true mystical experience may be beyond concepts and words while it is being experienced, once the experience is over the mystic will be able to attempt to conceptualise and describe it.[20] Naturally any subsequent description will rely very much on the conceptual and linguistic structures with which the mystic in question is familiar. So it is conceivable that a Sufi and a Hindu and a Christian may have identical experiences, but will use very different language and imagery to describe them.

Concluding Comments

In conclusion, a few comments about one or two of the issues I've been discussing in the context of an Evangelical Christian worldview. Despite its traditional apathy or even opposition towards mysticism,[21]

Evangelicalism as a whole has given religious experience, in the sense of a direct awareness and personal knowledge of God, a key place in its system. Its stress on personal, almost mystical, experience in fact goes back to its fountainheads, to Wesley's heart 'strangely warmed', to Whitefield, Edwards, and Howell Harris. I have argued in *Evangelicals and Truth* that the forms of Evangelicalism that have stressed intellectual assent and doctrinal beliefs at the expense of personal experience of God are aberrations, as are those forms that major on experience but neglect revealed and objective truth. 'The heart and the head' are both essential.

Evangelicals, then, despite a degree of ambivalence towards evidentialism, have tended to place a great deal of weight on their personal experience of God as key to their faith and as a justifiable basis for adopting it. The story of Paul's conversion, or the image of the vine and the branches, or the concept of knowing God personally, have often been paradigmatic. Experience of God, which can take many forms, is foundational; many evangelical sermons have agreed with Kierkegaard that mere head knowledge or intellectual acceptance of the truths of Christianity is insufficient; a personal relationship is essential.

But the religious experience that is at the heart of mainline Evangelicalism has a distinctive feature. It is seen very much as the work of God, and not of the individual. We do not engineer the experience; God comes to us.[22] So the emphasis tends to be less on my experience, and more on God's grace and self-revelation.

So the evangelical worldview is built very firmly on the concept of God as an external objective reality who comes to us, and whom we experience personally. But, complementing and balancing that concept is the equally significant one that, principally in the Scriptures, God has also revealed a noetic structure, an authorised interpretive framework in which to express and by which to interpret our experience. Here, for evangelicals, is the key to understanding and expressing our experience of God.

The emphasis on the Scriptures as an authorised expression of divine truth, however admirable, has perhaps had one detrimental effect. The wrong sort of emphasis on their completeness and sufficiency has tended to give rise to a self-satisfied attitude that has contributed to the sad lack of the sense of mystery among evangelicals. 'Ineffable' too infrequently appears in our vocabulary; we are too rarely speechless with wonder, love and praise. The current wave of interest in the range of spiritualities, not least mysticism, will perhaps help evangelicals to see that, however authoritative the words of Scripture may be, they can still never do justice to the greatness and glory of God. Mystery, the mystery that gave mysticism its name, will always remain.

Notes

1. A.J. Ayer's *Language, Truth and Logic* (1936) argued this position in its most notorious form. Ayer assumed 'the principle of verification' by which it can be determined whether or not a sentence is literally meaningful. A simple way to formulate it would be to say that a sentence had literal meaning if and only if the proposition it expressed was either analytic or empirically verifiable. As a result '... the mystic does not give us any information about the external world; he merely gives us indirect information about the condition of his own mind. These considerations dispose of the argument from religious experience ... the sentence.' 'There exists a transcendent "God" has, as we have seen, no literal significance.' A.J. Ayer, *Language, Truth and Logic* (London: Victor Gollanz, 1946²), 5, 119.

2. Richard Swinburne briefly discusses and dismisses the verificationist principle in *The Coherence of Theism* (Oxford: Oxford University Press, 1977), 22–9.

3. After taking mescaline, Aldous Huxley claimed to become aware of the Beatific Vision, of 'is-ness' as he contemplated flowers, the legs of a chair, or the cloth of his trousers. Cited in G. Parrinder, *Mysticism in the World's Religions* (Oxford: Oneworld, 1995), 177–8.

4. See Christopher Partridge's discussion of drugs and mystical experience above (ch. 7).

5. See M. Buber, *I and Thou*, tr. R.G. Smith (Edinburgh: T. & T. Clark, 1959).

6. William James, *The Varieties of Religious Experience* (London: Longmans, Green and Co., 1929), 422–4.

7. Richard Swinburne, *The Existence of God* (Oxford: Clarendon Press, 1979), 275. Cf. 244–76.

8. William P. Alston, *Perceiving God: the Epistemology of Religious Experience* (Ithaca: Cornell University Press, 1991).

9. James is commonly assumed to have argued that the evidential value of Mary's experience is wholly limited to her. What he actually says is that its authority is far greater for Mary than for 'outsiders', but that it can 'establish a presumption'. Swinburne and Alston argue that the 'presumption' can be substantial.

10. I have enlarged on this in my *Evangelicals and Truth: a Creative Proposal for a Postmodern Age* (Leicester: Apollos, 1998), 162–70.

11. James, *Varieties*, 380–1.

12. Ibid., 380.

13. Stace helpfully points out that the ineffability of a mystical experience while it is being experienced does not entail that it will be ineffable when subsequently recalled. W.T. Stace, *Mysticism and Philosophy* (London: Macmillan, 1960), 297.

14. James *Varieties*, 380–1.

15. E.g. Gen. 4:1, 17, 25, 2:24.

16. Hicks, *Evangelicals and Truth*, 166–70.

[17] I. T Ramsey developed his concept of 'disclosure' in several of his writings. See, for example, *Religious Language* (London: SCM, 1957).

[18] R. Descartes, *Third Meditation* para. 2, in E. Anscombe & P.T. Geach (eds.), *Descartes: Philosophical Writings* (London: Nelson/Open University Press, 1970), 76.

[19] Steven T. Katz, 'Language, Epistemology, and Mysticism', in Steven T. Katz (ed.), *Mysticism and Philosophical Analysis* (London: Sheldon Press, 1978), 22–74.

[20] Stace, *Mysticism and Philosophy*, 297.

[21] In his introduction to his very influential *Systematic Theology*, Charles Hodge spent forty-three pages considering and for the most part criticising 'mysticism'. Charles Hodge, *Systematic Theology*, Vol. 1 (New York: Charles Scribner, 1871), 61–103. The fact that the mystical way has its roots in the Catholic tradition may well be one of the sources of the evangelical mistrust of it. See also note 20.

[22] The suspicion that mystics somehow manipulate or produce their own experiences may be an additional factor that lies at the root of evangelicalism's suspicion of the mystic way.

Index